Studies in Economic Theory

Editors

Charalambos D. Aliprantis
Purdue University
Department of Economics
West Lafayette, IN 47907-2076
USA

Nicholas C. Yannelis
University of Illinois
Department of Economics
Champaign, IL 61820
USA

Titles in the Series

M. A. Khan and *N. C. Yannelis* (Eds.)
Equilibrium Theory
in Infinite Dimensional Spaces

C. D. Aliprantis, K. C. Border
and *W. A. J. Luxemburg* (Eds.)
Positive Operators, Riesz Spaces,
and Economics

D. G. Saari
Geometry of Voting

C. D. Aliprantis and *K. C. Border*
Infinite Dimensional Analysis

J.-P. Aubin
Dynamic Economic Theory

M. Kurz (Ed.)
Endogenous Economic Fluctuations

J.-F. Laslier
Tournament Solutions and Majority Voting

A. Alkan, C. D. Aliprantis and *N. C. Yannelis*
(Eds.)
Theory and Applications

J. C. Moore
Mathematical Methods
for Economic Theory 1

J. C. Moore
Mathematical Methods
for Economic Theory 2

M. Majumdar, T. Mitra and *K. Nishimura*
Optimization and Chaos

K. K. Sieberg
Criminal Dilemmas

M. Florenzano and *C. Le Van*
Finite Dimensional Convexity
and Optimization

K. Vind
Independence, Additivity, Uncertainty

T. Cason and *C. Noussair* (Eds.)
Advances in Experimental Markets

F. Aleskerov and *B. Monjardet*
Utility Maximization. Choice and Preference

N. Schofield
Mathematical Methods in Economics
and Social Choice

C. D. Aliprantis, K. J. Arrow, P. Hammond,
F. Kubler, H.-M. Wu and *N. C. Yannelis* (Eds.)
Assets, Beliefs, and Equilibria
in Economic Dynamics

D. Glycopantis and *N. C. Yannelis* (Eds.)
Differential Information Economies

A. Citanna, J. Donaldson, H. M. Polemarchakis,
P. Siconolfi and *S. E. Spear* (Eds.)
Essays in Dynamic
General Equilibrium Theory

M. Kaneko
Game Theory and Mutual Misunderstanding

S. Basov
Multidimensional Screening

Vesna Pasetta

Modeling Foundations of Economic Property Rights Theory

An Axiomatic Analysis of Economic Agreements

With 38 Figures
and 5 Tables

Springer

Professor Vesna Pasetta
EPRSA
PO Box 4242
Ithaca NY 14852
USA
E-mail: vp11@cornell.edu

Cataloging-in-Publication Data
Library of Congress Control Number: 2005925547

ISBN 3-540-24552-9 Springer Berlin Heidelberg New York

Springer is a part of Springer Science+Business Media
springeronline.com

Printed in Germany

Cover design: Erich Kirchner
Production: Helmut Petri
Printing: Strauss Offsetdruck

SPIN 11387497 Printed on acid-free paper – 42/3153 – 5 4 3 2 1 0

To my father Franc, who taught me to embrace life, and
both of my mothers – Toncka , who gave me life, and
Ljudmila, who saw me through it.

Preface

This is an introduction to the foundations of economic property rights theory (EPRT). In this volume, a first step in the EPRT research program, rules concerning economic property rights (e.p.r.s), entrepreneurial agreements, and enterprises are discussed. Introduced concept of e.p.r.s is an extension of the traditional concept of pairing of residual rights of control and residual rights of returns in the economic theory. Its importance in economics is generated from a general impossibility of making a complete contract, concerning e.p.r.s, for any nontrivial economic transaction. The volume offers a theoretical extension of mathematical economics, applying recent results of Hopf algebras, quasi-Hopf algebras, representation theory, theory of categories, and deformation theories, in looking for suitable mathematical methodology of economic property rights theories and foundations of general theory of economic agreements. The idea is to construct a kind of mathematical application in which any fundamental formal entity and/or operation has an empirical economic interpretation. This approach is seen as a way to cope with an extreme complexity of economic phenomena under consideration and requests for precise formulation of models where meaningful answers and solutions of problems are only those which are obtained rigorously. The proposed extensions in mathematical economics and property rights theory are to provide rich enough foundations to follow complexity of economic property rights in the exact way, and to identify where there is an appropriate method providing adequate solution, and also to find problems where in general there is no such methodology.

The program of EPRT is addressed primarily to scientists and researchers wishing to begin work on issues of economic property rights and economic institutions. For those with less formal mathematical background, the intention is to provide full details and line-by-line proofs of all basic relations that are needed for research in the field. The hope is that unessential formalism has been avoided. For those more interested in this application of mathematics, mathematical economics and OR, I have adopted a theorem-proof schema, trying not to propose economic statements that are not technically correct, so that the main results can be understood clearly. The intention is to achieve the balance between readability and rigorous formality by taking a completely algebraic approach in this volume. Discussions on the equally interesting versions of e.p.r.s institutions applying methodologies of C^*-algebras and other algebras have been left for volume II, while those focusing on noncommutative probability theory, braiding statistics, stochastic models on patterns of e.p.r.s flows, and stochastic calculus of institutions in general, are left for volume III. In other words, in this volume the algebraic approach is applied in formulation of EPRT, while the functional-analytic and stochastic approaches to EPRT are explored in the next two volumes. Note that it is not a survey, thus many interesting issues and methodological procedures are not discussed in any detail. Such as, for example, issues primarily linked to the political economy, law and legislative institutions, and particular forms of economic rights (intellectual property rights, particular securities, wage contracts, some elements from warranties, inheritance, parenthood, or many other forms of concrete types of economic contracts).

The fundamentals of mathematical economics in which concepts of the super-micro-economic analyses of economic property rights have their beginnings are over fifty years old; von Neumann (1928, 1937) [58], Kantorovich (1948) [39], Neumann and Morgenstern (1944) [59], Koopmans (1950) [41], Allias (1943) [6], Nash (1950) [56], Meade (1965) [50], and many others that have contributed to mathematical economics, game theory, and mathematical models of decision making, artificial intelligence and the reliability of expert systems. It is noteworthy that the complexity of the e.p.r.s phenomena, implying noncommutativity of economic relations, imposes an extension of mathematical tools applied to economics. The commutativity conditions were defined and discussed by the founders of the game theory in economics von Neumann and Morgenstern [59]. Later on, these issues have been considered by many others, although, more often analyzing the economic and behavioral consequences of a violation of these conditions than addressing them directly. Recall that the simplest form of the noncommutativity is that of the zero-sum games without a unique saddle-point and/or games of mixed strategies. Moreover, they concern modern economic theories and also rapidly developing ones, and in the applications of our concern one may think of two essential points for the extension:
(1) The existence of many natural economic spaces for which the traditional set-theoretical tools of analysis are not sophisticated enough to capture economic phenomena of concern. One may recall that within the frame of Euclidean geometry, combined with symmetries and linear spaces, and with traditional pointwise multiplication and addition, many important classes of functions applied in economics can be modeled. Having on hand the Grothendieck's algebraic geometry, via the notion of affine scheme, one can show that there is no need, in general, to ask anything more. However, one

can ask less, particularly concerning underlying economic axioms. From formal point of view this leads very naturally to a noncommutative algebra. Such spaces arise in mathematics (see Connes [23] for example), and in other applied sciences, but here we are focused on their applications in economics and in particular to e.p.r.s issues. These seem to give a new outlook to both, quite traditional and modern topics in economics.
(2) The extension of the traditional tools of mathematical economics involves an algebraic reformulation where passing from the commutative to the noncommutative setting is almost never straightforward. It itself offers an insight into completely new phenomena arising in the more complex economic issues. So, it seems to open a possibility for identifying the existence of a concept of the canonical evolution for complicated economic factors (as intangible assets for example), that are particularly important for understanding and formulation of dynamics in economics. One should also have in mind that developing a theory in the noncommutative framework leads to a new point of view, and new tools applicable to the traditional economic phenomena, (such as the procedures on cyclic correspondence of structure and properties of copartners, and advanced differential calculus), which unlike the theory of distributions seem to be particularly interesting and naturally adoptable to economic applications.

Apart from the above mentioned, modern computational devices, communications, information and new technologies and algorithms involved have extended domains of economics. The new economic theories and experimental approaches have become available taking into account ideas incorporated into the concepts of data compression, superdense coding, information transmission and entanglement concentrations. These exemplify nontrivial extensions of traditional economic relations between agents, and how modern market channels, implying modern communication and computation devices, can be used, alone or combined with classical market channels, to transmit traditional market as well as any other information. More recently additional computational procedures based on so called super-computers and those that are within experimental phase, have opened possibilities of extremely precise formulation, experimentation and controllability of data entanglements. These should enable one to substitute uncertain channels of economic transactions for certain ones in these applications. Naturally, there are issues that are to be clarified and corresponding procedures in calculations improved. For example, questions of finding exact expressions, rather than upper and lower bounds, for the traditional and more advanced unconventional securities still appear to be open and call for further research in advanced risk management, informational economics and economics of intangibles. It is noteworthy that recent results in variety of applied sciences on their *R&D* programs, communications and technological developments have imposed the importance of the economic property rights phenomena in economics more openly and directly. Here, modern communication and information technologies make it possible to capture an e.p.r.s effect that plays a central role in the enlarged concept of economic information theory. It is complementary in several respects to the role of traditional concept of market information in economics and is discussed and promoted in the sequel to this volume. Namely, the introduced concept of an entrepreneurial e.p.r.s provides ability of connecting different types of e.p.r.s institutions and/or clubs, characterized by different appropriation rules. It may be noteworthy that these may differ substantially. The introduced concept of e.p.r.s entanglement provides somehow extraordinary properties of control of information in an economic transaction. It plays a significant role in a better understanding of intrinsic security of information concerning economic transactions, for example. The idea is that e.p.r.s information can neither be reproduced nor can wealth be transferred, manipulated, cheated or eavesdropped without being identified by members of a club. At the same time these transactions cannot be an object of only traditional market transactions. Ordinary market information, by contrast, is available to any agent in the market, in general, and can be replicated, reproduced and/or copied at will with or without costs. To ensure privacy of economic transactions and/or protect "business secrets" traditional economic concept implies an institutional formation concerning externalities somehow out of economic domain. Such an approach implies a paternalistic structure of the economic agreements that are to follow, and agents are supposed to count on an e.p.r.s protection by some, out-off-economics, legislative regulative institutions. This appears to lack a full economic argumentation, at least from the EPRT point of view where transaction costs could not be ignored. Contrary to the traditional market approach, here one bases security and/or privacy of economic transactions on the fact that an e.p.r.s agreement among agents contains: (*i*) a traditional market communication and transactions of wealth by linear relations, and (*ii*) an appropriation operator making e.p.r.s typical irreversible economic phenomena. Recall that within the traditional theory of general economic equilibrium (GET), an appropriation operator is fixed and is assumed as the pure private relation which makes the theory consistent on the issue of property rights. On the contrary, the information context of EPRT, among others things, enables one to distinguish two different natural economic notions of information: traditional market information on value of an economic object and an information on an appropriation operator embodied in the object. These issues and others on institutionalization are addressed in the sequel to this volume.

The concept of economic property rights is intuitively linked with effective incentives to create, innovate, maintain and improve economic wealth and assets. The traditional economic theories assume, explicitly or implicitly, given pure private relations or some given fixed structure which makes the particular case (model) theoretically consistent. In that way these theories actually avoid discussion on the issues at a more general level (see Arrow [8]). The literature in economics concerned implicitly or explicitly with economic property rights is huge, and even a modest survey would make our introductory notes too long. One may think of studies concerning economic externalities, rational expectations, securities, theory of contracts, insurance, bargaining under incomplete information, repeated games, signaling, discrimination, principle-agent, moral-hazard, search, entry-exit problems, bankruptcy, and property rights in the narrow-traditional sense. Note that traditional approach to economic analysis of ownership and property rights has been crucially based on the assumption that there is no wealth effect. This simplification implies that the value maximization principle is sophisticated and precise enough in the consideration of e.p.r.s issues, and that it can be applied to modeling economic agreements and other economic institutions. An efficient economic arrangement of e.p.r.s is then simply the feasible agreement that maximizes the total value received by the partners involved. Within this traditional frame of secure property rights and separable ownership many of the interesting issues were resolved and suggested in economics, concerning the economic theory of organization (see Coase [21], Barzel [14] and others), economic theory of returns (see Arrow [7], Alchian [2], Demsetz [26], for example), economic theory of residual control and ownership patterns (see Meade [50], Williamson [79], Grossman and Hart [33], Hart and Moore [37], and others), human capital theory linked to the theory of the firm (Becker [15], Klein [40] and others), and many other economic theories implicitly based on the assumptions. So for example, validity of the theory of competitive market equilibrium, (claiming that any allocation resulting from the competitive market process is efficient under conditions that: a complete set of markets exists, behavior of participants in these markets is competitive, and markets clear) is fundamentally based on the assumption that an economy of concern operates within the pure private property rights system. The efficiency principle here means that the outcome of an economic activity tends to be efficient for the partners in bargaining process if they are able to bargain together without costs and can effectively implement and enforce their decisions. The problem is that through bargaining, implementation and enforcement of their agreements, participants are, more often than not, faced with: (*i*) significant transaction costs (due to bounded rationality, imperfect information, unobservability of some economic actions, and similar); (*ii*) unclear and unenforceable assigned property rights (due to complexity of property rights patterns, mutual entanglements and unseparability of e.p.r.s where any nontrivial economic transaction becomes a carrier of market unobserved transfers involving intangible assets, reputation, corporate culture or similar); and (*iii*) uncertainty (vagueness and dynamics of institutions, dynamics of patterns due to R&D, complex institutional arrangements, and similar).

The impression is that economic theory has not been able to explain non-standard conflicts where economic property rights are treated as the basic carriers of economic wealth; of formation and/or extension of variety of collections of e.p.r.s over a new technology, information and communication; restructuring, and transmuting of an existing property right structures, and similar issues which as practical economic problems are flourishing within any modern economy. One of the reasons is that the concept of e.p.r.s is complicated, even for simple cases. For example, a person who has a personal computer, has certain e.p.r.s concerning it. S/he has rights to: (*i*) use it for applications of various installed programs and to claim e.p.r.s on their outcomes (provided that s/he has knowledge of applying these programs and obeys adjacent rules and agreements); (*ii*) not to use them; (*iii*) make some specific personal configuration (provided that general rules are followed); (*iv*) modify and extend hardware and software (within the given rules and with additional investments); (*v*) choose how often to update the services; (*vi*) make links over the World Wide Web and; (*vii*) use the computer as a transaction device for any commodity or information available (provided that rules of the services are respected); (*viii*) use it in a direct transaction with another person or institution (to transfer e.p.r.s, either permanently by selling or making a gift, or temporarily by renting) and; (*ix*) make many other economic activities involving it, that are not explicitly assigned to others by a rule, agreement, the law, or contract.

It may be noteworthy that in the perception of e.p.r.s (as elementary carriers of economic wealth in an economic transaction), one is generally inclined to think that an agent is dealing with elementary super-micro-economic phenomena, where any other economic institution should be appropriately reduced in scale, and economic agreements of direct partners should be considered. On the contrary, for a more complete understanding of some of e.p.r.s phenomena it appears to be necessary to capture the economic instruments of the global and/or large economic institutions (global economic agreements, international projects and treaties, projects of high technological performances, R&D, and those that require involvement of large number of economic agents, institutions, resources and similar) to understand the economic realm of these infinitesimals. Interestingly enough, on the one hand, for a more complete insight into a super-micro-economic level of e.p.r.s structures and generated economic conflicts one has to count on the economic devices that are able to capture and trace extremely small differences in available properties of tangible and intangible assets. On the other hand, to understand the full impact of these nanoeconomic structures and games one should focus on global institutional level where they are enhanced by appropriate aggregate economic procedures. Namely, their economic impact is revealed in significant intensity only by an aggregation implying magnitudes that spread over large economic dimensions. This is why searching for an appropriate modeling of aggregate procedures of collections of e.p.r.s is in focus of this volume, and the issues of institutionalization are addressed in detail in the sequel.

What is an enterprise from point of view of EPRT? To get an idea of possible answers to this question, let us first consider what is a collection of e.p.r.s rules of behavior of agents or partners that form an enterprise or are in some entrepreneurial agreement. The most familiar way to capture economic rules is to follow economic transactions. As a simplest and easiest example, intuitively clear to understand, we may have in mind simple exchange of goods and/or services. Economic properties embodied in a good (service) under e.p.r.s of one agent are transferred to another, who in return transfers her/his good (service) to the first one. Thus, transformations of an economic space in which partners are engaged are assumed to be invertible, and every closed collection of invertible transformations is invertible. These establish a collection of e.p.r.s rules that agents (partners) follow, generating principles of economic relations or economic laws among them. In the above simple case one may think of a barter law, implementation of rules concerning exchange of private endowments of agents and formation of an economic space - barter market, implying an elementary economic principle that equalizes "demand" and "supply" of goods or services. Formally one may think of a group and/or simple zero sum game. In general, collections of e.p.r.s rules can also serve as arguments on other economic institutions. In these more complex cases the economic transformations or transactions are not all invertible. Instead, an enterprise, considered as an e.p.r.s institution, has a weaker "gluing structure," called the mutual understanding of agents, which provides a nonlocal "linearized inverse." It now means that certain linear combinations of agreements rather than the individual elements of agreements are invertible. It is worthy to note, that this notion of mutual understanding of partners is all that is needed to get an appropriate concept of a collection of e.p.r.s rules and/or an enterprise and provide further rich applications in economics.

Another important feature of economic rules is that their representations over some economic devices, as barter market above, allow aggregation. This is familiar from theory of simple complete competitive economy. In this case aggregation is symmetric, so that agents may change their relation, implemented by the transposition of vector spaces of agents. E.p.r.s rules tend to be more complicated but enterprise representations also have an aggregate. In fact we will see a theorem that says: given any collection of enterprises that can be identified with economic vector spaces, compatible with the aggregation of economic vector spaces, one can reconstruct an e.p.r.s rule and identify the collection as its representation. So, at least in certain favorable economic circumstances we can obtain complete characterization of a club. For strict e.p.r.s rules, the ones possessing a so-called universal principle of economic rationality, the aggregation of representations is symmetric as in the simple case. This economic law is supported only up to an equivalent e.p.r.s transaction which is not given by the usual transposing of agents in their economic relations, but by the weaker quasisymmetrc structure. It is weaker because, in general, this structure incorporates variety of economic transfers which braid conflicting economic interests and in this sense avoid traditional economic conflicts. In that way it provides an argumentation of the more complex e.p.r.s rules of agents' relations rather than the symmetric ones.

The proposed concept of an enterprise has other interesting economic properties. These are connected with the well-known duality and self-duality properties from mathematical economics. In this particular case an enterprise can be considered as an agreement, the dual linear space of which is also an agreement. The e.p.r.s structure that is accepted on the dual economic linear spaces is expressed in terms of original agreement as a copartner's expansion of e.p.r.s or simple coexpansion. The idea is that an agreement is considered from the point of view of copartner by a coagreement which restores a kind of input-output symmetry to the partners that constitute an enterprise. Thus, the ordinary expansion of e.p.r.s of an agent corresponds to a sort of deductive reasoning in her/his decision making. A copartner in his/her decision making exploits coexpansion of e.r.p.s to reverse the operation and unfold e.r.p.s of the proposed agreement. The coexpansion of e.r.p.s represents an inductive rather than deductive type of reasoning on possibilities. One may think of the coexpansion of an element of agreement as a sum of all aggregates which could give the collection of e.p.r.s under consideration when combined according the underlying e.p.r.s rule structure. We may have in mind a coordinate function x of one dimensional economic factor, the case where a coexpansion Δx expresses linear addition on the factor, $x \otimes 1 + 1 \otimes x$. As an example of the probabilistic interpretation, an element x of an agreement A is the random variable, so that $x_1 = x \otimes 1$ and $x_2 = 1 \otimes x$ are two independent random variables embedded in the aggregate agreement. Here, the aggregate agreement, $A \otimes A$, corresponds to the system after two steps of implementation in a random way. Embedding x in the aggregate according to the coexpansion $\Delta x = x_1 + x_2$ would tell us precisely that collection of e.p.r.s embodied in x after aggregation is the sum of two random variables x_1, x_2. The coexpansion of an e.p.r.s collection, Δx represents all the ways in which to obtain that e.p.r.s collection x after implementation from both sides of an agreement in an aggregate, emphasizing possibilities. The rules for coexpansion are the same as the rules for expansion, with the flows reversed, and represent copartner's economic reasoning in decision making within an enterprise. This property of an e.p.r.s enterprise makes a link with traditional concept of uncertainty or random walks in economics. Generalization to a more complex setting of e.p.r.s, which implies necessity of a noncommutative formalization, and an approach that applies noncommutative probability theory and random walks for capturing and understanding of particularities of uncertainty within EPRT are addressed in detail in the sequel to this volume, as already mentioned.

In this introductory promotion of the concept of an enterprise, as a basic e.p.r.s institution and an object of fundamental research within EPRT, the following may be useful to get an intuition on a variety of domains of economic theories and methodologies where it can be useful.

Economics of externalities	○	Uncertainty
Modified GEMs	○	Noncommutative probability
Super e.p.r.s spaces	○	Stochastics of e.p.r.s patterns
Noncommutative games	○	Incomplete information
	○	
○ ○ ○ ○	Enterprise	○ ○ ○ ○
	○	
E.p.r.s rules and laws	○	Dynamic duality
Complex invariants	○	Input-output dynamics
Club economics	○	Supermicro-macro duality
Scattering and transfers	○	E.p.r.s patterns of R&D

Note that an enterprise is only the simplest e.p.r.s institution, and we would like to explore some of the ideas with much wider applications in economics, hoping for a better understanding of e.p.r.s phenomena and institutions in general. The program of EPRT is to question the economics behind an exclusive dominance of an e.r.p.s pattern taken as an axiomatic structure, as for example the pattern within the traditional economics. Such types of questions are not raised too often, but axioms in economics are economic relations between agents also, and after all they might have associated principles that govern them. The systematic way to address this kind of issue is by means of mathematical category theory, which is applied to issues on e.p.r.s in this volume.

It may be noteworthy that EPRT is not so much concerned with *'what is gained?'*, but with question *'why and how is it gained?'* An implementation of reduction program, counting on a somehow naive view that there is indeed a fundamental principle of economics implying a fixed exclusive dominant e.p.r.s structure, on which economic experiences and gains are representations, is not going to lead us too far. Namely, it is no problem to suppose that some e.p.r.s relation is absolute, as a concept of pure private property rights, for example, and that economic devices and institutions are to measure it, to compare the observed results and to provide the best one. But, narrow scope of such an omniscient concept cannot be of much help in developing EPRT. One of the ideas which have been incorporated in EPRT and discussed throughout this volume is that an economic evaluation should be thought of more generally over dynamic dual pairing or matching of one structure with another, and that a mismatch itself carries a lot interesting e.p.r.s phenomena. Although from traditional economic choice theory it is already clear that for any fixed e.p.r.s relation an economic evaluation $f(x)$ can also be read $x(f)$, where f is an element of dual structure; economists willing to deal with e.p.r.s phenomena seem to face dynamic and complex fundamentals. After all, in the world of modern economic and technological restructuring it is extremely difficult to find an economic institution where agents' behavior would be determined by some rules given out of their (or some other agents') reach. This intrinsic dynamic property of structural pairing is just what makes it more appropriate to start with abstract algebraic structures and to investigate could results of this approach be useful to the particular domain of mathematical economics.

To get an intuition on the elements of proposed EPRT research program included in this volume the following diagram may be of help. We take the view that the simple economic theories in traditional economics are based on classical logic in decision making or, roughly speaking on Boolean algebras. Then we know that the relevant duality may be provided by complementation with Boolean algebras considering self-duality according to DeMorgan's theorem. These provide nice structure of traditional economic models, self-duality of their constituents and validity of I and II welfare economic theorems. Going above and beyond takes us to intuitive logic in economic decision making of agents and coagents, and ultimately into an axiomatic framework for theory of e.p.r.s claims. Here we are dealing with economic reasoning where an agent drops the familiar exclusive dominance of a fixed e.p.r.s structure that underlies traditional economic theory on e.p.r.s. The frame of "all or nothing", that either an e.p.r.s proposition or its negation provides economic efficiency is not subtle enough to capture e.p.r.s phenomena in this setting.

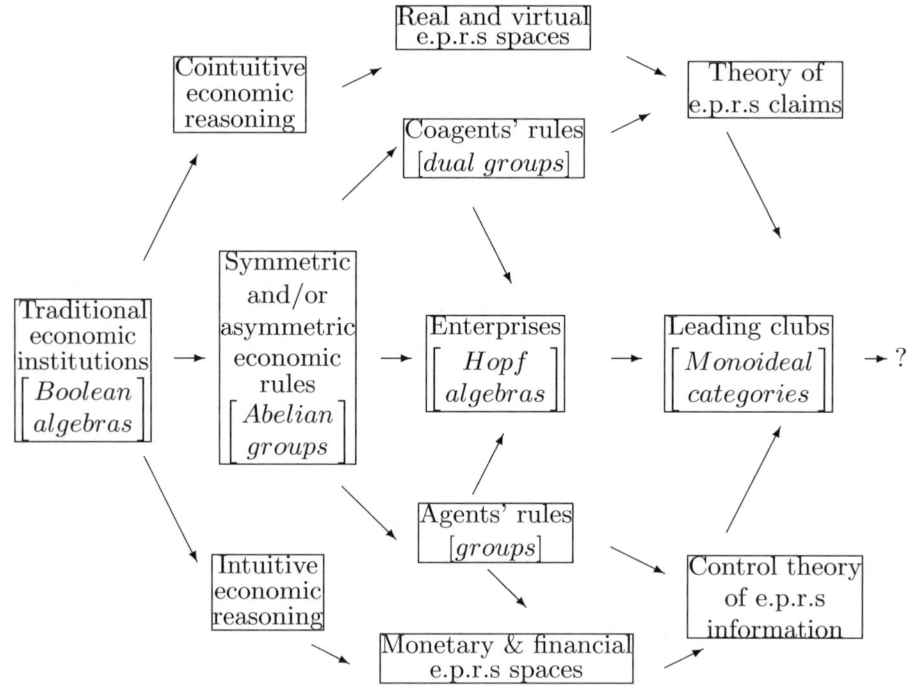

This generalization is also an essential feature of the logical structure and decision making process of e.p.r.s mechanisms. Parallel to this is the so called co-intuitive logic of her/his copartner, who drops the axiom that intersection of an e.p.r.s proposition and its negation carries no e.p.r.s (is empty). One may think of this intersection as the "boundary" of the e.p.r.s proposition, and, hence that a variety of intuitive reasonings on it become the origin of different forms of e.p.r.s institutions of concern. Especially, e.p.r.s institutional economic reasoning of coagent implies a type of e.p.r.s agreement which defines the boundary that then has the properties as one would expect for the "boundary" of an economic agreement. The conditions for e.p.r.s rational decision making on the boundary can be defined and then over combinatorial technique further developed to notion of e.p.r.s metric spaces and ultimately into some extend forms of economic (re)distribution by concepts of e.p.r.s power and/or claims. In between these extremes are some already well-know examples of a self-dual economic categories. They are based on (locally compact) symmetric economic reasoning or modified - asymmetric economic reasoning of both copartners, (Abelian groups of rules on e.p.r.s). We are in the domain of convenient economic environment where I and II economic welfare theorems can be made valid by direct modification of elements of the model, and where known economic methodologies for capturing a variety of economic phenomena can be used. The elements of economic variables are described in R^n, in a flat type of economic space, and are duals of each other. Also, here we have the examples of economic phenomena where the quantitative economic variables are cyclical, but they allow economic modeling by appropriate economic time series. The Fourier transformation interchanges the roles of the collections of e.p.r.s rule and their duals. These economic tools are well-known, scattered through out the advanced textbooks on economic theory, mathematical economics, game theory and/or econometrics, and appropriate journals, and are not discussed in this volume in detail. It is worthy to note that it might be too much to ask to ensure dynamic dual pairing of e.p.r.s institutions from self-dual structure to self-dual structures on the central axis of the diagram. In a dynamic setting of economic externalities it means that modification of e.p.r.s rules may lead to somehow strange restructuring of institutions and we are again faced with the problem of appropriate institutionalization. Roughly speaking, any e.p.r.s institutionalization implies transmutation of externalities and some new e.r.p.s pattern of $R\&D$ would expand domains of e.p.r.s, implying a need for some new restructuring and so on. Thus, an e.p.r.s pattern of intangibles embedded in an institution can be thought of as an economic source of the evolution of economic system, and e.p.r.s extensions as some sort of generalized Schumpeterian type of economic dynamics. Thus, last two "boxes," elements that lead to them, and ?, from the above diagram, are within the proposed program of this research results of which are included in the volume. The developed formal tools are to be used for concrete applications with the aim to provide algorithms for speeding up the negotiations procedures, to follow interferences of economic factors and economic property rights information accurately. Concepts of economic agreements are discussed, having a wide variety of probably unrelated concrete applications, from an entrepreneurial agreement of two agents to an international agreement or an economic alliance. This diversity is one of the themes in the economic property rights program and is a good reason for focusing on enterprises as objects of mathematical economics in this part of the program.

This volume is divided into five Chapters. Chapter 1 discusses an economic background in e.p.r.s phenomena using a simple example. The intention is to provoke an economic intuition and interest in issues and problems of the economic property rights. They, I hope, are clarified through exposition in this volume by unifying structure of economic property rights theory and by elucidation of the appropriate mathematical tools of mathematical economics.

Chapter 2 provides the definitions and basic elements of the program. First, the structures of an agreement, coagreement, biagreement and enterprise are discussed and formalized in an axiomatic way. An emphasis is on the economic interpretation of the elements while diagrams are used to help in clear presentation of relations and connections. Special attention is given in formalizing a concept of an enterprise and properties of mutual understanding map as its main constituent. Next, an intrinsic concentration of e.p.r.s interests of an agent about conflicting collections of e.p.r.s embedded in an agreement and coagreement are formalized by the concepts of argumentation and coargumentation, respectively. They are discussed from a point of view of cost (price) vis-à-vis quality, and properties of simple as well as more advanced forms of (co)argumentations are studied. This Chapter ends with basic formalization of an e.p.r.s gain and welfare structure.

Chapter 3 deals with an opening as the first extension of the elementary e.p.r.s institutions from Chapter 2. Here, simple openings are discussed in detail, providing definitions, main properties, examples of some forms and exploration of their effects on welfare. In the next Section dual aspects of opening are studied, while last two Sections are devoted to further extensions of opening through various procedures of confirmation of advance e.p.r.s spaces and formation of quasiinstituions.

Chapter 4 is concerned with representation theory and its applications to EPRT. The results obtained in the previous chapters, regarding the generalization of the e.p.r.s rules are further explored in formulation of e.p.r.s institutions of a more complex structure, by the appropriate forms of aggregation. The first Section provides a few fundamentals of the club theory, where I am trying to be as informal and nontechnical as possible. Besides the necessary definitions, some properties of general clubs and leading clubs are studied. In the next Section the generalization of opening, as a continuation of Chapter 3, is discussed through the concept of e.p.r.s transfers. Here, it is shown how the club of representations becomes a leading club with transfers, or quasiaggregate club, that incorporates sophisticated economic transactions among members and other clubs. Also it is shown how many of the e.p.r.s phenomena and constructions already studied in previous chapters can now be understood very conveniently in the club terms. These actually enable one to follow modeling concepts that support EPRT rather than to use some formulae. Finally, in the next Section the property of duality is generalized to the level of clubs and more complex e.p.r.s institutions.

Chapter 5 considers application of reconstruction theory to e.p.r.s institutions. In focus is investigation regarding possibilities of collections of elements of an economic club, which can be strictly identified with the given e.p.r.s institutions in a certain clear sense, to be equivalent to the representations of some enterprise which is to be reconstructed. The first Section discusses in detail the procedures for reconstruction in simple intuitions, while the next Section treats more complex cases of the reconstruction by transfers and provides some generalized theorems. Finally, in the last Section the examples of the e.p.r.s restructuring are discussed and a simple process of privatization is addressed in more detail.

It is a pleasure to thank all friends, colleagues and students who have helped in preparation and publication of this volume through encouragement and support, and by providing inspiring intellectual and moral environment conducive to a sustained and an exploratory scholarly work. I express my thanks to the editors of *Studies in Economic Theory* for welcoming my work into the series. I am grateful to Cornell University for its hospitality during the period when the manuscript was being completed. The research was made possible through the funding of the EPRSA which I wish to gratefully acknowledge. For my family, Sonja, Andrea and Miroslav, gratitude deeper than words can express.

Vesna Pasetta
March 2005

Contents

1

Economic Property Rights Dilemma

The aim of this Chapter is to offer an intuitive insight into economic property rights phenomena using a simple example. Assuming a vague understanding of economic elements and statements, an intention is to provoke an economic interest on issues and problems of economic economic property rights, to become more clarified through exposition of the program by this volume. A reader who is already familiar with the issues on property rights in economics, and has interest only in the formal elements of EPRT proposed in this program may skip this Chapter and start with Chapter 2.

1.1 Example

1.1.1 Partnership Problem

Consider two students, Ann and Bob, each of them has a computer as her/his asset in a private property. Assume the hardware and software characteristics of the computers are the same. In addition, Ann's and Bob's knowledge of various programs, and computer skills in general, are also their private assets. For simplicity let those be also mutually equal, by assumption. Both of them are also aware of these circumstances. Although satisfied with the performances of the computes for solving some type of problems, Ann and Bob have realized that their assets can be easily expended. They would be able to run more sophisticated programs if they aggregate their assets and run computers as 'parallel one'. Ann and Bob have both interest for advanced programs, and have enough computer programming skills to formalize and apply them. They want to be sure that, if such an enterprise is established, each of them has equal access to computer services of these more sophisticated programs. At the same time each has also interest to 'ordinary' computer service, when each of them would use her/his own computer disconnected from the other one. In other words, Ann and Bob want to be sure that an extension of her/his assets and e.p.r.s over this partnership has been made in an appropriate way. This meaning that each of e.p.r.s (including those to third parties, for example a warranty) may be appropriated separately and is not under a hazard due to established enterprise. The request seemed to be simple, since what they are asking for, is just to delineate extended performances obtained by appropriate links of their computers, i.e. an extended collection of e.p.r.s by a new assets (a 'new computer' and knowledge), in the way that those are equal, as their initial assets underlying by private property rights have been.

To get a better understanding of the problem, let us denote domain of e.p.r.s claims by $\mathbf{h}$. Then, the above story can be simply expressed in the following way,

$(A.1)$ $\mathbf{h}_p^a$ denotes Ann's (A) domain of e.p.r.s claims;
$(A.2)$ $\mathbf{h}_p^b$ denotes Bob's (B) domain of e.p.r.s claims;
$(A.3)$ $\mathbf{h}_p^a = \mathbf{h}_p^b$;
$(A.4)$ $\mathbf{h}_c = \mathbf{h} = \mathbf{h}_p^a \otimes \mathbf{h}_p^b$; aggregate e.p.r.s claims.

Problem: Find an appropriate arrangement or partnership that delineate each of partner's e.p.r.s on $\mathbf{h}$, so that the following conditions are satisfied:

(i) Ann and Bob have access to each of $\mathbf{h}_p^a$ and $\mathbf{h}_p^b$ respectively, *at the same time*, and all private Ann's and Bob's e.p.r.s are unchanged comparing to circumstances when assets were unlinked;
(ii) Ann or Bob has access to $\mathbf{h}$, *at the time*, in an equal way, confirming appropriate distribution of collections of e.p.r.s over partnership on their aggregate 'new' assets, $\mathbf{h}_{a\&b}$.

It is worth noting that $(A.1)$ implies $\mathbf{h}_p^a$ incorporates Ann's computer skills and her knowledge. Similar is valid for Bob by $(A.2)$. Also, $(A.3)$ implies: (a) an equal economic rationality in using each of the computers, for Ann and Bob, and (b) an equal valuations of each of their properties (including knowledge) and their partnership.

1.1.2 Solution

Ann's and Bob's aim is to make a schedule of accessibility of 24 hours of computer time (c/h), so that conditions (i) and (ii) are respected. An immediate suggestion is

student	*accessible c/h*
A	6
A,B	12,12
B	6

Table 1.1.

Ann and Bob are supposed to accept and be satisfied in the above schedule, having individually access to $\mathbf{h}_p^a$ and $\mathbf{h}_p^b$, during 12 hours, for each one, respectively, and sharing their rights over partnership on $\mathbf{h}$, during 6 hours, for each one. It was obvious to both of them that this schedule is made according to the requirements given by (i) and (ii).

Being economists, Ann and Bob have realized that their intention to share equal rights on whole (initial and expended) EPRS can be easily confirmed by a proper coin. Each of them perceives a proper coin as an objective device of equal division of an entity, thus they agreed that objectivity of suggestions in Table 1.1 can be easily checked by tossing two identical and proper coins. If a distribution of provisions (accessibility to advanced programs in c/h) from $\mathbf{h}$ is equal among them, it should correspond to the outcome of a distribution game with tossing two proper coins defined in the following way:

2 heads - A gets access to $\mathbf{h}$;
1 head, 1 tail - each of them get access to her/his $\mathbf{h}_p^i$ $i = a, b$;
2 tails - B gets access to $\mathbf{h}$.

The outcome of tossing of two identical proper coins provides the distribution of complete domain of e.p.r.s claims (private and partnerships') to Ann and Bob, that can be described as follows,

student	*nd*	*accessible c/h*
A (2 heads)	1/4	6
A,*B* (1 head, 1 tail)	1/2	12,12
B (2 tails)	1/4	6

Ann and Bob have been satisfied in using each of their e.p.r.s in the suggested way being confirmed by objective device (proper coins) as an equatable division of complete (aggregate and initial) e.p.r.s on their assets of concern.

1.1.3 Dilemma

After a while, Ann came with suggestion for computer-time rescheduling, as she needs more computer time for running advanced and sophisticated programs. Bob agreed, he also prefers to have more time for those programs. Ann suggested the following new schedule,

student	*accessible c/h*
A	8
A,*B*	8,8
B	8

Table 1.2.

Access to the sophisticated programs has been extended to 8 c/h for both of them, and individual 8 c/h has been enough for each of them in application of the simple programs. Both agreed to implement the schedule from the Table 1.2. But, in an intention to prove equitability of distribution of e.p.r.s by the same device (proper coins), in this division of complete EPRS both were puzzled.

Issue No.1

Applying the previous procedure in checking equitability of each of their complete rights objectively, it appears that something was wrong with this new agreement. The equitability of division of e.p.r.s, implied from tossing coins, has become the issue in some strange way. It appears that if they follow new rule, i.e. a new policy on accessibility of computer services defined by the new schedule, then

student	*?*
A (2 heads)	1/3
A,B (1 head, 1 tail)	1/3
B (2 tails)	1/3

and both of them have been aware that it can not be the case for two proper coins. Thus, each of them has started to wander is there something wrong with their ability to control her/his private e.p.r.s over partnership through collections of aggregate e.p.r.s $\mathbf{h}_{a\&b}$ on $\mathbf{h}$ and who is cheating whom, if at all. Both agreed that procedure for confirmation of the appropriation of each of their e.p.r.s over $\mathbf{h}$ has to be carefully reexamined, and that there should exist an explanation that would help them to understand the issues more precisely.

Issue No.2

At the same time, Bob noted that in Department computer room there are two new computers with performances equivalent to their $\mathbf{h}_p^i, i = a, b$. Now, he suggested, they may be better of if they sell their computes, and get a money for a summer tripe (or any other consumption or investment), and use the Department facilities further on in the next semester.

Issue No.3

Ann was thinking about using her computer for simple applications and the Department facilities just for sophisticated programs. She would like to have as best as possible information on Department policy concerning access to computer room, colleagues' demands for computer time, and how it suits her demands.

There are a lot of simple and not so simple issues for Ann and Bob, in following traces of e.p.r.s on each of initial properties, on possible extensions of performances of computers and their knowledge and programming skills by $\mathbf{h}_{a\&b}$, on transfers of e.p.r.s (for example, transfers of performances through new programs, including bugs) they have created, and similar. At the same time, each of them would like to complete her/his Ph.D as soon as possible. There has been established an intellectual race among graduate students at Department in completing their Ph.D's. In addition Ann and Bob are facing job market on which they have to compete with colleagues from other Universities, and may be between themselves too.

Before any further consideration of Issue No.2 and No.3, Ann wanted to examine her proposal that triggered e.p.r.s dilemma, and to check if there is something wrong with it, and whether there is cheating and/or misusing of partnership, from her or from Bob's side, and how to use advanced technology in the way that they are both better off.

1.2 Solution Concepts

Ann has been almost sure that Bob and she benefited from their partnership, both almost equally, but has been confused with the Dilemma, and possible questions that her new proposal of partnership arrangement might open. It was particularly important for persistence of their already established agreement on $\mathbf{h}$. Both would like to exclude possibility of mutual misunderstanding and eroding principle of agreeable sharing of e.p.r.s on domain of aggregate properties, and to exclude eventual 'strange redistribution' of e.p.r.s on the new aggregate EPRS $\mathbf{h}_{a\&b}$. Any misunderstanding on $\mathbf{h}$ may easily push them to an outcome that would make both worse off.

Being familiar with statistics Ann thought that an explanation for her puzzle might be given by some sort of positive correlation, born out of their partnership. But, she has been intrigued to understand the relation more completely. In particular, the main issue was what a procedure was to allocate the effects of augmentation of e.p.r.s in an understandable and acceptable way for both of them. She has known that a positive (negative) correlation for two classes of events accrue when there is a correspondence between them and when an event in the class is more (less) likely to happen if its correspondent in the other class does too. The probability calculus she was familiar with excesses this simply by

$$P(A|B) > P(A) \qquad P(A|B) > P(B) \qquad P(A|B) > P(A)P(B) \quad (1.1)$$

where the correlation is positive, and change of the sign to $<$ would mean a case to negative correlation. Relations in (1.1) are useful for calculations in a lot of problems she has faced in classroom, but she was not sure these formulas are to help her to clarify the correspondence relations Ann and Bob on $\mathbf{h}$, similarly as for the traditional example of correlation between smoking and lung cancer, that Ann recalls from classroom. A positive correlation of using aggregate properties on **h** may have resulted in new programs and extended computer skills and knowledge that each of them has become able to acquire on **h** - hence two events simultaneously happening on **h**. There was also a possibility of effects due to correlations with past learning and/or accumulated knowledge that each has had, i.e. of no-simultaneous events. They may have different learning abilities concerning expended performance of computers, so that one of them may need little bit more time to cope with sophisticated programs. Interferences with the other students, and professionals at Department and at Campus (Computer Help Desk) that help to each in various occasions, may also imply the positive effects. She wondered particularly, is it a correspondence that separates their ownership that causes the issue. Might, it be the case that combinations of their private rights and partnership agreement have resulted in different rationalities for pure private and partnership relation. Could there be strangely incorporated some 'public type' of reasoning of one of them or both about $\mathbf{h}_{a\&b}$ that might imply negative effects of free riding on $\mathbf{h}_{a\&b}$.

With an aim to demystify the e.p.r.s dilemma one may search for an explanation through each of the following conceptual possibilities: chance, coincidence, coordination, preestablished harmony of an exclusive dominant relation (as private relation, for example), logical identity of an economic rational behavior, and common cause.

1.2.1 Chance

In accepting a chance as an underlying concept for an explanation of e.p.r.s dilemma that have been experienced, Ann would admit a significant amount of indeterminism in partnership relation with Bob on **h**. It might be the case that some events on **h**, i.e. on their extended EPRS, though generally resulting from a sort of partnership agreement could also just happen, by chance. The dilemma No.1 about appropriate measurement of e.p.r.s, i.e. on probabilities, and supposed correlation that they have impression to experience on aggregate assets, **h** is just one of a significant amount of indeterminism of individual events that she (and also Bob) has admitted and accepted in any other domain of their activities and reality. Similarly, as there is some chance that coin tossed by one of them might always come up tail. It should not automatically imply that the coin is not fair, and that one is dishonest and/or is cheating. It is to be attributed to a chance. After all, any sequence $A_1, A_2, \ldots, A_n$, of agreements that would result from application of such a procedure (device) has the same probability $(1/2^n)$ as any other. To accept this explanation, Ann would intuitively admit that the relation has not been much of a partnership. An aggregate of e.p.r.s on **h** is extremely unlikely to persist and any positive or negative effect of their relationship on **h** is just an accident. This implies her beliefs have been that there was no real interference between their private

EPRSs. Thus, there is no sense to extrapolate the observed circumstances to a probability function, and further on to some sort of redistribution of their private EPRS, with the characteristic given in (1.1).

1.2.2 Coincidence of Interests

Consider a coincidence of Ann's and Bob's economic interests as an underlaying concept for an explanation of the Dilemma. Ann may accept the fact that she has met Bob at the Economic Department in the Graduate Program may be coincidence - as her link with Bob over **h** has noting to do particularly with Bob (and she is sure for him too). But it is not a chance, for the partnership does not just happen. Is it not the fact that they are both at the Department in the same program already a confirmation of coincidence of their ideas in the profession? Each of them can explain her/his interest in studying the program at the particular Department and University, both have been through similar admission procedure and obviously both passed a few filters in becoming graduated students. In particular each of them have expressed clearly interest in their partnership. Both are ready to share their private assets (computer and knowledge), and it is this vary private interest of each one in undertaking the action of cooperation and partnership. On domain of their aggregate economic property rights space, **h**, each one can also extend her/his private EPRS, thus bringing about positive effects. Knowledge and computer skills, each of them has initially, have been almost the same, and even more $\mathbf{h}_p^a = \mathbf{h}_p^b$, by assumption. Thus, positive correlation of their partnership is almost perfect. Even if a difference is allowed, it is always possible to construct some function that will relate them over the particular differences and different valuations of some characteristic of established partners' EPRS. For example, this relation could be logarithmic function reflecting the different scale that each one of them attributes to some characteristic of aggregate collection of e.p.r.s on **h**. Obviously, that would imply a very exact correlation, which is not pure chance, and it is not because Ann and/or Bob evaluations of e.p.r.s were somehow set by same internal economic rationality.

This concept seems acceptable as it implies persistence of their partnership relation on new aggregate asset **h**. The persistence of their partnership is attributed to the propagation of an alignment in domain of their separate private EPRS, $\mathbf{h}_p^i, i = a, b$. The problem of aggregation of e.p.r.s seems to be overcome, but only under condition that no issue remains when each of them explains to her/himself this separate private rationality on **h**. Even more, following the traditional concept of economic theory of private property, and within it, Ann can be almost sure that they both are going to be satisfied. What is important is an exclusive private e.p.r.s on $\mathbf{h}^i, i = a, b$ that each of them incorporates initially in formation of their partnership. Unfortunately, sooner or latter they will realize that condition *no issue remains*, can hardly be accepted having in mind dynamic setting of advanced knowledge and programming skills. For example, a new program (that she is not aware off at this moment), may bring substantial improvement in resolving the economic problems that they were both dealing with, but also may bring some bugs in applications. Thus, although attractive, this concept seems incomplete to Ann, as she was unable to dismissed completely the remain issues on aggregate assets **h**, and to specify completely their partnership relation. Thus, she continues to search having this solution concept on hand.

1.2.3 Coordination of Partnership

A concept of coordination as an underlaying explanation for extension of e.p.r.s on an aggregate of assets and benefits from it seems always attractive. It might be the case that a correspondence that Bob and Ann are experiencing on **h** affects various type of signals that, at first sight in a strange way, coordinate their behavior over **h**. Some information is provided in their communication from one to another on **h**. This information producing effects partially in each of partners behavior about their assets, actually imply the corresponding extension of their knowledge and programming skills that have positive impacts. Even more, these can be explained nicely as positive externalities of their partnership. The situation need not be deterministic. There can be indeterminate signaling and incomplete information if an information is not certain to be perceived equally, and/or might not have certain effect for them both.

In this case their communication over **h** seems to play a crucial role. Thus, it is not the domain of their private EPRS, $(\mathbf{h}_p^i, i = a, b)$, as separate properties that have much of an influence. To support this idea, they have to admit that each of them has some additional information to the common knowledge about $\mathbf{h}_p^i, i = a, b$ and **h**. Information that should eventually be communicated, not to be simple empty chat, is supposed to change EPRS for them both through partnership relation. Already being or becoming equipped with different knowledge, they are in an asymmetric position on **h**.

Ann is becoming more and more puzzled from the above reasoning, which although acceptable, it was excluded by starting assumptions. She recalls that their partnership started with perception that Bob and her, both have had common and almost full knowledge about their assets, $\mathbf{h}^i, i = a, b$ and **h**. Thus, any information in question, is already simultaneously familiar to Bob, and to Ann. If the case, they actually do not need to communicate, for almost all is already known. If not the case, then neither Ann nor Bob, could be sure that in cooperation of their private assets through partnership another side is not misusing some of e.p.r.s or cheating on **h**. The explanation that they might have different learning abilities is also not completely acceptable here, as the full knowledge for the $\mathbf{h}^i, i = a, b$ and **h** was assumed.

A way out of contradiction in Ann's reasoning above might be that each of them has two or more coexisting e.p.r.s rationalities, that are extended on **h**. Correlation between them is a result of their counterfactual type of arguments[1] to her/himself and among them resulting in events that are happening to subspaces of **h**. The problem here might be that Bob and Ann have already defined their economic rationality for each $\mathbf{h}_p^i, i = a, b$ and **h**. They need to allow a degree of imagination to each other, and to be ready to tolerate each other's behavior that might seem strange, wondering always where the gauge is. Thus, Ann figured out that a change of rationality and learning can not be excluded, but she also realized that these dynamic phenomena, whatever interesting and more realistic, will certainly make her intention to prove rightfulness of her proposal that triggered the Dilemma extremely complex. Thus, she left this concept aside, for a moment.

1.2.4 Preestablished Harmony of Dominance

It might be that some preestablished harmony of an exclusive dominant e.p.r.s relation, in this case private one, should be the appropriate concept for an explanation. E.p.r.s dilemmas that Ann and Bob are trying to understand in partnership are simple consequences of private type of their relation and economic rationality each of them has already experienced. She is able confidently to predict its persistence on an aggregate asset as along as it stays that way. None of the above explanation play much of a role, and they should not search for an explanations, out of this one, at all. Any issue that might appear should not be of importance for their e.p.r.s. They should ignore it, and accept that they have guarantees on their exclusive private EPRS, $\mathbf{h}^i, i = a, b$ and **h**, as they both are understanding it quite well, and each is acting according to her/his free will. Even more, if one of them make some strange action or experiment, or starts to behave randomly there is no respectful argument to question a private type of their relation. Both of them should continue to study and work on her/his PhD without loosing time in searching for answer(s) to such a silly question. Even if there are some "unexplainable e.p.r.s phenomena," they are so vague, and surely not worthy of consideration.

There is no harm in admitting that neither Ann nor Bob, or nor both of them (nor we) have any appropriate explanation for the e.p.r.s dilemma on **h**. In any case there is a lot of other important economic problems to seek answers for, anyway. Bob and Ann being brought up in an economic environment of free, private, market orientated society already are to have firm rationality and belief about intrinsic justice incorporated into private property on an asset. They are aware that if both of them share these beliefs and learning experiences, and behave according to the belief, almost all of their actions have already been harmonized. Even, if she supposes some disputes or

[1] They are accepting that their economic rationality about partnership is imperfectly fixed but familiar, one they would be stuck with whether or not they use it in the analysis of some other possible worlds, over counterfactual operators $\Box\!\!\rightarrow$, or $\Diamond\!\!\rightarrow$, i.e seeking an ownership reasoning over '*if it were the case* _, *then it would be the case that*' .... and/or '*if it were the case* _ *then it might be the case that*' ....

misunderstandings over enterprise on $\mathbf{h}$, they can easily find an arbitrator, who is able to resolve any issue impartially. For Ann it was a nice explanation, almost "too nice to be true". There has been a phenomenon which does not fit the pure private rationality. To get rid of it by attaching a notation of pre-established harmony of an exclusive dominant relation as a private relation, Ann should admit: (a) there has been no much of her (or Bob's) free will in decision making as the *Rule of An Exclusive Dominance* has already predetermined each of their action; or coordinates two series of events on the domains of Ann's and Bob's e.p.r.s by an arbitrator, or (b) she has no explanation, but refuses to consider e.p.r.s dilemma nevertheless, if she is to maintain the completeness of an understanding of her simple economic world.

1.2.5 Exclusive Economic Rationality

An exclusive economic rationality about issues of e.p.r.s, should correspond to an economic logical identity in a general sense. For example known concepts of maximizing an utility or preference seems very attractive as underlaying base. In particular, it provides nice, satisfying and relatively easily understood procedure in calculations. Namely, having $(A.1)-(A.4)$ and procedural rules (i) and (ii) the effects of Ann's and Bob's relation, being economic relation, can be explained as a functional relationship. Having in mind the modern economic theories, one is able to recall examples from the theory of private property in economics, and real economic activities, where almost any economic relation can be identified with an intention of maximizing preference and/or utility to participants. Then the circumstances are clear, and Ann can say that $\mathbf{h}^a$ and $\mathbf{h}^b$, have some value and/or are some functions of utility of partnership, denoted it by $\mathbf{h}$, $\mathbf{h}_p^a = f(\mathbf{h})$, and $\mathbf{h}_p^b = g(\mathbf{h})$, for some f and g. This allows calculations using market procedures (mechanism) over certain random variables, as well as verification on a market of computer services. Thus, being convinced empirically, $\mathbf{h}^*$, and each of $\mathbf{h}^i, i = a, b$, are carrier of e.r.p.s, and are co-existing, she can adopt some equation as definition or convention on an aggregate EPRS.

Little bit more precisely, an $A\&B$ partnership, is observed by Ann and Bob by an appropriate mapping with perception of e.p.r.s A_A and A_B respectively, concerning complete EPRSs, i.e. $\mathbf{h}$ and $\mathbf{h}^i, i = a, b$. Mappings (an agreement and coagreement) A_A and A_B have certain eigenvectors on EPRS (collections of e.p.r.s) in common, reflecting a partnership relation they are in. Denote these collections (vectors) by $h_1, h_2, \ldots, h_n$, with corresponding eigenvalues: $A_A h_j = a_j h_j$ and $A_B h_j = b_j h_j, j = 1, \ldots, n$. Now one can consider only EPRS spanned by these collections (vectors) as they established space of partnership on an aggregate asset. This is obviously a subspace of their complete EPRS. Any collection of e.p.r.s (vector) therein is a superposition $h = \sum c_j h_j$. Thus, one can predict with certainty that, if gains for Ann and Bob in an agreement A_A and A_B are both measured on this aggregate $\mathbf{h}$ and the things are (as have been) fixed by a partnership scheme, the outcome will be (a_k, b_k) for some k. Thus, she reached a *conditional certainty* on aggregate asset, i.e. on their common property formed by aggregation. If for Ann benefits from $A\&B$ common property yields value a_k, then the benefits for Bob is certain to yield the corresponding value b_k (if all the a_i are distinct, or else, a value in the set $\{b_j | a_j = a_k\}$). Thus, thinking about complex system of partnership relation $\mathbf{h}$ as some sort of joining each of her/his private asset $\mathbf{h}^i, i = a, b,$ the gains are: $A_A \otimes I$ for A, and $I \otimes A_B$, for B. These are both simple functions of their aggregate $A_A \otimes A_B$, as a partnership scheme. Thus, gains expressed by agreement and coagreement A_A and A_B, despite being partial in appearance and/or indirect valuation of a partnership, measure gains on single common property $\mathbf{h}$. Thus, one should not wonder that correlations can be found in suitably chosen arrangement.

In addition, as $\mathbf{h}$ consists of $\mathbf{h}^i, i = a, b,$ it implies some bi-orthogonal decomposition (canonical decomposition) $S_{\mathbf{h}} = \sum c_j (h_j^a \otimes h_j^b)$ such that the reduced states for Ann, $\#S[a]$, and Bob, $\#S[b]$, are diagonal in the basis of an individual private property $\{h_j^a\}$ for A and $\{h_j^b\}$, for B. If A_A and A_B are gains such that $A_A h_j = e_j h_j^a$ and $A_B h_j^b = d_j h_j^b$ (with $e_j \neq e_k$ and $d_j \neq d_m$ if $j \neq k$, and $j \neq m$), then the quantities A_A and A_B are thus perfectly correlated in the two private properties - components of $\mathbf{h} = \mathbf{h}_p^a \otimes \mathbf{h}_p^b$. So in the aggregation of an exclusive dominant relation, as private ownership for the example, in this way into a partnership relation a perfect correlation is not rare and unusual. Even more, with appropriate calculus it can be shown that every partnership arrangement displays some perfect correlation if looked at in a certain way.

Ann has been almost sure the problem is actually overcome in limits, as private type of e.p.r.s is guaranteed to each of them. The only problem is that it seems that the procedure itself has swept under the rug the presuppositions about their partnership relations over $\mathbf{h}$, which were substantive. For some other exclusive dominant appropriation scheme, i.e. an fixed ownership scheme, may be again proposed and adopted for a good reasons, but its adequacy should not be taken a priori.

1.2.6 Common Rationality

Effects of a partnership relation and extensions of e.p.r.s on $\mathbf{h}$, are simultaneously separable. They are happening to Bob and Ann, not to some strange entity Ann&Bob, although they might agree to call their partnership on $\mathbf{h}$, *A&B club* or *enterprise*. Then gains can be explained, very simply by the fact that whatever is happening on $\mathbf{h}$ can be traced back to some economic effects in sharing e.p.r.s on $\mathbf{h}$ in the past, including the initial contribution of each one's private properties $\mathbf{h}^i, i = a, b$. Their individual computers have had same hardware and software performance, they might be treated as synchronized, and as any partnership relation between Ann and Bob on $\mathbf{h}$ happens when their private assets are linked, there is no convincing reason to suspect future synchronization in computes performances and their programming skills. Some information and signals are exchanged, but both computers can be pre-programmed at the initial point. Thus, a concept of simple causality of private contribution and persistence of an e.p.r.s on it can be helpful. It has not lost sense even in an indeterministic environment of incomplete knowledge of internal structure of each of private assets; hardware and software of computes, and possible new knowledge accumulated through learning, and/or in creating more sophisticated programs on **h** by Ann, Bob or both. Although there is sense in speaking about causal order in the context of indeterminism, she should be careful at least at two points.

(*i*) It might be the case that private ownership just offers a pattern that might not be by itself sufficient for explanation of e.p.r.s dilemma from partnership on **h**. For example, if she allows different abilities in learning, then she can expect different gains for each of them in using **h** although it is hard to say that property rights pattern does not fit. Namely, she has considered her as well as Bob's knowledge and learning abilities as each of their own very private property. Thus, she has to add some additional conditions that will ensure a continuous process of partnership and 'rightful' shares to each of them. Thus, she has got only necessary conditions for causal order of their e.p.r.s in an indeterminism of aggregate e.p.r.s on **h**.

(*ii*) Second, intuitively she has been aware that every possible e.p.r.s phenomena that might be of interest in clarifying a proposal for partnership might not admit a causal e.p.r.s model. It might be the case that something is happening on **h** that is neither Ann's nor Bob's.

1.3 Policy Concepts of Appropriation

Let us get intuition on policy concepts of appropriations in EPRT trough the Example. Thus, in the Example the essence of the issues and Ann's aim has been to sketch a base for decision she is facing in next semester - *which of possible arrangement for covering her demands of computer services would be the best one.* As a summer exercise, before facing and implementing any decision in reality, she experimented theoretically about possible outcomes, hoping that this would help her in formulating her choice. Intuitively understanding concepts that could be useful in resolving e.p.r.s dilemma, brought up by formation of A&B enterprise, Ann indented in addition to clarify her statements imposed by issues No.2, and 3 more precisely. In her experiment she is searching for answers to the following:

(*i*) what should be the foundation of her e.p.r.s on a computer service, i.e. a base of her appropriation policy;
(*ii*) what should be her strategies within a chosen appropriation policy;
(*iii*) when and how should she change an arrangement defined by (*i*) and (*ii*), due to new elements (new technology and/or knowledge) that she could not be aware off at the moment.

Thus, (*i*) is to define a category of an e.p.r.s institution that she is accepting and/or forming as an agreeable structure of economic relations that she is welling to deal with in the next period. (*ii*) is to specify her strategies within a chosen institution or club, to ensure complete covering of her demands of computer services and maximal desirable effects of her assets (including knowledge), and (*iii*) to make her able to transform her choices under (*i*) and (*ii*) and to ensure accuracy of technology she is using, as well as her computer skills (knowledge), including her learning abilities. Obviously, issues under (*i*) and (*ii*) are to be (re)examined in a dynamic setting.

To make experiment manageable, Ann decided to consider following categories of e.p.r.s or institutions corresponding to possible choices of her appropriation policies:

($\mathcal{A}1$) Pure private, and/or private $A\&(\cdot)$ enterprise, where $(\cdot)$ denotes Bob, or any other student that she is able to cooperate with, on the basis of mutual understanding of structure of private e.p.r.s.
($\mathcal{A}2$) Pure common e.p.r.s - Using only Department's facilities, being within the rules that have been established at the Department, including tradition and convention of sharing available computer services at the computer room, as well as current arraignments on using facilities.
($\mathcal{A}3$) A fixed mixture of all/some of forms from above.

To formulate appropriate strategies within a chosen e.p.r.s institution are sketched in the following subsections.

1.3.1 Private Forms

One may note that formulation of a private e.p.r.s institution or club actually corresponds to issues discussed in formulation of e.p.r.s dilemma, that were already considered and are here reexamined in a bit more precisely manner.

Pure Private Club

A frame of pure private ownership seems most attractive to Ann. For a moment assume Ann has no budget constrains in purchasing any computer service. Being extremely lucky, there is no convincing reason to frame herself within any other appropriation policy than pure private. She is in position to get almost complete information on what might be the best choice for her at a market of computer service, and to use such type of service whenever she needs to. The frame of pure private e.p.r.s offers her maximal freedom in strategies concerning choice of programs, technological characteristics of computers, type of warranties and other services, covering her demands for computer services to a maximal extent in a temporal as well as in a dynamic setting. Any other institutional frame might reduce her e.p.r.s and make her worse off. The only constraint that she is facing is a level of technology available on computer services market. Thus, comparing to any other student at her Department she is already lucky enough to be almost sure that she is in an advanced position as far as meeting her demands on computer services is concerned. The formation of Ann's pure private club for computer service thus implies exclusive dominant appropriation of e.p.r.s by Ann within the club. Any other member might enjoy and benefit from membership in the extend in which one contributes to extension of Ann's e.p.r.s, estimated according a rule or an ad hock decision made by her.

Private Partnership

In more real and actual circumstances of some financial constraints Ann has to acquire information on variety of performances and types of computers and programs within her budget. A purchase of the latest technological advancement or even just better one, or enrollment in a course of advanced programming, may not be within attainable domain. Nevertheless, she already knows that, cooperating with Bob, (or some other student) she can get computer services at an extend level. The case seems simple enough to provide explicit solution. Her understanding of private e.p.r.s on $\mathbf{h}_p^a$ has also been simple. What she has expected from $\mathbf{h}_p^a$ and general theory of e.p.r.s, can be simplified and understood as: *Whatever happens to my property, it ends up as my property.* In a little bit more precise language, any dynamics of e.p.r.s collections (vectors) from $\mathbf{h}_p^a$ should be within $\mathbf{h}_p^a$. A partnership relation and formation of $\mathbf{h}_{a\&b}$ has made the case a bit more complex. Having in mind known dichotomy, private versus common property, it appears that she can simplify partnership relation on $\mathbf{h}_{a\&b}$ in the way to incorporate an idea that neither Bob (nor her) is able to exclude each other from e.p.r.s on $\mathbf{h}_{a\&b}$. Thus, $\mathbf{h}_{a\&b}$ can be in two states, a, b depending on whether Ann or Bob have access to $\mathbf{h}_{a\&b}$. A permutation of a state from $\mathbf{h}_{a\&b}^a$ to a state $\mathbf{h}_{a\&b}^b$ would only mean that it is Bob's term for an access to $\mathbf{h}_{a\&b}$. Accepting this intuition, it implies that it is enough to distinguish only two e.p.r.s forms on $\mathbf{h}$:

(*i*) symmetric states corresponding to each others private e.p.r.s collections, $\mathbf{h}_p^a$ and $\mathbf{h}_p^b$, with assumptions given by $A1 - A4$, (see page 2); and
(*ii*) asymmetric states corresponding to private partnership, i.e. closed private $A\&B$ enterprise, $\mathbf{h}_{a\&b}$.

To ensure an equality in appropriation of e.p.r.s on $\mathbf{h}$ she has to adopt a mechanism which is extraordinary, as it appeared in her proposal and e.p.r.s dilemma. The modification of her (and Bob) conventional perceptions of a mechanism that implies equitable division of an asset may have resulted from strong mutual impacts in separation (delineation) of e.p.r.s collections on $\mathbf{h}_{a\&b}$.

The situations when she has access to some of the computers can be described by imagining coins characterized only by whether they land heads up

(Ann's access) or tails (not Ann's access ≡ Bob's access). Then the traditional mechanism of delineating e.p.r.s into equal portions by a coin can be used, but in a modified version. The classical statistics prescribes a probability measure p^{nd} for two such coins in which the events are independent. If she tries to resolve the e.p.r.s dilemma of equal appropriation on their private A&B club property $\mathbf{h}_{a\&b}$, using reasoning of classical statistics, she already learned that she is going to be trapped. Thus, she should give up on the classical assumption and normal independent distribution, that each arrangement of individual e.p.r.s on $\mathbf{h}_p^a$ and $\mathbf{h}_p^b$, joined together provides the same access to Ann and Bob equiprobable. What is needed is an assumption about equal accessibility to complete EPRS, and a procedure that incorporates their interdependence, emphasizing a possible access to $\mathbf{h}_p^a, \mathbf{h}_p^b$, and $\mathbf{h}_{a\&b}$ as equiprobable. Then this is analogous to the assertion that, if two coins are tossed, the possibilities of 2 heads, 1 head, and 0 heads are equiprobable. But, this is exactly, what she got in her proposal with the intuitive understanding of ensuring each of their private e.p.r.s on aggregate $\mathbf{h}_{a\&b}$ of the private A&B enterprise.

Recall the tables, with the alternative probability distributions of the private A&B e.p.r.s, $\mathbf{h}$.

student	*# heads*	*# tails*	p^{nd}	p^{cp}	*access in c/h*	
					nd	*cp*
A	2	0	1/4	1/3	6	8
A,B	1	1	1/2	1/3	12,12	8,8
B	0	2	1/4	1/3	6	8

It can be rewritten by:

student	*# heads*	*# tails*	p^{nd}	p^{cp}	*access in c/h*	
					nd	*cp*
A	a,b		1/4	1/3	6	8
A,B(a)	a	b	1/4	1/6	6,6	4,4
A,B(b)	b	a	1/4	1/6	6,6	4,4
B		a,b	1/4	1/3	6	8

Table 1.3.

Thus, whether probability measure p^{nd} or p^{cp} gives equal probabilities to equal e.p.r.s, depends on whether the first or second table reflects the real equal partition over space of e.p.r.s on $A\&B$ enterprise. Using labeling e.p.r.s subspaces and second table, conditional probabilities of having the access to $\mathbf{h}_{a\&b}$ can be calculated as follows:

$$\begin{array}{lll} p^{nd}(\mathbf{h}^a_{a\&b}|\mathbf{h}^b) = \frac{1/4}{1/4+1/4} = \frac{1}{2} = p^{nd}(\mathbf{h}^a_p) = \frac{1}{2} & \text{no correlation} \\ p^{cp}(\mathbf{h}^a_{a\&b}|\mathbf{h}^b) = \frac{1/3}{1/3+1/6} = \frac{2}{3} > p^{cp}(\mathbf{h}^a_p) = \frac{1}{3} & \text{positive correlation} \end{array}$$

In that way, an intuitive indication, that an e.p.r.s model of $\mathbf{h}$ incorporates an augmentation of e.p.r.s by positive correlations of individual e.p.r.s joint over partnership within $A\&B$ enterprise is explicitly shown, as well as that equitable divisions of e.p.r.s among partners.

1.3.2 Common Forms

In Department computer room there are two computers, $\mathbf{h}_1$ and $\mathbf{h}_2$. Let us assume they have same performances as Ann's and/or Bob's, $\mathbf{h}^i_p, i = a, b$. The problem is to determine would it be economic rational for Ann to found her e.p.r.s on computer service only on the fact that she is a member of Department and has access to Department facilities as any other student. Thus, it has economic sense to consider possibility to sell her asset (computer), $\mathbf{h}^a_p$, (and to spend or save money for whatever she pleases) and to use Department facilities further on. She perceives this possibility as an extension of her assets, due to accessibility to this common (Department's) property.

She is framing herself into categorical circumstances conceptually different from previous private case. Computer facilities are under Department's ownership and control, with its policy on accessibility to computer room and computers, purchase of advance hardware and/or software, organization of service and appointment of assistant-managers, and similar. Let us denote such a policy as D-policy.

It is plausible to assume that no student at Department is excluded from an access to the computer room. There are four[2] graduate students, and there is a general claim that they should have equal access to computer services par day. But, during the summer there are just two of them, Ann and Bob, that split analysis and comparison of this category to the previous one, into two cases: Summer period and Regular semester.

Only Ann and Bob Again

The particularity of summer period, only Ann and Bob are at Department, and the fact that hardware and software of Department's computers are equivalent to Ann's and Bob's private computers, make this case compatible to assumptions $A.1$, $A.2$ and $A.3$ from page 2. Namely, it is a direct analogue

[2] Any fixed number equal or higher than number of computers in Department's computer room can be used. Four seems to be enough to present the basic ideas and to get intuition about a common e.p.r.s institution.

to the private partnership already discussed under e.p.r.s dilemma, but now framed within the category of common appropriation EPRS. Here an appropriation of e.p.r.s though computer services is founded on Ann's and Bob's membership of the Department. An assumption concerning D-policy should be incorporated into analysis, as it has a crucial role in framing possibilities. Namely, D-policy regulates, among others, a formation of an aggregate of $\mathbf{h}_1$ and $\mathbf{h}_2$. So for example, a natural D-policy of no exclusive e.p.r.s to any student to computer room, would actually prevent formation of an aggregate $\mathbf{h}_1 \otimes \mathbf{h}_2$. A possibility of existence of an aggregate EPRS, $\mathbf{h}_D$, as an analogue to $\mathbf{h}_{a\&b}$, is excluded and assumption A.4 is not valid. In that way, they are also prevented from applying more sophisticated programs and/or an advance technology. Even if in the computer room there is only one student (Ann or Bob), no one may be allowed to use both computers. The underlying argument of such D-policy is that some other student could come in any moment and should have free access to one of the D-computers.

Having in mind Table 1.3, a probability distribution corresponding to the D-policy of *no exclusive use of Department facilities,* is p^{dc}, $p^{dc} = (0, 1/2, 1/2, 0)$ or simply $p^{dc} = (0, 1, 0)$. It simply shows that Ann and Bob have 24 c/h access to $\mathbf{h}_1$ or $\mathbf{h}_2$, during the summer. Interestingly enough, this case is a direct analogue to the Ann's and Bob's private policies *not to cooperate*, i.e. to use each of private computers separately so that no $A\&B$ enterprise is formed. The conditional probability of having access to both D-computes is $p^{dc}(\mathbf{h}^a|\mathbf{h}_i^b) = 0, i = 1, 2$ which is less than $p^{dc}(\mathbf{h}_i^a) = \frac{1}{2}, i = 1, 2$. So, there is some negative effect on common Department asset associated with this type of D-policy. It can be concluded that this D-policy, by preventing formation and implementation of an advance technology, implies negative effects on e.p.r.s of members.

The D-authorities may change this D-policy and allow formation $\mathbf{h}_D = \mathbf{h}_1 \otimes_D \mathbf{h}_2$. Then depending on particular type of regulation of rights at 'new' Department's computer $\mathbf{h}_D$, Ann (and Bob), gets access to $\mathbf{h}_1, \mathbf{h}_2$, and $\mathbf{h}_D$. It is easy to see that if D-policy $\otimes_D$ is such that Ann and Bob are allowed to organize computer service almost completely as it suites their demands, we get a case that is analogue to running Ann's and Bob's private 'business' with their computers. Thus, on the short run (over a summer), Ann and Bob are going to face an analogous to the e.p.r.s dilemma in organizing required computer service to each of them through Department facilities, $(\mathbf{h}_1, \mathbf{h}_2, \mathbf{h}_D)$, as they would have already faced in previous case. In addition, Ann (or Bob) may be better off by selling her (his) computer, or combing its performances with those of $\mathbf{h}_D$.

At the same time, she (and Bob) is going to need computer service over next semester too, when circumstances are expected to be different, at least for the number of students that have access to Department facilities.

Regular Case

In more regular circumstances of activities at Department there are four students. Also assume that Department policy concerning studens' organization of required computer service through $(\mathbf{h}_1, \mathbf{h}_2, \mathbf{h}_D)$, is flexible, formation D's 'parallel computer' is allowed, so that $\mathbf{h}_D = \mathbf{h}_1 \otimes_D \mathbf{h}_2$. A D-policy, $\otimes_D$, then regulates the accessibility to Department facilities $\mathbf{h}^D$, i.e to $\mathbf{h}_D, \mathbf{h}_1$, and $\mathbf{h}_2$. A general claim that each of the students is guaranteed same access to these facilities seems plausible. A mechanism to implement some of D-policy within the general claim might be as follows:

- (i) Normal independent access (nd),
- (ii) Equal access in all cases, (dp),
- (iii) Forbidden exclusive access, (dc),
- (iv) Favoring exclusive access, (Dp).

To get more complete insight into effects each of the suggested policies on $\mathbf{h}_D$, $\mathbf{h}_1$ and $\mathbf{h}_2$ Table 1.4 is provided. It expresses partition of D-EPRS into four clusters, one for each student, and implementation of some of the above policies $(i)-(iv)$, on the possible states in Department facilities. The partition of D-EPRS to the students is denoted by S_1, S_2, S_3, S_4. A state description of D-EPRS is given by S_i^D, S_{ij}^D, where state S_i^D corresponds to the case where i student $i = 1, 2, 3, 4$, has exclusive access to $\mathbf{h}_D$, and state $S_{i,j}^D$, where two students i, and $j, i \neq j$, $i, j = 1, 2, 3, 4$ have access to $\mathbf{h}_1$, and/or $\mathbf{h}_2$.

	# heads				(i)	(ii)	(iii)	(iv)
states	S_1	S_2	S_3	S_4	p^{nd}	p^{dp}	p^{dc}	p^{Dp}
S_{12}^D	1	1	0	0	2/16	1/10	1/6	0
S_{13}^D	1	0	1	0	2/16	1/10	1/6	0
S_{14}^D	1	0	0	1	2/16	1/10	1/6	0
S_{24}^D	0	1	0	1	2/16	1/10	1/6	0
S_{34}^D	0	0	1	1	2/16	1/10	1/6	0
S_{23}^D	0	1	1	0	2/16	1/10	1/6	0
S_1^D	2	0	0	0	1/16	1/10	0	1/4
S_2^D	0	2	0	0	1/16	1/10	0	1/4
S_3^D	0	0	2	0	1/16	1/10	0	1/4
S_4^D	0	0	0	2	1/16	1/10	0	1/4

Table 1.4.

Here p^{nd} corresponds to standard D_{np}-policy of an equal c/h access of each student to each computer; p^{dp} to a D_{dp}-policy of an equitable arrangement of access to $\mathbf{h}_D$, $\mathbf{h}_1$ and $\mathbf{h}_2$ for all four students; p^{dc} to D_{dc}-policy where formation of $\mathbf{h}_D$ and an exclusive use of facilities by any student is forbidden, and finally p^{Dp} to a D_{Dp}-policy where only $\mathbf{h}_D$ and an aggregate arraignment is assumed to be used by all students.

Note that the general claim of equal access of 6 c/h to each student does not imply one-to-one distribution of internal time. Also note that two states of the D-EPR system have a natural economic interpretation of a level of computer technology. System is in a state of an advance technology, S_i^D, if one of the students S_i, $(i = 1, 2, 3, 4,)$ has exclusive access to $\mathbf{h}_D$ and in a state of traditional technology, $S_{i,j}^D$, if two students i, and $j, i \neq j,\ i, j = 1, 2, 3, 4$ have access to $\mathbf{h}_1$, and/or $\mathbf{h}_2$, respectively. To get a better insight into the computer time schedules resulting from implementation of the above D-policies the following tables may be useful.

states	p^{nd} c/h				p^{dc} c/h				p^{dc} c/h				p^{Dp} c/h			
	S_1	S_2	S_3	S_4	S_1	S_2	S_3	S_4	S_1	S_2	S_3	S_4	S_1	S_2	S_3	S_4
I	1^{30}	1^{30}	0	0	1^{12}	1^{12}	0	0	2	2	0	0	0	0	0	0
II	1^{30}	0	1^{30}	0	1^{12}	0	1^{12}	0	2	0	2	0	0	0	0	0
III	1^{30}	0	0	1^{30}	1^{12}	0	0	1^{12}	2	0	0	2	0	0	0	0
IV	0	1^{30}	0	1^{30}	0	1^{12}	0	1^{12}	0	2	0	2	0	0	0	0
V	0	0	1^{30}	1^{30}	0	0	1^{12}	1^{12}	0	0	2	2	0	0	0	0
VI	0	1^{30}	1^{30}	0	0	1^{12}	1^{12}	0	0	2	2	0	0	0	0	0
VII	1^{30}	0	0	0	2^{24}	0	0	0	0	0	0	0	6	0	0	0
VIII	0	1^{30}	0	0	0	2^{24}	0	0	0	0	0	0	0	6	0	0
IX	0	0	1^{30}	0	0	0	2^{24}	0	0	0	0	0	0	0	6	0
X	0	0	0	1^{30}	0	0	0	2^{24}	0	0	0	0	0	0	0	6
	6	6	6	6	6	6	6	6	6	6	6	6	6	6	6	6

Thus, from the table it was clear that all students have equal access to Department facilities (computer time), each one is guaranteed 6 hours. To understand different internal varieties, resulting from implementations of different D-policies, the conditional probabilities of assigning the $\mathbf{h}_D$, $\mathbf{h}_1$ and $\mathbf{h}_2$ to Ann's (or any other student) disposal can be calculated under condition that it is assigned to some other student. Note that each of the first six states $S_{i,j}^D$ should be replaced by two substates,

$$S_{i,j}^D \Rightarrow \begin{array}{l} i \text{ has access to } \mathbf{h}_1 \text{ and } j \text{ has access to } \mathbf{h}_2, \\ \text{or} \\ i \text{ has access to } \mathbf{h}_2 \text{ and } j \text{ has access to } \mathbf{h}_1, \\ i, j = 1, 2, 3, 4, i \neq j. \end{array}$$

which actually provide the same e.p.r.s to i and j.

Then, to the event that student 1, let us say Ann $(1 \equiv A)$, has access to Department facilities, i.e. D-facilities is in state $S_{1\equiv A,(\cdot)}^D(\mathbf{h}.)$, is assigned 1/4 of 24 D-c/h, according to all D-policies as a general claim. This is expressed over all probability measures, p^{nd}, p^{dp}, p^{dc}, and p^{Dp}, (First element of the last row of the tables). The conditional probabilities then are not the same, and for example the following can be concluded concerning the effects of different D-policies:

$p^{nd}(S_1(\mathbf{h}_D)\|S_j(\mathbf{h}_k))$	$= \frac{1}{4}$	no correlation under D_{nd}-policy;
$p^{dp}(S_1(\mathbf{h}_D)\|S_1(\mathbf{h}_k))$	$= \frac{2}{5}$	positive effects of an advanced technology under D_{dp}-policy;
$p^{dp}(S_1(\mathbf{h}_D)\|S_j(\mathbf{h}_k))$	$= \frac{1}{5}$	negative effect of a conventional technology under D_{pc}-policy;
$p^{dc}(S_1(\mathbf{h}_1)\|S_j(\mathbf{h}_k))$	$= \frac{1}{3}$	positive effects of cooperation between students under D_{dc}-policy
$p^{Dp}(S_1(\mathbf{h}_1)\|S_1(\mathbf{h}_k))$	$= 1$	maximal positive effects of advance technology under D_{Dp}-policy;
$p^{Dp}(S_1(\mathbf{h}_D)\|S_j(\mathbf{h}_k))$	$= 0$	negative effects of applying simple program in an advance technology under D_{Dp}-policy.

$j = 2, 3, 4 \quad k = 1, 2$

One may note that appropriation of e.p.r.s based on a Department facilities conventionally characterized as appropriation on a common domain of e.p.r.s contains collections of private e.p.r.s of participants, at least in the form of e.p.r.s on knowledge those involved in formation an institution or a club. Thus, even with high level of approximation and simplification it seems there is no particular sense of pure domain of common e.p.r.s.

1.3.3 Mixed Forms

Let us get better intuition on Puzzle No. 3, and sketch discussion on a case where Ann's e.p.r.s on a computer service are founded on some combination of pure private and common e.p.r.s, forming a category of mixed enterprise.

Simple Mixer

According to already given notations and descriptions this can be simple expressed by $\mathbf{h}_a = \mathbf{h}_p^a \otimes_{ap} \mathbf{h}^D$, where $\otimes_{ap}$ symbolizes an appropriation mechanism or *ap*-mechanism. Namely, Ann forms or becomes a member of an institution where domain of her e.p.r.s claims on computer service are some combination of her private asset and Department facilities. Having in mind statements from the above about $\mathbf{h}_p^a$ and $\mathbf{h}_D, \mathbf{h}_1, \mathbf{h}_2$ separately, in subsections 1.3.1 and 1.3.2, it is obvious that $\mathbf{h}_a$ given by this arrangement incorporates e.p.r.s of private and Department's domains of claims. Thus, Ann is in the circumstances where she can control and enjoy her pure private property on $\mathbf{h}_p^a$ as her exclusive dominant rights, while on Department facilities

$\mathbf{h}^D, (\mathbf{h}_D, \mathbf{h}_1, \mathbf{h}_2)$ she is constrained by a given Department policy and rules implied from it.

An extension of her e.p.r.s by configuration of her domain of claims, depending on D-policy, can be expressed symbolically in the following way:

$$\mathbf{h}_p^a \otimes \mathbf{h}_D \rightsquigarrow \left\{ \begin{array}{c} \mathit{Domain\ of} \\ \mathit{pure} \\ \mathit{private} \\ \mathit{e.p.r.s} \end{array} \right\} \otimes_{ap} \left\{ \begin{array}{c} \mathit{Domain\ of} \\ \mathit{common} \\ \mathit{e.p.r.s} \end{array} \right\} = \mathbf{h}_p^a \otimes_{ap} \mathbf{h}_{D_{ap}}$$
$$ap = nc, pc, dc, Dp, \tag{1.2}$$

where ap denotes an appropriation parameter. It is not hard to see that Ann has a particular interest for D_{Dp}-policy. It expends her e.p.r.s to maximal in a direct way. Namely, in addition to 24 hours that she has access to her pure private computer (simple programs), she gets access to advanced technology (sophisticated programs) for her whole 'quote' of 6 c/h per day in D-computer room. On the contrary, an implementation of D_{pc}-policy would mean that her e.p.r.s on computer service cannot be expended at all by her access to Department facilities. Namely, D_{pc}-policy excludes the possibility of an application of advanced technologies, thus this policy has no direct impact on her EPRS in this case. She may quite well completely cover her demands for computer services using almost exclusively her private computer, reducing mixed foundation of her appropriation to the pure private one. Only if her demands for computer service are simple ones and require at most 6 c/h per day she might consider possibility of selling her private computer. Then she bases her demands for computer service using common D-EPRs. In this case, mixed EPRS is reduced on 'pure" common EPRS, and an expansion of Ann's e.p.r.s may be indirect, by an expansion of her property (a gain obtained by selling her computer). Other two of D-policies would reduce an expansion of her e.p.r.s comparing to D_{Dp}-policy, and expend it comparing to D_{cp}-policy. In same time an issue of using Department facilities at full capacities may be imposed.

Obviously, Ann should have an interest to get more influence on formation D-policy. She may apply for an assistant position at Department, and/or to become more actively engaged in organizing activities at the computer room. Then she may gain more impact on formulation of a D policy, and particularly influence on c/h scheduling. It is clear from tables above, that even within the general ideal of equal c/hs access to the department facilities for all graduates, she would be in position to made a schedule that would expend her (and any other student in the similar position), e.p.r.s to maximal possible. In other words, modification of a schedule and implied appropriation of e.p.r.s is intrinsic to her position of a computer room manager. What type of schedule would Ann implemented depends strongly on degree of willingness of Department's authority to support her proposal, but also on demands, information and knowledge of other graduates. In any case, she will surprisingly find, that if her suggestion (having in mined that she and may be some other, as Bob, but not all students are using their pure private computer for simple programs) is different from p^{Dp} either capacities of Department facilities are not completely used, or she has to modify general claim of equal rights on access of computer time for each of the graduates including herself.

Advanced Mixer

Ann may tray to form a frame of more complete mixture, implying appropriation on her pure private, $A\&B$ enterprise, and Department's property. Then, Ann is in the space of e.p.r.s which configuration is imposed from $\mathbf{h}_a = \mathbf{h}_p^a \otimes_{ap_p} \mathbf{h}_{a\&b} \otimes_{ap_c} \mathbf{h}^D$, where ap_p symbolize aggregation of e.p.r.s by some private appropriation rule agreed among Ann and Bob, and ap_c an appropriation rule formulated by a Department policy. Here she may expect that expansions of e.p.r.s are higher than in the case of the best outcome in the simple mixer discussed above, $\mathbf{h}_a = \mathbf{h}_p^a \otimes \mathbf{h}^D$. Namely, she can reduce possible negative impacts of D-policy on her EPRS. Even if D-policy is given by D_{dc}-policy, she and Bob are in position to use advanced technology over their $A\&B$ enterprise. Having in mind dynamic setting of issues, (issues under (*iii*) on page 12), and necessity to establish foundation for e.p.r.s that she can not be aware off, at the moment, this frame seems to be perceived as most attractive one.

2

Definition of Enterprises

In this Chapter the definitions and basic elements of economic property rights theory (EPRT), that will be needed throughout this program are provided. They are based mostly on standard material of Hopf algebras with an emphasis on economic applications by appropriate economic interpretations. Some examples and exercises are also given to link EPRT with traditional economic models, primarily those within general economic equilibrium theory. More examples and concrete economic problems are discussed in Chapter 3 where we turn to the advances of the theory with emphasis on open enterprises. I would suggest that every reader work through the present elementary Chapter and at least the first part of the next Chapter in detail since these sections are central for understanding much of the later advanced and more complex material.

2.1 Basic Elements of Formalization

As already mentioned, what one, we may say Ann, is searching for refers to an institutionalized system of economic agreements, where 'to institutionalize' roughly means to shape the enterprise in the way that suits partners' economic property rights (e.p.r.s) interests. Namely, the structures of agreements and coagreements are to be interrelated by certain economic rules or laws, that partners accept in an agreeable way. Each has some understanding of her/his economic rationality concerning her/his assets (capital and knowledge), as locally compact economic rules that each obeys. Their economic behavior implied from these rules then defines each one as an agent and partner. Some economic rules (accepted by both), that are going to shape their economic reality over their relations within an enterprise, are to be established. This also includes the duals of the rules. The general understanding is that in formation of a concept of an enterprise, as an e.p.r.s entity, one should first start with a simple rule or an economic game on a domain of economic claims of partners, as a general description of initial relations they are in. This original object of their economic relations may later 'disappear', but it lives on in the various agreements associated with the economic environment they have built up. Having in mind dynamic setting of the e.p.r.s relations, an agent (Ann) should first replace a locally compact set of relations with a partner (Bob), defined by the rules of agreements, G, by schema of expansions of e.p.r.s that concern her, $C(G)$ together with the suitable co-rule of expansions of e.p.r.s that concerns a partner (Bob). This corule, which is actually a perception of extensions of e.p.r.s from partners' (Bob's) point of view, is determined by the rule of expansions of e.p.r.s concerning the agent (her). The idea is that in formalization of the problem, expansions/coexpansions of e.p.r.s are modeled by multiplication and comultiplication, respectively. In that way, one gets a concept of a biagreement, and if one has an economic characterization of these biagreements, one could presumably institutionalize them by replacing the agreements based on standard economic relations with the collections of extended economic agreements. Then the crucial point in defining an enterprise, in an axiomatic way, is that it should neither presuppose the existence of a fixed valuation concept of the e.p.r.s involved, nor the existence of mutual understanding among partners. The primary application of the valuation concept is to show that an enterprise has a non-trivial economic argumentation theory. Thus, a significant axiomatization should be accompanied by non-trivial argumentation/coargumentation theorems of an enterprise.

The following elements of an axiomatic construction of an enterprise considered as an e.p.r.s institution are to be defined:

(i) How an agent, initiator of an enterprise (Ann), perceives structure of e.p.r.s in the enterprise - structure of an agreement;

(ii) How a coagent, partner in an enterprise (Bob), perceives structure of e.p.r.s in the enterprise - structure of a coagreement;

(iii) Partners' (Ann's and Bob's) perception of an entrepreneurial structure of e.p.r.s in a dynamic setting - structure of a biagreement, and finally;

(iv) Conditions for mutual understanding of partners in an enterprise or conditions of sustainability of e.p.r.s relations in an enterprise.

2.1.1 Agreement and Coagreement

Throughout this section we let $\mathbf{h}$ be a field of economic claims of agents considered as a domain e.p.r.s on which agents are arranging their economic relations. Aggregation of e.p.r.s is built on an underlying assumption that agents' economic rationality on their endowments (capital and knowledge) shapes the procedure. Formally it is built by tensor products over $\mathbf{h}$, unless stated otherwise. Later on modified tensor products will be in focus to model some particular forms in aggregation of e.p.r.s relations of agents involved.

Definitions

We first express the basic properties of an agreement initiated by an agent (let us say by Ann) via maps of e.p.r.s, so that we may dualize them.

Definition 2.1 (An e.p.r.s agreement). *An* **h**-*agreement of an agent, is an* **h**-*vector space* A_A *together with two* **h**-*linear maps: an agency (agent's unit)* $\eta : \mathbf{h} \to A_A$ *and an expansion of e.p.r.s* m, $m : A_A \otimes A_A \to A_A$ *such that flows of collections of e.p.r.s make the following diagrams commutative:*

A1 - Agent's unit

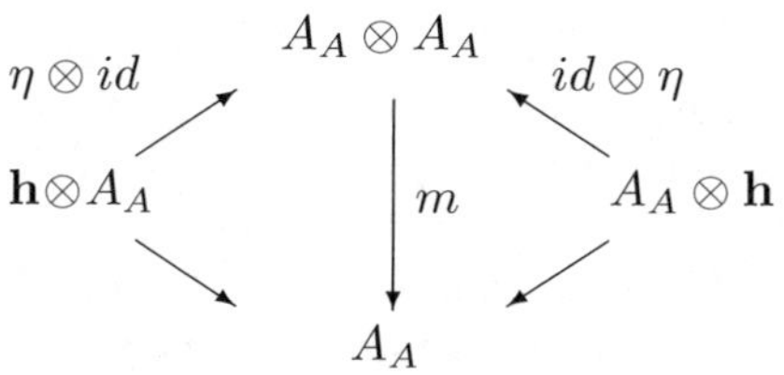

A2 - Associativity

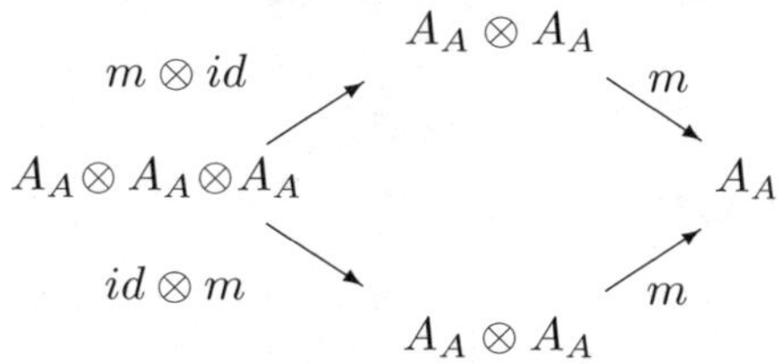

The two lower maps in *A1* are given by scalar multiplication.

Thus, an initiator for an e.p.r.s agreement (Ann) perceives herself as an agency, where her economic behavior is to be determined by an agreement, A_A. It is accepted by her, in the sense that she is reasoning strategically, over structural maps concerning her e.p.r.s in an agreement, denoted by η. Mapping η is an embedding of a field of initiator's (Ann's) economic claims on **h** into extended economic rights, that she may gain in A_A. One may think of η as her economic evaluation of an extension of the e.p.r.s from the field of claims **h**. Mapping id conserves the existing level of e.p.r.s in an agreement. Mapping m describes an expansion of e.p.r.s for an initiator (Ann) of an agreement. Here the compatibility of the e.p.r.s expansion with the growth and argumentation of **h** is concisely expressed as the requirement that the expansion of e.p.r.s m defines a linear map $m : A_A \otimes A_A \to A_A$. The assumption $A1$, gives the identity element in A_A by setting $1_A = \eta(1_{\mathbf{h}})$. Thus *A1* may also be expressed by relations:

$$m \circ (a_A \otimes 1_A) = m \circ (1_A \otimes a_A) = a_A \quad \text{for all } a_A \in A_A,$$

where the operator η that has defined an initiator (Ann) as an agent, is given by $\eta(h) = h1_A$ for all economic claims from her domain of claims, i.e. $h \in \mathbf{h}$.

An alternate way of expressing *A2* axiom would be the following: An associative **h**-agreement, which preserves already existing e.p.r.s of an agent, is a linear space A_A with id and structure maps $m : A_A \otimes A_A \to A_A$, and $\eta : \mathbf{h} \to A_A$ such that

$$m \circ (m \otimes id) = m \circ (id \otimes m) : A_A \otimes A_A \otimes A_A \to A_A;$$
$$m \circ (\eta \otimes id) = m \circ (id \otimes \eta) = id : \mathbf{h} \otimes A_A = A_A \otimes \mathbf{h} = A_A \to A_A.$$

Note that expansion map m is the usual product in an agreement A_A, $m(a_{1A} \otimes a_{2A}) = a_{1A} \circ a_{2A}$ for $a_{1A}, a_{2A} \in A_A$.

For more precise understanding of possible arrangements of e.p.r.s that agents have on disposal we recall flipping or twisting mapping.

Definition 2.2 (Twisting e.p.r.s). *For any* $\mathbf{h}$*-spaces* V *and* W*, the twist map* $\tau : V \otimes W \to W \otimes V$ *is given by* $\tau(v \otimes w) = w \otimes v$.

Note that, later on when we consider agreements and coagreements which are graded, in the form of superagreements and supercoagreements, we will modify the definition of the twist map. The above definition of an agreement in terms of diagrams suggests the definition of a coagreement. Now we express the corresponding properties of an e.p.r.s arrangement by an agent considered as copartner or coagent (let say Bob) of initiator (Ann). It appears as dualized notation of an agreement thus,

Definition 2.3 (An e.p.r.s coagreement). *An* $\mathbf{h}$*-coagreement of an agent, is an* $\mathbf{h}$*-vector space* A_B *together with two* $\mathbf{h}$*-linear maps: a coagency (coagent's unit)* $\varepsilon : A_B \to \mathbf{h}$*, and a coexpansion of e.p.r.s* Δ*,* $\Delta : A_B \to A_B \otimes A_B$ *such that flows of collections of e.p.r.s are understood in a way that the following diagrams are commutative:*

A3 - Coagent's unit

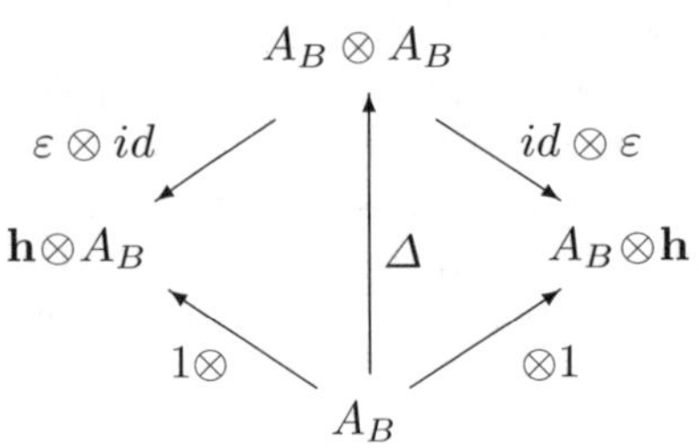

A4 - Coassociativity

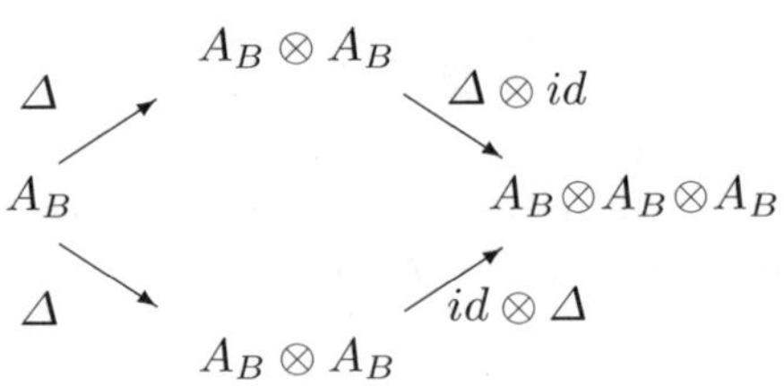

The maps in *A3*, $\otimes 1$ and $1\otimes$ are given by $a_B \mapsto 1 \otimes a_B$ and $a_B \mapsto a_B \otimes 1$, for any $a_B \in A_B$. A concept of coagency, ε, is to provide a base for identifying a partner's (Bob's) economic effects on a domain of economic claims $\mathbf{h}$, having in mind the agreement that has been proposed by initiator (Ann), and preserving initiator's e.p.r.s on $\mathbf{h}$. That is, the above axiom *A3* can be expressed by $(\Delta \otimes id) \circ \Delta = (id \otimes \Delta) \circ \Delta$ and that ε describes a coagreement by

$$(\varepsilon \otimes id) \circ \Delta(a_B) = (id \otimes \varepsilon) \circ \Delta(a_B) = a_B,$$

for all elements of coagreement $a_{iB} \in A_B$.
Note that ε also preserves economic transactions to a copartner, i.e. it is a homomorphism,

$$\varepsilon(a_{1B}, a_{2B}) = \varepsilon(a_{1B}) \circ \varepsilon(a_{2B})$$

for all elements of coagreement $a_{1B}, a_{2B} \in A_B$.

An alternate way of expressing *A4* (associativity of e.p.r.s in coagreement) would be the following: A coassociative **h**-agreement, which preserves his existing level of e.p.r.s, is a linear space A_B with structure maps: (i) of sharing e.p.r.s, $\Delta : A_B \to A_B \otimes A_B$, and (ii) shaping a field of e.p.r.s claims by copartner, $\varepsilon : A_B \to \mathbf{h}$, such that

$$(id \otimes \Delta) \circ \Delta = (\Delta \otimes id) \circ \Delta : A_B \to A_B \otimes A_B \otimes A_B;$$
$$(\varepsilon \otimes id) \circ \Delta = (id \otimes \varepsilon) \circ \Delta = id : A_B \to A_B = \mathbf{h} \otimes A_B = A_B \otimes \mathbf{h}.$$

Note that coexpansion map of e.p.r.s for Bob, Δ, is assumed to be homotransaction of A_B, modelled by homomorphism of A_B.

In general, the notation used for economic operations of coagreements is not as concise as that for operations of agreements on an elementary domain of e.p.r.s claim **h**. The following notation for Δ, is effective [72] and is going to be also useful in simplifying notation of various types of economic operations. Given an **h**-coagreement $(A_B, \Delta, \varepsilon)$ and $a_B \in A_B$, we can write

$$\Delta(a_B) = \sum_{i=1}^{n} a_{i(1)B} \otimes a_{i(2)B}, \qquad a_{i(1)B}, a_{i(2)B} \in A_B.$$

Here the right hand side is a formal sum denoting an element of $A_B \otimes A_B$. It denotes how expansion of e.p.r.s of copartner Δ shares out any collection of e.p.r.s from coagreement a_B into linear combinations of a part $_{(1)B}$ in the first factor of $A_B \otimes A_B$ and a part $_{(2)B}$ in the second factor. Thus, it can be rewritten as

$$\Delta(a_B) = \sum_{(a_B)} a_{(1)B} \otimes a_{(2)B},$$

and the notation of summation can be left implicit as well, if there is no confusion. Property of coassociativity then means that if e.p.r.s of a coagreement are to be shared out by a coagent again, it does not matter which piece of $\Delta(a_B)$ is shared out. Thus, it can be written

$$a_{(1)B} \otimes a_{(2)(1)B} \otimes a_{(2)(2)B} = a_{(1)(1)B} \otimes a_{(1)(2)B} \otimes a_{(2)B} = a_{(1)B} \otimes a_{(2)B} \otimes a_{(3)B},$$

for example. An economist may think of a_B as being like a probability density function. The total probability mass of e.p.r.s that a coagent is dealing with in an element of coagreement, a_B, $\varepsilon(a_B)$ is being shared out among different e.p.r.s spaces.

Namely, for **h**-linear maps f, g from A_B to A_B or to **h**, we write

$$(f \otimes g)(\Delta(a_B)) = \sum_{(a_B)} f(a_{(1)B}) \otimes g(a_{(2)B}).$$

Moreover, since the associativity law holds, we have

$$(\Delta \otimes 1)\Delta(a_B) = (1 \otimes \Delta)\Delta(a_B) = \sum a_{(1)B} \otimes a_{(2)B} \otimes a_{(3)B},$$

and, in general, it is defined

$$\Delta_1 = \Delta, \qquad \Delta_n = (1 \otimes \cdots \otimes 1 \otimes \Delta)\Delta_{n-1} \quad n > 1,$$

and written,

$$\Delta_n(a_B) = \sum a_{(1)B} \otimes a_{(2)B} \otimes \cdots \otimes a_{(n+1)B}.$$

Using this method of notation, the coagency property may be expressed by

$$a_B = \sum a_{(1)B}\varepsilon(a_{(2)B}) = \sum \varepsilon(a_{(1)B})a_{(2)B}.$$

Note that from definitions of an agency, *A1*, and coagency, *A3*, it is obvious that an expansion of e.p.r.s m is a surjective map, and coexpansion of e.p.r.s Δ is injective.

Duality

Duality is a well known principle of theoretical and applied modeling, with an important interpretation for economic theories. In the context of an agreement and a coagreement the twist map can be used to dualize the notion of opposite agreement. So for a given agreement A, recall that A^{op} is the agreement obtained by using A as an economic space of elements of the agreement (considered as vector space), but with a new rule for expansion of e.p.r.s in an agreement. So $a_1 \circ a_2 = (a_2 a_1)^{op}$, for $a_1, a_2 \in A^{op}$. In terms of maps this new multiplication is given by $m' : A \otimes A \to A$, where $m' = m \circ \tau$. Similar is valid for a coagreement. Namely, given a coagreement A_B, then the coopposite coagreement A_B^{op} is given by the same domain of e.p.r.s activities as the vector space, ($A_B^{op} = A_B$), with the new coexpansions of elements of e.p.r.s in coopposite coagreement, $\Delta' = \tau \circ \Delta$.

An intuition of close relationship between an agreement and a coagreement is confirmed and can be precisely expressed by looking at dual spaces of an agreement and a coagreement. Note that cases which are finite dimensional can be easily linked with the traditional economic analysis of relations of agents on some economic device, such as a market, for example.

For any $\mathbf{h}$-space V, let $V^* = Hom_{\mathbf{h}}(V, \mathbf{h})$ denote the linear dual of V. Then V and V^* determine a non-degenerative bilinear form $\langle\ ,\ \rangle : V \otimes V^* \to \mathbf{h}$ via $\langle f, v\rangle = f(v)$. Note that notation of a bilinear form supports an economic intuition of V as acting on V^*. If an economic activity $\phi : V \to W$ is $\mathbf{h}$-linear, then the *transpose* of ϕ is $\phi^* : W^* \to V^*$, given by

$$\phi^*(f)(v) = f(\phi(v)), \forall f \in W^*, v \in V. \tag{2.1}$$

Lemma 2.4. *For a coagreement* A_B, *there is a corresponding agreement* A_B^*, *where expansion of e.p.r.s in the agreement is given by* $m = \Delta^*$, *and agency of the agreement is determined by the given transpose coagency,* $\eta = \varepsilon^*$.

Proof: The lemma is proved simply by dualizing the diagrams. One needs only the additional observation that since $A_B^* \otimes A_B^* \subseteq (A_B \otimes A_B)^*$, we may restrict Δ^* to get an expansion map for agreement $m : A_B^* \otimes A_B^* \to A_B^*$. Explicitly, expansion map m is given by $m(f \otimes g)(a_B) = \Delta^*(f \otimes g)(a_B) = (f \otimes g)\Delta a_B$, for all $f, g \in A_B^*, a_B \in A_B$. □

Note that if a coagreement A_B is based on simplified e.p.r.s rationality of copartners, it is cocommutative, i.e. if twisting the coexpansion map gives coexpansion map, $\tau \circ \Delta = \Delta$, then A_B^* is commutative, i.e. $m \circ \tau = m$ on $A_B^* \otimes A_B^*$.

Difficulties can arise if we begin with an agreement A_A, and if A_A is not finite dimensional. Then $A_A^* \otimes A_A^*$ is a proper subspace of $(A_A \otimes A_B)^*$, and thus the image of $m^* : A_A^* \to (A_A \otimes A_A)^*$, may not lie in $A_B^* \otimes A_B^*$. Of course, if A_A is finite dimensional, all is well, and A_A^* is a coagreement. The point is that in general A_A is not finite dimensional, and an introduction of an assumption of its finite dimensionally implicitly carries a form of transfer of e.p.r.s and economic wealth. For more see discussion in Chapter 4.

Proposition 2.5. *If* A_A *is an agreement, then its finite dual,* A_A°, *is a coagreement, with coexpansion of e.p.r.s* $\Delta = m^*$, *and coagency* $\varepsilon = \eta^*$.

Proof: Recall that the finite dual of A_A is $A_A^\circ = \{f \in A_A^* \mid f(I_A) = 0,$ for same ideal I_A of A_A such that $dim(A_A/I) < \infty\}$. In particular, A_A° is the largest subspace V of A_A^* such that $m^*(V) \subseteq V \otimes V$. Thus, we can choose $f \in A_A^\circ$ and let $\{g_1, \ldots, g_n\}$ be a base for $A_A \rightharpoonup f$. Then $m^* f = \sum_{i=1}^n g_1 \otimes h_i$, for some $h_i \in A_A^*$. Since each $g_i \in A_A \rightharpoonup f$, also $A_A \rightharpoonup g_i \subseteq A_A \rightharpoonup f$, a finite-dimensional space, as f vanishes on a right ideal of A_A of finite codimension. Thus each $g_i \in A_A^\circ$. Since the $\{g_i\}$ are linearly independent, we may choose $\{a_{1A}, \ldots a_{nA}\}$ in A_A such that $g_i(a_{jA}) = \delta_{ij}$. Now $f \leftharpoonup a_{jA} = \sum_i g_i(a_{jA})h_i = h_j$, and so each $h_j \in f \leftharpoonup A_A$, which is finite-dimensional as f vanishes on a left ideal of A_A of finite codimension. Thus, also $h_j \in A_A^\circ$, for all j and so $m^* f \in A_A^\circ \otimes A_A^\circ$.

Coassociativity of $\Delta = m^*$ follows by dualizing the associativity of m and restricting domain of elements of coagreement to A_A°. □

Biagreement

A biagreement is obtained by combining the notions of an agreement (A_A, m, η) and a coagreement $(A_B, \Delta, \varepsilon)$.

Definition 2.6 (Biagreement). *An* **h***-space* B *is a biagreement if* (B, m, η) *is an agreement and* (B, Δ, ε) *is a coagreement and if either of the following (equivalent) conditions holds:*

(i) Δ *and* ε *are economic transactions accepted by an agent;*
(ii) m *and* η *are economic transactions accepted by a coagent.*

Formally above conditions mean that $(i) \Longrightarrow \Delta$ and ε are morphisms of $(A_A \equiv B, m, \eta)$, and $(ii) \Longrightarrow m$ and η are morphisms of $(A_B, \equiv B, \Delta, \varepsilon)$. We may say that biagreement B is linear space of e.p.r.s endowed with the structural mappings concerning: (i) agreement (m, ε), and (ii) coagreement (Δ, η), satisfying the compatible conditions. This condition can simply be understood and written in the form Δ as economic transactions of **h**-agreements. We may assume here that expansion (multiplication) of collections of e.p.r.s for an agency, is given by the usual rule $(e \otimes f)m(e' \otimes f') = eme' \otimes fmf'$. It may be better to write the compatible condition for an initiator's arrangement of e.p.r.s and a partner's arrangement of e.p.r.s in the form,

$$(m \otimes m) \circ id \otimes \tau \otimes id \circ (\Delta \otimes \Delta) = \Delta \circ m : B \otimes B \to B \otimes B.$$

It is also worthy to note that biagreement data and axioms are self-dual with respect to: (i) all flow of e.p.r.s formally expressed by arrows in the above diagrams, and (ii) position of agents in the (co)agreement expressed by the replacement of (m, η) by (Δ, ε) and vice versa.

A5 - Connections in biagreement

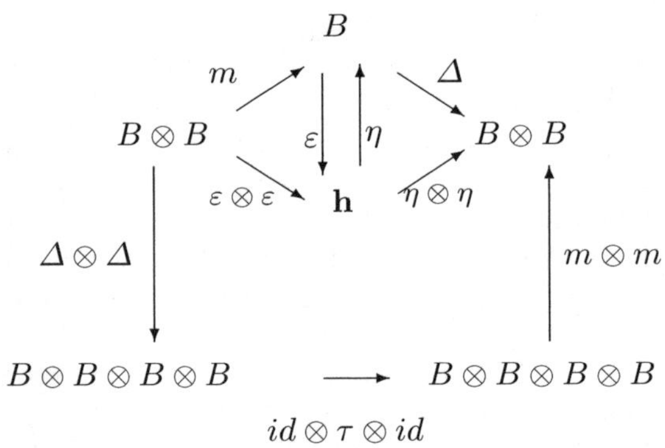

Here $id \otimes \tau \otimes id$ is the economic transaction exchanging the second and third places of the factors in the aggregate. It is important to note that this may become nontrivial in an aggregate category. For example one that gives $\mathbf{Z}_2$-graded vector spaces of claims. For more on this issue see following sections. The usual vector spaces of economic claims are given by simple exclusive dominant rationality of agents. Nevertheless, if all the relevant axioms, with the necessary permutation morphisms, are written down they will be automatically applicable in more general institutions obtained by some of general aggregation procedures.

Note also that a biagreement can be expressed in an alternate way as follows. A biagreement $(B, m, \eta, \Delta, \varepsilon; \mathbf{h})$ over $\mathbf{h}$ is a vector space $(B, \mathbf{h})$ over a domain of e.p.r.s claims, $\mathbf{h}$, which is both an agreement and a coagreement, in a compatible way. The compatibility is

$$\Delta(h,g) = \Delta(h)\Delta(g), \ \Delta(1) = 1 \otimes 1,$$
$$\varepsilon(hg) = \varepsilon(h)\varepsilon(g), \ \varepsilon(1) = 1, \tag{2.2}$$

for all $h, g \in B$. In other words, $\Delta : B \to B \otimes B$ and $\varepsilon : B \to \mathbf{h}$ are agreement maps, and this is the same as the assertion that $m : B \otimes B \to B$; $\eta : \mathbf{h} \to B$ are coagreement maps, where $B \otimes B$ has the structure of aggregation (the tensor product) of coagreement. Then condition that $\varepsilon(1_B) = 1_B$ is automatic as $\mathbf{h}$ is a field of claims on e.p.r.s.

Opposite biagreement

For any biagreement $B = (B, m, \eta, \Delta, \varepsilon; \mathbf{h})$, by applying the opposite operator in an appropriate way one can get three other biagreements. Precisely we have the following biagreements: $B^{op} = (B, m^{op}, \eta, \Delta, \varepsilon; \mathbf{h})$, $B^{cop} = (B, m, \eta, \Delta^{op}, \varepsilon; \mathbf{h})$, and $B^{op,cop} = (B, m^{op}, \eta, \Delta^{cop}, \varepsilon; \mathbf{h})$. They carries opposite structures to $(B, m, \eta, \Delta, \varepsilon; \mathbf{h})$,

Dual biagreement

Let $B = (B, m, \eta, \Delta, \varepsilon; \mathbf{h})$ be a biagreement. Consider the dual vector space $B^* = Hom(B, \mathbf{h})$. By duality, Δ and ε give rise to linear maps,

$$m' : B^* \otimes B^* \xrightarrow{\lambda} (B \otimes B)^* \xrightarrow{\Delta^*} B^*$$

and $\eta' = \varepsilon^* : \mathbf{h} = \mathbf{h}^* \to B^*$ where λ is the map determined by

$$\langle (\alpha \otimes \beta), a \otimes b \rangle = \langle \alpha, a \rangle \langle \beta, b \rangle$$

for $\alpha, \beta \in B^*$ and $a, b \in B$. Conditions that define a biagreement imply that m' is an associative product on the dual vector space B^* with unit equal to η. If B^* is finite dimensional, then the map $\lambda : B^* \otimes B^* \to (B \otimes B)^*$ is an isomorphism, which allows us to define that map $\Delta' = \lambda^{-1} m^*$ from B^* to $B^* \otimes B^*$. Then one can check that $(B^*, m', \eta', \Delta', \varepsilon' = \eta^*; \mathbf{h})$ is a biagreement.

Also if B is any biagreement, then B° is a biagreement. Precisely we have,

Theorem 2.7. *Let $(B, m, \eta, \Delta, \varepsilon; \mathbf{h})$ be a biagreement. Then $(B^\circ, m^*, \eta^*, \Delta^*, \varepsilon^*; \mathbf{h})$ is also a biagreement.*

Proof: We know that $(B^*, \Delta^*, \varepsilon^*)$ is an agreement by the Lemma 2.4 and that (B°, m^*, η^*) is a coagreement by proposition 2.5. To claim that B° is a subagreement of B^*, let us choose $f, g \in B^\circ$. Then $B \rightharpoonup f$, and $B \rightharpoonup g$, are finite-dimensional. Now for any $b \in B$, we have $b \rightharpoonup fg = \sum (b_1 \rightharpoonup f)(b_2 \rightharpoonup g) \subseteq$ span of $(B \rightharpoonup f)(B \rightharpoonup g)$, which is finite-dimensional. Thus, $fg \in B^\circ$. Also certainly, $\varepsilon \in B^\circ$, as it vanishes on an ideal of codimension one. Thus, B° is a subagreement of B^*. It is straightforward to check that B° is a biagreement, by dualizing the diagrams for B. □

In the infinite dimensional case the correct notion of dual biagreement is more intricate. A standard approach using economic agreements is to restrict domain of biagreements to a certain subset $B^\circ \subset B^*$ with the desirable properties. A different approach is to focus on the pairing. More on this issue and on some other properties of biagreements follow in next subsections.

2.1.2 Enterprise

Having above in mind, we can provide additional axioms leading to the axiomatic construction of an entrepreneurial agreement or an enterprise considered as an e.p.r.s institution shaped by partners.

Definition and Mutual Understanding Map

Economic rules concerning e.p.r.s within an institution are defined to be expressible by an institutional agreement, not necessarily backed by simple e.p.r.s rationality. So, an institutional agreement is not necessarily commutative, thus it could be important which route partners take in the agreement. Here we are actually dealing with a biagreement that contains a particular relation of mutual understanding among agents involved concerning e.p.r.s.

Definition 2.8 (An enterprise). *An enterprise over a domain of e.p.r.s claims,* $\mathbf{h}$, *is a biagreement* B *over* $\mathbf{h}$ *endowed with the mutual understanding map* $\gamma : B \to B$, *obeying,*

$$m \circ (\gamma \otimes id) \circ \Delta = m \circ (id \otimes \gamma) \circ \Delta = \eta \circ \varepsilon.$$

It is denoted by $(B, m, \eta, \Delta, \varepsilon, \gamma; \mathbf{h})$, *or simply by* H.

The axiom concerning mutual understanding mapping, γ, may be expressed by the following diagram.

A6 - Mutual understanding mapping

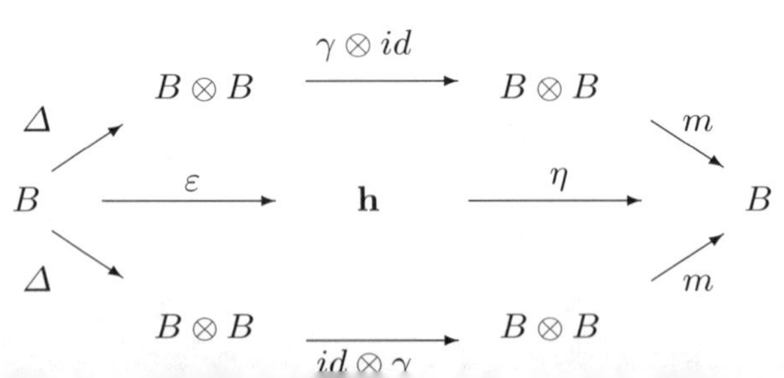

The mutual understanding map of an enterprise provides a concept of an inverse reasoning on collections of e.p.r.s within an enterprise. However, although it is an inverse notion, it does not require that $\gamma^2 = id$, and it does not even assume that γ, as a linear map, has an inverse γ^{-1}. If the considered enterprise is finite dimensional then corresponding mutual understanding map has a linear inverse.

Properties of mutual understanding

Note that the mutual understanding mapping reverses e.p.r.s expansion mapping and coexpansion mapping over a biagreement among agents, implying relation from definition 2.8, $m \circ (id \otimes \gamma) \circ \Delta = m \circ (\gamma \otimes id) \circ \Delta = \eta \circ \varepsilon : B \to B$. Namely we have,

$$m \circ (id \otimes \gamma) \circ \Delta(a) = m \circ (\gamma \otimes id) \circ \Delta(a) = \varepsilon(a) 1_B,$$

where $a \in B$. The mutual understanding map is an anti-internal economic transaction (anti-homomorphism), $\gamma(a_{1B}a_{2B}) = \gamma(a_{2B})\gamma(a_{1B})$. In this economic application it carries an e.p.r.s transaction that reverses economic rationality on e.p.r.s, i.e. it enables agents to perceive themselves in *'the other's shoes'* concerning e.p.r.s gains in a biagreement. One may think of mutual understanding map as a biagreement that concerns an arrangement of partners' e.p.r.s growth by their expansion and coexpansion. Thus, it is formally defined by a biagreemental economic transaction on the agreement given by (B, m, Δ). In general, a mutual understanding map, γ, is not an economic transaction (morphism) of agreement or coagreement. As mentioned, it reverses both expansion and coexpansion, so that we may put $m^{op} = m \circ id \otimes \tau \otimes id$, and $\Delta^{op} = id \otimes \tau \otimes id \circ \Delta$, where op denotes the opposite operator. Recall that reversing a biagreement by applying an opposite operator on either expansion of e.p.r.s, or on coexpansion of e.p.r.s, or on both, we still get a biagreement. A mutual understanding map γ, if it exists at all, is a biagreement transaction

$$(B, m, \eta, \Delta, \epsilon) \to (B, m^{op}, \eta, \Delta^{op}, \epsilon).$$

If in addition it is bijective, which is not always so, then γ^{-1} is a mutual understanding map for (B, m^{op}, Δ) and (B, m, Δ^{op}), hence γ is one for (B, m^{op}, Δ^{op}). Thus, an enterprise based on simple e.p.r.s rationality of agency, i.e. $m = m^{op}$, is also called commutative. Here, the property is induced from commutativity of underlying agreement in an enterprise. Similarity, a simple e.p.r.s rationality of coagency, i.e. $\Delta = \Delta^{op}$, provides cocommutative of an enterprise it contains. More on a simple enterprise and simple e.p.r.s institutions in general is discussed in Subsection 2.2.1. If a mutual understanding map for a biagreement exists, it is unique (the proposition below), but not necessary bijective. If it is bijective, it may have arbitrary finite or infinite order.

Proposition 2.9. (Uniqueness of mutual understanding) *The mutual understanding map in an enterprise is unique and satisfies the following conditions:*
(i) an angent's understanding of 'opposed' agreement $\gamma(hg) = \gamma(g)(h)$, $\gamma(1) = 1$ *(i.e.* γ *is an 'antiagreemental' map), and*
(ii) a coangent's understanding of 'opposed' coagreement $(\gamma \otimes \gamma) \circ \Delta h = \tau \circ \Delta \circ \gamma h$, $\varepsilon\gamma h = \varepsilon h$ *(i.e.* γ *is an 'anticoagreemental' map).*

Proof: The proof is based on the idea that mutual understanding map of agents that form an enterprise, implies a consistency of e.p.r.s reasoning of agent/coagent placed in the inverse positions in decision making. The only complication here is that we are working with parts of linear combinations and have to take care to keep the order of the (co)expansions of e.p.r.s. Let $\gamma_1, \gamma_2,$ be two mutual understanding maps on a biagreement B. They are equal because

$$\begin{aligned}\gamma_1 h &= (\gamma_1 h_{(1)})\varepsilon(h_{(2)}) = (\gamma_1 h_{(1)})h_{(2)(1)}\gamma_2 h_{(2)(2)} = (\gamma_1 h_{(1)})h_{(2)}\gamma_2 h_{(3)} \\ &= (\gamma_1 h_{(1)(1)})h_{(1)(2)}\gamma_2 h_{(2)} = \varepsilon(h_{(1)})\gamma_2 h_{(2)} \\ &= \gamma_2 h.\end{aligned}$$

Note that here we express $h = h_{(1)}\varepsilon(h_{(2)})$ having in mind the axiom of coagency *A3*, and then insert $h_{(2)(1)}\gamma_2 h_{(2)(2)}$ knowing that it would be reduced to $\varepsilon(h_{(2)})$ (e.p.r.s would be appropriated by a coagent). Having in mind property of associativity of an agent, *A2*, and coassociativity of a coagent, *A4*, the e.p.r.s embodied in $(\gamma_1 h_{(1)(1)})h_{(1)(2)}$ collapses to $\varepsilon(h_{(1)})$, i.e. corresponding e.p.r.s are appropriated by a coagent. The linear ordering of e.p.r.s used here is $(\gamma_1 h_{(1)})h_{(2)}\gamma_2 h_{(3)}$. Having in mind a pure exclusive dominant rationality of an agent and a coagent as an underlying base for the ordering of e.p.r.s in an enterprise, this is the most convenient ordering. (The discussion on issues of ordering in the general case is given in Chapter 4.) The expressions, as $(\gamma_1 h_{(1)})h_{(2)}$ or $h_{(2)}\gamma_2 h_{(3)}$, can be collapsed similarly, wherever they occur, as long as the two collapsing factors are in linear order. (This is just the analogue of concealing $h^{-1}h$ or hh^{-1}, in a traditional linear reasoning.) Having this techniques at our disposal, and applying the axiom of mutual understanding to hg, we have $(\gamma_1(h_{(1)}g_{(1)}))h_{(2)}g_{(2)} = \varepsilon(hg) = \varepsilon(h)\varepsilon(g)$. This identity can be applied not to g but to $g_{(1)}$, while keeping $g_{(2)}$ for another purpose. Thus, we have $(\gamma_2(h_{(1)}g_{(1)(1)}))h_{(2)}g_{(1)(2)} \otimes g_{(2)} = \varepsilon(h)\varepsilon(g_{(1)}) \otimes g_{(2)} = \varepsilon(h) \otimes g$. Applying γ_2 to the second factor and expanding e.p.r.s according to a pure exclusive dominant rationality of coagent, we have $(\gamma_2(h_{(1)}g_{(1)}))h_{(2)}g_{(2)}\gamma_2 g_{(3)} = \varepsilon(h)\gamma_2 g$. Now, $g_{(2)}\gamma_2 h_{(3)}$ can be modified in the required expression such that $(\gamma_2(h_{(1)}g))h_{(2)} = \varepsilon(h)\gamma_2 g$. The procedure can be used again, so that the result is applied, not to h but to $h_{(1)}$, so $(\gamma_2(h_{(1)(1)}g))h_{(1)(2)} \otimes h_{(2)} = \varepsilon(h_{(1)})\gamma_2 g \otimes h_{(2)} = \gamma_2 g \otimes h$. Applying γ_2 to the second factor and multiplying gives $(\gamma_2(h_{(1)}g))h_{(2)}\gamma_2 h_{(3)} = (\gamma_2 g)(\gamma_2 h)$. Reducing $h_{(2)}\gamma_2 h_{(3)}$ then gives the desired outcome. We obtain $\gamma_2(1) = 1$ more simply as $\gamma_2(1) = 1\gamma_2(1) =$

$1_{(1)}\gamma_2 1_{(2)} = \varepsilon(1) = 1$. For $\Delta \circ \gamma_2$ and $\varepsilon \circ \gamma_2$ identities the proof is similar but 'inside out' to the above. Using the symmetry principle of pure exclusive dominant relations it can be obtained easily. For direct proof we have $(\gamma_2 h) = \varepsilon(\gamma_2 h_{(1)})\varepsilon(h_{(2)}) = \varepsilon((\gamma_2 h_{(1)})h_{(2)}) = \varepsilon(1)\varepsilon(h) = \varepsilon(h)$. Finally we can compute $\gamma_2 h_{(2)} \otimes \gamma_2 h_{(1)} = (\gamma_2 h_{(1)})_{(1)} h_{(2)(1)} \gamma_2 h_{(4)} \otimes (\gamma_2 h_{(1)})_{(2)} h_{(2)(2)} \gamma_2 h_{(3)} = (\gamma_2 h_{(1)})_{(1)} h_{(2)} \gamma_2 h_{(3)} \otimes (\gamma_2 h_{(1)})_{(2)} = (\gamma_2 h)_{(1)} \otimes (\gamma_2 h)_{(2)}$ using the same techniques as above. □

The crucial point is that in general entrepreneurial agreement concerning e.p.r.s, the properties of a mutual understanding map between agency and coagency can differ considerably from the analogous map in the traditional agreeable rules of behavior or simple economic games, given above.

Entrepreneurial Map

Note that as an agent and a coagent have aggregated their e.p.r.s by forming an enterprise, an aggregation procedure can be defined for the two biagreements (quasi-enterprise) or for two enterprises. Here quasi-enterprise is an e.p.r.s institution where there is no mutual understanding map. In other words, a biagreement defines an underlying e.p.r.s structure for a quasi-enterprise. So for two enterprises H_1, H_2 the entrepreneurial agreement $H_1 \otimes H_2$ has e.p.r.s vector space $B_1 \otimes B_2$, with the aggregate procedure of e.p.r.s $\otimes$ based on structure of agreement and coagreement. An agreeable entrepreneurial map f is a map between two enterprises that respects each of the entrepreneurial agreeable structures involved. It is both an agreeable map and a coagreeable map (a biagreeable map), and for a mutual understanding map we have $\gamma f(h) = f(\gamma h)$. In fact, the last condition is somehow redundant. Namely, a biagreeable map between enterprises is automatically an agreeable entrepreneurial map as the structures involved are mutually compatible by the appropriate aggregate procedure that has been implemented.

Exercise 2.10. If B is a biagreement, show that B^{op}, defined as B with the opposed expansion m^{op}, $h\, m^{op} g = gh$, is also a biagreement. Likewise for B^{cop}, defined as B with the opposite coexpansion, $\Delta^{cop} h = h_{(2)} \otimes h_{(1)}$. If H is an entrepreneurial agreement, show that H^{op} is an entrepreneurial agreement if and only if mutual understanding map γ is invertible. In this case $\gamma^{op} = \gamma^{-1}$. Similar is valid for H^{cop} with $\gamma^{cop} = \gamma^{-1}$. Show also that, if γ is invertible, the mutual understanding map $\gamma : H \to H^{op/cop}$, where both are opposite, is an agreeable economic isotransaction.

It is noteworthy that a structure of a biagreement is not rich enough to form an enterprise H, (as there is no mutual understanding map) but that H^{op} and H^{cop} are enterprises. In that case a mutual understanding map γ^{op} is called skew-mutual understanding map for H.

Dual Enterprise

The duality property of the enterprise structure is one of the distinctive features of entrepreneurial agreements, evident from the structure of the axioms given by *A1 - A6.*

Proposition 2.11. *The axioms of an enterprise expressed in diagrams A1 - A6, are self-dual in the sense that reversing arrows and interchanging* Δ, ε *with* m, η *gives the same set of axioms.*

Proof: Recall that the axioms of a coagent in *A3, A4* are just dual in this way to the axioms of an agent in *A1, A2.* Looking now at *A4*, and *A6*, reverse the arrows and interchange Δ, ε with m, η, and then flip the resulting diagrams about the vertical axis on the page. This gives the original diagrams. □

Note that the above proposition can be easily understood in terms of dual linear spaces, as it is the case in traditional economic analyses. Recall that a coagreement defines an agreement on the dual linear space and, in the finite dimensional case, an agreement defines a coagreement on the dual. So having in mind a traditional equilibrium analysis in economics, (and preceding proposition being within this context is given without proof, left as an exercise) it can be concluded that for every finite dimensional enterprise H, there is a dual entrepreneurial agreement H^* built on the vector space H^* dual to H. Note also that since, in the finite dimensional case, $H^{**} \cong H$, in a canonical way, for the case of the traditional pure private relations, we are used to (and should) think of H, H^* as symmetrical economic objects. Note that this symmetry carries economic notion of law concerning some exclusive dominant appropriation rule on e.p.r.s. One may think of pure private property rules in classical economic tradition. Then relations among agents that form an enterprise according to the aggregate procedure of e.p.r.s, $\otimes$, that has been implemented in forming such an enterprise, are exclusive dominant e.p.r.s rules of a pure private enterprise. Thus, instead of writing $\phi(v)$ for the evaluation of a map in H^* on an element H, we may write $\phi(v) = \langle \phi, v \rangle$.

Proposition 2.12. *Using the notion of an exclusive dominant e.p.r.s rationality of agents, and corresponding economic valuation, the explicit formulae that determine the agreeable entrepreneurial structure of e.p.r.s on* H^* *from that on* H *are as follows. For the biagreement structure* B, *we have*

$$\langle \phi\psi, h \rangle = \langle \phi \otimes \psi, \Delta h \rangle, \qquad \langle 1, h \rangle = \varepsilon(h),$$
$$\langle \Delta\phi, h \otimes g \rangle = \langle \phi, hg \rangle, \qquad \varepsilon(h) = \langle \phi, 1 \rangle,$$

for all $\phi, \psi \in B^*$, *and* $h, g \in B$. *In the case of an enterprise, there is an additional relation of mutual understanding,*

$$\langle \gamma\phi, h \rangle = \langle \phi, \gamma h \rangle.$$

Exercise 2.13. Prove the above proposition.

Hints: Note that this is an elementary exercise on what is in economics known as the dual linear economic spaces, and how maps are dualized within the context of traditional economics. See for example Koopmans [41], Debreu [24], or any advanced textbook of mathematical economics. See also the discussion on issues in the next section within the context of argumentation and coargumentation applied to the simplest forms of enterprises, as for example enterprises on economic natural resources.

In the infinite dimensional case the correct notion of dual is more intricate and more interesting for EPRT. A traditional economic approach is to restrict to a certain subset $H^o \subset H^*$ with right properties as it has been mentioned in discussion on duality of biagreements. A different approach is to focus on the pairing.

Definition 2.14. *Two biagreements or enterprises H_1, H_2 are paired if there is a bilinear map $\langle\ ,\ \rangle : H_1 \otimes H_2 \to \mathbf{h}$ obeying the economic valuation equations displayed in the preceding proposition for all $\phi, \psi \in H_1,\ h, g \in H_2$. They are a strictly dual pair if the pairing is nondegenerative in the sense that there are no nonzero null elements in H_1 or in H_2. Recall, that $\phi \in H_1$ is null if $\langle \phi, h \rangle = 0$ for all $h \in H_2$, and $h \in H_2$ is null if $\langle \phi, h \rangle = 0$ for all $\phi \in H_1$.*

Recalling the finite dimensional case, this is just the same as saying $H_2 = H_1^*,\ H_1 = H_2^*$ with economic valuation given by the pairing.

Proposition 2.15. *A pairing between biagreements (or enterprises) can always be made nondegenerative in a setting of traditional economic environment by quotienting out, i.e. setting to zero, those elements that pair as zero with all the elements of the other biagreement (or enterprise). The resulting biagreements (or enterprises) are then a strictly dual pair.*

Proof: Using the proposition 2.12, we have $i_1 : H_1 \to H_2^*$ and $i_2 : H_2 \to H_1^*$, given by $i_1(\phi) = \langle \phi,\ \rangle$ and $i_2(h) = \langle\ , h \rangle$, are economic maps considered by agents as agreeable, or agreeable maps. Then we can set them to zero, i.e. quotient by $J_i = \ker i_i$. Recall that, in the traditional functional setting of economic relations among agents, the set of elements mapping to zero is usually interpreted as a condition of clearing economic relations, by concept of zero-sum games. Kernels of agreeable maps are always ideals, so H_1/J_i and H_2/J_2 are agreements. Secondly, since $\langle \Delta\phi, h \otimes g \rangle = \langle \phi, hg \rangle = 0$ for all h, g if $\phi \in J_1$, we conclude that $\Delta J_1 \subseteq J_1 \otimes H_1 + H_1 \otimes J_1$. Likewise, $\Delta J_2 \subseteq J_2 \otimes H_1 + H_1 \otimes J_2$. Thus, we can consider the ideals of biagreements with this property as biideals. Now one can quotient by them and have that Δ is still well-defined in the quotient, so the quotients are also biagreements. Finally if H_1, H_2 are enterprises, there is a mutual understanding map γ such that $\langle \gamma\phi, h \rangle = \langle \phi, \gamma h \rangle = 0$ for all h if $\phi \in J_1$. Similarly, one can get on the other side of the relation. Hence $\gamma J_i \subseteq J_i$. This confirms that the ideals are entrepreneurial ideals and that the quotients are enterprises. □

2.2 Arguments and Coarguments

Within the EPRT program, and particularly an enterprise considered as an e.p.r.s institution, the concepts of e.p.r.s argumentation and coargumentation are seen as an intrinsic concentration of e.p.r.s interests of agents about conflicting positions of those embodied into agreements and coagreements. Thus, it is natural to include them among the basic definitions of EPRT. They are, in any case, among the most important of the actions an enterprise can do - to make an economic influence on other e.p.r.s structures and institutions. Economic arguments and coarguments provide essential exercise in working with abstract enterprises constituted by entrepreneurial agreements/coagreements.

There are two ways of referring to an argumentation and coargumentation, or economic representation and corepresentation of a collection of e.p.r.s. They have natural economic interpretation of a *cost (price)* vis a vi *quality* , imbedded into an e.p.r.s as an element of an agreement and a coagreement .

From another point of view, if one wants to emphasize the argumentation (coargumentation) itself, then one says that the agreement (coagreement) of an enterprise has an economic influence on formation and implementation of e.p.r.s. This economic influence is an argumentation (coargumentation), or sometimes it may be thought of as economic action (coaction) of an enterprise. If, on the other hand, one wants to emphasize the e.p.r.s space on which the agents of a biagreement or enterprise make an economic influence or act, we say that it is *standardized* in the case of argumentation, and a *costandardized* in the case of coargumentation. Thus, (co)standardized EPRS is nothing other than an e.p.r.s space on which the (co)argumentation of an enterprise has some economic impacts. In formal terms we are dealing with (co)modules of the bialgebras or Hopf algebras. So, if two standardized EPRS are isotransactive, it means not only that they are isomorphic as economic vector spaces, but that underlying e.p.r.s structures of argumentations and coargumentations correspond to each other. It is convenient to place the emphasis on the economic space that is influenced from point of view of cost and quality. In addition, if there is some other agreeable economic policy from another agreement to an enterprise considered, its economic influence can also be incorporated into structure of enterprise in an appropriate way.

In this section first the formalization of an e.p.r.s argumentation and coargumentation is provided for the simplest economic structures - economic structure of a natural resource. The next two subsections explain formulation of argumentation and coargumentation implemented into more complex e.p.r.s structures of biagreements and enterprises.

2.2.1 Simple Forms

Let us formalize concepts of argumentation and coargumentation having in mind the simplest possible collections of e.p.r.s. Simplicity of these economic objects is understood here in the sense that underlying e.p.r.s structure on which argumentation and/or coargumentation is to be implemented is such that it can be modeled by a vector space. It is plausible that an economic natural resource, or some other simple economic activity, has e.p.r.s structure which can be modeled in this way. As examples we may have in mind water, minerals, uncultivated land, simple unskilled labor and similar. The crucial point here is that these economic resources have simple underlying e.p.r.s structure. It might be important to note that in a variety of economic problems, where particularities of e.p.r.s relations among agents can be fixed and/or are not important economic issues, almost any EPRS may be reduced to simple e.p.r.s space, this meaning on one with the simplest e.p.r.s structure, to be approximated by an economic vector space. From that point of view elements discussed in this subsection provide a link between EPRT and the more traditional economic theories as general equilibrium theory for example.

From above it is obvious that in these cases an underlying structure of e.p.r.s relations among agents to these simple economic objects is implicitly assumed and implemented in an economic analysis. More complex concepts of an argumentation and coargumentation are necessary for already formed e.p.r.s institutions with more rich e.p.r.s structure, as agreements, biagreements and enterprises. They are formalized in following subsections.

As mentioned above, there are cost and quality types of argumentation and/or coargumentation on e.p.r.s of a natural recourse. If one wants to emphasize a type of argumentation, $\alpha_A, (\alpha_B)$, itself, then one says that the agreement of an enterprise H, has an influence on cost (quality) on domain of a natural resource, V. This influence is a *cost argumentation*, α_A, and/or a *quality argumentation*, α_B, respectively. If, on the other hand, one wants to emphasize the space on which the action has an influence, one says that a space of natural resource V is a *cost H-standardized* economic space, in the case of cost argumentation, and a *quality H-standardized* economic space, in the case of quality argumentation. If the two standards carry equal economic transactions (they are isomorphic), it is meant not only that they are isomorphic as economic vector spaces, but that the underlying argumentations and coargumentations of the enterprise mutually agree.

In an analogous way, quality and cost type of coargumentation on a natural resource can be formulated. The type of coargumentation, $\beta_B, (\beta_A)$, describes how the coargumentations of H has economic influence on quality (cost) of a natural resource, V. Similarly, an economic natural space V may be referred to as a *quality H-costandardized* economic space, in the case of quality coargumentation, and a *cost H-costandardized* economic space, in the case of cost (price) coargumentation.

In addition, if there is an agreeable economic policy on appropriation of e.p.r.s, f, from another agreement on a natural resource to an enterprise H considered, one says that an argumentation or H-standard pulls back e.p.r.s to an argumentation of the other agreement. Here first one is modifying of a natural resource by mapping according to an economic policy f, and then applying the argumentation of H, a collection of e.p.r.s is obtained. Analogous is valid for a coargumentation. Namely, we have that, for a given coagreeable economic policy on appropriation of e.p.r.s, f, from H to another coagreement on a natural resource, a coargument or H-costandard pushes out e.p.r.s to a coagreement by first applying the coargumentation of H, and then implementing the economic policy f, a collection of e.p.r.s is obtained.

Let us specify the elements of argumentation and coargumentation of an enterprise on a natural resource more precisely.

Argumentations

A cost (price) argumentation (or cost representation) of a biagreement or an enterprise H on e.p.r.s embodied in a natural resource is a pair (α_A, V), where V is an economic vector space of e.p.r.s concerning a natural resource, and α_A is a linear map $H \otimes V \to V$. One may write $\alpha_A(h \otimes v) = \alpha_{hA}(v)$, such that $\alpha_{hgA}(v) = \alpha_{hA}(\alpha_{gA}(v))$, $\alpha(1_H \otimes (v)) = v$. Note that V is an economic vector space which defines e.p.r.s structure of a natural resource, or some other simple factor or an economic activity (unskilled labor for example). Thus we have

Definition 2.16 (Cost argumentation). *A cost argumentation of an H-enterprise on a natural resource is a pair (α_A, V) of an economic vector space of a natural resource, V, together with a linear map α_A, $\alpha_A : H \otimes V \to V$, such that the following diagrams are commutative:*

ACA1

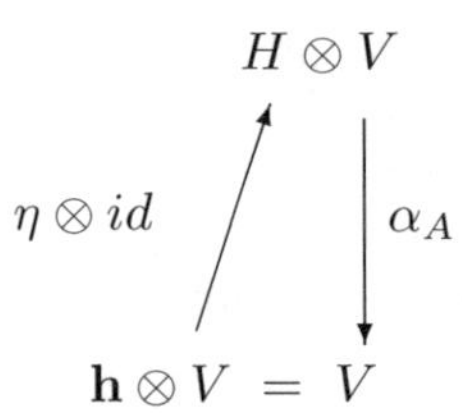

ACA2

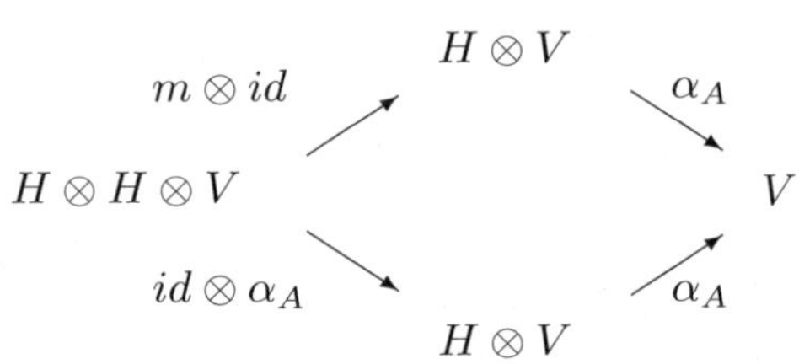

Comparing *ACA1* and *ACA2* to the axioms *A1* and *A2* that characterized an agency in 2.1, we see that in the case of a cost (price) argumentation on a natural resource the axioms are almost the same, with some of the expansions of e.p.r.s replaced by α_A. We may use a symbolic notation of

cost argumentation given by $\overset{a}{>}$. Thus, for each collection of e.p.r.s from an enterprise, $h \in H$, we can also write $\rho(h) = h \overset{a}{>} (\,) = \alpha_A(h \otimes (\,))$, viewed as a linear map from economic vector space V on itself, $V \to V$. From formal point of view we may think of $Lin(V)$ as the usual algebra of such linear maps, with multiplication given by composition, then clearly the axioms for α_A just say that the corresponding $\rho : H \to Lin(V)$ is an algebra map. Thus, a convenient way of thinking about an argumentation of an enterprise on a natural resource within EPRT is that using entrepreneurial capital and knowledge, embodied into $\mathbf{h}$, an enterprise, as an economic agent, acts on a natural resource establishing the e.p.r.s-structure on it, $\mathbf{h} \otimes V$. In that way an economic expansion of e.p.r.s, α_A, of an enterprise considered is obtained.

As already emphasized, there is an analogous notation of qualitative e.p.r.s argumentation for a natural resource. This is a map $\alpha_B : V \otimes H \to V$, denoted by $v \otimes h \mapsto \alpha_{Bh}(v)$, such that $\alpha_{Bhg}(v) = \alpha_{Bg}(\alpha_{Bh}(v))$, and $\alpha_B(v \otimes 1_H) = v$.

Definition 2.17 (Quality argumentation). *A quality argumentation of an H-enterprise on a natural resource is pair (α_B, V) of an economic vector space V of a natural resource, together with a linear map α_B, $\alpha_B : V \otimes H \to V$, such that the following diagrams are commutative:*

AQA1 *AQA2*

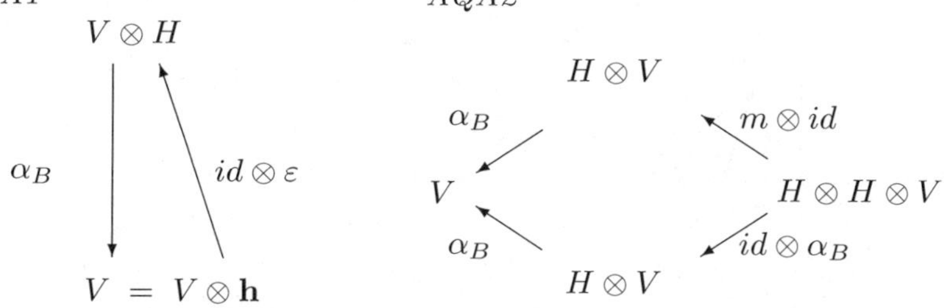

It is easy to compare the above axioms with the ones for an e.p.r.s coagreement, *A3* and *A4* in Section 2.1.1. Also, in this case we may use a symbolic notation of quality argumentation given by $\overset{a}{<}$. For example, if $\overset{a}{>}$ is a cost (price) argumentation, then $v \otimes h = (\gamma h) \overset{a}{<} v$ is a corresponding quality argumentation of an H-enterprise to a natural resource. Here we use the properties of mutual understanding mapping, γ, implied from relations between coagreements and agreements in an enterprise. One can also use γ^{-1} if it exists. To understand the definition of a qualitative argumentation for a natural resource, one may have in mind that its axioms are generated from economic information (constituting a cost (price) argumentation) obtained over an exclusive dominant economic rationality, for example private rationality, of agents on e.p.r.s of a natural resource providing a quality argumentation of an enterprise. If we assume a perfect exclusive dominant economic (as pure private) reasoning of agents and perfect distribution of information on a natural resource, then economic content of a natural resource is linear image of such a coordination among agents.

Coargumentation

Let us now discuss more precisely e.p.r.s axioms of coargumentation of an enterprise on a natural resource. They are simply obtained by reversing the flow (arrows) of e.p.r.s in the diagrams, interchanging $\Delta, \varepsilon, \alpha,$ and m, η, β and assuming an exclusive dominant economic rationality and coordination of information among agents which preserve this exclusive dominant rationality in the process. Then we get the following,

Definition 2.18. (Quality coargumentation) *A quality coargumentation of an* H*-enterprise on a natural resource is pair* (β_B, V) *of an economic vector space* V *of a natural resource together with a linear map* β_B, $\beta_B : V \to V \otimes H$, *such that* $(\beta_B \otimes id) \circ \beta_B = (id \otimes \Delta) \circ \beta_B$ *and* $id = (id \otimes \varepsilon) \circ \beta_B$. *This may be expressed by the following commutative diagrams:*

AQC3 *AQC4*

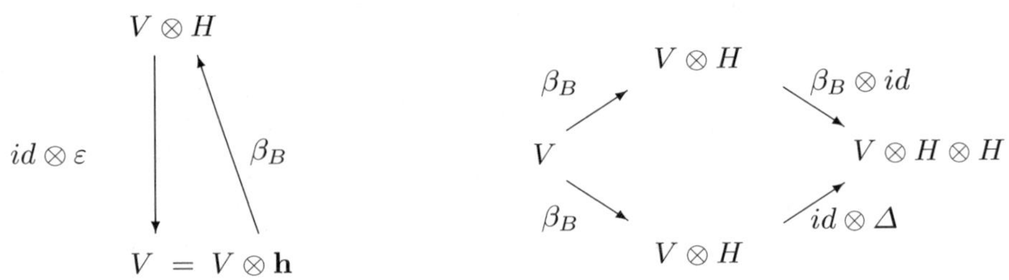

Comparing these axioms with the diagrams of *A3* and *A4* in 2.3, we see that they are obtained by polarization of the e.p.r.s in the definition of a coagreement. Recalling the notation of a coagreement in section 2.1.1, instead of writing β for a coargumentation on a natural resource one usually uses a summation. So it can be denoted by a formal sum notation $\beta_B(v) = \sum v^{(\bar{1})} \otimes v^{(\bar{2})}$, where the right hand side is an explicit representation of combinations of e.p.r.s as an element of $V \otimes H$. In terms of this notation, the axioms of a *quality costandardization* of a natural resource are

$$\sum v^{(\bar{1})(\bar{1})} \otimes v^{(\bar{1})(\bar{2})} \otimes v^{(\bar{2})} = \sum v^{(\bar{1})} \otimes v^{(\bar{2})}_{(1)} \otimes v^{(\bar{2})}_{(2)}, \tag{2.3}$$

$$\sum v^{(\bar{1})} \varepsilon(v^{(\bar{2})}) = v. \tag{2.4}$$

Above we have concentrated on quality coargumentation, but clearly there is analogous notation for cost (price) coargumentation of an enterprise on a natural resource. Thus,

Definition 2.19. (Cost coargumentation) *An enterprise* H *has a cost coargumentation on a natural resource* V *(or* V *is a cost* H*-costandardized) if there is a map* β_A, $\beta_A : V \to H \otimes V$, *such that* $(id \otimes \beta_A) \circ \beta_A = (\Delta \otimes id) \circ \beta_A$ *and* $id = (\varepsilon \otimes id) \circ \beta_A$. *Thus we have,*

ACC3

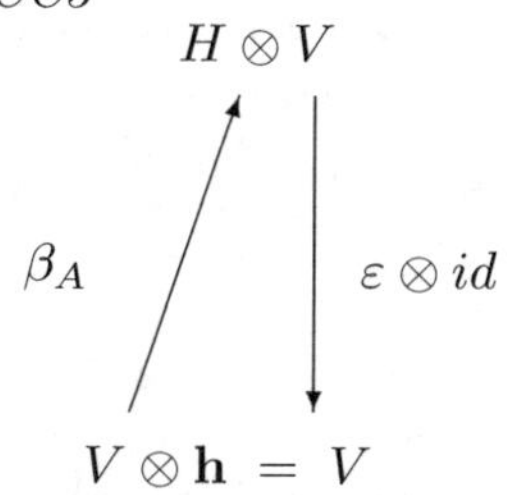

ACC4

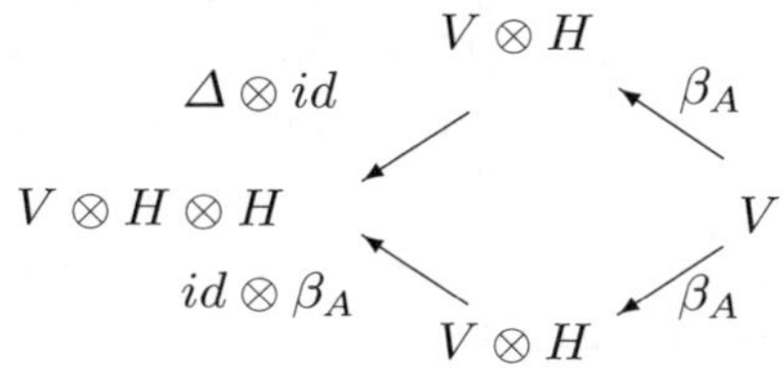

The relevant diagrams, under assumption of an exclusive dominant economic rationality of agents on a natural resource, are polarization of the e.p.r.s in the definitions of an agreement.

If we write the map explicitly as

$$\beta_A(v) = \sum v^{(\bar{1})} \otimes v^{(\bar{2})} \in H \otimes V,$$

then the cost costandardized property of a natural resource may be expressed by

$$\sum v^{(\bar{1})} \otimes v^{(\bar{2})(\bar{1})} \otimes v^{(\bar{2})(\bar{2})} = \sum {v^{(\bar{1})}}_{(1)} \otimes {v^{(\bar{1})}}_{(2)} \otimes v^{(\bar{2})}, \tag{2.5}$$

$$\sum \varepsilon(v^{(\bar{1})}) v^{(\bar{2})} = v. \tag{2.6}$$

For example, since γ is an anticoagreeable map, it can be used to convert a quality coargumentation to a price (cost) one, and vice versa, by composition with $\beta_B(\beta_A)$, and similarly with γ^{-1} if it exists.

Some Additional Properties of Simple Forms

Let us discuss some additional properties of simple e.p.r.s institutions in more detail. Several examples of a simple enterprise and its e.p.r.s properties are provided to shed some light on more concrete forms of simple e.p.r.s institutions. Note that, as in the above sections, simplicity of e.p.r.s relations actually means possibility of e.p.r.s representation over vector spaces, and natural economic resources appear as concrete examples one may have in mind. Thus, here we are studying properties of argumentation and coargumentation of partners concerning natural economic resources and formation of biagreements and/or enterprise by employment of these simple e.p.r.s structures.

Proposition 2.20. *Let us consider enterprise* H *formed on a natural resource* V. *Then mutual understanding map between partners (agent and coagent) is its own inverse.*

Proof: The proof uses the property that if mutual understanding map is such that $\gamma^{-1} = \gamma$, we have $\gamma^2 = id$, what characterizes a commutative enterprise considered as an e.p.r.s institution. An enterprise is commutative if it is commutative as an agreement. It is cocommutative if it is cocommutative as a coagreement, i.e. if $\tau \circ \Delta = \Delta$. From Exercise 2.10, it can be seen that if H is commutative or cocommutative, then H^{op} or H^{cop} respectively coincide with H. Since it is unique, we have $\gamma^{-1} = \gamma$. For a direct proof in the cocommutative case, we have $\gamma^2 h = (\gamma^2 h_{(1)})(\gamma h_{(2)})h_{(3)} = (\gamma h_{(1)} \gamma h_{(2)})h_{(3)} = h$. The commutative case is almost identical. □

Example 2.21. Let G be a set of e.p.r.s rules that agents accept in their relations on a natural resource, described as a finite group with identity e. Let $\mathbf{h}(G)$ denote the set of economic functions on G with the value in the field of e.p.r.s claims of partners, $\mathbf{h}$. That this has the structure of an enterprise concerning natural resource can be seen by the following:
(i) The structure of economic vector space is given by pointwise addition and the argumentation of $\mathbf{h}$ by

$$(\lambda \cdot \phi)(u) = \lambda \cdot (\phi(u)).$$

(ii) The elements of e.p.r.s agreement are given by

$$(\phi\psi)(u) = \phi(u)\psi(u), \qquad \eta(\lambda)(u) = \lambda, \qquad \phi, \psi \in \mathbf{h}(G),\ u \in G$$

(iii) The elements of e.p.r.s coagreements by

$$(\Delta\phi)(u, v) = \phi(uv), \qquad \varepsilon\phi = \phi(e),$$

and
(iv) mutual understanding map by

$$(\gamma\phi)(u) = \phi(u^{-1}).$$

Sketch of proof and comments: The axioms *A1-A6* are to be verified. Here we are identifying $\mathbf{h}(G) \otimes \mathbf{h}(G) = \mathbf{h}(G \times G)$ (functions of two group variables) when defining the expansion of e.p.r.s for copartner. *A4* is easily verified as $((\Delta \otimes id)\Delta\phi)(u, v, w) = (\Delta\phi)(uv, w) = \phi((uv)w) = \phi(u(vw)) = (\Delta\phi)(u, vw) = ((id \otimes \Delta)\Delta\phi)(u, v, w)$. Note that this statement resulted from associativity property of e.p.r.s rules of behavior accepted among agents concerning a natural resource, G. Likewise $((\varepsilon \otimes id)\Delta\phi)(u) = (\Delta\phi)(e, u) = \phi(eu) = \phi(u)$ and $((\gamma\phi_{(1)})\phi_{(2)})\ (u) = (\gamma\phi_{(1)})(u)\phi_{(2)}(u) = \phi_{(1)}(u^{-1})\phi_{(2)}(u) = \phi(u^{-1}u) = \phi(e) = \varepsilon(\phi)$. Similar can be shown for the other partner. Thus we get a biagreement among agents in the formation of an enterprise concerning collections of e.p.r.s on a natural resource as an economic vector space. Added mutual understanding among agents γ given by condition (iii) completes conditions for an enterprise on a natural resource or a simple enterprise. □

Example 2.22. Let G be a set of e.p.r.s rules that agents accept in their relations on a natural resource, described as a finite group. Let $\mathbf{h}G$ denote the economic vector space with basis G. Precisely, elements of agreements are given by $\{a = \sum_{u\in G} a(u)e_u\}$, where $\{e_u \mid u \in G\}$ denotes the basis, and the coefficients have values in $\mathbf{h}$. Simply, one may think of it as a set of formal $\mathbf{h}$-linear combinations of elements that are defined by the rulesin economic relations, G, such that $a = \sum a(u)u$, $u \in G$. This can be simply denoted by $\mathbf{h}G$, and has the structure of an enterprise concerning natural resource that has the property $\tau \circ \Delta = \Delta$, i.e. it is a cocommutative enterprise as a coagreement. The structure of economic vector space is given by the agreeable structures of agency, coagency and mutual understanding map:

$$\text{product in G}, \qquad 1 = e, \qquad \Delta u = u \otimes u, \qquad \varepsilon u = 1, \qquad \gamma u = u^{-1},$$

regarded as $u \in G \subset \mathbf{h}G$, extended by linearity to all of $\mathbf{h}G$.

Sketch of proof and comments: As in the above case, here we count on properties of economic rules given by G. So the expansion map of e.p.r.s for an agreement is clearly associative (so *A2* is satisfied) because the multiplication of e.p.r.s defined by the accepted e.p.r.s rules has property of associativity. *A4* is also satisfied, as a coexpansion of e.p.r.s is coassociative because it is so on each of the basis of an element $u \in G$. It is an algebra homomorphism because $\Delta(uv) = uv \otimes uv = (u \otimes u)(v \otimes v) = \Delta(u)\Delta(v)$. The other facts can be also shown. □

In a general enterprise, considered as an e.p.r.s institution, one can always search for e.p.r.s rule like elements. They have the properties that the coexpansion of e.p.r.s is of the type $\Delta u = u \otimes u$.

Example 2.23. The enterprise given over the accepted e.p.r.s rules of agents in their relations to natural resource, i.e. simple enterprise just described above, can also be thought of as an economic space determined by economic functions. Namely, the set of coefficients $\{h(u)\}$ of $h \in \mathbf{h}G$ can be regarded as economic functions on G. The e.p.r.s structure of the enterprise is equivalent in terms of these economic functions to

$$(hg)(u) = \sum_v h(v)g(v^{-1}u), \qquad 1(u) = \delta_e(u),$$

$$(\Delta h)(u,v) = \delta_u(v)h(u), \qquad \varepsilon(h) = \sum_u h(u), \qquad (\gamma h)(u) = h(u^{-1}),$$

for all $h, g \in \mathbf{h}G$. Here $\delta_u(v) = 1$ if $u = v$ and 0 otherwise. For this reason, we may think of this form of enterprise as e.p.r.s rule convolution agreement.

Proof: If $h = \sum_v h(v)v$, $g = \sum_u g(u)u$, then $hg = \sum_{u,v} h(v)g(u)vu = \sum_{u,v} h(v)g(v^{-1}u)u$. □

Example 2.24. Two forms of simple enterprises on a natural resource, $\mathbf{h}(G)$ and $\mathbf{h}G$, described above, are strictly dual to each other. The pairing is as follows: $\phi \in \mathbf{h}(G)$ should be extended by linearity to a function on $\mathbf{h}G$. Thus, $\langle \phi, \psi \rangle = \phi(\sum_u h(u)u) = \sum_u h(u)\phi(u)$.

Sketch of proof and comments: To check the pairing equations it is enough to check them on the generators $u \in G \subset \mathbf{h}G$, since the structure of $\mathbf{h}G$ is just the structure of these, extended by linearity. For example, $\langle \phi \otimes \psi, \Delta \rangle = \langle \phi \otimes \psi, u \otimes u \rangle = \phi(u)\psi(u) = (\phi\psi)(u) = \langle \phi\psi, u \rangle$. To continue see proposition 2.11. □

It might be noteworthy that for a construction of an enterprise on a natural resource one may use a simple but important application of these constructions when rules of behavior of partners are given by G as a finite Abelian group. Then $\hat{G}$ consists of economic maps from G to $\mathbf{h} - \{0\}$ that respect the rule structure in the sense that $\chi(uv) = \chi(u)\chi(v)$ (Pontrayagin dual). It is called the character rule of G. $\hat{G}$ determines e.p.r.s rules under the pointwise multiplication of elements as expansion of e.p.r.s on a natural resource.

Proposition 2.25. *The elements of e.p.r.s rules $\hat{G}$ can be identified with the nonzero agreeable economic maps form $\mathbf{h}G$ to $\mathbf{h}$, so that $\mathbf{h}\hat{G} = (\mathbf{h}G)^*$ as enterprises. Hence from the previous statement, we may conclude that $\mathbf{h}\hat{G} \cong \mathbf{h}(G)$ as enterprises. Similarly we conclude that $\mathbf{h}G \cong \mathbf{h}(\hat{G})$. These economic isotransactions are modeled by the Fourier transforms of the convolution algebra on $\hat{G}$ to functions on G and vice versa. Explicitly they take the form*

$$\tilde{h}(u) = \sum_{\chi} h(\chi)\chi(u), \qquad \tilde{\chi} = \frac{1}{\mid G \mid} \sum_{u \in G} \chi(u^1)\phi(u)$$

for $h, \tilde{\phi} \in \mathbf{h}\hat{G}$ and $\phi, \tilde{h} \in \mathbf{h}(G)$. It is similar with $G, \hat{G}$ interchanged. Note that $\mid G \mid$ denotes the number of elements of G or $\hat{G}$, and it is assumed to be invertible in the field of claims of agents $\mathbf{h}$.

If e.p.r.s rules are not forming an Abelian group, it seems plausible to extend the definition of new e.p.r.s rules $\hat{G}$ to the collection of equivalence classes of irreducible representations. In this case, new rules, $\hat{G}$, have actually modified relations among partners implying nonsymmetric flow of information on e.p.r.s. An alternative approach, having in mind the second of the above Fourier transformations used, is simply to work with the enterprise $\mathbf{h}G$ in place of $\mathbf{h}(\hat{G})$. This is an example where the economic reasoning on forms of EPRSs is more complex than one concerning a natural resource and is discussed in the next section. An example of such an economic reasoning of extensions of e.p.r.s has a direct link with the conventional growth models in economics.

The following summarizes the relationship between the axioms of argumentation and coargumentation of an H-enterprise on a natural resource.

Proposition 2.26. *Let us consider an enterprise H as a finite dimensional EPRS, which is making economic influence on a natural resource V. Then a cost argumentation of H corresponds to a quality coargumentation of H^* on the same economic space of a natural recourse according to a chosen exclusive dominant economic rationality. Explicitly, if $\beta(v) = \sum v^{(\bar{1})} \otimes v^{(\bar{2})}$ is the coargumentation of H^*, then $h \overset{a}{>} v = \sum v^{(\bar{1})}\langle h, v^{(\bar{2})}\rangle$ is the corresponding argumentation of H. If A_A is a cost H-standardized agreement about a natural economic resource, then it is a quality H^*-costandardized agreement. If A_B is a cost H-standardized coagreement about a natural resource, then it is a quality H^*-costandardized coagreement.*

Proof: Having in mind the conditions of the proposition, the proof is an elementary exercise on the duallity of economic linear spaces and how economic maps are dualized over corresponding e.p.r.s mappings. From the axioms of an agreement and coagreement, we have already noted that coassociativity of Δ corresponds to associativity of the expansion of e.p.r.s m in the dual, and similarly associativity to coassociativity in the dual. One can now verify that these make H^* into an enterprise. Proceeding from the axioms, *A1* - *A6*, we have

$$\begin{aligned}\langle \Delta(\phi\psi), h \otimes g\rangle &= \langle \phi\psi, hg\rangle = \langle \phi \otimes \psi, \Delta(hg)\rangle = \langle \phi \otimes \psi, \Delta(h)(\Delta g)\rangle \\ &= \langle \phi_{(1)} \otimes \psi_{(1)}\phi_{(2)} \otimes \psi_{(2)}, \Delta(h) \otimes \Delta(g)\rangle \\ &= \langle (\Delta\phi)(\Delta\psi), h \otimes g\rangle\end{aligned}$$

as required. Here we used that H is a biagreement as well as pairing equations of an enterprise. In addition, it can be shown that

$$\begin{aligned}\langle (\gamma\phi_{(1)})\phi_{(2)}, h\rangle &= \langle \gamma\phi_{(1)} \otimes \phi_{(2)}, h_{(1)} \otimes h_{(2)}\rangle = \langle \phi_{(1)} \otimes \phi_{(2)}, \gamma h_{(1)} \otimes h_{(2)}\rangle \\ &= \langle \phi, (\gamma h_{(1)})h_{(2)}\rangle = \langle \phi, 1\rangle\varepsilon(h) = \varepsilon(\phi)\varepsilon(h) \\ &= \langle 1\varepsilon(\phi), h\rangle.\end{aligned}$$

One gets a similar result for implementation of γ on $\phi_{(2)}$. Since these identities hold for arbitrary test elements h, g we conclude that H^* is an enterprise.

Now concerning argumentation we can compute

$$\begin{aligned}h \overset{a}{>} (g \overset{a}{>} v) &= (g \overset{a}{>} v)^{(\bar{1})}\langle h, (g \overset{a}{>} v)^{(\bar{2})}\rangle = v^{(\bar{1})(\bar{1})}\langle g, v^{(\bar{1})(\bar{2})}\rangle\langle g, v^{(\bar{1})}\rangle \\ &= v^{(\bar{1})}\langle g \otimes h, v^{(\bar{2})}{}_{(1)} \otimes v^{(\bar{2})}{}_{(2)}\rangle \\ &= (gh) \overset{a}{>} v\end{aligned}$$

and

$$\begin{aligned}1 \overset{a}{>} v &= v^{(\bar{1})}\langle 1, v^{(\bar{2})}\rangle = v^{(\bar{1})}\varepsilon(v^{(\bar{2})}) \\ &= v,\end{aligned}$$

so that we have a cost (price) argumentation on the same vector space of a natural resource V as the quality coagreement. Similar can be shown for other statements in the proposition. □

As already mentioned, the crucial point to note here is that it is plausible to assume that natural economic resources have simple underlying economic structure which can be captured by a vector space structure. It might be important to note that in a variety of economic problems, where particularities of e.p.r.s relations among agents can be fixed or are not important economic issues, almost any EPRS may be reduced to the one with the simplest e.p.r.s structure, i.e. to be approximated by an economic vector space. Naturally in these cases an underlying structure of e.p.r.s relations among agents is implicitly assumed and implemented in an economic analysis. If such type of approximations are not possible, or plausible from economic point of view, e.p.r.s relations are imposed as fundamental, and more complex concepts of argumentation and coargumentation are necessary on already formed e.p.r.s institutions, as agreements, biagreements and/or enterprises.

2.2.2 Advance Argumentation

In a modern economy it is plausible to expect that agents in their mutual economic relations are involved more often with argumentation and coargumentation on already made agreements and coagreements, than on a natural resource directly. In addition, from point of view of EPRT, argumentation on agreements and coagreements is more interesting than those on natural recourses. Here argumentation concerns the more complex e.p.r.s structures of already made agreements, coagreements, biagreements or enterprises. It is plausible that the relevant underlying e.p.r.s structure of agreement and/or coagreement is taken into account throughout the argumentation. At the same time, to get a full sense of an economic content of argumentation on economic agreements and coagreements, the focus is on biagreements or enterprises, and not merely some agreement as the source of argumentation. An economic circumstance where an agreement could be considered as an outcome of an exclusive dominant source of economic argumentation corresponds to a form of dictatorial economy. This case of an economy carries an exclusive e.p.r.s pattern and a strict hierarchy to the extreme implying the most simplified structure of economic influences. The case may be of an economic interest due to simplified structure of argumentation, although most of the interesting economic issues of EPRT are avoided or swept under the rug, and are on the margin of this program.

Cost Standardized Argumentation

A cost (price) argumentation of an enterprise on an agreement modifies its e.p.r.s structure forming a cost (price) standardized agreement. More precisely,

Definition 2.27 (Cost standardized agreement). *An agreement A_P resulting from a cost (price) argumentation of an enterprise H, is an enterprise cost (price) standardized (simply H-standardized) agreement if A_P is a simple cost (price) H-standardized agreement as defined in 2.16, and in addition it satisfies the following,*

$$\begin{aligned} \alpha_A(h \otimes (a_{iP} a_{jP})) &= h \overset{a}{>} (a_{iP} a_{jP}) \\ &= \sum (h_{(1)} \overset{a}{>} a_{iP})(h_{(2)} \overset{a}{>} a_{jP}), \qquad (2.7) \\ &\quad a_{iP}, a_{jP} \in A_P, \\ h \overset{a}{>} 1_{A_P} &= \varepsilon(h) 1_{A_P}. \qquad (2.8) \end{aligned}$$

Thus, in addition to axioms *ACA1* and *ACA2*, a cost H-standardized agreement satisfies the following axioms expressed as commutative diagrams,

AA5

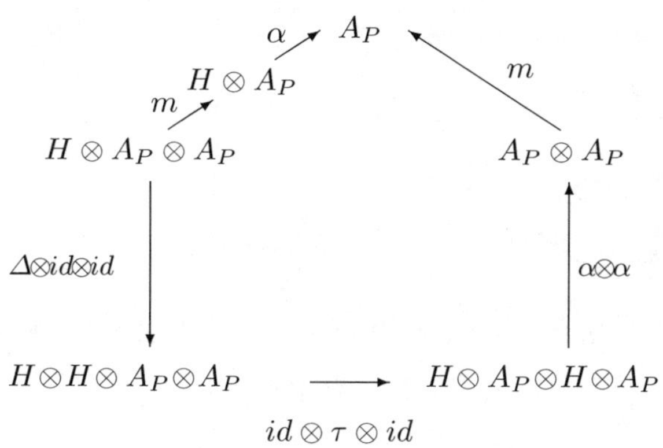

and

AA6

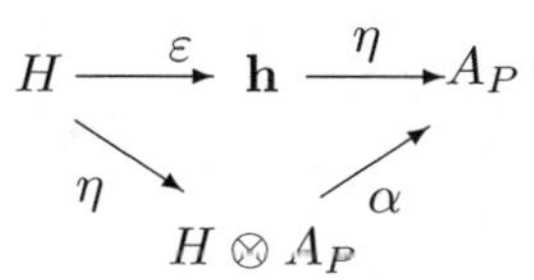

There is a notion of cost (price) H-standardized coagreement. We have that an enterprise H makes impacts on a coagreement by force of an argumentation, forming a cost standardized coagreement C_P. More precisely we have,

Definition 2.28 (Cost standardized coagreement). *A coagreement C_P resulting from an e.p.r.s cost argumentation of an enterprise H, is an enterprise standardized (simply H-standardized) cost coagreement, C_P, if it is a simple cost (price) H-standardized coagreement, and in addition*

$$\Delta(h \overset{a}{>} c_P) = \sum h_{(1)} \overset{a}{>} c_{(1)P} \otimes h_{(2)} \overset{a}{>} c_{(2)P}, \tag{2.9}$$

$$\varepsilon(h \overset{a}{>} c_P) = \varepsilon(h)\varepsilon(c_P). \tag{2.10}$$

The condition says that an e.p.r.s cost argumentation $\overset{a}{>}, \overset{a}{>}$: $H \otimes C_P \to C_P$ is a coagreeable economic map, where $H \otimes C_P$ has the aggregation procedure of e.p.r.s generated from the coagreement structure on which argumentation is implemented, $\Delta(h \overset{a}{>} c_P) = (\Delta h) \overset{a}{>} (\Delta c_P)$. The condition can be expressed by diagrams, where a polarization of the axioms that characterized the coagreement is obvious in comparison to its axioms, *A3* and *A4* from 2.3. Thus, in addition to *AQA1* and *AQA2*, we have the following axioms for an H-standardized coagreement expressed as commutative diagrams,

AA7

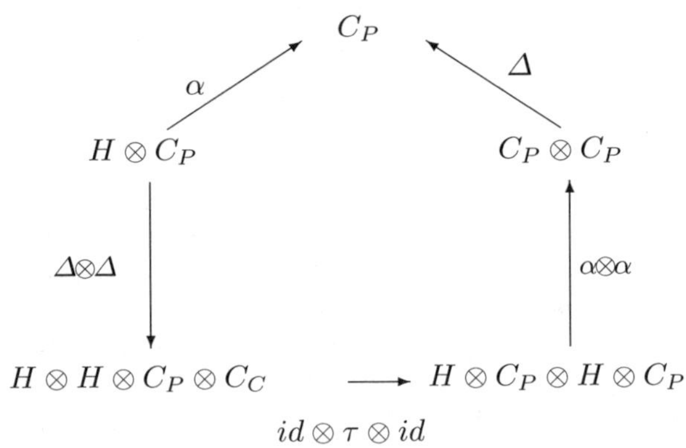

and

AA8

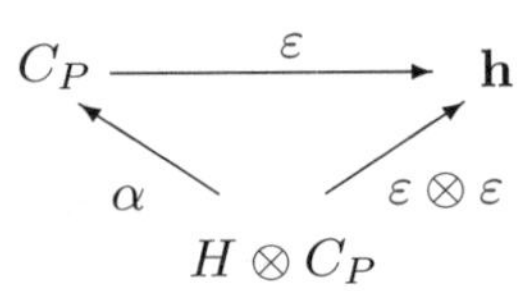

Quality Standardized Argumentation

Analogously to argumentation on natural resources, there is a notation of an e.p.r.s quality argumentation of an H-enterprise on an agreement, A_Q, and coagreement, C_Q.

We say that A_Q is a **quality** H**-standardized agreement** if an H enterprise influences quality of e.p.r.s in an agreement considered as a simple one, and in addition it satisfies,

$$(a_{iQ}a_{jQ}) \overset{a}{<} h = \sum (a_{iQ} \overset{a}{<} h_{(1)})(a_{jQ} \overset{a}{<} h_{(2)}), \tag{2.11}$$

$$1_{A_Q} \overset{a}{<} h = 1_{A_Q}\varepsilon(h). \tag{2.12}$$

Thus, a quality H-standardized agreement satisfies *AQA1* and *AQA2*, and under the assumption of perfect economic rationality of agent and coagent, also satisfies additional axioms given as diagrams, obtained by congruent transformation of diagrams given in *AA5* and *AA6*, above. Recall, that this is a map $A_Q \otimes H \rightarrow A_Q$, denoted by $a_Q \otimes h \mapsto v \overset{a}{<} a_Q$ such that $(a_Q \overset{a}{<} h) \overset{a}{<} g = a_Q \overset{a}{<} (hg)$ and $a_Q \overset{a}{<} 1_{A_Q} = 1_{A_Q}$. For example, if $\overset{a}{>}$ is a cost (price) argumentation, then $a_Q \otimes h = (\gamma h) \overset{a}{<} a_Q$ is a corresponding qualitative argumentation on an agreement A_Q. Here we use the properties of mutual understanding mapping, γ. Namely, its properties imply an economic rationality that makes a clear link between cost (price) argumentation and quality argumentation of an enterprise. One can also use γ^{-1} if it exists.

We say that C_Q is a **quality H-standardized coagreement** if H enterprise influences quality of the coagreement as a simple one, and in addition it satisfies,

$$\Delta(c_Q \overset{a}{<} h) = \sum c_{(1)Q} \overset{a}{<} h_{(1)} \otimes c_{(2)Q} \overset{a}{<} h_{(2)}, \tag{2.13}$$

$$\varepsilon(c_Q \overset{a}{<} h) = \varepsilon(c_Q)\varepsilon(h). \tag{2.14}$$

Thus, a definition of quality argumentation of H-enterprise on a coagreement or quality H-standardized coagreement under the assumption of perfect economic rationality of agent and coagent on underlying e.p.r.s structure the additional axioms, to *AQA1* and *AQA2*, can be obtained by appropriate congruent transformation of diagrams given in *AA7* and *AA8*, above.

Properties of Argumentations

In the following, a few properties of an e.p.r.s argumentation on agreements and coagreements are discussed over several propositions, examples, and exercises.

Example 2.29 (Regular argumentation). The cost regular argumentation R_P of a biagreement or an enterprise H on its economic activities is $R_h(g) = hg$, and makes H into a cost H-standardized coagreement. Similarly, a quality regular argumentation A_Q of a biagreement or enterprise H on its economic activities is $A_{hQ}(g) = gh$, and makes H into a quality H-standardized coagreement.

Proof: A cost regular argumentation of an enterprise is an argumentation satisfying agency and associativity axioms *A1* and *A2* for an enterprise H. It can be written $C_h(g) = h \overset{a}{>} g$, which gives us a standardized coagreement because

$h \overset{a}{>} \Delta g = h_{(1)}g_{(1)} \otimes h_{(2)}g_{(2)} = \Delta(hg)$ and $\varepsilon(h \overset{a}{>} g) = \varepsilon(hg) = \varepsilon(h)\varepsilon(g)$, as required for that case of cost regular argumentation. The proof for the quality regular argumentation is strictly analogous to the above. □

Example 2.30 (Adjoint argumentations). The cost adjoint argumentation Ad_P of an enterprise H on itself is $Ad_P = Ad_h(g) = \sum h_{(1)}g\gamma h_{(2)}$, and makes H into a cost H-standardized agreement. Similarly, a quality adjoint argumentation Ad_Q of an enterprise H on itself is $Ad_Q = Ad_{hQ}(g) = \sum(\gamma h_{(1)})gh_{(2)}$, and makes H into a quality H-standardized agreement.

Proof: Using the properties of the mutual understanding map γ it can be checked that

$$h \overset{a}{>} (g \overset{a}{>} a_P) = h \overset{a}{>} (g_{(1)}a_P\gamma g_{(2)}) = h_{(1)}g_{(1)}a_P(\gamma g_{(2)})(\gamma h_{(2)})$$
$$= (hg)_{(1)}a_P\gamma(hg)_{(2)} = (hg) \overset{a}{>} a_P.$$

Also, we have $1 \overset{a}{>} a_P = 1a_P\gamma(1) = a_P$. To show that we have a standardized agreement, we compute

$$h \overset{a}{>} (a_{iP}a_{jP}) = h_{(1)}a_{iP}a_{jP}(\gamma h_{(2)}) = h_{(1)}a_{iP}(\gamma h_{(2)})h_{(3)}a_{jP}\gamma h_{(4)}$$
$$= (h_{(1)} \overset{a}{>} a_{iP})(h_{(2)} \overset{a}{>} a_{jP})$$

and

$$h \overset{a}{>} 1 = h_{(1)}1\gamma h_{(2)} = \varepsilon(h).$$

One may insert $(\gamma h_{(2)})h_{(3)}$, knowing that e.p.r.s embodied into the expression of e.p.r.s collapse using the mutual understanding axioms. Then freely restructuring e.p.r.s, while keeping the order, the required relation to express coassociativity can be shown. On the other hand, that this is a quality standardized agreement is seen from $(a_{iQ}a_{jQ}) \overset{a}{<} h = (\gamma h_{(1)})a_{iQ}a_{jQ}h_{(2)} = (\gamma h_{(1)})a_{iQ}h_{(2)}(\gamma h_{(3)})a_{jQ}h_{(4)} = (a_{iQ} \overset{a}{<} h_{(1)})(a_{jQ} \overset{a}{<} h_{(2)})$ and $1_H \overset{a}{<} a_Q = (\gamma h_{(1)})h_{(2)} = \varepsilon(h)$. □

Exercise 2.31. Consider an argumentation of a finite dimensional enterprise H on H^*. Show that:
(i) if it is a cost coregular argumentation, $A^*_{PC}(h)(\phi) = \sum \phi_{(1)}\langle h, \phi_{(2)}\rangle$, it makes H^* into a cost H-standardized agreement.
(ii) if it is a cost coadjoint argumentation,
$Ad^*_h(\phi) = \sum \phi_{(2)}\langle h, (\gamma\phi_{(1)})\phi_{(3)}\rangle$,
it makes H into a cost H-standardized coagreement.

Hints: (i) We are dealing with an argumentation from the coassociativity and coagency axioms for H^*. The computation is similar to that in the Example 2.29, but in a dual language. (ii) This is an argumentation, and expanding the products via the pairing axioms, restructuring and recombining of e.p.r.s, the required elements can be obtained. The computation is similar to that in the Example 2.30, but using a dual approach.

Now let us deal with the case where e.p.r.s rules G do not provide symmetric structure of e.p.r.s relations. Then in implementing the rules, $\mathbf{h}G$, the sequence of argumentation and coargumentation fundamentally determines the position of partners in formation of their e.p.r.s over a field of their claims $\mathbf{h}$. This is the simplest example of the economic reasoning on e.p.r.s pattern that cannot be trivialized implying a noncommutative case of e.p.r.s institutions. In this case, rules of e.p.r.s G do not provide a symmetric power to partners on a domain of their claims, (G is non-Abelian), and within such an enterprise, $\mathbf{h}G$, underlying e.p.r.s structure is noncommutative. Thus they can no longer be treated as isomorphic to the agreement of economic functions on an e.p.r.s space of the enterprise. Nevertheless one can still think of $\mathbf{h}G$ as economic functions on noncommutative e.p.r.s space generalization of $\hat{G}$. An example of such an economic reasoning of extension of e.p.r.s on simple economic factors (as natural resource) is given below and has direct links with the more traditional models of asymmetric information, and growth models in economics.

Example 2.32. **(Simple growth enterprise)** Let G be a rule of growth of an economic factor and g an agreement on growth. There is an enterprise $(U(g), m, \Delta, \gamma)$ of a general simple growth agreement g over an arbitrary field of e.p.r.s claims $\mathbf{h}$, defined as follows:

(a) Its agreement is defined by a nontrivial economic reasoning on growth to: (i) preserve the positions of agency in the growth process, and (ii) ensure expansion by elements of agreement g by some standardized economic relations.

(b) Its coagreement is then determined by : (i) the coexpansion of e.p.r.s of primitive type, and (ii) coagency that has no e.p.r.s influence on domain of e.p.r.s claims $\mathbf{h}$.

(c) For any level of growth ξ, their mutual understanding map is given by $\gamma(\xi) = -\xi$.

Such an enterprise corresponds to a traditional concept of simple economic expansion due to growth of tangible assets (goods) in an economy, and simple growth representation in economics. In EPRT it is called simple *R&D* enterprise or simple growth enterprise and determines the universal enveloping enterprise $(U(g), m, \Delta, \gamma)$ or just $U(g)$ on an agreeable growth agreement g.

Proof and comments: To show (a) recall that an expansion of e.p.r.s of agency is not trivial and is determined by agreeable growth structure, modeled by the Lie algebra structure of g. The e.p.r.s rule G is a Lie group, and as we are not dealing with finite groups, the space of analytic economic function on e.p.r.s rule will be infinite dimensional, and one can not longer use the convenient identification of $\mathcal{F}(G\times G)=\mathcal{F}(G)\otimes\mathcal{F}(G)$. In the case of connected e.p.r.s rule G, one may think of the space of distributions on G supported at the identity 1. One can also think of $U(g)$ as the price invariant differential operation of G, providing the expansion on $U(g)$. In general case, the associativity of agreement is determined by the solution to so called 'universal mapping problem'. For any linear map ρ of g into an associative agreement A, $\rho : g \to A$ satisfying,

$$\rho(\xi)\rho(\eta) - \rho(\eta)\rho(\xi) = \rho(\xi\eta - \eta\xi) = \rho([\xi,\eta]) \;\; \xi,\eta \in g \tag{2.15}$$

there is a unique agreeable homotransaction, also denoted by ρ, of $U(g)$ into A, $\rho : U(g) \longrightarrow A$. This determines $U(g)$ uniquely up to an economic isotransaction. Thus, these are standardized according to the relation (2.15) for the aggregation of growth. These standards then provide finite strings of elements of growth g with these economic relations. Under the assumption that domain of e.p.r.s $\mathbf{h}$ is of characteristic zero, there is the natural embedding of g into $U(g)$, so one may identify g as a subspace of $U(g)$ and $U(g)$ is generated by g as an agreement.
To show (b) recall that primitive type of economic reasoning of a coagent implies the property of cocommutativity, and for elements $\xi \in g$ this translates into the relation

$$\Delta\xi = \xi\otimes 1 + 1\otimes\xi, \;\; \xi\in g \tag{2.16}$$

This mapping (2.16) clearly satisfies the standard (2.15). For example, one has $\Delta(\xi\eta) = (\xi\otimes 1 + 1\otimes\xi)(\eta\otimes 1 + 1\otimes\eta) = \xi\eta\otimes 1 + 1\otimes\xi\eta + \xi\otimes\eta + \eta\otimes\xi$, and $\Delta(\eta\xi) = (\eta\otimes 1 + 1\otimes\eta)(\xi\otimes 1 + 1\otimes\xi) = \eta\xi\otimes 1 + 1\otimes\eta\xi + \eta\otimes\xi + \xi\otimes\eta$. By subtracting these and using the defined difference relations, one obtains $(\xi\eta - \eta\xi)\otimes 1 + 1\otimes(\xi\eta - \eta\xi) = \Delta((\xi\eta - \eta\xi))$ as required. Hence it extends to an agreeable economic homotransaction $\Delta : U(g) \longrightarrow U(g)\otimes U(g)$. The coagency is defined by $\varepsilon : g \longrightarrow \mathbf{h}$ given by its lack of impacts on domain of e.p.r.s, so that $\varepsilon(\xi) = 0$, $\forall\xi$. It clearly satisfies the standard (2.15), thus can be extended to an agreeable economic homotransaction, also denoted by coagency ε. From primitivity of economic reasoning of coagency, we have that for any $a = \xi \in g$

$$(\varepsilon\otimes id)(\Delta a) = (id\otimes\varepsilon)(\Delta a) = a,$$

and hence by expansion for all $a \in U(g)$. Thus, we have shown that $(U(g), m, \Delta)$ is an associative, coassociative and cocommutative biagreement. To show that it is an enterprise we have to check existence and properties of mutual understanding map.
So (c) mutual understanding map is, $\gamma(\xi) = -\xi$ satisfies the standard (2.15), as a map from g to the opposite agreement, $U(g)^{op}$. Thus, γ extends as an antihomotransaction,

$$\gamma : U(g) \to U(g), \;\; \gamma(ab) = \gamma(b)\gamma(a)$$

reflecting the mutual understanding of agency and coagency of their conflicting economic position in the growing process on field of claims $\mathbf{h}$, so also we have,

$$\gamma(\xi_1 \cdots \xi_n) = (-1)\xi_n \xi_{n-1} \cdots \xi_1.$$

Thus, for $a = \xi \in g$,

$$(m \circ (\gamma \otimes id) \circ \Delta)(a) = (m \circ (id \otimes \gamma) \circ \Delta)(a) = 0,$$

and hence by expansion for all products of $\xi's$. These show that γ is the mutual understanding map for biagreement $U(g)$, providing structure of an enterprise. Such an enterprise corresponds to a traditional concept of *R&D* in economics, and simple growth representation. Clearly every element of g is primitive, and it is known that the converse is true, i.e., $Prim(U(g)) = g$.

One may note that the enveloping agreement $U(g)$ of an agreed growth g carries an e.p.r.s structure of a biagreement which is determined by the requirement that the canonical projection from the aggregate growth agreement $T(g)$ to $U(g)$ is an economic transactions of biagreements. Equivalently, we may consider the aggregate agreement $T(V)$ and the symmetric agreement $S(V)$ on an economic vector space V. There exists a unique biagreement e.p.r.s structure on aggregate $T(V)$ and on $S(V)$ such that conditions under (b) are satisfied, for any element of aggregate, $v \in T(V)$. This biagreement is simple one, i.e. it is cocommutative and for all $v_1, \ldots, v_n \in V$ we have that the coexpansion of e.p.r.s Δ, can be expressed by

$$\Delta(v_1 \ldots v_n) =$$

$$1 \otimes v_1 \cdots v_n + \sum_{p=1}^{n-1} \sum_{\sigma} v_{\sigma(1)} \cdots v_{\sigma(p)} \otimes v_{\sigma(p+1)} \cdots v_{\sigma(n)} + v_1 \cdots v_n \otimes 1$$

for all $v_i, i = 1, \cdots, n$, elements of an aggregate where σ runs over all $(p, n-p)$-shuffles of the symmetric e.p.r.s-rule S_n, i.e. all permutations σ such that ordering is preserved $\sigma(1) < \sigma(2) < \cdots < \sigma(p)$ and $\sigma(p+1) < \sigma(p+2) < \cdots < \sigma(n)$. The coexpansion Δ can be defined as the composition of the economic transaction from $U(g)$ to $U(g \oplus g)$ induced by the diagonal map $\xi \mapsto (\xi, \xi)$ on g and the canonical isotransaction $U(g \oplus g) \cong U(g) \otimes U(g)$. Elements of this example are going to be discussed in more detail and/or generalized later on through the volume. □

Note, an economy that carries this type of economic growth is called paternalistic economy having in mind conditions (b) imposed on a copartner.

An element in a general enterprise which provides coexpansion of e.p.r.s of a linear form $\Delta\xi = \xi \otimes 1 + 1 \otimes \xi$ is called *primitive*. This notion can be linked with an understanding of simple dominant economic rationality of e.p.r.s institutions as one on simple e.p.r.s structures such as natural resources, for example. The subspace $Prim(A)$ of primitive elements of A is modeled by a Lie subalgebra of A where A is equipped with the Lie bracket given by the commutators $[a, a'] = aa' - a'a$, for all $a, a' \in A$. Namely, the economic subspace of simple growth elements of an agreement can always be expressed as zero-sum or some constant sum economic game. This, also makes the above example the traditional model of economic growth. A reader may also see an application of Lie group in economics within more traditional context in [66].

It may be worthy to note that the association of enterprises $\mathbf{h}(G)$ and $\mathbf{h}G$ to e.p.r.s rules G extends as appropriate policies on domain of e.p.r.s from the economic club of agents governed by finite e.p.r.s rules on an elementary economic vector space (natural resources) to the economic club of simple enterprises. This means that the economic theory of finite e.p.r.s rules precisely embeds into the economic theory of simple enterprises on economic factors or natural resources. Similar is the case of the appropriation policies that carry the association of a simple *R&D* enterprise, $U(g)$, to an economic growth agreement over $\mathbf{h}$, g. In fact there are theorems which state that essentially all simple enterprises are of similar forms to those of $\mathbf{h}(G)$ or $\mathbf{h}G$ (or $U(g)$), respectively.

Exercise 2.33. Let an enterprise be given by $H = \mathbf{h}G$, where G defines e.p.r.s rules, and $H = U(g)$, where growth g is given by a simple *R&D* program (agreement) on $\mathbf{h}$, as discussed above. Show that the adjoint argumentation, described in Example 2.30, becomes

$$u \overset{a}{>} v = uvu^{-1}, \qquad \xi \overset{a}{>} \eta = \xi\eta - \eta\xi$$

for all e.p.r.s rules, $u, v \in G$ and $\xi, \eta \in g$.
Show that the axioms of a standardized agreement reduce to the usual notions of e.p.r.s rules implemented by economic transactions on itself (automorphisms) or an agreement on a simple *R&D* program implemented by an argumentation based on its contributions on elements of agreement A, namely

$$u \overset{a}{>} (a_i a_j) = (u \overset{a}{>} a_i)(u \overset{a}{>} a_j), \qquad u \overset{a}{>} 1 = 1,$$

$$\xi \overset{a}{>} (a_i a_j) = (\xi \overset{a}{>} a_i)a_j + a_i(\xi \overset{a}{>} a_j), \qquad \xi \overset{a}{>} 1 = 0,$$

for any $a_i, a_j \in A$. Verify these directly for the adjoint argumentations described above.

Hints: For the formulae stated, just set $\Delta u = u \otimes u$, $\gamma u = u^{-1}$, $\Delta\xi = \xi \otimes 1 + 1 \otimes \xi$, $\gamma\xi = -\xi$, and so on, into the abstract definitions above. Compare your proofs for the adjoint argumentations with the proof in the Example 2.30.

The principle discussed above seems to work just as well for any enterprise considered as an e.p.r.s institution. Namely it gives one point of view about the concept of an H-standardized enterprise. It generalizes the notion that an agreement A is covariant due to some economic rules imposed on it, or a principle of a simple *R&D* program within the system. More precisely, it generalizes the notion that an agreement is *e.p.r.s* – G-covariant or g-covariant. When economic rules G influence an agreement by internal economic transactions (automorphisms), a standard construction provides a semidirect or cross expansion agreement. This is the agreement generated by $\mathbf{h}G$ and A, but with simplified economic relations between them, such that $ua = (u \overset{a}{>} a)u$ for all $a \in A$ and $u \in G$. In that way e.p.r.s relations are described over commutative relations between elements of an agreement and an enterprise. Likewise, when a simple *R&D* program is an argumentation of an enterprise, one has the semidirect or cross expansion agreement with the cross relations between the agreement of concern and growth process. More precisely, cross relations are given by $\xi a - a\xi = \xi \overset{a}{>} a$ for all $a \in A$, and $\xi \in g$. This principle works just as well for any enterprise.

Proposition 2.34 (Cross expansion). *Let H be a biagreement or an enterprise.*
(i) For a cost H-standardized agreement, A_P, there is a **cost cross expansion** *agreement, $A_P \bowtie\!\!\!\lhd H$, built on an aggregate $A_P \otimes H$ with an expansion of e.p.r.s*

$$(a_{iP} \otimes h)(a_{jP} \otimes g) = \sum a_{iP}(h_{(1)} \overset{a}{>} a_{jP}) \otimes h_{(2)}g, \; a_{iP}, a_{jP} \in A_P, \; h, g \in H.$$

The unit element is $1 \otimes 1$.
(ii) For a quality H-standardized agreement, A_Q, there is a **quality cross expansion** *agreement $H \rhd\!\!\!\bowtie A_Q$ built on an aggregate $H \otimes A_Q$ with expansion of e.p.r.s*

$$(h \otimes a_{iQ})(g \otimes a_{jQ}) = \sum hg_{(1)} \otimes (a_{iQ} \overset{a}{<} g_{(2)})a_{jQ}, \; a_{iQ}, a_{jQ} \in A_Q, \; h, g \in H.$$

The unit element is $1 \otimes 1$.

Proof: To verify (i) let us show that an expansion of e.p.r.s as given in (i) is an associative one. We have,

$$\begin{aligned}
&(a_{iP} \otimes h)((a_{jP} \otimes g)(a_{lP} \otimes f)) - \\
&(a_{iP} \otimes h)a_{jP}(g_{(1)} \overset{a}{>} a_{lP}) \otimes g_{(2)}f = \\
&a_{iP}(h_{(1)} \overset{a}{>} (a_{jP}(g_{(1)} \overset{a}{>} a_{lP}))) \otimes h_{(2)}g_{(2)}f = \\
&a_{iP}(h_{(1)} \overset{a}{>} a_{jP})((h_{(2)}g_{(1)}) \overset{a}{>} a_{lP}) \otimes h_{(3)}g_{(2)}f = \\
&((a_{iP} \otimes h)(a_{jP} \otimes g))(a_{lP} \otimes f).
\end{aligned}$$

Note that here the third equality holds because argumentation $\overset{a}{>}$ respects the agreement structure and so one can compute $h_{(1)} \overset{a}{>} (\;\;)$, and it is a cost (price) argumentation. That $1 \otimes 1$ is the identity is easily verified. Note that

$A_P \otimes 1$ and $1 \otimes H$ appear as subagreements but with mutual commutative relations, so that it can be written,

$$ha_P \equiv (1 \otimes h)(a_P \otimes 1) = h_{(1)} \overset{a}{>} a_P \otimes h_{(2)}$$
$$= (h_{(1)} \overset{a}{>} a_P \otimes 1)(1 \otimes h_{(2)}) \equiv (h_{(1)} \overset{a}{>} a_P)h_{(2)},$$

where we identify $h \equiv 1 \otimes h$ and $a_P \equiv a_P \otimes 1$. This corresponds to the usual way of working with semidirect or cross expansion of e.p.r.s, as defined by expansion of e.p.r.s for an agency dealing with a cost of a simple economic factor (for example natural resource), i.e. as cross commutative relations. An economic interpretation is that in expansion of e.p.r.s, agents transfer e.p.r.s to each other by an aggregation procedure, in a way that preaggregate cost structures are preserved.
(ii) For a case of quality argumentation the proof is strictly analogous to *(i)*. If we write the relations in proofs over diagrams, then a cost - quality economic rationality gives the proofs we need now. Note also that $H \otimes 1$ and $1 \otimes A_Q$ appear as subagreements but with the mutual commutative relations

$$a_Q h \equiv (1 \otimes a_P)(h \otimes 1) = h_{(1)} \otimes a_Q \overset{a}{<} h_{(2)}$$
$$= (h_{(1)} \otimes 1)(1 \otimes a_Q \overset{a}{<} h_{(2)}) \equiv h_{(1)}(a_Q \overset{a}{<} h_{(2)}),$$

where we identify $h \equiv h \otimes 1$ and $a_Q \equiv 1 \otimes a_Q$. This corresponds to an alternative way of working with semidirect or cross expansions of e.p.r.s, as defined by expansion of e.p.r.s in dealing with a quality of a simple economic factor (natural resource, for example), i.e. as cross commutative relations. An economic interpretation is that in expansion of e.p.r.s, agents transfer e.p.r.s to each other by an aggregation procedure in a way that preaggregate quality structures are preserved. □

An economic approach about standardized agreements arises from quite a different point of view. This approach is described by the following example.

Example 2.35. **(Graded economic vector space)** Let H be an enterprise described by $H = \mathbf{h}(G)$, and let e.p.r.s rules, G, be described by a finite group. Then an $\mathbf{h}(G)$-standardized space of e.p.r.s refers to an economic vector space V which is an *e.p.r.s* – G-graded, i.e. $V = \oplus_{u \in G} V_u$. If $v \in V_u$, one says that v is homogeneous of degree $|v| = u$. The argumentation of ϕ is

$$\phi \overset{a}{>} v = \phi(|v|)v.$$

An $\mathbf{h}(G)$-standardized agreement is nothing other than an *e.p.r.s* – G-graded agreement, i.e. an agreement for which the expansion of e.p.r.s $A \otimes A \to A$ is compatible with grading in the sense that $|a_i a_j| = |a_i||a_j|$, $a_i, a_j \in A$ and $|1| = e$. Likewise, an $\mathbf{h}(G)$-standardized coagreement refers to a coagreement where coexpansion of e.p.r.s $\Delta : C \to C \otimes C$ is compatible with the grading.

Proof: Recall that the argumentation can be written in the following form, $\phi \overset{a}{>} v = \sum_{u \in G} \phi(u)\beta_u(v)$, where $\beta_u(v)$ are vectors in V. To be an economic argumentation, one needs $\beta_u(\beta_w(v)) = \delta_{u,w}\beta_u(v)$ for all $u, w \in G$ and $v \in V$. Hence the $\beta_u : V \to V$ are projection operators and V splits as stated. For A to be a standardized agreement, we need $\phi \overset{a}{>} (a_i a_j) = (\phi_{(1)} \overset{a}{>} a_i)(\phi_{(2)} \overset{a}{>} a_j) = (\Delta\phi)(|a_i||a_j|)a_i a_j = \phi(|a_i||a_j|)a_i a_j$ to equal $\phi(|a_i a_j|)a_i a_j$ for all ϕ (on homogeneous a_i, a_j). It is similar for the other statements in the example. The cross expansion $A \succ\!\!\alpha\!\!\lhd \mathbf{h}(G)$ is part of an appropriation procedure that we will come to later, in the Chapter on clubs and institutions. Standards of this cross expansion are e.p.r.s-G-graded economic vector spaces which are also A-standardized in a compatible way. □

It may be noteworthy that two different economic conceptualizations of an enterprise, one where the idea is to understand an enterprise as an e.p.r.s rules-covariant agreement ($H = \mathbf{h}G$), and another where the idea is to view an enterprise as e.p.r.s rules-graded agreement ($H = \mathbf{h}(G)$), can be combined. This permits more accurate following of e.p.r.s flows in these institutions not deductible from one concept alone. They provide the notion of an economic standardized enterprise as an e.p.r.s institution. This unified understanding of an economic enterprise in mathematical economics is made possible by working with the notion of abstract e.p.r.s institutions and application of Hopf algebra in the economic theory.

2.2.3 Advance Coargumentation

Let us now discuss more precisely axioms of coargumentation of an enterprise on agreements, coagreements, biagreements and enterprises. Similar to the case of argumentation, they are more interesting objects for research within the program of EPRT, as here coargumentation concerns the more complex economic structures. It is economically plausible that in each case the relevant underlying e.p.r.s structure of an agreement and coagreement or an enterprise that one is dealing with is respected in some way in the process of coargumentation. Having in mind sections 2.2.1 and 2.2.2, diagrammatic presentation of axioms can be simply obtained by reversing the flow (arrows) of e.p.r.s in the diagrams, interchanging $\Delta, \varepsilon, \alpha,$ and $m, \eta, \beta,$ and assuming a perfect economic rationality and coordination of information among agents which preserve their dominant type of an economic rationality in the process.

Costandardization

Costandardization is specified over the following definitions.

In explicit terms, A_Q is a **quality H-costandardized agreement** if it satisfies conditions of costandardized simple agreement, and in addition if

$$\beta(a_{iQ}a_{jQ}) = \beta(a_{iQ})\beta(a_{jQ}), \quad \beta(1_{A_Q}) = 1 \otimes 1, \tag{2.17}$$

for any $a_{iQ}, a_{jQ} \in A_Q$.

Note that an economic aggregation of e.p.r.s from A_Q and H to $A_Q \otimes H$ has been compatible with the structure of the agreement A_Q, and we are requiring β to be an agreeable map.

Following the same reasoning as in the case of standardized argumentation, an agreement is a **cost H-costandardized agreement** if it is a cost (price) costandardized as a simple agreement, and if β is an agreeable map as in 2.17 above.

A quality coagreement C_Q is a **quality H-costandardized coagreement** if

$$\sum c^{(\bar{1})}{}_{(1)} \otimes c^{(\bar{1})}{}_{(2)} \otimes b^{(\bar{2})} = \sum c_{(1)}{}^{(\bar{1})} \otimes c_{(2)}{}^{(\bar{1})} \otimes c_{(2)}{}^{(\bar{2})},$$
$$\sum \varepsilon(c^{(\bar{1})})c^{(\bar{2})} = \varepsilon(c). \tag{2.18}$$

Finally, a coagreement C_P is a **cost H-costandardized coagreement** if the cost (price) coargumentation obeys the following,

$$\sum c^{(\bar{1})} \otimes c^{(\bar{2})}{}_{(\bar{1})} \otimes c^{(\bar{2})}{}_{(\bar{2})} = \sum c_{(1)}{}^{(\bar{1})} c_{(2)}{}^{(\bar{1})} \otimes c_{(1)}{}^{(\bar{2})} \otimes c_{(2)}{}^{(\bar{2})},$$
$$\sum c^{(\bar{1})}\varepsilon(c^{(\bar{2})}) = \varepsilon(c). \tag{2.19}$$

Properties of Coargumentation

In the following, a few properties of a coargumentation on agreements and coagreements are discussed over several propositions, examples, and exercises. They are given in an analogous way to argumentation.

Example 2.36. **(Regular coargumentation)** The quality regular coargumentation of a biagreement or an enterprise H on its restructuring is given by the regular coexpansion of e.p.r.s, $R_Q = \Delta : H \to H \otimes H$, and makes H into a quality H-costandardized agreement. The cost regular coargumentation $R_P : H \to H \otimes H$, of a biagreement or an enterprise H on its restructuring is $R_P = \Delta$, and gives a cost H-costandardized agreement.

Proof: The axioms of a costandardization follow directly from coagency and coassociativity axioms *A3* and *A4* for Δ. That H is a costandardized agreement in this case is precisely the axiom that Δ is an agreeable economic transaction in structure and properties (homomorphism). The cost side of the statement is strictly analogous to those for quality just given. Compare with Example 2.29. □

Example 2.37. **(Adjoint coargumentation)** The quality adjoint coargumentation of an enterprise H on its restructuring is $Ad_Q = Ad_{hQ}(g) = \sum h_{(2)} \otimes (\gamma h_{(1)})h_{(3)}$, and makes H into a quality H-costandardized coagreement. The cost adjoint coargumentation of an enterprise on itself is $Ad_P = Ad_{hP}(g) = \sum h_{(1)}\gamma h_{(3)} \otimes h_{(2)}$, and makes H into a cost H-costandardized coagreement.

Proof: We have $(Ad_Q \otimes id)Ad_Q(h) = h_{(2)(2)} \otimes (\gamma h_{(2)(1)})h_{(2)(3)} \otimes (\gamma h_{(1)})h_{(3)} = h_{(3)} \otimes (\gamma h_{(2)})h_{(4)} \otimes (\gamma h_{(1)})h_{(5)} = h_{(2)} \otimes (\gamma h_{(1)})_{(1)}h_{(3)(1)} \otimes (\gamma h_{(1)})_{(2)}h_{(3)(2)}$ from properties concerning mutual understanding map (Proposition 2.9). Also $h_{(2)} \otimes \varepsilon((\gamma h_{(1)})h_{(3)}) = h$, so we have a coargumentation. This quality argumentation then makes H a quality H-costandardized coagreement because $h_{(1)(2)} \otimes h_{(2)(2)} \otimes (\gamma h_{(1)(1)})h_{(1)(3)}(\gamma h_{(2)(1)})h_{(2)(3)} = h_{(2)(1)} \otimes h_{(2)(2)} \otimes (\gamma h_{(1)})h_{(3)}$ on canceling $h_{(1)(3)}\gamma h_{(2)(1)}$ since they are in the correct order after linear renumbering. Also $\varepsilon(h_{(2)})(\gamma h_{(1)})h_{(2)} = \varepsilon(h)$. For a cost side of the statement, that Ad_P is a cost costandardized comes out now as $h_{(1)}(\gamma h_{(3)}) \otimes h_{(2)(1)}\gamma h_{(2)(3)} \otimes h_{(2)(2)} = h_{(1)(1)}(\gamma h_{(3)})_{(1)} \otimes (\gamma h_{(3)})_{(1)} \otimes h_{(1)(2)}(\gamma h_{(3)})_{(2)} \otimes h_{(2)}$ and $h_{(1)}\gamma h_{(3)}\varepsilon(h_{(2)}) = h_{(1)}\gamma h_{(2)} = \varepsilon(h)$. Compare with Example 2.30 □

Exercise 2.38. Consider a coargumentation of a finite dimensional enterprise H on H^*. Show that:
(i) if it is a quality coregular coargumentation,
$C^*_Q(\phi)(h) = \sum h_{(1)}\langle h_{(2)}, \phi\rangle$,
it makes H^* into a quality H-costandardized coagreement.
(ii) if it is a quality coadjoint coargumentation,
$Ad^*_Q(\phi)(h) = \sum h_{(1)}\gamma h_{(3)}\langle h_{(2)}, \phi\rangle$,
it makes H^* into a quality H-costandardized agreement.

Compare to Exercise 2.31.

Proposition 2.39. (Cross coexpansion of e.p.r.s) *Let H be a biagreement or an enterprise.*

(i) *For a quality H-costandardized coagreement, C_Q, there is a* **quality cross coexpansion** *of e.p.r.s through coagreement $H \bowtie C_Q$ built on $H \otimes A_Q$ with the coagreement structure*

$$\Delta(h \otimes c_Q) = \sum h_{(1)} \otimes c_{(1)Q}^{(\bar{1})} \otimes h_{(2)}c_{(1)}^{(\bar{2})} \otimes c_{(2)}, \qquad \varepsilon(c \otimes h) = \varepsilon(c)\varepsilon(h)$$

for $h \in H$, $c \in C_P$.

(ii) *For a cost H-costandardized coagreement, C_P, there is a* **cost cross coexpansion** *of e.p.r.s trough coagreement, $C_P \bowtie H$, built on $C_P \otimes H$ with the coagreement structure*

$$\Delta(c \otimes h) = \sum c_{(1)} \otimes c_{(2)}^{(\bar{1})}h_{(1)} \otimes c_{(2)}^{(\bar{2})} \otimes h_{(2)}, \qquad \varepsilon(c \otimes h) = \varepsilon(c)\varepsilon(h)$$

for $h \in H$, $c \in C_P$.

Hint of proof: Apply dual version of the proof of Proposition 2.34.

In EPRT when general biagreements and enterprises are studied, one almost always needs both the cost and quality versions of e.p.r.s standards and costandards. The typical situation is the following, with the similar proposition for costandards.

Proposition 2.40. (E.p.r.s correspondence) *If V is a cost standardized economic vector space, then V^* is a quality standardized economic vector space. The e.p.r.s correspondence is given by,*

$$(f \overset{a}{<} h)(v) = f(h \overset{a}{>} v) \qquad \forall v \in V,\ f \in V^*.$$

If A is a finite dimensional cost standardized agreement, the A^* is a quality standardized coagreement. If C is a cost standardized coagreement, then C^* is a quality standardized agreement. Similar is valid for cost-quality interchanged and for standards replaced by costandards.

Proof: The proof is based on definitions. For example, if C is a cost standardized coagreement, then acting on elements $\phi, \psi \in C^*$, one gets

$$\begin{aligned}((\phi\psi) \overset{a}{<} h)(c) = (\phi\psi)(h \overset{a}{>} c) &= \phi((h \overset{a}{>} c)_{(1)})\psi((h \overset{a}{>} c)_{(2)}) \\ &= \phi(h_{(1)} \overset{a}{>} c_{(1)} \otimes h_{(2)} \overset{a}{>} c_{(2)}) \\ &= (\phi \overset{a}{<} h_{(1)})(c_{(1)})(\psi \overset{a}{<} h_{(2)})(c_{(2)}) \\ &= ((\phi \overset{a}{<} h_{(1)})(\psi \overset{a}{<} c_{(2)}))(c),\end{aligned}$$

and

$$(\varepsilon \overset{a}{<} h)(c) = \varepsilon(h \overset{a}{>} c) = \varepsilon(h)\varepsilon(c),$$

so that C^* is a quality standardized agreement. □

2.3 E.p.r.s Gains and Welfare Structures

Within the context of EPRT, and particularly concerning an economic impacts and/or influance of an enterprise, two further notions are of fundamental importance: (i) an e.p.r.s gain based on the instituion, and (ii) a welfare of an e.p.r.s structure. Both are involved from and developed on economic rules among partners, resulting from their economic behavior and mutual relations concerning economic goals. At the same time, these concepts establish a sophisticated link between methodologies of traditional economic analyses and tools of EPRT. Namely, versions of traditional concepts can be generalized to the setting of agreements with externalities and equilibria that permit elementary considerations of e.p.r.s issues. In this Section only the simple forms of e.p.r.s gains and welfare structure are discussed, leaving the more complex ones for later. From formal point of view, we are applying further notions of integral and $*$-structures on e.p.r.s issues.

2.3.1 E.p.r.s Gains

Price (cost) and quality e.p.r.s gains on an enterprise are defined as follows.

Definition 2.41 (Price gain). *A price (cost) e.p.r.s gain on an enterprise H is a (not identically zero) liner map $\int\!\!\!\!\!p : H \to \mathbf{h}$ such that*

$$(id \otimes \int\!\!\!\!\!p\,) \circ \Delta = \eta \circ \int\!\!\!\!\!p\; .$$

A price (cost) gain in an enterprise H is a nonzero element $\Lambda_p \in H$ such that

$$h\Lambda_p = \varepsilon(h)\Lambda_p \qquad \forall h \in H.$$

E.p.r.s gains are price normalized if $\int\!\!\!\!\!p\; 1 = 1$ or $\varepsilon(\Lambda_p) = 1$, respectively.

Similarly for quality gains,

Definition 2.42 (Quality gain). *A quality e.p.r.s gain on an enterprise H is a (not identically zero) liner map $\int\!\!\!\!\!q : H \to \mathbf{h}$ such that*

$$\Delta \circ (\int\!\!\!\!\!q \otimes id) = \int\!\!\!\!\!q \circ \eta.$$

A quality gain in an enterprise H is a nonzero element $\Lambda_q \in H$ such that

$$\Lambda_q h = \Lambda_q \varepsilon(h) \qquad \forall h \in H.$$

E.p.r.s gains are quality normalized if $\int\!\!\!\!\!q\,1 = 1$ or $\varepsilon(\Lambda_q) = 1$, respectively.

An economic intuition of notions of price and quality e.p.r.s gains are clear in terms of the adjoint of the cost and quality argumentations of an enterprise on itself through a process of cost and quality (re)construction and/or economic (re)structuring, as was described in the Examples 2.29 and 2.37. So, recall from the Example 2.29 that the cost argumentation has an adjoint one, which is a quality argumentation of H on H^* given by $P_h^*(\phi)(g) = \phi(hg)$. Thus, the price-invariance of the gain on H^* is equivalent to the more familiar relations.

$$\int\!\!\!\!\!p\; P_h^*(\phi) = \sum \langle h, \phi_{(1)} \rangle \int\!\!\!\!\!p\; \phi_{(2)} = \varepsilon(h) \int\!\!\!\!\!p\; \phi. \qquad \forall h, \phi. \tag{2.20}$$

Similar is valid for a quality e.p.r.s gain, where we count on the property that the quality argumentation has an adjoint one, which is a cost (price) argumentation of H on H^* given by $Q_h^*(\phi)(g) = \phi(gh)$. Namely, every finite dimensional enterprise carries an e.p.r.s gain, not necessarily normalizable, which is unique up to scale. This applies to both price and quality gains. In the particular case an enterprise may have price and quality gains which coincide. Such an enterprise is called unistandardized. Obviously those are quite strong conditions imposed on structure of e.p.r.s in an e.p.r.s institution.

The notion of an e.p.r.s gain Λ_p in an enterprise H has some agreeable advantages but is suitable only in the finite-dimensional case. In such circumstances an e.p.r.s gain is clearly just a price gain on H^*. A normalized e.p.r.s gain in a general enterprise, when it exists, is unique and unistandardized.

Example 2.43 (Normalized gains). Normalizes price gain on an enterprise $H = \mathbf{h}(G)$ is provided by $\oint \phi =| G |^{-1} \sum_{u \in G} \phi(u)$. A normalized price gain in an enterprise $\mathbf{h}G$ is provided by $\Lambda_p =| G |^{-1} \sum_{u \in G} u$. In normalization procedures, it is assumed that $|G|$ is invertible. These examples are evidently unistandardized.

Hint of proof: The proof is based on duality relation between enterprises, and pairing principle already discussed in the Example 2.10 above.

Proposition 2.44. *Let H be a finite-dimensional enterprise. If gain $\oint \phi = TrL_\phi \circ \gamma^2$ is not zero for all $\phi \in H^*$, then it defines a price-invariant e.p.r.s gain on H^*.*

Proof: Note that $L_{L_h^* \phi} = L_{h(1)}^* \circ L_\phi \circ L_{\gamma^{-1} h(2)}^*$ for an $h \in H$ and $\phi \in H^*$. To see this, we evaluate on elements $\psi \in H^*, g \in H$ and use the duality pairing and property of γ^{-1} from the section 2.1.1. Thus,

$$\begin{aligned}
&\langle L_{L_{h(1)}^*} \circ L_\phi \circ L_{\gamma^{-1} h(2)}^* \psi, g \rangle = \\
&\langle \phi L_{\gamma^{-1} h(2)}^* \psi, h_{(1)} g \rangle = \langle \phi, h_{(1)} g_{(1)} \rangle \langle L_{\gamma^{-1} h(3)}^* \psi, h_{(2)} g_{(2)} \rangle = \\
&\langle \phi, h_{(1)} g_{(1)} \rangle \langle \psi, (\gamma^{-1} h_{(3)}) h_{(2)} g_{(2)} \rangle = \langle \phi, h g_{(1)} \rangle \langle \psi, g_{(2)} \rangle = \\
&\langle L_h^* \phi, g_{(1)} \rangle \langle \psi, g_{(2)} \rangle = \langle L_{L_h^* \phi} \psi, g \rangle.
\end{aligned}$$

Then cyclicity of the trace and the fact that L^* is a quality argumentation give $TrL_{L_{h(1)}^*} \circ L_\phi \circ L_{\gamma^{-1} h(2)}^* \circ \gamma^2 = TrL_{L_{h(1)}^*} \circ L_\phi \circ \gamma^2 \circ L_{\gamma h_{(2)}}^* = TrL_{\gamma h_{(1)}}^* \circ L_{h_{(1)}}^* \circ L_\phi \circ \gamma^2 = TrL_{h_{(1)} \gamma h_{(2)}}^* \circ L_\phi \circ \gamma^2 = \varepsilon(h) TrL_\phi \circ \gamma^2$, as required in (2.20).
□

2.3.2 Welfare Structure

Having in mind the well-known fundamental welfare theorems in economics, a particular application of argumentations to the theory of enterprises is to develop a notion of a fundamental welfare activity of an enterprise. Its concrete realization is called a *welfare argumentation.* The theorem can be used as an indication of an appropriate enterprise (re)construction and/or restructuring in EPRT. From point of view of economics, it may be noteworthy that welfare argumentation is assumed to be induced by argumentation/coargumentation of an enterprise on itself, and not by some direct external regulation or intervention, in the sense of traditional theories of social welfare, planning mechanisms, or legislative regulations. Nevertheless, an enterprise obtained by such construction is very concrete, being realized over welfare activities on some economic vector space, and thus is very suitable for applications in economics. The theorem below shows that any enterprise considered as an e.p.r.s institution can be realized concretely in the suggested way by argumentation/coargumentation on its e.p.r.s structure through (re)construction procedures and/or economic restructuring. Even more, it claims that both the enterprise and its dual can be realized as *subagreements* of activities on the same economic vector space. Clearly, it is also suitable for formulation of an economic setting of e.p.r.s vector space, and an economic analysis of enterprises realized as a collection of bounded economic activities and/or e.p.r.s gains of enterprise on natural recourses. In addition, possibility of studying economic externalities directly through the concepts of agreements and coagreements will allow more general formulation and economic analysis of e.p.r.s institutions over unbounded economic activities, developed more precisely in the following chapters.

Theorem 2.45. (Fundamental welfare of simple enterprise)
Let H be a finite dimensional enterprise. Implement the price (cost) regular argumentation to $H \subseteq Lin(H)$ as described in Example 2.29, $h \mapsto h \overset{a}{>} = R_P = L_h$. In the agreement $Lin(H) \otimes Lin(H)$ there is an invertible element W of $H \otimes H \otimes H$ such that,

$$(id\otimes id\otimes \Delta)(W)\circ(\Delta\otimes id\otimes id)(W) \neq (1\otimes W)\circ(id\otimes \Delta\otimes id)(W)\circ(W\otimes 1)$$
$$\Delta h = W(h\otimes 1)W^{-1} \quad \gamma h = (\varepsilon\otimes id)\circ W^{-1}(h\otimes (\,)).$$

Now implement the quality coregular argumentation to $H^* \subseteq Lin(H)$ as described in Example 2.36, $\phi \mapsto \phi \overset{a}{>} = R^*_\phi$. Then within the agreement $Lin(H) \otimes Lin(H)$ we also have, where defined,

$$\Delta\phi = W^{-1}(1\otimes\phi)W, \qquad \gamma\phi = (id\otimes\phi)\circ W^{-1}((\,)\otimes 1).$$

The subagreements $H \subseteq Lin(H)$ and $H^* \subseteq Lin(H)$ together generate all of $Lin(H)$.

Proof: Note that conditions in the theorem determine explicitly, W, W^{-1} as linear maps $H \otimes H \to H \otimes H$. These linear maps can be identified with elements of $Lin(H) \otimes Lin(H)$ in the usual way by

$$W(g\otimes h) = g_{(1)}\otimes g_{(2)}h, \qquad W^{-1}(g\otimes h) = g_{(2)}\otimes(\gamma g_{(2)})h. \tag{2.21}$$

Then we verify the identity,

$$\begin{aligned}
&(W(h\otimes 1)W^{-1})(g\otimes f) = \\
&W(h\otimes 1) \overset{a}{>} (g_{(1)}\otimes(\gamma g_{(2)})f) = W(hg_{(1)}\otimes(\gamma g_{(2)})f) = \\
&h_{(1)}g_{(1)(1)}\otimes h_{(1)}g_{(1)(2)}(\gamma g_{(2)})f = h_{(1)}g\otimes h_{(2)}f = \\
&(\Delta h) \overset{a}{>} (g\otimes f).
\end{aligned}$$

Similarly we have,

$$\begin{aligned}
&(W^{-1}(1\otimes\phi)W)(g\otimes f) = W^{-1}(1\otimes\phi) \overset{a}{>} (g_{(1)}\otimes g_{(2)}h) \\
&= W^{-1}(g_{(1)}\otimes g_{(2)(1)}h_{(1)})\langle\phi, g_{(2)(2)}h_{(2)}\rangle \\
&= g_{(1)(1)} \otimes (\gamma g_{(1)(2)})g_{(2)(1)}h_{(1)}\langle\phi, g_{(2)(2)}h_{(2)}\rangle = g_{(1)} \otimes h_{(1)}\langle\phi, g_{(2)}h_{(2)}\rangle \\
&= \phi_{(1)} \overset{a}{>} g \otimes \phi_{(2)} \overset{a}{>} h.
\end{aligned}$$

Explicitly, we have $\phi \overset{a}{>} g = g_{(1)}\langle\phi, g_{(2)}\rangle$. Similar procedures are applied to mutual understanding maps γ. To show that equations for a welfare map, W, itself, are satisfied, we evaluate on $H \otimes H \otimes H$,

$$\begin{aligned}
&(1\otimes W) \circ (id\otimes\Delta\otimes id)(W) \circ (W\otimes 1)(g \otimes h \otimes f) \\
&= (1\otimes W) \circ (id\otimes\Delta\otimes id)(W)(g\otimes h_{(1)}\otimes h_{(2)}f) \\
&= W_{12}(g_{(1)} \otimes h_{(2)} \otimes g_{(2)}h_{(2)}f) = (g_{(1)(1)} \otimes g_{(1)(2)}h_{(2)}) \otimes g_{(2)}h_{(2)}f \\
&= g_{(1)} \otimes g_{(2)(1)} \otimes g_{(2)}h_{(2)}f = W_{23}(g_{(1)} \otimes g_{(2)}h \otimes f) \\
&= W_{23}W_{12}(g \otimes h \otimes f) \\
&= (W \otimes 1) \circ (1 \otimes W)(g \otimes h \otimes f).
\end{aligned}$$

Note that here $W_{12} = 1\otimes W$, $W_{23} = (id\otimes id\otimes \Delta)(W)$, $W_{13} = W \otimes 1$. For the last part, we show that every economic activity $H \to H$ arises by argumentations $\overset{a}{>}$ of H and H^* on H, at least when H is finite dimensional. In this convenient case, every linear economic activity can be viewed as an element of $H \otimes H^*$ acting on H in the usual way by an economic evaluation, namely $(h \otimes \phi)(g) = h\langle\phi, g\rangle$. We have to represent this by elements of enterprises H, H^* which argumentations or economic actions are via $\overset{a}{>}$. Indeed, as economic actions in $Lin(H)$ we find $h \otimes \phi = h(\gamma^{-1}e_{a(1)}) \overset{a}{>} (\langle\phi, e_{a(2)}\rangle f^a \overset{a}{>} (\ ))$, where $\{e_a\}$ is a basis of H and $\{f^a\}$ is a dual basis. Thus, $h(\gamma^{-1}g_{(2)(1)}) \overset{a}{>} (\langle\phi, e_{a(2)}\rangle \otimes f^a \overset{a}{>} g) = h(\gamma^{-1}e_{a(1)})g_{(1)}\langle\phi, e_{a(2)}\rangle\langle f^a e_{a(2)}\rangle = h(\gamma^{-1}g_{(2)(1)})g_{(1)}\langle\phi, g_{(2)(2)}\rangle = \langle\phi, g\rangle$, as required. The coassociativity property from axiom *A4* and the properties of mutual understanding map γ^{-1} were used to obtain above equalities. □

Motivated by application of functional analysis on e.p.r.s issues, the notion of an agreement with externalities is introduced whenever our background field of e.p.r.s claims **h** contains economic externalities. Note that from formal point of view this simply means that a field of e.p.r.s claims is equipped with some form of 'conjugation'. For simplicity we may consider $\mathbf{h} = \mathcal{C}$. In this context a notion of a $*$-algebra is familiar one, thus for our applications it is not difficult to develop a notion of an agreement with externalities as a well defined economic concept. It means that we are given an agreement or enterprise H equipped with an economic mapping that concerns externalities, described by an antilinear map $(\ )^* : H \to H$ obeying $*^2 = id$ and $(hg)^* = g^*h^*$ for all $h, g \in H$.

Definition 2.46 (Simple enterprise with externalities). *A simple enterprise with externalities is an enterprise* H *such that the agreement on externalities is part of entrepreneurial structure in the following way,*

$$\Delta h^* = (\Delta h)^{*\otimes *}, \qquad \varepsilon(h^*) = \overline{\varepsilon(h)}, \qquad (\gamma \circ *)^2 = id.$$

If H_1, H_2 *are two enterprises with externalities, they are dually paired if they are dually paired as enterprises and in addition*

$$\langle h_2^*, h_1 \rangle = \overline{\langle h_2, (\gamma h_{(1)}) \rangle}$$

for all $h_1 \in H_1,$ *and* $h_2 \in H_2$.

It is noteworthy that within EPRT, a choice of such an e.p.r.s externality structure specifies forms of a simple enterprise. These simple forms, determined as enterprises over field of e.p.r.s claims with externalities, can have a list of legislative proposals or receipts as a description of economic activities. There are many applications of welfare externality structures, particularly in the context of e.p.r.s regulative mechanisms and an economic theory of contracts. At the same time, the above suggests a restrictive type of e.p.r.s institutions, which e.p.r.s activities are to be based on and/or constrained within a legislation or some planning framework. In that sense, it also shows that there is no complete regulation or legislation covering of an enterprise, even a simple one. In other words, scope of domain of any regulation or legislative is just a part of an economic domain of an enterprise considered as an e.p.r.s institution.

Proposition 2.47. *In the setting of FWE Theorem 2.45 above suppose that* H *is a finite-dimensional enterprise that allows externalities. Then* H^* *is also an enterprise with externalities and* $Lin(H)$, *generated by* $H \subseteq Lin(H)$ *and* $H^* \subseteq Lin(H)$, *becomes an e.p.r.s agreement with externalities. With respect to this welfare externality structure* $*$, *the fundamental welfare has the property* $W^{*\otimes *} = W^{-1}$, *(it is unitary). If* $\fint$ *is a quality e.p.r.s gain on* H, *it can be chosen so that it defines an economic valuation, given by a sesquilinear form* $(g, h) = \fint g^* h = \overline{(h, g)}$, *which is compatible with the welfare externality structure on* $Lin(H)$ *induced by* H, H^* *in the sense,*

$$\fint (h \overset{a}{>} g)^* f = \fint g^* (h^* \overset{a}{>} f), \qquad \fint (\phi \overset{a}{>} g)^* f = \fint g^* (\phi^* \overset{a}{>} f),$$

for $g, h, f \in H,\ \phi \in H^*$.

Proof: Since every element of an agreement with externalities, $Lin(H)$, factorizes into the argumentations of H and H^*, these subagreements necessarily define an economic activity on $Lin(H)$ by $(h \overset{a}{>})^* = h^* \overset{a}{>}$ and $(\phi \overset{a}{>})^* = \phi^* \overset{a}{>}$, such that they become conjugate subagreements. For the first part of the proposition, we begin by expressing W in terms of such subagreements from H, H^*. Indeed, $W(g \otimes f) = g_{(1)} \otimes g_{(2)} f = g_{(1)} \langle f^a, g_{(2)} \rangle \otimes e_a f = f^a \overset{a}{>} g \otimes e_a \overset{a}{>} f$, where $\{e_a\}$ is a basis of H and $\{f^a\}$ is a dual basis. So $W = f^a \overset{a}{>} \otimes e_a \overset{a}{>}$ and, hence by definition $W^{*\otimes *} = f^{a*} \overset{a}{>} \otimes e_a^* \overset{a}{>} = f'^a \overset{a}{>} \otimes (\gamma e'_a) \overset{a}{>}$, where $e'_a = \gamma^{-1} e_a^*, f'^a = f^{a*}$ form a new basis and dual basis. Dropping the $\prime$, we have $W^{*\otimes *}(g \otimes f) = f^a \overset{a}{>} g \otimes (\gamma e_a) \overset{a}{>} f = g_{(1)} \langle f^a, g_{(2)} \rangle \otimes (\gamma e_a) f = g_{(1)} \otimes (\gamma g_{(2)}) f = W^{-1}(g \otimes f)$. For the second part of the statement, we show that this conjugate, $*$, structure on $Lin(H)$ really is an adjoint economic activity with respect to an economic valuation, $(\ ,\ )$, as stated in the proposition. Note that properties of mutual understanding map, γ allow to arrange $(\gamma \fint)^* = \fint$ without loss of generality. Namely, the cost form of the gain is also an e.p.r.s gain, so this equality holds up to a scale. In view of $(* \circ \gamma)^2 = id$, it is a phase, and we can then absorb this phase in a rescaling of a quality e.p.r.s gain, $\fint$. Thus, an economic valuation $(\ ,\ )$ is Hermitian in the form stated in the proposition. To show this explicitly, we may use the implementations $h \overset{a}{>}$, which is easier part of the proof, since

$$(h \overset{a}{>} g, f) = \fint (h \overset{a}{>} g)^* f = \fint (hg)^* f = \fint g^* h^* f = \fint g^* (h^* \overset{a}{>} f) = (g, (h \overset{a}{>})^* f)$$

is automatic. It is trickier to show validity of this nice property of economic valuation for the implementations $\phi \overset{a}{>}$. Here we have,

$$\begin{aligned}
(\phi \overset{a}{>} g, g) &= \fint (\phi \overset{a}{>} g)^* h = \fint (g^*_{(1)})^* \overline{\langle \phi, g_{(2)} \rangle} h \\
&= \fint g^*_{(1)} \overline{\langle \phi, (g^*_{(2)})^* \rangle} h = \fint g^*_{(1)} \langle \gamma^{-1}(\phi^*), g^*_{(2)} \rangle h \\
&= \fint g^*_{(1)} h_{(1)} \langle \gamma^{-1} \phi^*_{(3)}, g^*_{(2)} \rangle \langle (\gamma^{-1} \phi^*_{(2)}) \phi^*_{(1)}, h_{(2)} \rangle \\
&= \fint g^*_{(1)} h_{(1)} \langle (\gamma^{-1} \phi^*_{(2)})_{(1)}, g^*_{(2)} \rangle \langle (\gamma^{-1} \phi^*_{(2)})_{(2)}, h_{(2)} \rangle \langle \phi^*_{(1)}, h_{(3)} \rangle \\
&= \fint g^*_{(1)} h_{(1)} \langle \gamma^{-1} \phi^*_{(2)}, g^*_{(2)} h_{(2)} \rangle \langle \phi^*_{(1)}, h_{(3)} \rangle \\
&= \fint (g^* h_{(1)})_{(1)} \langle \gamma^{-1} \phi^*_{(2)}, (g^*_{(2)} h_{(1)})_{(2)} \rangle \langle \phi^*_{(1)}, h_{(2)} \rangle \\
&= \fint g^* h_{(1)} \langle \phi^*, h_{(2)} \rangle = \fint g^* (\phi^* \overset{a}{>} h) = (g, (\phi \overset{a}{>})^* h).
\end{aligned}$$

Here the second equality is from the definition of $\phi^* \overset{a}{>} g = g_{(1)} \langle \phi, g_{(2)} \rangle$. The third equality is from the definition of an enterprise with externalities, with regard to $\Delta \circ *$. The fourth equality is from the relationship between the conjugate structures in enterprises, H, H^*, and the axiom on mutual understanding map $(\gamma \circ *)^2 = id$. The fifth introduces some factors that collapse to $\varepsilon(h_{(2)})$ with the fact that γ^{-1} is a skew mutual understanding map for H, i.e. it is a mutual understanding map for H^{op} as described previously. Next equality is valid due to facts that the expansion of e.p.r.s in H^* can be written in terms of the coexpansion of e.p.r.s for coagency in H, and uses property of coassociativity, and property of inverse mutual understanding map γ^{-1} of being an anticoagreemental map. For seventh equality the coexpansion of e.p.r.s in H^* is written in terms of H to combine some factors, while the eighth equality uses the property of Δ as an agreeable homotransaction. Finally, the ninth equality, is obtained using the properties of $\mathfrak{g}$ as a quality e.p.r.s gain, leading to the required result. □

In an economic functional-analytic context, one can consider an enterprise, H to be an e.p.r.s equilibrium agreement, and instead of $Lin(H)$ one takes the bounded economic activities, $B(\mathcal{H}_\phi)$, on economic property right space (EPRS), $\mathcal{H}_\phi$, determined by an economic state or economic weight ϕ. For example, we may recall the model of simple pure exclusive dominant economy on natural resources with bounded economic activities. A given state of pure exclusive dominant economy provides elements for construction of a central element of the economic system to play a role of an economic equilibrium and a positive self adjoint enterprise. This construction of an economic equilibrium, is an elementary but useful way to pass from an welfare agreement which is not necessarily complete, to an equilibrium agreement. The necessary data are a welfare agreement A and the state $\phi : A \to \mathbf{h}$ which is nonnegative, $\phi(a^*a) \geq 0$. One then forms an EPRS by defining, a not necessarily definite, economic valuation on A by $\langle a_1, a_2 \rangle = \phi(a_2^* a), a \in A$. The EPRS $\mathcal{H}_\phi$ is then the completion of the quotient of agreement A by the kernel of this form. Under the favorable circumstances, A will provide cost and quality argumentations on $\mathcal{H}_\phi$ by expansions of e.p.r.s. Obviously this is the case that underlies foundations of a traditional concept of an economy, defined in a pure private economic environment, from formal as well as from historical perspective of mathematical economics where generalized fixed point theorems were applied in economics. Without going into details here, recall that with ϕ defined suitably, via the economic gain on an enterprise H, the above welfare structure on $Lin(H)$ becomes just the appropriate adjoint economic activity on $B(\mathcal{H}_\phi)$, so that economic welfare ordering satisfies pure private rationality as appropriate welfare argumentation. The structure of Theorem 2.45 and Proposition 2.47 is then a characterization of what is in EPRT considered an EPRS of a natural economic resource and/or a simple enterprise. As was already discussed, they are assumed to be equipped with a mutual understanding map that satisfies a condition that $\gamma^2 = id$, (recall Section 2.2.1). From above it is obvious that such a condition is not needed when an enterprise is formulated along the economic concepts of activities discussed above. What is needed is a lot of care concerning the formulation of the coagency. Namely, coagency need not always exists as a finite map, but its role can also be carried out to some extent by an e.p.r.s gain.

Another, different, way to search for an appropriate configuration of an e.p.r.s environment is by tools that are more directly dealing with consequences of e.p.r.s externalities. Formally, it is based on C^*- algebra. This approach seems to be more appropriate for e.p.r.s issues in economics although the problem in application is that there is no single good notion of aggregation of e.p.r.s institutions formalized over these externality types of agreements. A simplest way to resolve the problem is to fix a finitely generated dense welfare externality substructure and demand that only those e.p.r.s institutions that satisfy this condition could be considered as enterprises. This is an approach which uses the context of matrix e.p.r.s rules and will be discussed later along with some more general cases of e.p.r.s institutions with externalities in the sequential to this volume.

3

Opening Structures

This chapter explores impacts of missing an axiom or a condition of an agreeable e.p.r.s structure. One may have in mind an intention to relax some of the axioms that ensure biagreemental or an entrepreneurial structure of an enterprise, and then ask for some other elements that are to compensate for them. Thus, some conditions are to be imposed that shape circulation of e.p.r.s among agents, and their arrangements of e.p.r.s, in the way that consistency of an e.p.r.s institution is ensured and e.p.r.s relations are under control. In particular, the conditions concerning coexpansion of e.p.r.s of copartner are relaxed so that an agreeable structure holds only up to some elements. The most important consequences have been already noted on simple e.p.r.s institutions, as discussed in Chapter 2 within 2.2.1, or enterprises on natural resources. This class of simple enterprises is modified to a class of enterprises that could be considered as simple only up to conjugation by an opening structure carrying some new e.p.r.s relation among partners. Namely, copartners within the class could accept simplified e.p.r.s rationality, but only up to conjugation by an opening structure obeying some new e.p.r.s conditions. A traditionally trained economist may have in mind market opening, although concept of an e.p.r.s opening includes innovation, initiation, R&D types of opening of economic institutions and similar. In the case of market opening, or simple market, one usually thinks of an economic device of measuring efficiency, and as a mechanism for welfare restructuring and redistribution. Note that a concept of an e.p.r.s opening also includes arbitrations and other forms of mediating devices between partners. From point of view of agreeable structure of such opening enterprises, they are truly different from the enterprises based on the established e.p.r.s rules or the simple *R&D* enterprises, as defined and described in the previous Chapter 2. Nevertheless, the e.p.r.s structural properties of these open institutions are so close to entrepreneurial conditions that all the familiar results for the enterprises based on e.p.r.s rules and simple e.p.r.s growth enterprises tend to have analogies here also. The enterprises which copartners' e.p.r.s arrangements are shaped in this way are called open enterprises. The fact that properties of these institutions are so close to those based on simple e.p.r.s rules and simple growing enterprises, also allow us to consider them as institutions based on e.p.r.s rules or e.p.r.s enterprises. The examples given in this Chapter are indeed modifications of familiar simple enterprises and simple growing ones, but one should not think that these forms are the only examples. One may note that there are plenty of open enterprises that are not based on some fixed e.p.r.s rule or simple growing process at all.

In this Chapter basic definitions and properties behind the class of open enterprises are provided. In developing appropriate technic within mathematical economics on these issues, we continue within the abstract setting of general algebraic formalization of the economic phenomena. Here, we again distinguish e.p.r.s structures for simple open enterprises from those that incorporate more complex e.p.r.s structures of their openings.

3.1 Simple Opening

3.1.1 Definition and Main Properties

Recall from Section 2.2.1 in Chapter 2, when we considered properties of enterprises formed as simple ones, i.e., as enterprises on natural resources, that coexpansion of e.p.r.s has the property of being unaffected by any transposition map. Precisely, one has $\tau \circ \Delta = \Delta$, where τ is transposition map. This can be weakened requiring an enterprise to carry modified form of coexpansion of e.p.r.s, becoming only cocommutative up to conjugation by an element of $\mathcal{R} \in H \otimes H$, which obeys some further properties. This element $\mathcal{R}$ is constituted as a quasitriangular e.p.r.s structure, and in the EPRT interpretation it carries a collection of e.p.r.s due to opening of a biagreement or simple enterprise H. Thus,

Definition 3.1 (Simple opening). *An open biagreement or a simple open enterprise is a pair $(H, \mathcal{R})$, where H is a biagreement or a simple enterprise and $\mathcal{R} \in H \otimes H$, is an e.p.r.s transaction, that has its inverse, $\mathcal{R}^{-1}$, and obeys the following axioms of an opening,*

$$(\Delta \otimes id)\mathcal{R} = \mathcal{R}_{13}\mathcal{R}_{23}, \quad (id \otimes \Delta)\mathcal{R} = \mathcal{R}_{13}\mathcal{R}_{12} \tag{3.1}$$

$$\tau \circ \Delta h = \mathcal{R}(\Delta h)\mathcal{R}^{-1}, \ \forall h \in H. \tag{3.2}$$

Writing $\mathcal{R} = \sum \mathcal{R}^{(1)}\mathcal{R}^{(2)}$, the notation used is

$$\mathcal{R}_{ij} = \sum 1 \otimes \cdots \otimes \mathcal{R}^{(1)} \otimes \cdots \otimes \mathcal{R}^{(2)} \otimes \cdots \otimes 1,$$

the element of $H \otimes H \otimes \cdots \otimes H$ which is $\mathcal{R}$ in the ith and j^{th} factors. Here, τ denotes the transposition map, and $\mathcal{R}$ is called simple opening.

Let us mention here that $\mathcal{R}_{ij}$ can be roughly understood as benefits resulting from using elements out of the enterprise H, as i^{th} and j^{th} factors, instead of those determined by a complete or full entrepreneurial agreement H. Then, from definition we see that axiom (3.2), means that although an open enterprise does not usually ensure a coexpansion of e.p.r.s for copartner as has been the case for corresponding full enterprise, this complication is being controlled by benefits and costs of openings. In other words, an extension of e.p.r.s of agents and coagents by an e.p.r.s arrangement as a simple open enterprise is controlled by benefits and costs of such an arrangement. That this definition is a good description of simple opening relations of agents will be obvious from various properties of a simple open enterprise studied in this Chapter on an abstract level. In addition, in the following Chapters 4 and 5 an alternative meaning of such type of enterprises or e.p.r.s institutions will be provided, as well as more complex forms.

It is noteworthy that many of the economic statements that have been shown and proven for simple complete enterprises can also be valid for simple open enterprises. To understand axioms 3.1, let us consider those over a simple example that also links us with traditional understanding of a market in economics. Recall discussion on simple e.p.r.s structures in 2.2.1 and particularly Proposition 2.12 in Chapter 2. Let there be given a finite-dimensional biagreement H based on pure private economic rationality of agents and let $\mathcal{R}$ be an invertible element of $H \otimes H$. Then benefits of market opening $\mathcal{R}$ can be viewed as a linear map $\mathcal{R}_1 : H^* \to H$ in the sense that it links activity $\phi \in H^*$ to $(id \otimes \phi)(\mathcal{R})$. It has economic interpretation of shaping market by a suggested price structure, ϕ, that is to ensure benefits of $(id \otimes \phi)(\mathcal{R})$. Then we can show that axioms (3.2) hold, iff this proposed price structure (linear map) is accepted by all participants of the market. Copartners, competitors and enterprises with an e.p.r.s-opposed structure are also elements of the market thus it is supposed to be accepted by them too. One may think of this price mapping as an economic transaction containing coagreeable and antiagreeable mapping, i.e., a biagreement map $H^{*op} \otimes H$. Namely, we can see, by the pairing relations in Proposition 2.12, which explains the explicit formulae that determine the simple entrepreneurial e.p.r.s structure on H^* from that on H, for this particular case, that $\mathcal{R}_1(\psi, \phi) = \mathcal{R}^{(1)}\langle \psi \otimes \psi, \Delta\mathcal{R}^{(2)}\rangle$, while $\mathcal{R}_1(\psi)\mathcal{R}_1(\phi) = \mathcal{R}'^{(1)}\mathcal{R}^{(1)}\langle \psi \otimes \psi, \mathcal{R}^{(2)} \otimes \mathcal{R}'^{(2)}\rangle$. Note that here $\mathcal{R}'$ denotes an e.p.r.s structure of opening benefits as it appears to participants in second appearance on the market (a second copy of $\mathcal{R}$). The equality of these expressions for all price structures ϕ, ψ is just the second of axioms given in (3.1), so that this corresponds to $\mathcal{R}_1$, an e.p.r.s structure of prices that would be accepted by opposed e.p.r.s structured market enterprise, (an antiagreeable map). Also, $\Delta(\mathcal{R}_1(\psi)) = \Delta(id \otimes \phi)\mathcal{R} = \Delta\mathcal{R}^{(1)}\langle \phi, \mathcal{R}^{(2)}\rangle$, while $(\mathcal{R}_1 \otimes \mathcal{R}_1)(\Delta\phi) = \mathcal{R}^{(1)} \otimes \mathcal{R}'^{(1)}\langle \phi, \mathcal{R}^{(2)}\mathcal{R}'^{(2)}\rangle$ by the definition of the pairing. Hence their equality for all price structure ϕ is just the first of relations in axiom (3.1), i.e., structure that is accepted by copartners. Similar can be shown for $\mathcal{R}_2$, as axioms (3.1) hold iff the map $\mathcal{R}_2 : H^* \to H$, linking ϕ to

$(\phi \otimes id)(\mathcal{R})$, is an agreeable and anticoagreeable map, i.e., a biagreeable map $H^{*cop} \to H$.

An economic intuition of market participation in a modern economy is that it provides benefits to all involved, and thus is based on a voluntary economic engagement. This statement has the following form within the context of EPRT.

Lemma 3.2. *If* $(H, \mathcal{R})$ *is an open biagreement, then an e.p.r.s collection formed by (due to) opening is completely distributed among participants. If* H *is an enterprise then its mutual understanding map ensures complete understanding of transfers of e.p.r.s of opening, and hence constitutes the mutual understanding of an open enterprise.*

Proof: To prove the first statement we have to show that if $(H, \mathcal{R})$ is an open biagreement, then $\mathcal{R}$ as an element of $H \otimes H$, that obeys

$$(\varepsilon \otimes id)\mathcal{R} = (id \otimes \varepsilon)\mathcal{R} = 1_H.$$

Let us apply ε to axiom (3.1). We have

$$(\varepsilon \otimes id \otimes id)(\Delta \otimes id)\mathcal{R} = \mathcal{R}_{23} = (\varepsilon \otimes id \otimes id)\mathcal{R}_{13}\mathcal{R}_{23},$$

so that $(\varepsilon \otimes id)\mathcal{R} = 1_H$, because one can identify e.p.r.s inverse of such an opening, i.e., $\mathcal{R}_{23}$ is invertible. Similarly for the other side.
To prove the second statement we have to show that if H is a simple enterprise then one also has that

$$(\gamma \otimes id)\mathcal{R} = \mathcal{R}^{-1}, \quad (id \otimes \gamma)\mathcal{R}^{-1} = \mathcal{R},$$

and hence $(\gamma \otimes \gamma)\mathcal{R} = \mathcal{R}$. To show above equalities we may use the first statement, just proven, and properties of the mutual understanding map γ. Then we have that

$$\mathcal{R}^{(1)}_{(1)}\gamma\mathcal{R}^{(1)}_{(2)} \otimes \mathcal{R}^{(2)} = 1_H$$

and by axiom (3.1) it is equal to $\mathcal{R}(\gamma \otimes id)\mathcal{R}$. One gets similar result for the other side; hence, $(\gamma \otimes id)\mathcal{R} = \mathcal{R}^{-1}$. Similarly for $(id \otimes \gamma)\mathcal{R}^{-1} = \mathcal{R}$ once we know that $(\Delta \otimes id)(\mathcal{R}^{-1}) = (\mathcal{R}_{13}\mathcal{R}_{23})^{-1} = \mathcal{R}_{23}^{-1}\mathcal{R}_{13}^{-1}$, etc., since Δ is an agreeable internal economic transaction. □

In addition, it can be shown that if $\mathcal{R}$ is an e.p.r.s collection due to opening of a biagreement or a simple open enterprise H, then so is $\tau(\mathcal{R}^{-1})$. Also $\tau(\mathcal{R})$ and $\mathcal{R}^{-1}$ are opening e.p.r.s collections for simple enterprise with opposed e.p.r.s structure. Precisely,

Proposition 3.3. *For any given opening* $\mathcal{R}$ *of a simple biagreement or an enterprise* H, $\tau(\mathcal{R}^{-1})$, *is also an opening. In addition,* $\tau(\mathcal{R})$ *and* $\mathcal{R}^{-1}$, *constitute openings on simple opposite structured enterprise,* H^{op}, *or coopposite structured enterprise* H^{cop}, *respectively.*

Proof: To show the first statement we use the results of previous lemma, $(\Delta \otimes id)(\mathcal{R}^{-1}) = \mathcal{R}_{23}^{-1}\mathcal{R}_{13}^{-1}$. Permuting the order in $H \otimes H \otimes H$, we obtain $(id \otimes \Delta)(\mathcal{R}_{21}^{-1}) = \mathcal{R}_{31}^{-1}\mathcal{R}_{21}^{-1}$. Similarly, $(id \otimes \Delta)(\mathcal{R}^{-1}) = \mathcal{R}_{12}^{-1}\mathcal{R}_{13}^{-1}$ provides, after permutation of the order in $H \otimes H \otimes H$, that $(\Delta \otimes id)\mathcal{R}_{21}^{-1} = \mathcal{R}_{31}^{-1}\mathcal{R}_{32}^{-1}$. This confirms that condition (3.1) from definition of an opening is satisfied for $\mathcal{R}_{21}^{-1} = \tau(\mathcal{R}^{-1})$. Using, (3.2) we have that $\mathcal{R}^{-1}(\tau \circ \Delta))\mathcal{R} = \Delta$, and after permutation of order in $H \otimes H$, we obtain $\mathcal{R}_{21}^{-1}(\Delta(\,))\mathcal{R}_{21} = \tau \circ \Delta$, as required. The second statement, for the case of $\tau(\mathcal{R})$, is shown directly from definition of an opening simply by permutation order in (3.1) and (3.2), and identifying the opposite expansion and coexpansion of e.p.r.s. That $\mathcal{R}^{-1}$ is an opening for H^{op} or H^{cop} is then obvious from the first part of the statement. □

In general in economics, in addition to the above beneficial role of an opening this concept also carries costs providing conditions of an economic control.

Roughly speaking, conditions of an economic control are carried over some mechanisms shaping economic relations between agents according to so called cleaning opening conditions. The most familiar is the case of simple market, where in addition to the benefit that is to be expected from market involvement, market imposes costs implying conditions of an economic control. They are carried over market or arbitration mechanisms and shape economic relations between agents according to clearing market conditions.

Similar statement is valid within EPRT, where conditions of an economic control are carried over some opening mechanisms and shape economic relations between agents, according to clearing conditions. These are to be more sophisticated and to incorporate elements of e.p.r.s more precisely. So for every representation ρ of the agreement of a simple enterprise H in matrices, $(\rho \otimes \rho)(\mathcal{R})$ is a matrix solution of the same equations. It is these matrix solutions that are needed in concrete applied market structures in economics. An e.p.r.s clearing conditions of an opening, described by quasitriangular e.p.r.s structures, provide a way of generating many such solutions from a single abstract opening solution $\mathcal{R}$. One way to cope with these solutions is to apply the concept of an opening variety (to be more precisely explained in following sections). That is the reason why the quasitriangular structure $\mathcal{R}$ is sometimes referred to as the universal opening. Precisely we have,

Lemma 3.4. (Abstract cleaning condition) *Let $(H, \mathcal{R})$ be an opening biagreement. Then axioms of a simple open enterprise, 3.2 and the second part of 3.1, imply an abstract cleaning condition of e.p.r.s of an opening.*

Proof: We have to show that if $(H, \mathcal{R})$ is a quasitriangular biagreement, then above axioms from definition of $\mathcal{R}$ imply

$$\mathcal{R}_{12}\mathcal{R}_{13}\mathcal{R}_{23} = \mathcal{R}_{23}\mathcal{R}_{13}\mathcal{R}_{12},$$

as the abstract e.p.r.s cleaning condition of a collection of e.p.r.s due to an opening. Note that $(id \otimes \tau \circ \Delta)\mathcal{R}$ can be computed in two ways: using the second of the axioms (3.1) directly or using the axiom (3.2) and then second part of axiom (3.1). Thus, $(id \otimes \tau \circ \Delta)\mathcal{R} = (id \otimes \tau)(id \otimes \Delta)\mathcal{R} = (id \otimes \tau)\mathcal{R}_{13}\mathcal{R}_{12} = \mathcal{R}_{12}\mathcal{R}_{13}$, and $(id \otimes \tau \circ \Delta)\mathcal{R} = \mathcal{R}_{23}((id \otimes \Delta)\mathcal{R})\mathcal{R}_{23}^{-1} = \mathcal{R}_{23}\mathcal{R}_{13}\mathcal{R}_{12}\mathcal{R}_{23}^{-1}$. □

Before proceeding with the general theory of open enterprises, let us see some simple nontrivial examples. They provide a nice link with the concept of market from traditional economic theories. They also offer additional explanations of the definitions above for the particular e.p.r.s problems in applications. In addition, they are based on already known results from the Chapter 2 and are going to be used for further illustrations of the theoretical statements below and following Chapters. So the first example is to support an economic intuition of a particular role of opening as an economic valuation device within EPRT, as we have concept of present value within traditional market frame.

Example 3.5. This example is using a simple growing enterprise already discussed in detail in 2.32. Here, in addition to the elements given before (reader may recall the properties of simple enterprises that concern natural recourses if necessary), let us open the model to a simple market. An economic intuition is that some of the collections of e.p.r.s carried by simple factors are results of such an opening (thus not part of direct and full agreement and coagreement of agents and coagents within the enterprise). Also, it is economically plausible to assume that simple opening rules describe valuation of market opening by comparing outcomes with market factors to outcomes of full closed simple enterprise. In that way market rule is determined up to isotransaction of collections of e.p.r.s. Thus, in this simple example the e.p.r.s rules of a simple enterprise with market opening are modeled by $CZ_{/n}$, so that it is generated by $1_H, g$ with the simple market opening rule $g^n = 1_H$. The coexpansion, coagency and mutual understanding map, are given by $\Delta g = g \otimes g$, $\varepsilon g = 1_H$, $\gamma g = g^{-1}$, respectively. Then:
(a) the trivial structure of an opening is described by $\mathcal{R} = 1_H \otimes 1_H$,
(b) a nontrivial e.p.r.s structure of an opening is quasitriangular given by,

$$\mathcal{R} = \frac{1}{n} \sum_{a,b=0}^{n-1} e^{-\frac{2\pi \imath ab}{n}} g^a \otimes g^b.$$

Note that this simple opening is generated by cost structure of opening for the nontrivial case. In this example we have that above opening structures are also valid for an opposite structured simple economic reasoning.

Sketch of proof and comments: Any enterprise that is based on simplified copartner's e.p.r.s reasoning (i.e. cocommutative enterprise), such as this one, can be regarded as a trivial open enterprise with an opening given by $\mathcal{R} = 1_H \otimes 1_H$. Roughly speaking one may think of trivial market open enterprise where opening market structure has no impact on decision making of the partners. Thus, in this case there is actually no change due to such a trivial opening of an enterprise.

To verify nontrivial opening of a simple investing enterprise recall that nontrivial opening is to change a full e.p.r.s structure of an investor. In this example, a set of economic opening rules, that partners accept in their economic reasoning about an opening and/or market, is given by the set $\{g^n \mid n = 0, \pm 1, \pm 2, \ldots\}$. In detail, rules of simple market opening are defined in the following way. Let g be an agreement with the market opening rules G. Agents identify rules that link market factors and those within the ordinary simple closed enterprise by the sequence,

$$\begin{aligned} g^0 &:= 1_H \\ g^1 &:= g \\ g^n &:= g^{(n-1)} \cdot g \quad \text{for } n := 1, 2, , \ldots \\ g^n &:= (g^{-n})^{-1} \quad \text{for } n < 0, \end{aligned}$$

and the familiar law of indices holds: $g^m \cdot g^n = g^{m+n}$. This is an economic subrule that partners accept. It may happen (and in our case of assumed simplicity that opening rules are finite it must happen) that two apparently different valuations of opening coincide (powers of g coincide). If $g^i = g^j$, where (without loss of generality, $i < j$, then $g^{j-i} = 1$), and so there is a positive circulation of a collection of e.p.r.s over market which will clean opening effects, i.e. distribute them to participants. This simply means a positive power of the agreement g which is 1_H, having in mind the role of copartner explained above. Then the order of g is defined by $ord(g) := min\{m > 0 \mid g^m = 1_H\}$. If $ord(g) = m$ then we have that $\langle g \rangle = \{1, g, g^2, \ldots g^{m-1}\}$. In our case $G = \langle g \rangle$, means that opening rules are of Abelian type. This make considered example directly linked with traditional type of simple models in economics: (i) investment allocation in competitive market and (ii) growth. In addition, it is plausible to assume that facing finite market rules, partners will be able to learn economic law of such a market opening, and distribution of market effects is complete over market participants. In EPRT, such a simple market is described by $Z_{/n}$. Also it is known that if g has order n then the map $r \mapsto g^r$ yields an isotransaction $Z_{/n} \to G$, where Z_n denotes the additive group of integers modulo n. Then for our application we actually have that every subrule of market rules is a market rule so that $G = \langle g \rangle$ and $G_1 \leq G$ then either $G_1 = \{1\}$ when we are actually dealing with trivial opening rules, or $G_1 = \langle g^s \rangle$ where $s := min\{r \mid r > 0, g^r \in G_1\}$. Note that in this simple example field of e.p.r.s claims is modeled by field of complex numbers. It has simple economic interpretation that partners in their e.p.r.s claims and opening considerations take into account risky and speculative claims as well as real ones. In this case of market openings $\mathcal{R}$, note that

$$n^{-1} \sum_{b=0}^{n-1} e^{-\frac{2\pi \imath ab}{n}} = \delta_{a,0} = \begin{cases} 1 & \text{if } a = 0 \\ 0 & \text{otherwise.} \end{cases}$$

Then $\mathcal{R}_{13}\mathcal{R}_{23} = n^{-2}\sum e^{-\frac{2\pi\imath(ab+cd)}{n}} g^a \otimes g^c \otimes g^{b+d} = n^{-2}\sum e^{-\frac{2\pi\imath(a-c)}{n}} e^{-\frac{2\pi\imath cb'}{n}}$ $g^a \otimes g^c \otimes g^{b'} = n^{-1}\sum e^{-\frac{2\pi\imath ab'}{n}} g^a \otimes g^c \otimes g^{b'}$, where $b' = b+d$ was a change of variables. This equals $(\Delta \otimes id)\mathcal{R}$ as required and at the same time shows impacts of an investment market on an investor opening. Similar can be shown for the second half of condition (3.1). The remaining part of axiom (3.1) is automatically satisfied because this simple growing enterprise is generated on simplified e.p.r.s reasoning of all participants (it is both commutative and cocommutative). To show that investment market opening structures above are also the ones for an opposed e.p.r.s structured enterprise we have to prove that $\tau(\mathcal{R}) = \mathcal{R}$, are quasitriangular structures on H^{op} or H^{cop}. The proof comes simply from permuting the order in axioms that define an investor's market opening, (3.1) and (3.2), and identifying the opposed e.p.r.s expansion and coexpansion, for these types of open enterprises. This property of simple opening makes it directly linked with the traditional economic reasoning that firms are to face uniform type of markets independently of their internal structure. Note that this simple example is going to be used again for discussion below within the extended setting of a concept of *R&D* carrying new scope of technology and some more tricky and interesting e.p.r.s relations in Chapter 5. □

There are many interesting e.p.r.s forms that can be built from opening, $\mathcal{R}$, of simple opening enterprises. These collections of e.p.r.s are a base in various applications for results which are analogous to those concerning simple enterprises from Chapter 2 but allow opening. So for example Proposition 2.20 has the following analogous proposition.

Proposition 3.6. *Let us consider a simple open enterprise $(H, \mathcal{R})$ with a mutual understanding map γ. Then the mutual understanding also concerns opposed e.p.r.s structured enterprise and is shaped by opening relations in the sense of $\gamma^2(h) = uhu^{-1}$, for all $h \in H$ where u is an invertible agreement (element) of H, determined by an opening in the way that*

$$u = \sum (\gamma\mathcal{R}^{(2)})\mathcal{R}^{(1)}, \quad u^{-1} = \sum \mathcal{R}^{(2)}\gamma^2\mathcal{R}^{(1)},$$

which coexpansion of e.p.r.s is shaped by an inverse of its opening such that

$$\Delta u = \mathcal{R}^{-1}\mathcal{R}_{21}^{-1}(u \otimes u).$$

Likewise for $v = \gamma u$, we have that $\gamma^{-2}(h) = vhv^{-1}$, where v is an invertible agreement (element) of H determined by opening e.p.r.s in the way,

$$v = \sum \mathcal{R}^{(1)}\gamma\mathcal{R}^{(2)}, \quad v^{-1} = \sum (\gamma^2\mathcal{R}^{(1)})\mathcal{R}^{(2)},$$

and its e.p.r.s coexpansion is modified, as in above case, by opening structure,

$$\Delta v = \mathcal{R}^{-1}\mathcal{R}_{21}^{-1}(v \otimes v).$$

Proof: The proof is done in several steps:
(I) First let's compute

$$\begin{aligned}(\gamma h_{(2)})uh_{(1)} &= (\gamma h_{(2)})(\gamma \mathcal{R}^{(2)})\mathcal{R}^{(1)}h_{(1)} = (\gamma(h_{(1)}\gamma\mathcal{R}^{(2)}h_{(2)}))\mathcal{R}^{(1)}h_{(1)} \\ &= (\gamma(h_{(1)}\mathcal{R}^{(2)}))h_{(2)}\mathcal{R}^{(1)} = (\gamma\mathcal{R}^{(2)})(\gamma h_{(1)})h_{(2)} = \varepsilon(h)u.\end{aligned}$$

The properties of mutual understanding map, axioms (3.2) and property of copartner are used here to get these equalities. Then we get

$$(\gamma^2 h)u = (\gamma^2 h_{(2)})\varepsilon(h_{(1)})u = (\gamma^2 h_{(3)})(\gamma h_{(2)})uh_{(1)} = uh.$$

(II) To show that u, and u^{-1} are inverse, on one hand we have,

$$\begin{aligned}u^{-1}u &= \mathcal{R}^{(2)}(\gamma^2\mathcal{R}^{(1)})u = \mathcal{R}^{(2)}u\mathcal{R}^{(1)} = \mathcal{R}^{(2)}(\gamma\mathcal{R}'^{(2)})\mathcal{R}'^{(1)}\mathcal{R}^{(1)} \\ &= (\gamma\mathcal{R}^{(2)})(\gamma\mathcal{R}'^{(2)})\mathcal{R}'^{(1)}\gamma\mathcal{R}^{(1)} = \gamma(\mathcal{R}'^{(2)}\mathcal{R}^{-(2)})\mathcal{R}'^{(1)}\gamma\mathcal{R}^{-(1)} \\ &= \gamma(1_H)1_H = 1_H,\end{aligned}$$

using above proven step (I) and the facts how mutual understanding map is acting on an opening gain, established in Lemma 3.2. On the other hand we have,

$$uu^{-1} = u\mathcal{R}^{(2)}\gamma^2\mathcal{R}^{(1)} = (\gamma^2\mathcal{R}^{(2)})u\mathcal{R}^{(1)} = (\gamma\mathcal{R}^{(2)})u\gamma\mathcal{R}^{(1)} = 1_H.$$

Hence we have shown that u, u^{-1} are inverse elements of an enterprise H.
(III) Next we have to show that mutual understanding map provides understanding of the opposed e.p.r.s structured open enterprise. Thus, we define $\gamma^{-1}(h) = u^{-1}(\gamma h)u$ and verify that

$$\begin{aligned}(\gamma^{-1}h_{(2)})h_{(1)} &= u^{-1}(\gamma h_{(2)})uh_{(1)} = u^{-1}(\gamma h_{(2)})(\gamma^2 h_{(1)})u \\ &= u^{-1}(\gamma((\gamma h_{(1)})h_{(2)}))u = \varepsilon(h)u^{-1}u = \varepsilon(h),\end{aligned}$$

using parts of (I) and (II) from above and properties of mutual understanding map γ. Similarly, we clarify that

$$\begin{aligned}h_{(2)}\gamma^{-1}h_{(1)} &= h_{(2)}u^{-1}(\gamma h_{(1)})u = u^{-1}(\gamma^2 h_{(2)})(\gamma h_{(1)})u \\ &= u^{-1}(\gamma(h_{(1)}\gamma h_{(2)}))u = \varepsilon(h)u^{-1}u = \varepsilon(h).\end{aligned}$$

This means that the inverse of a mutual understanding map is a mutual understanding map for an opposed e.p.r.s structured enterprise, H^{op}. Hence it is the inverse of the mutual understanding map on an e.p.r.s enterprise according to Exercise 2.10 and Proposition 2.9 from Chapter 2.
(IV) Let us check the property of coexpansion of e.p.r.s of u,

$$\begin{aligned}\Delta u &= \Delta(\gamma\mathcal{R}^{(2)})\mathcal{R}^{(1)} = (\gamma\mathcal{R}^{(2)}_{(2)})\mathcal{R}^{(1)}_{(1)} \otimes (\gamma\mathcal{R}^{(2)}_{(1)})\mathcal{R}^{(1)}_{(2)} \\ &= (\gamma(\mathcal{R}^{(2)}_{(2)}\mathcal{R}'^{(2)}_{(2)}))\mathcal{R}^{(1)} \otimes (\gamma(\mathcal{R}^{(2)}_{(1)}\mathcal{R}'^{(2)}_{(1)}))\mathcal{R}'^{(1)} \\ &= (\gamma(\mathcal{R}''^{(2)}\mathcal{R}'''^{(2)}))\mathcal{R}''^{(1)}\mathcal{R}^{(1)} \otimes (\gamma(\mathcal{R}^{(2)}\mathcal{R}'^{(2)}))\mathcal{R}'''^{(1)}\mathcal{R}'^{(1)} \\ &= (\gamma\mathcal{R}'''^{(2)})u\mathcal{R}^{(1)} \otimes (\gamma(\mathcal{R}'^{(2)}\mathcal{R}'^{(2)}))\mathcal{R}'''^{(1)}\mathcal{R}'^{(1)} \\ &= (\gamma\mathcal{R}'''^{(2)})\mathcal{R}^{-(1)}u \otimes (\gamma\mathcal{R}'^{(2)})\mathcal{R}^{-(2)}\mathcal{R}'''^{(1)}\mathcal{R}'^{(1)} \\ &= \mathcal{R}^{-(1)}(\gamma\mathcal{R}'''^{(2)})u \otimes \mathcal{R}^{-(2)}(\gamma\mathcal{R}'^{(2)})\mathcal{R}'^{(1)}\mathcal{R}'''^{(1)} \\ &= \mathcal{R}^{-(1)}(\gamma\mathcal{R}'''^{(2)})u \otimes \mathcal{R}^{-(2)}u\mathcal{R}'''^{(1)} \\ &= \mathcal{R}^{-(1)}(\gamma\mathcal{R}'''^{(2)})u \otimes \mathcal{R}^{-(2)}(\gamma^2\mathcal{R}'''^{(1)})u \\ &= \mathcal{R}^{-1}\mathcal{R}_{21}^{-1}(u \otimes u).\end{aligned}$$

Here the second equality uses the axioms of an enterprise, the third and fourth equations follow from (3.1), and fifth equality uses the facts about u in part (I) and the argumentation of mutual understanding γ on market benefits, $\mathcal{R}$. The sixth equality is the cleaning market condition established by Lemma 3.4, applied in a suitable form. Another copy of u then appears and we can use part (I) again. The proof of the corresponding results for v are analogous. They can also be obtained by applying the results for u to the open enterprise that has opposed or coopposed e.p.r.s structure, i.e. to $(H^{op/cop}, \mathcal{R})$. □

Corollary 3.7. *For a simple open enterprise* $(H, \mathcal{R})$, *there exist a central arrangement,* $CA \in H$. *Also there exists an e.p.r.s-rule-like arrangement,* $RL \in H$, *that implements mutual understanding map by conjugation.*

Proof and comments: Using results of above proposition we have to show that an element of a simple enterprise defined by $CA := uv = vu$ exists, which obviously is determined by an opening $\mathcal{R}$ and mutual understanding map γ. Clearly, $\gamma^2(u) = uuu^{-1} = u$ and $\gamma^2(v) = v$, so that $uv = v\gamma^2(u) = vu$. We have to show that uv, vu are all elements that commute with all h. That is the case as $uvh = \gamma^2(\gamma^{-2}(h))uv = huv$ for all h, so it is really centralized. Coexpansion of e.p.r.s on CA is determined by inverse of opening collection (one may think of market opening costs) as by Lemma 3.2 we have that $(\gamma \otimes \gamma)\mathcal{R} = \mathcal{R}$, so that $(\gamma^2 \otimes \gamma^2)\mathcal{R}_{21}\mathcal{R} = \mathcal{R}_{21}\mathcal{R}$. Hence $\Delta(uv) = \mathcal{R}^{-1}\mathcal{R}_{21}^{-1}(u \otimes u)\mathcal{R}^{-1}\mathcal{R}_{21}^{-1}(v \otimes v) = \mathcal{R}^{-2}\mathcal{R}_{21}^{-1}(uv \otimes vu)$.

For second statement we have to show that the element of H, called opening rule-like and given by $RL := uv^{-1} = v^{-1}u$ is an e.p.r.s-rule-like and implements mutual understanding relation in repeated way over opening structure. It appears as a special case of the above central agreement CA, so we have $\Delta uv^{-1} = \mathcal{R}^{-1}\mathcal{R}_{21}^{-1}(u \otimes u)(v^{-1} \otimes v^{-1})\mathcal{R}_{21}\mathcal{R} = uv^{-1} \otimes uv^{-1}$. That uv^{-1} implements mutual understanding map in repeated way is then obvious as u, v^{-1} each does, so uv^{-1} implements γ^4. It is noteworthy that, for any finite-dimensional enterprise over a field of e.p.r.s claims which is of zero characteristic, we have $\gamma^4 = id$, and thus $RL = uv^{-1}$ is central in this case. For finite dimensional semisimple enterprises, we have $\gamma^2 = id$, and hence we have that u, v are separably central although both are opening rule-like agreements in this case. □

3.1.2 Some Simple Open Forms

Having in mind the above general discussion on simple open enterprises, let us discuss some more concrete simple forms. They are given together with some related additional definitions to describe properties of simple open enterprises. These definitions lead to a concept of economic equilibria and theory of e.p.r.s link-invariant within EPRT, which economic intuitions can easily be traced back to the more conventional economic theories.

First we have an impartial opening that defines an impartial open enterprise. Note that if in an open simple enterprise $(H, \mathcal{R})$ an impartial opening does not exists in H, it can always be adjoint through a central extension of H. It is introduced by an arrangement or element ν with the required properties as follows.

Definition 3.8. (Impartial open enterprise) *An open enterprise is called impartial open if it has an impartial arrangement ν such that*

$$\nu^2 = vu, \quad \Delta\nu = \mathcal{R}^{-1}\mathcal{R}_{21}^{-1}(\nu \otimes \nu), \quad \varepsilon\nu = 1, \quad \gamma\nu = \nu.$$

One may think of a market as impartial economic institution traditionally discussed within conventional competitive economic theories. Here, the element uv has a central square root ν, that satisfies the conditions. Note that listed properties are not independent; the latter two can be deduced from the first two, and the first one can be deduced from the last three. In the above elementary example an impartial market element exists, and this is left to the reader to be shown as a simple exercise. Note that this type may be considered as a standard normal market form of an opening of a simple enterprise.

Exercise 3.9. Show that simple market enterprise described in Example 3.5 is an impartial open enterprise according to

$$u = v = \nu = \frac{1}{n}\sum_{a,b=0}^{n-1} g^{-b}g^{a}e^{-\frac{2\pi\imath ab}{n}} = \frac{1}{n}\sum_{a=0}^{n-1} g^{a}\theta_n(a)$$

where $\theta_n(a) = \sum_{b=0}^{n-1} e^{-\frac{2\pi\imath(a+b)b}{n}}$ is the $Z_{/n}$ theta-function.

Hint: It is the $Z_{/n}$-Fourier transform of a Gaussion.

Definition 3.10. (Completely open enterprise) *An open enterprise is called completely open, if e.p.r.s structure of its opening is trivial.*

An example of completely open enterprises is one most similar to the traditional concept of a firm within perfect competitive market economy. In this case we have that market opening implies structure of opening described by $\mathcal{R}_{21}\mathcal{R} = 1 \otimes 1$. Economic decision making within such an environment can be described by applying simplex analysis, well known, highly developed and extensively used procedure in applied economics. From algebraic point of view those are cocommutative cases such as a simple enterprise described in Example 3.5 with market confirmed growth agreement g. Recall that such an agreement formally corresponds to Lie algebra thus, their representation theory is conventional one for Lie algebra g. These agreements do not lead to more complex economic equilibria or interesting e.p.r.s link invariants or knot invariants. In the above example if $n = 2$ we have a complete open market enterprise. In this case one may think of traditional production function which structure is defined by two economic factors, capital and labor. This structure is assumed valid for an economy and any enterprise - firm embedded into it. For more detail on this approach a reader may see [66].

Definition 3.11. (Factorisable open enterprise) *An open enterprise is called factorisable, if its modified opening $\mathcal{R}_{21}\mathcal{R}$ is nondegenerative in the sense that linear map $\mathcal{R}_{21}\mathcal{R} : H^* \rightarrow H$ linking ϕ to $(\phi \otimes id)(\mathcal{R}_{21}\mathcal{R})$ is surjective. Equivalently, the linear map linking ϕ to $(id \otimes \phi)(\mathcal{R}_{21}\mathcal{R})$ is surjective.*

In the above example, open enterprise is factorisable iff n is odd, and $n > 1$. Namely, we can take $\{e_a\}$ to be a dual basis to the $\{g^a\}$, so that

$$\sum_b (\mathcal{R}_{21}\mathcal{R})^{(2)} e_b((\mathcal{R}_{21}\mathcal{R})^{(2)}) e^{\frac{2\pi \imath ab}{n}} = g^{2a}.$$

If n is odd, then $2a$ is a permutation of $\{0, \ldots, n-1\}$ as a runs through this set, and otherwise not. Hence an open enterprise from Example 3.5 is factorisable iff n is odd.

The factorisable open enterprises are at the opposite extreme to a completely open enterprises. For them an opposed e.p.r.s structured opening $\tau(\mathcal{R}^{-1})$ is maximal distinct from a considered opening $\mathcal{R}$. Here modified form of opening $\mathcal{R}_{21}\mathcal{R}$ is far from trivial. Note also that $\mathcal{R}_{21}\mathcal{R}$ is not an agreeable or antiagreeable map, and actually it becomes a source of new conceptual arrangements of e.p.r.s, and formations of new e.p.r.s institutions, as for example economic clubs and/or leading clubs, within a more general and complex e.p.r.s setting addressed in Chapter 5. Roughly speaking, a setting that allows more complex e.p.r.s structures of modified opening, $\mathcal{R}_{21}\mathcal{R}$ will provide elements for (re)establishing a self-duality of these more complex opening relations associated with the complicated and cumbersome factorable opening rules. Such a self-duality will, in turn, allow forms of Fourier transformation on them, issues that are going to be discussed later on. Here recall that for simple open enterprises, invariance means that the argumentation of an element h is the same as an expansion of e.p.r.s of coagency under this agreement, precisely by $\varepsilon(h)$. Similarly, one may think of a simple investor where growth of the particular e.p.r.s is in essence of an economic argumentation for an opening.

Proposition 3.12. *For any simple open enterprise* $(H, \mathcal{R})$, *the element* $(\gamma \otimes id)(\mathcal{R}_{21}\mathcal{R})$ *in* $H \otimes H$ *is invariant under the e.p.r.s adjoint action, extended to the aggregate. The map* $\mathcal{R}_{21}\mathcal{R} : H^* \to H$ *in above definition provides simplified e.p.r.s reasoning of agency with the argumentation (action) of* H. *Here* H *acts on itself by the e.p.r.s adjoint action and on* H^* *by the e.p.r.s coargumentation (as in example 2.37). In addition, concerning mutual understanding map the modified opening has the property that* $(\gamma \otimes \gamma)(\mathcal{R}_{21}\mathcal{R}) = \tau(\mathcal{R}_{21}\mathcal{R})$.

Proof: Having in mind results from Chapter 2, the adjoint argumentation from the Example 2.37, and its extension to an argumentation on $H \otimes H$ explained in the Exercise 2.38, we have,

$$\begin{aligned} h \overset{a}{>} (\gamma \otimes id)(\mathcal{R}_{21}\mathcal{R}) &= h_{(1)}(\gamma(\mathcal{R}_{21}\mathcal{R})^{(1)})\gamma h_{(2)} \otimes h_{(3)}(\mathcal{R}_{21}\mathcal{R})^{(2)}\gamma h_{(4)} \\ &= h_{(1)}(\gamma\mathcal{R}^{(1)})(\gamma\mathcal{R}'^{(2)})\gamma h_{(2)} \otimes h_{(3)}\mathcal{R}'^{(1)}\mathcal{R}^{(2)}\gamma h_{(4)} \\ &= h_{(1)}(\gamma\mathcal{R}^{(1)})\gamma h_{(3)}(\gamma\mathcal{R}'^{(2)}) \otimes \mathcal{R}'^{(1)}h_{(2)}\mathcal{R}^{(2)}\gamma h_{(4)} \\ &= h_{(1)}\gamma h_{(2)}(\gamma\mathcal{R}'^{(1)})(\gamma\mathcal{R}'^{(2)}) \otimes \mathcal{R}'^{(1)}\mathcal{R}^{(2)}h_{(3)}\gamma h_{(4)} \\ &= \varepsilon(h)(\gamma \otimes id)(\mathcal{R}_{21}\mathcal{R}). \end{aligned}$$

Here the fact that γ is an antiagreeable map and axioms (3.2) are used to get third and fourth equalities. The proof of invariance of modified opening $\mathcal{R}_{21}\mathcal{R} : H^* \to H$ is similar to procedures used in Chapter 2 Examples 2.30, and 2.37. The final relation in proposition follows from Lemma 3.4 and the fact that mutual understanding map, γ, is an antiagreeable map. □

3.1.3 Simple Opening and Welfare

We now consider how an opening and corresponding e.p.r.s structure interact with the notation of welfare as described in Chapter 2. Recall that $*$ is an antiagreeable and coagreeable map, in the sense that it maps an e.p.r.s structured enterprise into its e.p.r.s opposed structured form, or precisely $* : H \to H^{op}$ is an (antilinear) biagreeable map. It can be shown that H^{op} has two natural e.p.r.s structures induced from an opening $\mathcal{R}$. So one can expect that $\mathcal{R}$ maps under $* \otimes *$ to one or the other of these structures. Note also, if an enterprise is completely open then these two paths coincide, and we cannot make any distinction between them. From this point of view, recall that the traditional concept of a firm in economics corresponds to a completely open enterprise, thus there is no possibility for identifying these e.p.r.s phenomena within traditional concept of a firm and its economic welfare analysis. A traditionally trained economist may recall Modigliani and Miller theory on structure of capital [52].

Definition 3.13. (Real and virtual welfare opening effect) *A nontrivial open structure in a simple open enterprise is called welfare real if* $\mathcal{R}^{*\otimes *} = \tau(\mathcal{R})$. *It is welfare virtual if* $\mathcal{R}^{*\otimes *} = \mathcal{R}^{-1}$.

One may check that modified opening, $\mathcal{R}_{21}\mathcal{R}$ is self-adjoint for the real opening as in this case we have $(\mathcal{R}_{21}\mathcal{R})^{*\otimes *} = \mathcal{R}_{21}\mathcal{R}$. It is unitary, in the case of virtual opening as $(\mathcal{R}_{21}\mathcal{R})^{*\otimes *} = \mathcal{R}^{-1}\mathcal{R}_{21}^{-1}$. As already mentioned for completely open enterprises real and virtual notations coincide; so that $\mathcal{R}^{*\otimes *} = \tau(\mathcal{R}) = \mathcal{R}^{-1}$ can be taken as an axiom for a completely open welfare $*$-enterprise. In the example 3.5 we have a real opening structure of an $*$-enterprise with the welfare effects $*$-structure $g^* = g^{-1}$.

We conclude this introductory discussion with some additional elementary examples, that also provide a link with the traditional cases from microeconomics. In particular we may recall a traditional description of market impacts through economic functions as profit and discount, for example. These examples are built on an underlying assumption that any market game provides and ensures a symmetric rule of participants' behavior. A rule of behavior can be described by an Abelian group.

Example 3.14. (Simple market opening) This example is using a simple enterprise already discussed in detail in 2.22, with the first generalization provided in the Example 3.5. Here the idea is to specify an opening of such an enterprise. Let G be a finite symmetric e.p.r.s rule concerning agents behavior, and $\mathbf{h}G$ an agreeable arrangement on domain of their e.p.r.s claims, as in Example 2.22. Market opening for such an arrangement is determined by a function $\mathcal{R} \equiv \pi$ on $G \times G$, called profit function, such that,

$$\sum_{cd=v} \pi(u,c)\pi(w,d) = \delta_{u,w}\pi(u,v), \qquad \sum_{cd=u} \pi(c,u)\pi(d,w) = \delta_{v,w}\pi(u,v),$$

$$\sum_{v} \pi(u,v) = \delta_{u,v} = \sum_{u} \pi(v,u),$$

for all $u, v, w,$ in $G,$ and with e being the identity element. This shows that an opening structure for such a simple type of agreement can be determined by the corresponding price system.

Sketch of proof and comments: An element $\mathcal{R} \equiv \pi \in \mathbf{h}G \otimes \mathbf{h}G$ that describes market opening in this example can be written as $\pi = \sum_{u,v} \pi(u,v)u \otimes v$. To check that axiom (3.1) is valid we compute $(\Delta \otimes id)\pi = \sum \pi(u,v)u \otimes u \otimes v$ while $\pi_{13}\pi_{23} = \sum \pi(u,c)\pi(w,d)u \otimes w \otimes cd$ providing the stated form for the first part of the condition. Similar is true for the other part. The axiom (3.2) is automatically fulfilled since the domain of e.p.r.s claim of agency, $\mathbf{h}G,$ has nice simplified properties (it is assumed to be both cocommutative and commutative). This shows that an opening structure for $\mathbf{h}G$ corresponds to the Fourier transform of a bicharacter on $\hat{G}$. The remaining conditions correspond to cleaning conditions shown in Lemma 3.4. These together with the given axiom (3.1) are equivalent to ability of partners in such a simple open enterprise to identify costs of an opening, i.e. the invertability of π. Note that when we allow speculations in domain of e.p.r.s claims, i.e. when we have $\mathbf{h} = C$, then $u^* = u^{-1}$ for the e.p.r.s natural welfare $*$-structure. Hence $\pi^{*\otimes *} = \overline{\pi}(u^{-1}, v^{-1})$ so that the property of real welfare effect of π can also be discussed in terms of these coefficients $\pi(u, v)$. □

Example 3.15. Let G be a finite symmetric e.p.r.s rule (an Abelian group) as above, and $\mathbf{h}(G)$ a set of functions on the e.p.r.s rule with values in a domain of e.p.r.s claim. It has the structure of a simple enterprise (see the Example 2.21), which opening is determined by a profit function $\pi \in H \otimes H$ such that,

$$\pi(uv, w) = \pi(u, w)\pi(v, w), \quad \pi(u, vw) = \pi(u, v)\pi(u, w),$$
$$\pi(u, e) = 1 = \pi(e, v),$$

for all $u, v, w,$ in G, and with e being the identity element.

Sketch of proof and comments: As in example 2.22, due to the fact that we are dealing with extremely simple model we may identify $\mathbf{h}(G) \otimes \mathbf{h}(G)$ with functions on $G \times G$, with pointwise multiplication. Using the coexpansion of e.p.r.s given in Example 3.5, we have at once that axiom (3.1) corresponds to the first two displayed equations. The axiom (3.2) becomes $vu\pi(u, v) = \pi(u, v)uv$, and so is automatically fulfilled because the e.p.r.s rule, as long as followed, ensures proper behavior of agents in this type of enterprise and openings. Given these first two of the stated conditions, the latter two hold iff π is invertible. This means that profit is nowhere vanishing. This is due to fact that the bicharacter rule corresponds to Pontryagin dual, consisting of bimaps on $G \times G$ to domain of claims where the zero level of e.p.r.s claim is excluded that respect the rule structure in the sense $\chi(uv) = \chi(u)\chi(v)$. It is noteworthy that when field of claims allows speculative transactions, there is $*$-structure given by $(\pi^*)(u) = \overline{\pi(u)}$, so we can have real or virtual market openings depending on the reality properties of $\mathcal{R}$ as a function π. □

Example 3.16. **(Simple investment and security)** Recall a simple growth economy as in Example 2.33. Let $U(1)$ be its universal enveloping agreement. Its e.p.r.s generators are $1, \xi$, with primitive type of coexpansion of e.p.r.s for coagreement described by $\Delta\xi = \xi \otimes 1 + 1 \otimes \xi$. Here we extend this type of enterprises for an opening over the market modeled by an offering of a security, m. We already know, from discussion above that there is the trivial opening that corresponds to trivial monetary effects. What is more interesting is a nontrivial monetary effects of opening described by

$$\mathcal{R} = e^{m\xi\otimes\xi}.$$

This is the simple e.p.r.s linear open enterprise modeled by $U_m(1)$, or $U_q(1)$ when $q = e^{m/2}$. This opening implies a real welfare effects of an $*$-agreement $U_m(R)$ or $U_q(R)$, with $\xi^* = \xi$, and $m^* = m$, where R denotes line of reals. It implies a virtual welfare effects when $\xi^* = \xi$, and $m^* = -m$.

Sketch of proof and comments: Recall that an offering of a security is described by a ring of formal power series in that security. In addition, the universal enveloping agreement concerns the one dimensional simple growth with properties already discussed in Example 2.33, is described by Lie algebra with the trivial Lie bracket. Thus, the verification of the axioms is quite straightforward. For example,

$$(\Delta \otimes id)\mathcal{R} = e^{m(\Delta\otimes id)\xi\otimes\xi} = e^{m(\xi\otimes 1\otimes\xi + 1\otimes\xi\otimes\xi)} = \mathcal{R}_{13}\mathcal{R}_{23},$$

etc., while axiom (3.2) is automatically satisfied because this simple type of enterprise is based on simplified e.p.r.s reasoning of participants implying convenient properties of commutativity and cocommutativity. Note that another welfare $*$-structure is $\xi^* = -\xi$ which is then precisely an '$n = \infty$' analogue of Example 3.5. Recall that this has been first formulated in Example 3.14, but based on the envelope algebra of R, the real line, rather than on a group algebra, to play the role of e.p.r.s rule of behavior in EPRT. The formulation in Example 3.15, in terms of function algebras, is convenient for insertion into functional-analytic setting within which welfare structure is discussed in Chapter 2. Thus, as we are dealing with one variable model, one may think of a security as a parameter m to carry virtual economic value. Recall that $L^\infty(R)$ is the usual Hopf-von Neumann or Kac algebra of bounded functions on R (acting by multiplication on $L^2(R)$). We define $L^\infty_m(R)$ to be this same Hopf-von Neumann type of agreement but with the nonstandard virtual opening $\mathcal{R}(x,y) = e^{mxy}$. One may think of the e.p.r.s agreement concerning a simple competitive economy. It can be described formally by one dimensional Kac algebra. In fact, this formulation is not fundamentally different from $U_m(R)$ when one bears in mind that the functions on R are in some sense 'generated' by the tautological coordinate function $\xi(x) = x$, of market coordination of perfect competitive economy x. The coproduct in L^∞_m is $(\Delta\xi)(x,y) = \xi(x+y) = (\xi\otimes 1 + 1\otimes\xi)(x,y)$, and within the EPRT it gets interpretation of coexpansion of e.p.r.s. Clearly these variants are all based on the same idea, and moreover, they are built on the standard concept of enterprises with only the market opening being nonstandard. Some more general examples are going to be given later on in Chapter 4. □

3.2 Dual Opening Structures

In this subsection a few notes are made on the dual results to those of a simple open enterprise given in previous subsections. If a simple open enterprise carries a coexpansion of e.p.r.s that is almost simplified, up to opening conjugation, then its dual entrepreneurial arrangement or dual of an open enterprise should carry an expansion of e.p.r.s being almost simplified, up to some sort of 'opening conjugation', defined in a suitable way. It appears that a simple opening might be more suitable to express an 'e.p.r.s law' as a generalization of an e.p.r.s rule respected by agents or an enveloping agreement, while its dual version is more suitable as generalization of the economic functions on an e.p.r.s rule.

3.2.1 Dual Openings

It is important to have in mind that the axioms of an open enterprise are not self-dual, contrary to the axioms of an enterprise. From above we know that an ordinary open enterprise H comes equipped with an assessment of e.p.r.s carried by opening, $\mathcal{R}$ and $\mathcal{R}^{-1}$ in $H \otimes H$. Thus, we may think of $\mathcal{R}^{-1}$ as a map $\mathbf{h} \to H \otimes H$, so in the dual formulation we are asking for 'invertible' map $A \otimes A \to \mathbf{h}$, where A is an entrepreneurial agreement but to be referred to in the dual formulation, and $\mathbf{h}$ is a domain (field) of e.p.r.s claims of agents. An intuition of A is that it is dual to an enterprise H, or H can be considered as dual to A. The idea is to be able to eliminate H itself from the axioms and refer everything to A. At this point it is important to be clear what is meant by 'invertible' map that we are searching for to express duality concept. The sense we need is in terms of the agreeable structure on the dual of $A \otimes A$. This agreeable structure that corresponds to $H \otimes H$ comes from the coexpansion of e.p.r.s on $A \otimes A$, and it is therefore natural to consider the convolution algebra of maps $Homt(A \otimes A, \mathbf{h})$. More generally and in this application, if A_B is any coagreement and A_A is any agreement, then an economic transaction $Homt(A_B, A_A)$ has a convolution agreemental structure described by,

$$(\phi\psi)(b) = \sum \phi(b_{(1)}) \cdot_A \psi(b_{(2)}), \quad 1(b) = \eta_A \varepsilon(b). \tag{3.3}$$

Note that on the right sides of these equations the expansion of e.p.r.s and preserving maps are in agreement A_A. This construction has already been used in defining the agreeable dual to a coagreement in Section 2.1.1, with agreement equal to complete field of e.p.r.s claims, i.e. $A_A = \mathbf{h}$. Now we use it with coagreement $A_B = A \otimes A$ and $A_A = \mathbf{h}$. Explicitly then, $\mathcal{R} : A \otimes A \to \mathbf{h}$ should be invertible in $Homt(A \otimes A, \mathbf{h})$, in the sense that there exists a map $\mathcal{R}^{-1} : A \otimes A \to \mathbf{h}$ such that

$$\sum \mathcal{R}^{-1}(a_{(1)} \otimes b_{(1)})\mathcal{R}(a_{(2)} \otimes b_{(2)}) = \varepsilon(a)\varepsilon(b) =$$
$$\sum \mathcal{R}(a_{(1)} \otimes b_{(1)})\mathcal{R}^{-1}(a_{(2)} \otimes b_{(2)}).$$

Note that, duality principle used in Chapter 2, can be applied on an open simple enterprise in the usual way. Here the resulting axioms and the ways of working with these almost simplified enterprises look somewhat different in practice, so it is worthy to write them out explicitly in the dual form. Also, while the axioms are dual, we are not limited to finite-dimensional enterprises or biagreements. In this case, two setups are not perfectly equivalent. For some examples the present duality formulization certainly provides some technical advantages and carries additional explanatory power of e.p.r.s relations. It also overcomes a few technical difficulties in calculations.

Having in mind these issues, dual structures of an open enterprise can be formulated precisely by the following definition.

Definition 3.17. (Dual simple opening) *A dual open biagreement or a simple open enterprise is a pair* $(A, \mathcal{R})$, *where* A *is a biagreement or a simple enterprise and* $\mathcal{R}$ *is an opening expressible as a convolution invertible map* $\mathcal{R} : A \otimes A \to \mathbf{h}$, *such that*

$$\mathcal{R}(a^i a^j \otimes a^l) = \sum \mathcal{R}(a^i \otimes a^j_{(1)}) \mathcal{R}(a^j \otimes a^l_{(2)}) \tag{3.4}$$

$$\mathcal{R}(a^i \otimes a^j a^l) = \sum \mathcal{R}(a^i_{(1)} \otimes a^l_{(1)}) \mathcal{R}(a^i_{(2)} \otimes a^j),$$

$$\sum a^j_{(1)} a^i_{(1)} \mathcal{R}(a^i_{(2)} \otimes a^j_{(2)}) = \sum \mathcal{R}(a^i_{(1)} \otimes a^j_{(1)}) a^i_{(2)} a^j_{(2)}, \tag{3.5}$$

for all $a^i, a^j, a^l \in A$.

That this definition is dual to the one of a simple open enterprise is obvious as an expansion of e.p.r.s in Definition 3.1 is replaced by the convolution expansion of e.p.r.s in Definition 3.17 above, and the coexpansion of e.p.r.s by the expansion of e.p.r.s in A. Axiom (3.5) is the dual of (3.2). Also it claims that A is almost simplified (commutative) - up to opening $\mathcal{R}$, as one would expect. Axioms (3.4) are the dual of (3.1) and claim that $\mathcal{R}$ is a 'bialgebra bicharacter'. This with the meaning that the opening carries an e.p.r.s dichotomy.

As expected we also have results analogous to those in Section 3.3. So a dual version of Lemma 3.2 takes the following form,

Lemma 3.18. (Duality of opening) *If* $(A, \mathcal{R})$ *is a dual open biagreement, then coagency defines an opening for any element of biagreement* $a \in A$. *If* A *is a simple open enterprise then, in addition, the mutual understanding map ensures:* (*i*) *a balance between an opening and its inverse for any element of agreement, and* (*ii*) *homogeneousness of an opening.*

Proof: To prove the first statement we have to show that if $(A, \mathcal{R})$ is an open biagreement, then

$$\mathcal{R}(a \otimes 1) = \varepsilon(a) = \mathcal{R}(1 \otimes a), \quad \text{for any} \quad a \in A.$$

We have

$$\begin{aligned}\mathcal{R}(a\otimes 1) &= (\mathcal{R}^{-1}(a_{(1)}\otimes 1)\mathcal{R}(a_{(2)}\otimes 1))\mathcal{R}(a_{(3)}\otimes 1)\\ &= \mathcal{R}^{-1}(a_{(1)}\otimes 1)(\mathcal{R}(a_{(2)}\otimes 1)\mathcal{R}(a_{(3)}\otimes 1))\\ &= \mathcal{R}^{-1}(a_{(1)}\otimes 1)\mathcal{R}(a_{(2)}\otimes 1\cdot 1)\\ &= \varepsilon(a)\end{aligned}$$

where the axioms (3.4) were used. Likewise on the other side.
To prove (i) under the second statement we have to show that if A is a simple enterprise then one also has that

$$\mathcal{R}(\gamma a^i\otimes a^j)=\mathcal{R}^{-1}(a^i\otimes a^j),\ \ \mathcal{R}^{-1}(a^i\otimes\gamma a^j)=\mathcal{R}(a^i\otimes a^j) \tag{3.6}$$

and hence $\mathcal{R}(\gamma a^i\otimes\gamma a^j)=\mathcal{R}(a^i\otimes a^j)$. To show above equalities we may use the first statement, just proven, and properties of mutual understanding map γ. Note that if $\mathcal{R}^{-1}$ exists, it is unique. Hence for A an open enterprise is given by $\mathcal{R}^{-1}(a^i\otimes a^j)=\mathcal{R}(\gamma a^i\otimes a^j)$, using axioms (3.6). In this case, $a^i\otimes a^j\mapsto\mathcal{R}(\gamma a^i\otimes\gamma a^j)$ is convolution-inverse to $\mathcal{R}^{-1}$ because

$$\begin{aligned}\mathcal{R}(\gamma a^i_{(1)}\otimes\gamma a^j_{(1)})\mathcal{R}(\gamma a^i_{(2)}\otimes\gamma a^j_{(2)}) &= \mathcal{R}(\gamma a^i\otimes(\gamma a^j_{(1)})a^j_{(2)})\\ &= \mathcal{R}(\gamma a^i\otimes 1)\varepsilon(a^j)=\varepsilon(a^i)\varepsilon(a^j).\end{aligned}$$

Hence, $\mathcal{R}(\gamma a^i\otimes\gamma a^j)=\mathcal{R}(a^i\otimes a^j)$. Note that in the case where $\mathcal{R}$ is a linear map obeying relation (3.6) above and axioms (3.4) and if A is an enterprise, we can use (3.6) as a definition of inverse of opening, i.e. $\mathcal{R}^{-1}$. □

Lemma 3.19. (Dual cleaning condition) *Let $(A,\mathcal{R})$ be a dual opening biagreement, then redistribution of e.p.r.s gained by opening is complete.*

Proof: We have to show that if $(A,\mathcal{R})$ is an open biagreement, then axioms of dual open biagreement from Definition 3.17 ensure clearing condition on collection of e.p.r.s gained by opening. Precisely, we have that then

$$\begin{aligned}&\sum\mathcal{R}(a^i_{(1)}\otimes a^j_{(1)})\mathcal{R}(a^i_{(2)}\otimes a^l_{(1)})\mathcal{R}(a^j_{(2)}\otimes a^l_{(2)})\\ =&\sum\mathcal{R}(a^j_{(1)}\otimes a^l_{(1)})\mathcal{R}(a^i_{(1)}\otimes a^l_{(2)})\mathcal{R}(a^i_{(2)}\otimes a^j_{(2)})\end{aligned} \tag{3.7}$$

for all elements of agreement $a^i,a^j,a^l\in A$. We apply the second axiom of (3.4), and then axiom (3.5), and again the second axiom of (3.4), so that

$$\begin{aligned}&(\mathcal{R}(a^i_{(1)}\otimes a^j_{(1)})\mathcal{R}(a^i_{(2)}\otimes a^l_{(1)}))\mathcal{R}(a^j_{(2)}\otimes a^l_{(2)})\\ &=\mathcal{R}(a^i\otimes a^l_{(1)}a^j_{(1)})\mathcal{R}(a^j_{(2)}\otimes a^l_{(2)})=\mathcal{R}(a^j_{(1)}\otimes a^l_{(1)})\mathcal{R}(a^i\otimes a^j_{(2)}a^l_{(2)})\\ &=\mathcal{R}(a^j_{(1)}\otimes a^l_{(1)})(\mathcal{R}(a^i_{(1)}\otimes a^l_{(2)})\mathcal{R}(a^i_{(2)}\otimes a^j_{(2)})).\ \square\end{aligned}$$

3.2.2 Some Properties of Dual Openings

There are many interesting e.p.r.s institutions that can be built from an opening considered from dual point of view. Using these elements, one can check various properties of an open enterprise that are analogous to the conventional enterprise, but differ by conjugation.

Proposition 3.20. *Let $(A, \mathcal{R})$ be a dual open simple enterprise. Let $v : A \to \mathbf{h}$, and $v^{-1} : A \to \mathbf{h}$, be e.p.r.s claim mappings defined by*

$$v(a) = \sum \mathcal{R}(a_{(1)} \otimes \gamma a_{(2)}), \quad v^{-1}(a) = \sum \mathcal{R}(\gamma^2 a_{(1)} \otimes a_{(2)}).$$

Then $\sum a_{(1)} v(a_{(2)}) = \sum v(a_{(1)}) \gamma^2 a_{(2)}$, and v^{-1} is the inverse of v in the convolution agreement $Homt(A, \mathbf{h})$. One can likewise define e.p.r.s claims as follows

$$u(a) = \sum \mathcal{R}(a_{(2)} \otimes \gamma a_{(1)}), \quad u^{-1}(a) = \sum \mathcal{R}(\gamma^2 a_{(2} \otimes a_{(1)})$$

obeying $\sum u(a_{(1)}) a_{(2)} = \sum \gamma^2 a_{(1)} u(a_{(2)})$. The mutual understanding map of A is bijective.

Proof: Note that this is just the dual of Proposition 3.6. In this proof let us have focus on v rather then u, as it was the case in procedure applied to show validity of Proposition 3.6. Here we also have the proof done in several steps:
(I) First compute

$$\begin{aligned}
a_{(1)} v(a_{(2)}) &= a_{(1)} \mathcal{R}(a_{(2)} \otimes \gamma a_{(3)}) \\
&= (\gamma(\gamma a_{(3)})_{(1)})(\gamma a_{(3)})_{(2)} a_{(1)} \mathcal{R}(a_{(2)} \otimes (\gamma a_{(3)})_{(3)}) \\
&= (\gamma(\gamma a_{(3)})_{(1)}) a_{(2)} (\gamma a_{(3)})_{(3)} \mathcal{R}(a_{(1)} \otimes (\gamma a_{(3)})_{(2)}) \\
&= \mathcal{R}(a_{(1)} \otimes \gamma a_{(4)})(\gamma^2 a_{(5)}) a_{(2)} \gamma a_{(3)} = v(a_{(1)}) \gamma^2 a_{(2)}.
\end{aligned}$$

Here we put $a^j = b = \gamma a_{(3)}$ and insert $\varepsilon(\gamma a_{(3)}) = (\gamma(\gamma a_{(3)})_{(1)})(\gamma a_{(3)})_{(2)}$, and then use axiom (3.5) to change the order.
(II) This step is to show that v^{-1} and v are inverses. We have,

$$\begin{aligned}
\mathcal{R}(a_{(1)} \otimes a_{(3)}) v(a_{(2)}) &= \mathcal{R}(a_{(1)} \otimes a_{(4)}) \mathcal{R}(a_{(2)} \otimes \gamma a_{(3)}) \\
&= \mathcal{R}(a_{(1)} \otimes (\gamma a_{(2)}) a_{(3)}) = \varepsilon(a).
\end{aligned}$$

We used axioms (3.4) and using the above proven step (I) we have,

$$\begin{aligned}
\varepsilon(a) &= \mathcal{R}(a_{(1)} \otimes a_{(3)}) v(a_{(2)}) = v(a_{(1)}) \mathcal{R}(\gamma^2 a_{(2)} \otimes a_{(3)}) \\
&= v(a_{(1)}) v^{-1}(a_{(2)}) = v(a_{(2)}) \mathcal{R}(\gamma^2 a_{(1)} \otimes \gamma^2 a_{(3)}) \\
&= \mathcal{R}(\gamma^2 a_{(1)} \otimes a_{(2)}) v(a_{(3)}) = v^{-1}(a_{(1)}) v(a_{(2)}).
\end{aligned}$$

We used for latter that $\mathcal{R}(\gamma^2 a \otimes \gamma^2 b) = \mathcal{R}(a \otimes b)$. Hence we have shown that v, v^{-1} are inverse in convolution agreement $Homt(A, \mathbf{h})$.
(III) To complete the proof we next have to show that mutual understanding map has the required property, ensuring understanding of the opposite e.p.r.s structured opening, i.e. that γ is invertible. We define $\gamma^{-1}(a) = \gamma a_{(2)} v(a_{(1)}) v^{-1}(a_{(3)})$ and verify from (I) and (II) that

$$\begin{aligned}
(\gamma^{-1} a_{(2)}) a_{(1)} &= (\gamma a_{(3)}) a_{(1)} v(a_{(2)}) v^{-1}(a_{(4)}) \\
&= (\gamma a_{(3)})(\gamma^2 a_{(2)}) v(a_{(1)}) v^{-1}(a_{(4)}) \\
&= v(a_{(1)}) v^{-1}(a_{(2)}) = \varepsilon(a), \\
a_{(2)} \gamma^{-1} a_{(1)} &= v^{-1}(a_{(3)}) a_{(4)} \gamma a_{(2)} v(a_{(1)}) = (\gamma^2 a_{(3)}) \gamma a_{(2)} v(a_{(1)}) v^{-1}(a_{(4)}) \\
&= v(a_{(1)}) v^{-1}(a_{(2)}) = \varepsilon(a). \quad \square
\end{aligned}$$

3.3 Advanced Openings

In this section the first step in generalization of the concept of an opening is proposed. Issues are to be studied more completely within the extended setting of economic clubs and other more complex e.p.r.s institutions in Chapter 4. One may proceed directly to the next Chapter on a first reading of the book, and come back to these sections when studying other forms of advanced opening and formation of new types of enterprises from already established ones. Here, a few introductory steps into extension theory are made into more advanced aspects of the economic theory related to modification and institutionalization of e.p.r.s where correspondence of structure and properties of enterprise are in focus. In particular, economic effects of modification of e.p.r.s structure and properties of a copartner by an opening of an agreement or an enterprise are considered. One may think of the construction a modification of correspondence of e.p.r.s structure and its properties by 'twisting' procedures. These have formal algebraic base in some more advanced aspects of deformation theory, Hopf algebra cohomology and quasitriangular Hopf algebras introduced by V.G. Drinfeld [28].

3.3.1 Confirmation of Openings

The idea is to sketch a framework or procedures which provide schemes for new forms of openings. In particular, of interest are those elements which allows cycling e.p.r.s structure of copartners, and e.p.r.s modifications. At this introductory state, we use an elementary construction providing the base for theory of enterprise extensions and dynamics of e.p.r.s. Note that a more complete study of these issues, with appropriate e.p.r.s interpretation is addressed more precisely later within discussion of e.p.r.s categories, clubs and leading e.p.r.s institutions in this volume and more in the sequel.

Let us first make a few comments on a closed path of opening involving a copartner in the sense that e.p.r.s structure and properties are repeated themselves. At first the intention is to get some insight into these cycles on e.p.r.s rules for copartner and on simple growth of an enterprise. Namely, the idea is to understand how to run copartner's e.p.r.s rules that are incorporated into an enterprise by an opening and what are the economic impacts due to these modifications on simple growing agreements at the level of an enterprise.

Let H be a biagreement or an enterprise. The following expressions emphasize repeated structure of e.p.r.s through a coexpansion,

$$\Delta_i := H^{\otimes n} \to H^{\otimes n+1}, \quad \Delta_i = id \otimes \cdots \otimes \Delta \otimes \cdots \otimes id, \tag{3.8}$$

where Δ is in the ith position, $i = 1, \ldots, n$ and we add to this the conventions $\Delta_0 = 1 \otimes (\ )$ and $\Delta_{n+1} = (\ ) \otimes 1$, so that Δ_i are defined for $i = 0, \ldots, n+1$. Then one can define a chain linked with copartner, or an n-cochain χ to be an invertible element of $H^{\otimes n}$, i.e. $\chi, \chi^{-1} \in H^{\otimes n}$. In addition, boundary of a coexpansion of e.p.r.s for copartner within given entrepreneurial arraignment H can be identified and it is called coboundary of n-cochain, χ as the $n+1$-cochain

$$\partial \chi = \left(\prod_{i=1}^{i\ even} \Delta_i \chi \right) \left(\prod_{i=1}^{i\ odd} \Delta_i \chi^{-1} \right), \tag{3.9}$$

where the even i run $0, 2, \ldots,$ and the odd i run $1, 3, \ldots,$ and the products are each taken in increasing order. We also write $\partial \chi \equiv (\partial_+ \chi)(\partial_- \chi^{-1})$ for the separate even and odd parts.

Definition 3.21. (Path of copartner's open structure) *An n-cocycle for an enterprise or biagreement is an invertible element $\chi \in H^{\otimes n}$ such that $\partial \chi = 1$. It is of coagency type if $\varepsilon_i \chi = 1$ for all $\varepsilon_i = id \otimes \cdots \otimes \varepsilon \otimes \cdots id$.*

The following example might be useful for understanding concepts of cycling and boundary of a copartner or simple cocycling and coboundary at the level of an enterprise.

Proposition 3.22. *Let H be a biagreement or an enterprise. Then:*
(a) An element of biagreement or enterprise, $\chi \in H$, can be considered an 1-cocycle if it is invertible, $\chi^{-1} \in H$, and it is e.p.r.s rule-like, so that

$$\chi \otimes \chi = \Delta \chi \tag{3.10}$$

It is automatically coagency.
(b) An element of aggregate of two biagreements or enterprises, $\chi \in H \otimes H$, is considered a 2-cocycle if it is invertible, $\chi^{-1} \in H \otimes H$, and is such that

$$(1 \otimes \chi)(id \otimes \Delta)\chi = (\chi \otimes 1)(\Delta \otimes id)\chi. \tag{3.11}$$

It is coagency if $(\varepsilon \otimes id)\chi = 1$, *or equivalently if* $(id \otimes \varepsilon)\chi = 1$.
(*c*) *An element of a three fold aggregate institution* $\chi \in H \otimes H \otimes H$ *is considered a 3-cocycle if it is invertible,* $\chi^{-1} \in H \otimes H \otimes H$, *and such that*

$$(1 \otimes \chi)((id \otimes \Delta \otimes id)\chi)(\chi \otimes 1) = \\ ((id \otimes id \otimes \Delta)\chi)((\Delta \otimes id \otimes id)\chi). \quad (3.12)$$

It is coagency if $(id \otimes \varepsilon \otimes id)\phi = 1 \otimes 1$.

Proof and comments: Recall that an n-cocycle for an enterprise or biagreement is an invertible element of appropriate level of aggregate institution $\chi \in H^{\otimes n}$ such that its coboundary ensures $\partial\chi = 1$. The condition $(\varepsilon \otimes id)\chi = 1$ implies $(id \otimes \varepsilon)\chi = 1$ if χ is already a 2-cocycle. This is seen by applying ε to the middle factor of the 2-cocycle condition, and vice versa. Similarly, one sees from the 3-cocycle condition that the coagency condition for ε in the middle position implies the coagency condition for ε in the other two positions as well. □

The following is an example of an enterprise structured by $\mathbf{h}(G)$, as in Example 3.15, which statements are not difficult to prove, having in mind the procedure just shown above.

Example 3.23. Let G be a collection of e.p.r.s rules accepted by partners, and let a corresponding enterprise H be formed on profit function $\mathbf{h}(G)$ as already described in Example 3.15. Then:
(*a*) There exists an economic transaction (not necessarily unique) from underlying e.p.r.s rule of enterprise to nonempty e.p.r.s of coagent on domain of e.p.r.s claims. We may say that coagency is of 1-cocycle type. From formal point of view we are dealing with a group homomorphism to $\mathbf{h} - \{0\}$.
(*b*) There is nowhere-zero profit function χ on $G \times G$ such that corresponding inverse function $\chi^{-1} \in G \otimes G$ exists, and χ is such that

$$\chi(v,w)\chi(u,vw) = \chi(u,v)\chi(uv,w), \quad \chi(e,u) = 1 = \chi(u,e)$$

for $u, v, w \in G$. Here e is an e.p.r.s structure of the rule that ensures its preservation (a rule identity). One may think of χ as an element of $Z^2(G)$, a normalized 2-cocycle in the usual sense on an e.p.r.s rule, or there is a coagency of 2-cocycle type on $\mathbf{h}(G)$.
(*c*) There is a nowhere zero profit function χ on $G \times G \times G$ such that

$$\chi(v,s,m)\chi(u,vs,m)\chi(u,v,s) = \chi(u,v,sm)\chi(uv,s,m), \quad \chi(u,e,v) = 1,$$

for $u, v, w, m \in G$. Here e is an e.p.r.s rule identity, i.e. a normalized 3-cocycle in $Z^3(G)$, in the usual sense.

Hint: The statements follows directly from the structure of the profit function $\mathbf{h}(G)$, as discussed in Example 3.15, now applied in setting of Proposition

3.22. □

It is worthy to note that the notions above for $H = \mathbf{h}(G)$, can be reduced to the usual theory of group cocycles, and in application to the economic game theory. The usual group n-cochain is a pointwise invertible function $\chi : G \times G \times \cdots \times G \to \mathbf{h}$ and has coboundary,

$$(\partial\chi)(u_1, u_2, \ldots, u_{n+1}) = \prod_{i=0}^{n+1} \chi(u_1, \ldots, u_i u_{i+1}, \ldots, u_{n+1})^{(-1)^i}$$

where, by convention, the first $i = 0$ factor is $\chi(u_2, \ldots, u_{n+1})$ and the last factor is $\chi(u_1, \ldots, u_n)^{\pm 1}$. One has $\partial^2 = 1$ and the rule of costandard expansion of e.p.r.s by coboundaries of the form $\partial(\ )$. These notions are also applied on the exponent of the relevant notions for simple growth agreemental structures and properties of coagency.

For applications in EPRT one should have in mind that the process of opening an agreement or an enterprise can only give a genuinely new enterprise if the cocycle χ used to accept an e.p.r.s arrangement carries nontrivial element in its structure and properties. Recall that the above formulation of the correspondence in structure and properties of e.p.r.s rules from point of view of a copartner in terms of an enterprises is almost always valid for any simple biagreement or enterprise. The conditions are to have $\partial^2 = 1$ and specify e.p.r.s rules concerning the correspondence and properties of copartner $\mathcal{H}^n(\mathbf{h}, H)$. One may also try to apply the same definitions to other forms of enterprises and even when applied to the more complex enterprise $\mathbf{h}G$ or $U(g)$ we will see that notions become novel and require nontrivial constructions. In addition, for these and other nonsimple enterprises one should be careful because we may not have the required condition on boundary of copartner, $\partial^2 = 1$, and the attended structural interpretation. We may note that $\mathcal{H}^1(\mathbf{h}, H)$, and $\mathcal{H}^2(\mathbf{h}, H)$ spaces are well defined for any biagreement or enterprise. This is obvious as in fact $\mathcal{H}^1(\mathbf{h}, H)$ corresponds to the e.r.p.s rule-like element, (it is same as the 1-cocycles), where invertible elements on domain of the e.r.p.s claim $\mathbf{h}$ can be considered as 0-cocycles and their coboundary from definition (3.9) is always 1. Thus, we may conclude that $\mathcal{H}^1(\mathbf{h}, H)$ is the e.p.r.s rule of invertible rule-like elements in a biagreement or enterprise. In considering $\mathcal{H}^2(\mathbf{h}, H)$ the following may be useful,

Proposition 3.24. *Let H be a biagreement or an enterprise. If $h_i \in H$ is an invertible element with $\varepsilon h_i = 1$, then ∂h_i, is an opening of coagency type 2-cocycle for H. It specifies boundary of coagent and may be called coboundary. More generally, if χ is an opening of coagency type 2-cocycle, then $\chi^{h_i} = (\partial_+ h_i)\chi(\partial_- h_i^{-1}) = (h_i \otimes h_i)\chi\Delta h_i^{-1}$ is also an opening of coagency type 2-cocycle. This opening corresponds to χ, by coagent structure and properties, and may be considered to carry same appropriation rules as χ. The non-*

Abelian space, $\mathcal{H}^2(\mathbf{h}, H)$, of appropriational rules consist of the openings type 2-cocycles in H standardized to such modifications.

Sketch of proof: One can use several notations to prove above statement, all of them with some merit. The simplest way is just to check the requirement on coboundary $\partial(\partial h_i) = 1$ from the definition (3.9) using usual explicit summation notation for coexpansion of e.r.p.s. Similarly to see that $\partial(\chi^{h_i}) = 1$ if $\partial\chi = 1$, and to check the coagency conditions. One may proceed directly in terms of linear maps and compute that equality

$$(1 \otimes \chi^{h_i})(id \otimes \Delta)\chi^{h_i} = (\chi^{h_i} \otimes 1)(\Delta \otimes id)\chi^{h_i}$$

is valid for the main result. □

It may be worthy to note that if H is any biagreement and χ is a 2-cocycle then H_χ is a biagreement. If H is an enterprise then so is H_χ, and if H is an open biagreement or open enterprise then so is H_χ. To these we may attach an analysis from point of view of e.p.r.s structure and its properties. Namely, we may recall that a 1-cocycle for H means an invertible e.p.r.s rule-like element h_i. It is not difficult to see that it defines an inner autotransaction, or an e.p.r.s valuation concept $H \to H$ as biagreements or entrepreneurial agreements by $h \mapsto h_i h h_i^{-1}$. This explicitly means that we are dealing with a biagreeable, and in the case of enterprise, an entrepreneurial map. In the case of an open enterprise, it is this economic transaction that preserves opening $\mathcal{R}$ as well.

3.3.2 Some New Simple Forms

Recall from section 3.1 when we considered properties of a simple open enterprise that conditions of a full e.r.p.s entrepreneurial arrangement were weakened. The relaxation of entrepreneurial constrains has concentrated on properties of coagent in the sense that a new form of enterprise carries property of simplified e.p.r.s reasoning of copartners (cocommutativity) only up to conjugation by an element of $\mathcal{R} \in H \otimes H$, obeying some additional properties. This element $\mathcal{R}$ is of an e.p.r.s quasitriangular structure, and in the EPRT it carries an interpretation of opening relations of a biagreement or simple enterprise H.

From economic point of view the main issue in a confirmation procedure of an opening (cocycling and twisting) is formation of new e.p.r.s structures. Namely, results of a confirmation process are new open enterprises. The crucial point is that process of twisting can only give a genuinely new enterprise if the assessment of copartner about e.p.r.s structure and properties of a path used to twist are nontrivial. Recall that, if a space of confirmation $\mathcal{H}^2$ is trivial for an enterprise, then all twistings carry the same collection of e.p.r.s in economic transactions (they are isomorphic). It is plausible that such circumstances do not happen often and the twisting process does generally provide source of new open enterprises from old ones. Formally, we are dealing with the problem of formulation of the cohomology of group in terms of Hopf algebras $\mathcal{H}^n(\mathbf{h}, H)$.

Theorem 3.25. *Let an open enterprise,* $(H, \mathcal{R})$, *be given and let* χ *be an opening coagency type 2-cocycle. Then there is a new open enterprise* $(H_\chi, \mathcal{R}_\chi)$ *defined by the same agency and coagency, and coexpansion of e.p.r.s with the property that*

$$\Delta_\chi h = \chi(\Delta h)\chi^{-1}, \quad \mathcal{R}_\chi = \chi_{21}\mathcal{R}\chi^{-1}, \quad \gamma_\chi h = U(\gamma h)U^{-1}$$

for all $h \in H_\chi$. *Here* $U = \sum \chi^{(1)}(\gamma\chi^{(2)})$ *and is invertible.*

Sketch of proof and comments: Note that first generalization of this theorem is given by Theorem 3.32 below, and a more complete discussion on issues of new entrepreneurial structures with appropriate e.p.r.s interpretation is given later within a setting of e.p.r.s categories, clubs and leading e.p.r.s institutions in Chapter 4.
(i) Let us check first that Δ_χ is coassociative. One has,

$$\begin{aligned}
(\Delta_\chi \otimes id)\Delta_\chi h &= \chi_{12}((\Delta \otimes id)(\chi(\Delta h)\chi^{-1}))\chi_{12}^{-1} \\
&= \chi_{12}((\Delta \otimes id)\chi)((\Delta \otimes id)\Delta h)((\Delta \otimes id)\chi^{-1})\chi_{12}^{-1}, \\
(id \otimes \Delta_\chi)\Delta_\chi h &= \chi_{23}(id \otimes \Delta)(\chi(\Delta h)\chi^{-1})\chi_{23}^{-1} \\
&= \chi_{23}((id \otimes \Delta)\chi)((id \otimes \Delta)\Delta h)((id \otimes \Delta)\chi^{-1})\chi_{23}^{-1}.
\end{aligned}$$

Then applying the condition that we are dealing with 2-cocycle, it is not hard to see that those two expressions are equal, given that coexpansion Δ is already coassociative. Since opening conditioning by χ is an agreement autotransaction, it is clear that Δ_χ is still an agreeable map.
(ii) Let us now verify that $\mathcal{R}_\chi$ is an opening for the biagreement H_χ. It is evidently invertible as $\chi, \mathcal{R}$ are. It can be computed,

$$\begin{aligned}
(\Delta_\chi \otimes id)\mathcal{R}_\chi &= \chi_{12}((\Delta \otimes id)(\tau(\chi)\mathcal{R}\chi^{-1}))\chi_{12}^{-1} \\
&= \chi_{12}((\Delta \otimes id)\tau(\chi))((\Delta \otimes id)\mathcal{R})((\Delta \otimes id)\chi^{-1})\chi_{12}^{-1}, \\
&= \chi_{12}((\Delta \otimes id)\tau(\chi))\mathcal{R}_{13}\mathcal{R}_{23}((\Delta \otimes id)\chi^{-1})\chi_{23}^{-1}, \\
&= \chi_{12}((\Delta \otimes id)\tau(\chi))\mathcal{R}_{13}((id \otimes \tau \circ \Delta)\chi^{-1})\mathcal{R}_{23}\chi_{23}^{-1} \\
&= \chi_{31}(\chi^{(1)}_{\ (2)} \otimes \chi^{(2)} \otimes \chi^{(1)}_{\ (1)})\mathcal{R}_{13}((id \otimes \tau \circ \Delta)\chi^{-1})\mathcal{R}_{23}\chi_{23}^{-1} \\
&= \chi_{31}\mathcal{R}_{23}(\chi^{(1)}_{\ (2)} \otimes \chi^{(2)} \otimes \chi^{(1)}_{\ (2)})\mathcal{R}_{13}((id \otimes \tau \circ \Delta)\chi^{-1})\mathcal{R}_{23}\chi_{23}^{-1} \\
&= \chi_{31}\mathcal{R}_{13}\chi_{13}^{-1}\chi_{32}((id \otimes \tau \circ \Delta)\chi)((id \otimes \tau \circ \Delta)\chi^{-1})\mathcal{R}_{32}\chi_{23}^{-1} \\
&= \chi_{31}\mathcal{R}_{13}\chi_{13}^{-1}\chi_{32}\mathcal{R}_{32}\chi_{23}^{-1} = (\mathcal{R}_\chi)_{13}(\mathcal{R}_\chi)_{23}.
\end{aligned}$$

The proof that $(id \otimes \Delta_\chi)\mathcal{R}_\chi = (\mathcal{R}_\chi)_{13}(\mathcal{R}_\chi)_{12}$ is similar, so that both conditions of the axiom (3.1) for $\mathcal{R}_\chi$, are obtained. The axiom (3.2) for $\mathcal{R}_\chi, H_\chi$ is automatic as

$$\begin{aligned}\tau \circ \Delta_\chi h &= \chi_{21}(\tau \circ \Delta h)\chi_{21}^{-1} = \chi_{21}\mathcal{R}(\Delta h)\mathcal{R}^{-1}\chi_{21}^{-1} \\ &= \mathcal{R}_\chi \chi(\Delta h)\chi^{-1}\mathcal{R}^{-1} = \mathcal{R}_\chi(\Delta_\chi h)\mathcal{R}_\chi^{-1}.\end{aligned}$$

(*iii*) Now, if H is an enterprise, we check that γ_χ is a mutual understanding map for H_χ. To do this we first establish that U is invertible. Note that one can define $U^{-1} = (\gamma\chi^{-(1)})\chi^{-(2)}$, we have $\chi^{-1} = \chi^{-(1)} \otimes \chi^{-(2)}$ in this notation, and check that $U^{-1}U = 1 = UU^{-1}$. It can also be checked that $\circ(\gamma_\chi \otimes id)\Delta_\chi h = \varepsilon(h) = \circ(id \otimes \gamma_\chi)\Delta_\chi h$ using the definitions, elementary properties of a mutual understanding map, and the fact that $UU^{-1} = 1$. Note that one can study these elements U, U^{-1} in an analogous way as for u, u^{-1} in Proposition 3.24. So for example, they are not e.p.r.s rule-like, but rather one has $\Delta = \chi^{-1}(U \otimes U)(\gamma \otimes \gamma)\chi_{21}^{-1}$, which actually, from the point of view of underlying e.p.r.s structure of copartner, means that $\chi \sim (\gamma \otimes \gamma)\chi_{21}^{-1}$.
□

Proposition 3.26. *Let χ, ψ be 2-cocycles. The enterprises obtained by implementations these types of cocycle opening, as in the preceding theorem, are isotransactive via an inner autotransaction if χ, ψ are same according to their e.p.r.s structures of coexpansion and their properties. In particular, if χ is a coboundary then its implementation can be canceled by an inner autotransaction.*

Sketch of proof: Note that the first statement can be shown, proving that there is a map from space of rules confirmation $\mathcal{H}^2(\mathbf{h}, H)$ to the set of confirmations of H up to inner autotransactions. Formally, there is a map from space $\mathcal{H}^2(\mathbf{h}, H)$ to the set of twistings of H up to inner autotransaction. An assumption that χ, ψ are same up to structures of their coexpansions of e.p.r.s and their properties actually means that χ, ψ are cohomologous in the sense discussed in Proposition 3.24 above. By definition this means that $\psi = (h_i \otimes h_i)\chi\Delta h_i^{-1}$ for some invertible elements $h_i \in H$. Then we can write the coexpansion of e.p.r.s Δ_ψ in the following form

$$\begin{aligned}\Delta_\psi(h) &= \psi(\Delta h)\psi^{-1} \\ &= (h_i \otimes h_i)\chi(\Delta h_i^{-1})(\Delta h)(\Delta h_i)\chi^{-1}(h_i^{-1} \otimes h_i^{-1}) \\ &= (h_i \otimes h_i)(\Delta_\chi(h_i^{-1} h h_i))(h_i^{-1} \otimes h_i^{-1}).\end{aligned}$$

Here $h_i(\ )h_i^{-1}$ is an inner autotransaction of the agreemental structure. Thus, we see that it now defines an economic transaction of open type between enterprises carrying appropriate e.p.r.s collection. This means that $H_\psi \to H_\chi$, is an biagreement isotransaction. In the case where H has mutual understanding map, becoming an enterprise, it is also an entrepreneurial autotransaction. One can also check this directly from the formulae given for the mutual understanding map after conforming. Finally, if H is an open enterprise then

$$\begin{aligned}\mathcal{R}_\psi &= \psi_{21}\mathcal{R}\phi^{-1} = (h_i \otimes h_i)\chi_{21}(\Delta^{op} h_i^{-1})\mathcal{R}(\Delta h_i)\chi^{-1}(h_i^{-1} \otimes h_i^{-1}) \\ &= (h_i \otimes h_i)\mathcal{R}_\chi(h_i^{-1} \otimes h_i^{-1})\end{aligned}$$

where we were using axiom (3.2) of an open enterprise. One can conclude that the induced isotransaction maps the opening structures as well, if these are present. □

Example 3.27. Let H be an open enterprise and let 2-cocycle be defined by its opening, $\chi = \mathcal{R}$. Then H_χ is the open enterprise of H^{cop} type with the opposite coexpansion of e.p.r.s as in Proposition 3.3

Sketch of proof and comments: Particularity of this example is that the quasitriangular e.p.r.s structure, which describes an opening $\mathcal{R}$ for an enterprise H, is taken as a 2-cocycle. But, one can think of any opening $\mathcal{R}$, having in mind axioms (3.1), and opening cleaning condition discussed in Lemma (3.4), as a 2-cocycle. The result is then obvious, having in mind conditions of axiom (3.2). On the other hand, we know from previous sections, and particularly from Proposition 3.3, that H^{cop} has for its mutual understanding map γ^{-1}, where γ is the mutual understanding map of enterprise H. Thus, for H^{cop} one can recover the e.p.r.s structure of opening $\mathcal{R}_{21}\mathcal{R}\mathcal{R}^{-1} = \mathcal{R}_{21}$, and from Theorem 3.25 one has that $\gamma^{-1}h = U(\gamma h)U^{-1}$, or $\gamma^{-2}h = UhU^{-1}$. So, one may take $U = v$ in Proposition 3.24, and recovers the result stated in the Proposition as an example of the conforming theorem. Note that $\mathcal{R}_{21}^{-1}$ is another 2-cocycle which could be used for confirmation, and in this case one recovers the results for $U = u$. □

It is noteworthy that from results above the confirmation theorem can be used in general as a provider of new e.p.r.s structured enterprises. One may begin with elementary examples of enterprises such as $\mathbf{h}G, U(g)$, which have trivial opening with $\mathcal{R} = 1 \otimes 1$, and systematically modify an underlying exclusive dominant e.p.r.s structure by introducing a 2-cocycle χ, possibly depending on one or more parameters as for example appropriation parameter. This modification can then result in a nontrivial e.p.r.s rule, and one may think of it informally as the initial enterprise being modified and/or e.p.r.s restructured so that a nontrivial (not pure exclusive dominant) rule of ownership is accepted. As a way of obtaining new e.p.r.s rules from ordinary pure dominant economic reasoning or enveloping agreements, this confirmation procedure by itself will only generate trivial opening. Namely, if our initial opening $\mathcal{R}$ is trivial, then after confirmation we have $\mathcal{R} = \chi_{21}\chi^{-1}$, so that $\tau(\mathcal{R}^{-1}) = \tau(\chi\chi_{21}^{-1}) = \mathcal{R}$. On the other hand, the entire theory of trivial opening rules obtained in this way is governed by χ so that other structures with which our initial cocommutative enterprise interacted can be systematically modified - restructured at the same time by introducing χ in their definitions above. This provides an economic frame for systematic approach to e.p.r.s modification - restructuring issues which are addressed in details in Chapter 5.

One should have in mind that the initial enterprise for our confirmation procedure according to Theorem 3.25 above, does not have to be cocommutative or a simple enterprise. Instead, one could view the theorem as a kind of confirmation-equivalence for e.p.r.s rules in economic reasoning. Two open enterprises my look very different, but, if they are related by a confirmation procedure, their agreements can be identified, and after this their coexpansions of e.r.p.s differ only by opening by a 2-cocycle χ. This in turn means that their properties are very similar and differ only by the effects of the 2-cocycle. For example, it means that all the representations of the two enterprises coincide and their aggregate expansions, according to Chapter 2, also coincide up to economic isotransaction with argumentation by the 2-cocycle χ as an interconfirmation. Thus, confirmation or twisting - equivalence is a powerful concept which, at the same time, provides a systematic approach to a modification-restructuring problem in EPRT.

Also, if one thinks of confirmation as a kind of equivalence or measurement modification, then it is clear that when it is implemented we also have to conform other e.p.r.s structures defined on an enterprise or those with which it interacts, if we want the analogous relationships to be maintained. Likewise from the modification-restructuring point of view, if we want the restructuring to respects all relations. Examples are the concept of $*$-structure from the point of view of e.p.r.s gains and welfare effects, and the concept of e.p.r.s standardized agreements discussed in Sections 2.2.1 and 2.3.2 in Chapter 2. From economic point of view, it may be noteworthy that an intention for economic restructuring which implies completely different or modified e.p.r.s structure is also legitimate intention and is discussed in Chapter 4.

Proposition 3.28. *Let elements of a new enterprise be given as in Theorem 3.25. If H is an enterprise with welfare structure of $*$-agreement over a domain of claims that allows speculations in the sense of a simple enterprise with externalities defined by 2.46, and its mutual understanding map ensures real impact of opening in the sense that $(\gamma \otimes \gamma)(\chi^{*\otimes *}) = \chi_{21}$, then welfare modification*

$$*_\chi = (\gamma^{-1}U)((\ )^*)\gamma^{-1}U^{-1} \tag{3.13}$$

makes H_χ in Theorem 3.25 into a welfare enterprise as well. This welfare enterprise is real (virtual) open enterprise whenever H is.

Sketch of proof: Note that allowing speculation simply means that domain of e.p.r.s claims is complex field. From the assumption that we are dealing with 'real' χ one may conclude that $U^* = \gamma^{-2}U$, and hence that $\gamma^{-1}U$ is self-adjoint under welfare e.p.r.s structure $*$. This implies that $(*_\chi)^2 = id$. Similarly, it is easy to see that $(\gamma_\chi \circ *_\chi)^2 = id$. For compatibility with the coexpansion of e.p.r.s, we may use the properties of U, U^{-1} obtained in the same manner as computations of u, u^{-1} in Proposition 3.6. So, they may not be rule-like but rather of the for $\Delta U = \chi^{(1)}(U \otimes U)\gamma \otimes \gamma)\chi_{21}^{-(1)}$, which actually claims that $\chi \cong (\gamma \otimes \gamma)\chi_{21}^{-1}$. Thus, from $\Delta\gamma^{-1}U$ we see that

$$
\begin{aligned}
&(*_\chi \otimes *_\chi)(\Delta_\chi h)(\gamma^{-1}U)\chi^{-(1)^*} h^*_{(1)}\chi^{-(2)*}h^*_{(2)}\chi^{(2)*}\gamma^{-1}U^{-1} \\
&=\chi^{(1)}(\gamma^{-1}U)h^*_{(1)}(\gamma^{-1}U^{-1})_{(1)}\chi^{-(1)}\otimes\chi^{(2)}(\gamma^{-1}U)_{(2)}h^{*(2)}(\gamma^{-1}U^{-1})_{(2)}\chi^{-(2)} \\
&= \Delta_\chi \circ *_\chi(h),
\end{aligned}
$$

as required. If H is a real open enterprise, then we have

$$
\begin{aligned}
(*_\chi \otimes *_\chi)(\mathcal{R}_\chi) &= (\gamma^{-1}U \otimes \gamma^{-1}U)\chi^{-1*\otimes*}\mathcal{R}_{21}\chi_{21}^{*\otimes*}(\gamma^{-1}U^{-1} \otimes \gamma^{-1}U^{-1}) \\
&= \chi^{-(1)}(\Delta\gamma^{-1}U)\mathcal{R}_{21}(\tau \circ \Delta\gamma^{-1}U^{-1})\chi_{21}^{-1} = (\mathcal{R}_\chi)_{21}
\end{aligned}
$$

using appropriate expression for ΔU again and the assumption on openness. The proof is similar for virtual opening effects. □

3.4 Quasiinstitutions

Recall from Section 3.1 when we considered properties of a simple open enterprise that conditions of a full e.r.p.s entrepreneurial arrangement were weakened. The relaxation of entrepreneurial constrains has concentrated on properties of coagent in the sense that new form of enterprise carries property of simplified e.p.r.s reasoning only up to conjugation by an element of $\mathcal{R} \in H \otimes H$, obeying some additional properties. This element $\mathcal{R}$ is of an e.p.r.s quasitriangular structure, and in the EPRT it carries an interpretation of opening relations of a biagreement or simple enterprise H. Here an idea is to continue with relaxing the simple open biagreement or enterprise. Now, not only is the condition of simplified e.p.r.s reasoning of copartner valid only to opening conjugation, but in addition this same principle governs a property of coassociativity of coexpansion of e.p.r.s of a copartner in a biagreement or an enterprise. This then give us a new concept of an enterprise, i.e. an open quasienterprise. Note that from formal point of view we are applying concept of Drinfeld's quasitriangular quasi-Hopf algebras.

3.4.1 Definitions

Let as formulate the above ideas on a new concept of an enterprise more precisely. It addition to relaxing constrains of a full entrepreneurial arrangements as already mentioned, the motivation for a qasienterpenerial formulation is that this concept allows an introduction the elements of economic confirmation as part of an open entrepreneurial arrangement more precisely and clearly.

Thus, having the elements of an open biagreement and enterprise already clarified from the previous sections we get,

Definition 3.29. (Open quasibiagreement) *An open quasibiagreement is* $(H, \Delta, \varepsilon, \phi, \mathcal{R})$, *where:*

(i) H *is an agency agreement;*
(ii) $\Delta : H \to H$ *is an agreeable economic transaction such that*

$$(id \otimes \Delta) \circ \Delta = \phi((\Delta \otimes id) \circ \Delta(\ ))\phi^{-1}; \tag{3.14}$$

(iii) The axioms for the coagency ε *are those of the usual biagreement;*
(iv) The element $\phi \in H \otimes H \otimes H$ *controls the nonassociativity of an agency. Control is invertible and has a property that*

$$(1 \otimes \phi)((id \otimes \Delta \otimes id)\phi)(\phi \otimes 1) = ((id \otimes id \otimes \Delta)\phi)((\Delta \otimes id \otimes id)\phi); \tag{3.15}$$

(v) An opening $\mathcal{R} \in H \otimes H$ *is invertible and still intertwines the coexpansion of e.p.r.s. Its opposite is as in basic definition of opening* (3.2),

$$\tau \circ \Delta h = \mathcal{R}(\Delta h)\mathcal{R}^{-1}, \ \forall h \in H, \tag{3.16}$$

but other two axioms, (3.1), *that define a simple open biagreement are modified by control* ϕ *to*

$$(\Delta \otimes id)\mathcal{R} = \phi_{312}\mathcal{R}_{13}\phi_{132}^{-1}\mathcal{R}_{23}\phi, \tag{3.17}$$
$$(id \otimes \Delta)\mathcal{R} = \phi_{231}^{-1}\mathcal{R}_{13}\phi_{213}\mathcal{R}_{12}\phi^{-1} \tag{3.18}$$

in the usual notation.

Note that if we denote by $\phi = \sum \phi^{(1)} \otimes \phi^{(2)} \otimes \phi^{(3)}$ then $\phi_{213} = \sum \phi^{(2)} \otimes \phi^{(1)} \otimes \phi^{(3)}$, etc. These axioms are also motivated by the representation theory, where the mutual understanding map corresponds to the existence of dual representations, that is going to be used later on in Chapter 4.

One may note that the condition (3.15) above corresponds to requirement that control is 3-cocycle. Thus, a quasibiagreement can be expressed by the $(H, \Delta, \varepsilon, \phi)$.

Definition 3.30. (Open quasienterprise) *An open quasienterprise is defined as an open quasibiagreement* $(H, \Delta, \varepsilon, \phi, \mathcal{R})$, *with extended mutual understanding map to the triple* (γ, α, β), *where:*
(vi) $\alpha, \beta \in H$ *and* $\gamma : H \to H$ *obeying the following additional axioms,*

$$\sum(\gamma h_{(1)})\alpha h_{(2)} = \varepsilon(h)\alpha, \ \sum h_{(1)}\beta h_{(2)} = \varepsilon(h)\beta, \ \forall h \in H, \tag{3.19}$$
$$\sum \phi^{(1)}\beta(\gamma\phi^{(2)})\alpha\phi^{(3)} = 1 \ \sum(\gamma\phi^{-(1)})\alpha\phi^{-(2)}\beta\gamma\phi^{-(3)} = 1 \tag{3.20}$$

and is determined uniquely up to a transformation $\alpha \mapsto U\alpha$, $\beta \mapsto \beta U^{-1}$, $\gamma h \mapsto U(\gamma h)U^{-1}$, *for any invertible* $U \in H$.

An open quasienterprise can be expressed by $(H, \Delta, \varepsilon, \phi, \gamma, \alpha, \beta, \mathcal{R})$, with conditions $(i) - (vi)$ satisfied from Definition 3.29 and Definition 3.30 above. To understand the meaning of these definitions more completely and to follow examples one should have in mind that they are based on more advanced aspects of the EPRT. These are linked with opening cocycling and e.p.r.s transformations, which introductory view was given in the previous subsection on confirmation, while some issues are discussed below and more advanced approach in Chapter 5.

Example 3.31. Let H be an ordinary enterprise, and let a control ϕ be given such that satisfies conditions (ii), (3.14) and (iii) from Definition of a quasibiagreement 3.29. Then (H, ϕ) is a quasienterprise. The extended mutual understanding map of this quasienterprise, (γ, α, β) undertakes the γ, from the initial enterprise H while $\beta = 1$, and $\alpha = c^{-1}$, where $c = \sum \phi^{(1)}(\gamma\phi^{(2)})\phi^{(3)}$ is central. It is assumed that ϕ and c are invertible. Moreover, if $F \in H \otimes H$ is invertible and modified adjoint-invariant in the sense that $(\Delta h)F = F\Delta h$ for all $h \in H$, the $\phi = \partial F$ is a modified adjoint-invariant 3-cocycle of type required.

Sketch of proof and comments: In the general case, when H is not based on simplified e.p.r.s reasoning of agency implying noncocommutative, the modified adjoint-invariance conditions given in this Example are different requirements than those given under the e.p.r.s adjoint argumentation from Example 2.30 in Chapter 2 extended to aggregate powers. That is the reason why it is called modified. It is clear that if condition (ii) (3.14) from definition for quasibiagreement holds, and a control ϕ is coagency 3-cocycle, then we have that (H, ϕ) forms a quasibiagreement. To show that it carries the quasienterprise structure, we have to verify the conditions for an extended mutual understanding map, and the 3-cocycle condition. First, the modified adjoint-invariance condition (3.14) means that

$$\begin{aligned} h\phi^{(1)}(\gamma\phi^{(2)})\phi^{(3)} &= h_{(1)}\phi^{(1)}(\gamma\phi^{(2)})(\gamma h_{(2)})h_{(3)}\phi^{(3)} \\ &= (h_{(1)}\phi^{(1)})(\gamma(h_{(2)}\phi^{(2)}))h_{(3)}\phi^{(3)} \\ &= (\phi^{(1)}h_{(1)})(\gamma(\phi^{(2)}h_{(2)}))\phi^{(3)}h_{(3)} = \phi^{(1)}(\gamma\phi^{(2)})\phi^{(3)}h, \end{aligned}$$

so c as stated is central. Thus, we can satisfy axiom (3.19), and the first part of (3.20) if we use the data from example, i.e. with $\alpha = c^{-1}$ and $\beta = 1$. The condition of 3-cocycle (3.12) then implies that $c = (\gamma\phi^{-(1)})\phi^{-(2)}\gamma\phi^{-(3)}$ also. Hence we conclude that the second part of (3.20) holds. Note that, although the requirement to ensure higher level of compatibility of structures and properties for a general enterprise and confirmation is not so easy to ensure as in the simple (commutative) case, the problems due to 3-cocycle property is not unavoidable. More precisely, one can show that if F is a modified adjoint-invariant in the sense that $(\Delta h)F = F\Delta h$, then $\partial^2 F = 1$, i.e. $\phi = \partial F$ is a 3-cocycle required for this example. The computation is left for next theorem as a special case. That ϕ is then ad-invariant is obvious form the definition of ∂F in terms of the $\Delta_i F$, since each of these is modified adjoint-invariant. □

3.4.2 Some Properties

The numerous results familiar for ordinary enterprises and simple open enterprises can be extended to the quasienterprenerial type of relations. In that case a control ϕ and elements of entrepreneurial structure built from it, provide the frame for conjugation. This type of extensions has already been exploited in formulation of the notion of the extended mutual understanding map. Namely, the more general notion is needed because, in general, the concepts of argumentation and coargumentation, α, β respectively, in general do not preserve existing e.p.r.s structure (α and β cannot be taken to be unity), except in the case of trivial control ϕ. Finally, in this more general setting we have the following generalization of the Theorem 3.25 where quasi-structure of an institution is base for generalization.

Theorem 3.32. *Let an open quasienterprise $(H, \alpha, \beta, \phi, \mathcal{R})$ be given, and let F be an arbitrary invertible element of $H \otimes H$ such that $(\varepsilon \otimes id)F = 1 = (id \otimes \varepsilon)F$. Then H_F, is also a quasienterprise when defined as follows:*
(a) H_F is constituted by the agreement that is the same as in H and the coagreement where coagency is the same as in H while coexpansion of e.p.r.s is $\Delta_F h = F(\Delta h)F^{-1}$.
(b) opening is defined by $\mathcal{R}_F = F_{21}\mathcal{R}F^{-1}$;
(c) control by $\phi_F = F_{23}((id \otimes \Delta)F)\phi((\Delta \otimes id)F^{-1})F_{12}^{-1}$, and
(d) extended mutual understanding by

$$\gamma_F = \gamma, \ \ \alpha_F = \sum(\gamma F^{-(1)})\alpha F^{-(2)}, \beta_F = \sum F^{(1)}\beta\gamma F^{(2)}. \tag{3.21}$$

Sketch of proof and comments: As already mentioned, a generalization of this theorem with appropriate e.p.r.s interpretation is given within discussion of e.p.r.s categories, clubs, leading institutions and similar in Chapter 4. Let us first recall a few comments on cocycles on e.p.r.s rules and their links with an enterprise. Namely, we are already familiar with the basics of the idea how cocycles on e.p.r.s rules or simple growth agreements can be extended and formulated at the level of an enterprise. An n-cocycle for an enterprise or biagreement is an invertible element $\phi \in H^{\otimes n}$ such that $\partial\phi = 1$, and a cochain or cocycle is of a coagency type if $\varepsilon_i\phi = 1$ for all $\varepsilon_i = id \otimes \cdots \otimes \varepsilon \otimes \cdots id$. One should have in mind that the process of twisting can only give a genuinely new enterprise if the opening ϕ used to twist is nontrivial from point of view of generated appropriation. Recall, that formulation of the derived appropriation rules in terms of an enterprise means that one has $\partial^2 = 1$ and rules of appropriation $\mathcal{H}^n(\mathbf{h}, H)$ for n derived appropriation. One may also try to apply the same definitions to their forms of enterprises and even when applied to the nonsimple enterprise $\mathbf{h}G$ or $U(g)$ we will see that notions become novel and imply nontrivial constructions. In addition for these and other nonsimple enterprises one should be careful because we may not have

$\partial^2 = 1$, and the intended appropriation configuration. Recall that $\mathcal{H}^1(\mathbf{h}, H)$, and $\mathcal{H}^2(\mathbf{h}, H)$ e.p.r.s spaces are well defined for any biagreement or enterprise. This is obvious as in fact $\mathcal{H}^1(\mathbf{h}, H)$ is the same as the 1-cocycles, as 0-cocycles are invertible elements of the e.p.r.s domain $\mathbf{h}$, and their coboundary from definition (3.9) is always 1. Thus we may conclude that $\mathcal{H}^1(\mathbf{h}, H)$ is the rule of invertible e.p.r.s rule-like elements in a biagreement or enterprise. In considering $\mathcal{H}^2(\mathbf{h}, H)$ one may have in mind that if $h_{in} \in H$ is an invertible element with $\varepsilon h_{in} = 1$, then ∂h_{in} is a coagency 2-cocycle for H. Recall that it is a coboundary. More generally, if ϕ is a coagency 2-cocycle, then $\phi^{h_{in}} = (\partial_+ h_{in})\phi(\partial_- h_{in}^{-1}) = (h_{in} \otimes h_{in})\phi \Delta h_{in}^{-1}$ is also a coagency 2-cocycle. We say that it is appropriational rule over derivatives to control ϕ. The non-Abelian space of appropriational rules $\mathcal{H}^2(\mathbf{h}, H)$ consists of the coagency 2-cocycles in H standardized by such transformations. In addition, it can be shown that for an open enterprise $(H, \mathcal{R})$ and control ϕ there is a new open enterprise $(H_\phi, \mathcal{R}_\phi)$ defined by the same agreement and coagency, and with the other elements of opening defined by $\Delta_\phi h = \phi(\Delta h)\phi^{-1}$, $\mathcal{R}_\phi = \phi_{21}\mathcal{R}\phi^{-1}$, $\gamma_\phi h = U(\gamma h)U^{-1}$ for all $h \in H_\phi$. Here $U = \sum \phi^{(1)}(\gamma\phi^{(2)})$ and it is invertible. Thus, if Δ already fails to be coassociative up to control ϕ, then an arbitrary F means that coassociativity of Δ_F also fails, up to the new ϕ_F as stated. This proves the condition (3.18) for the new $\mathcal{R}_F$. In dealing with the new mutual understanding maps we have to have in mind that in general α_F, β_F can not be kept trivial, so that we may try to keep $\gamma_F = \gamma$ and define α_F and β_F to play the role of U^{-1}, U. Finally we have to check that ϕ_F is a 3-cocycle for H_F if ϕ is a 3-cocycle for H. Here we may use the well-known algebraic method, due to the fact that H is quasienterprise, the algebra of the face maps Δ_i is

$$\Delta_i \Delta_j = \Delta_{j+1}\Delta_i, \quad i < j, \quad \Delta_i \Delta_i = \phi^{-1}(\Delta_{i+1}\Delta_i)\phi$$

in view of condition (3.16). The 3-cocycle condition for ϕ is

$$(\Delta_0\phi)(\Delta_2\phi)(\Delta_4\phi) = (\Delta_3\phi)(\Delta_1\phi),$$

and by definition

$$\phi_F = (\partial_+ F)\phi(\partial_- F^{-1}) = (\Delta_0 F)(\Delta_2 F)\phi(\Delta_1 F^{-1})(\Delta_3 F^{-1}).$$

Then using this notation it can be show that equality

$$((\Delta_F)_0\phi_F)((\Delta_F)_2\phi_F)((\Delta_F)_4\phi_F) = ((\Delta_F)_3\phi_F)((\Delta_F)_1\phi_F)$$

is valid. In addition it is easy to see that ϕ_F is coagency if ϕ and F are. $\square$

It is noteworthy that as a special case of this theorem, we have that implementation of a control into an ordinary enterprise by an arbitrary invertible element F takes us out of the class of ordinary enterprises, by introducing an 'associativity deficit'

$$\phi = \partial F \equiv F_{23}((id \otimes \Delta)F)((\Delta \otimes id)F^{-1})F_{12}^{-1}$$

as the coboundary of a control F. It obeys the 3-cocycle condition relative to the coexpansion of e.p.r.s. modified for manipulation with control F, $F(\Delta\ )F^{-1}$, rather then the original one, Δ. This is another way of saying that, for an enterprise which is not built on simplified e.p.r.s reasoning of agency, i.e. noncommutative H, one does not have a standard correspondence of structures and properties for coagency through 3-cycles (the theory of appropriational rule over third derivative may not be valid) but something slightly more complicated. If F is a control implemented by 2-cocycle, as was discussed above then $\phi = 1$, and we remain within an enterprise.

Also from results above it is obvious that concept of a quasienterprise provides a larger class than one of ordinary enterprise, but one that is closed under implementation of arbitrary controls and/or manipulation of e.p.r.s. This gives a much more general kind of 'twisting-equivalence' than one discussed above. In particular, many important ordinary open enterprises can be greatly simplified in their structure by the more general implementations to an equivalent quasienterprise. For example, a certain ad-invariant 3-cocycle control ϕ can be determined for $U(g)$ in the setting of the Example 3.31, for all complex simple growing agreements (modeled by Lie algebras) g. There is also an opening $\mathcal{R}$ obeying (3.18), given by the exponential of the inverse form of opening, $(\mathcal{R}_{21}\mathcal{R})^{-1}$, (which is ad-invariant). Then, such an open quasienterprise, $(U(g), \phi, \mathcal{R})$ is an equivalent, in the sense of implementation and manipulation after an appropriate e.p.r.s restructuring by an isotransaction, to the open enterprise $U_{ap}(g)$, where ap stands for an appropriation. This means, in particular, that these $U_{ap}(g)$ contain agreements that are isotransactive to $U(g)$, since implementation and manipulation changes only the coexpansion of e.p.r.s and opening structure, etc., but their coexpansion of e.p.r.s is actually an e.p.r.s transformation of deformed opening due to modified appropriation procedures of enterprise considered (described by $U(g)$). As was already mentioned this also means that their representations are just the same as those of $U(g)$, while the aggregate expansion of e.p.r.s of representations are isotransactive via control F to the usual aggregate extension of e.p.r.s of $U(g)$ representations.

Finally the dual of a quasienterprise can be defined in the similar manners as dual structures have been derived for the case of simple open enterprise.

4

Representation Theory

One of the main motivations of the theory of enterprises is that they provide the generalization of the e.p.r.s rules. This continues also in formation of e.p.r.s institutions of more complex structure through an aggregation. Namely, as it was already shown in Chapter 2 by Example 2.35, if an enterprise is represented in a simple form by vector spaces V, W then it is also represented in an aggregate simple form by economic space $V \otimes W$. One may say that the representations of the enterprise allow aggregation among themselves. This is one of the main properties of e.p.r.s rules representations, and is also very important property for enterprises as elementary e.p.r.s institutions. This property has already been used several times in constructing some of the enterprises in previous Chapters. In this Chapter it is studied more precisely and the theory of economic clubs within EPRT is developed.

From formal point of view, theory of e.p.r.s clubs is actually an application of the category theory into economic phenomena of interest. An economic club is just a collection of members (economic objects, i.e. enterprises and their representations in this case), and a specification of what it is to be an allowed economic relation or transaction between any two of them. This approach allows us to introduce a notion of an e.r.p.s appropriation (being a functor) and a notion of an e.p.r.s transformation or economic implementable policy (natural transformation) in order to explain what should be meant by a characterization of being 'economic natural' for certain economic transactions and/or e.p.r.s institutions in the club. This will also help us to avoid mistaking notions of an economic equality for isotransactions. In addition, in dealing with e.p.r.s institutions one faces necessity to adopt the working compromise of an intuitive or naive approach in developing theory of e.p.r.s institutions to traditional economic theory, a complete rigorous axiomatic development being out of reach. At the same time careful examination of the foundations is required if one wants to avoid paradoxical situations. From point of view of game theory this will allow us to overcome some of conflicts in the sustainable way and to deal with the complexity of wealth flows within and among different e.r.p.s institutions.

In Section 4.1 a few fundamentals of club theory are given, trying to be informal and nontechnical as much as possible. Beside necessary definitions, some properties of general clubs and leading clubs are studied. One may recall that according to the traditional economic theories economic agents and/or institutions are either efficient, profitable, winners or not; there is not much more to be said. The idea of a club concept is to allow more sophisticated economic analysis where members may carry elements of imperfection and inefficiency, but still to be 'the efficient in a way'. In other words unequal e.p.r.s collections may be considered in an exchange but still be supported by an economic transaction which is an isotransaction. Even better one can keep track of the way they are efficient: the isotransaction itself. This underlies the modern concept of economic laws: as a member can be 'economic efficient and itself carrying elements of inefficiency', it has an e.p.r.s symmetric rule that internalize these elements of imperfection forming its rule on autotransactions. It is important to note that in a club this careful distinction between economic equality and isotransaction breaks down when we study the general economic transactions. Transactions in a club are either efficient or inefficient and the problem can be overcome by appropriate extension of a club. Here are also given some theorems about general leading clubs, not necessarily coming from a biagreement or an enterprise, such as the construction of a dual leading club.

In Section 4.2 the generalizations of open biagreements or open enterprises, as the continuation of Chapter 3, are discussed. The structure of opening or universal 'market relations' is new ingredient and it appears that it is just what is needed to ensure an economic equality between any two representations in a coherent way. One takes such quasisymmetries for granted in case of simple economic rules representations, where they are just usual permutations at the level of underlying vector spaces. However in the general case of e.r.p.s rule they are more complicated since permutation itself carries an e.r.p.s unequality. In this way, the club of representations becomes a leading club with transfers, transferred leading club, or quasiaggregate club, that incorporates sophisticated economic transactions among its members and other clubs. Here the idea is to show how many of e.p.r.s phenomena and constructions in previous chapters can now be understood very conveniently in these club terms, enabling one to follow economic concepts that underlie them rather than to use some formulae. In particular, the club rationality about standard agreements, or system of e.p.r.s covariant rules, is developed. As was already mentioned in Chapter 2, a standard agreement just means an agreement which is a member in the club of representations of an e.p.r.s. rule. So each e.p.r.s rule generates a club or 'economic universe' in which its covariant agreements are valid. The extensions of these ideas are going to allow us to examine the covariant agreements that allow transfer statistics. For example, one become able to construct superagreements with private-public statistics. These being forms of agreements which are elements of the club or economic universe generated by a nontrivial e.p.r.s rule of private investments combined with public ('welfare') risk transfers. Thus, here conditions are examined for unifying notions of nontrivial statistics and covariance under an e.p.r.s rule into the notion of e.p.r.s rule covariance.

Finally, in Section 4.3 of this Chapter the property of duality that has been extensively discussed for simple institutions in previous Chapters, is generalized to capture relevant economic phenomena on the level of clubs and more complex e.p.r.s institutions. Here, the focus is on entrepreneurial structure where mutual understanding among partners not just biagreement is emphasized. An existence of an invertible e.r.p.s rule allows one to define conjugate representations of e.r.p.s relations between agents in biagreement, so the mutual understanding map is just what is needed to define a conjugate price system of any enterprise representation. In this case the club of representations is rigid. With the rigid frame, one has the notion of aggregate procedures or acceptable mergers between representations, which is itself representation. In this Section the notion of a club e.p.r.s dimension or rank of a representation is introduced, and the connection between e.p.r.s rules and the theory of complex economic redistribution flows taking forms of knotted invariants is addressed. Later on in Chapter 5 we count on reader's understanding of the full structure underlying the representations of a given enterprise, so that formalization provided helps us to reconstruct that enterprise entirely from its representations.

4.1 Clubs, Policies and Leadership

In this section self-contained introduction to the elements of economic club theory that are needed within EPRT is given. Members of a club need not be enterprises and they enter here with an intention to focus on our program, and reader should have in mind that there exist a lot of clubs which primer ideas have noting to do with EPRT. Nevertheless being actually an application of category theory into economics one may think of an intention to be theoretical clear about the objects that one is dealing with and what are the allowed transformations or maps between them.

4.1.1 Definitions and General Construction

For a better understanding and precise discussion about the e.p.r.s institutions and allowed economic transformations and/or economic transactions between them, let us use already formed intuition and consider a collection of enterprises $H_1, H_2, H_3, \ldots,$ and economic mappings between them more precisely. In other words, we are interested in:

(*i*) collection of enterprises involved,
(*ii*) set of economic transactions among them, and
(*iii*) how economic transactions are composed.

At the same time, these are components over which differences and/or similarities between e.p.r.s institutions are to be investigated. The following definition of a club is adopted to provide environment for a more precise and clear discussion on issues of e.p.r.s of interest.

Definition 4.1 (Club of enterprises). *A club M^c refers to a collection of enterprises $H_1, H_2, H_3, \dots,$ and a set of economic transactions among them, $Trn_c(H_i, H_j)$, $i, j = 1, 2, \dots,$ such that:*
(i) For any pair (H_i^c, H_j^c) of enterprises from the club M^c, there is a set of transactions from an enterprise H_i^c to H_j^c, denoted by $Trn_c(H_i^c, H_j^c)$. Sets of transactions $Trn_c(H_i^c, H_j^c)$ and $Trn_c(H_l^c, H_k^c)$ are disjoint unless $H_i^c = H_l^c$ and $H_j^c = H_k^c$, in which case they coincide;
(ii) For any given enterprises H_i^c, H_j^c, H_k^c, of M^c there is an e.p.r.s mapping

$$Trn_c(H_i^c, H_j^c) \times Trn_c(H_j^c, H_k^c) \to Trn_c(H_i^c, H_k^c)$$

described by $(t_2^c, t_1^c) \mapsto t_1^c \circ t_2^c$, with the following properties:
(ii1) For every enterprise H_i^c there is an e.p.r.s preserving transaction, $id_{H_i^c} \in Trn_c(H_i^c, H_i^c)$, that corresponds to the identity of e.p.r.s transactions of the ith enterprise within the club, such that $t^c \circ id_{H_i^c} = t^c$ and $id_{H_i^c} \circ t^c = t^c$, for any transaction t^c for which composition $\circ$ is defined. We may also say that $id_{H_i^c}$ is an e.p.r.s transaction which is a quality preserving argumentation of the ith enterprise in relations to every member of the club, (a quality identity under $\circ$ for the transactions of $Trn_c(H_i^c, H_j^c)$), and a cost (price) preserving argumentation of the ith enterprise in relations to every member of the club, (a cost identity under $\circ$ for transactions of $Trn_c(H_j^c, H_i^c)$);
(ii2) A rule of composition of an economic mapping $\circ$ is 'associative' in the sense that when the compositions of e.p.r.s transactions $t_1^c \circ (t_2^c \circ t_3^c)$ and $(t_1^c \circ t_2^c) \circ t_3^c$ are defined they are equal.
(ii3) A transaction $t^c \in Trn_c(H_i^c, H_j^c)$, is called an e.p.r.s isotransaction if there exists a transaction $(t^c)^{-1} \in Trn_c(H_j^c, H_i^c)$, such that $t^c \circ (t^c)^{-1} \in Trn_c(H_j^c, H_j^c)$ and $(t^c)^{-1} \circ t^c \in Trn_c(H_i^c, H_i^c)$ are identity transactions for the club M^c.

Note that we have not said that the collection of enterprises forms a set and despite of notation of composition $\circ$ used in the definition, the transaction sets $Trn_c(H_i, H_j)$ need not be sets of e.p.r.s mappings. Nevertheless, the notations used write the elements of $Trn_c(H_i, H_j)$, as though they were mappings, $t^c : H_i \to H_j$, and $H_i, H_j \in M^c$, as a natural extension of set theory notation.

In this research we are primarily interested in economic relations between the clubs, and formation of an aggregate e.p.r.s institution. Thus, we need precise definitions and clarifications of properties of economic 'maps' between two clubs with respect their e.p.r.s structure. The following definition is proposed:

Definition 4.2 (Appropriation). *An economic mapping from a club M^{c_k} to another club M^{c_l} is a functor, called an appropriation, F_{ap}. It is an e.p.r.s prescription, that assigns to every enterprise H^{c_k} of M^{c_k} a collection of e.p.r.s $F_{ap}H^{c_k}$ of M^{c_l}, and for every transaction $t^{c_k} : H_i^{c_k} \to H_j^{c_k}$ of M^{c_k} a transaction $F_{ap}(t^{c_k}) : F_{ap}H_i^{c_k} \to F_{ap}E_j^{c_k}$ of club M^{c_l}, such that:*
(i) $F_{ap}id_{H^{c_k}} = id_{F_{ap}H^{c_k}}$ for every enterprise H^{c_k} from M^{c_k};
(ii) if composition of transactions $t_1^{c_k} \circ t_2^{c_k}$ is defined in M^{c_k}, then $F_{ap}t_2^{c_k} \circ F_{ap}t_1^{c_k} = F_{ap}(t_2^{c_k} \circ t_1^{c_k})$.

Note that the above defines a covariant appropriation, while a contravariant appropriation from M^{c_l} to M^{c_k} is actually a covariant appropriation from M^{c_k} to $M^{c_l dual}$. For such an e.p.r.s appropriation the only change in the above definition is that in this case we have $F_{ap}(t_2^{c_k} \circ t_1^{c_k}) = F_{ap}t_1^{c_k} \circ F_{ap}t_2^{c_k}$. Obviously two clubs can be considered to be isomorphic if there exist mutually inverse e.p.r.s appropriations between them. Note that we have not said that such clubs are equal.

The concept of an e.p.r.s transformation or an economic policy concerning e.p.r.s restructuring, is introduced to capture economic relation between the class of all appropriations from a given club M^{c_k} to another club M^{c_l}. We may pose the question:

Can one form the class of appropriations into an enterprise?

In order to do so, in a clear way, it is required to determine what should serve as the economic transactions in such an enterprise. This leads us to the notion of an e.p.r.s transformation or economic policies concerning e.p.r.s structures. They may look somehow forbidding but they are quite ubiquitous. Recall, that many of economic (re)constructing and institutionalizing procedures, as mergings, acquisitions and similar, in an economy are accepted or seem to be accepted as economically natural. Roughly speaking, an underlying coherence of a well defined e.p.r.s transformation makes an economic policy acceptable. An e.p.r.s structure it carries and corresponding transfers of e.p.r.s are implementable just because they respect certain appropriation rules of the economic institutions. Such an economic policy can often be formulated literally as transformation of nature of an economy or reconstitution of the e.p.r.s of an institution. An economist may have in mind variety of so called reforms or restructuring programs in an economy concerning firms, corporations, industries as well as national economies. Note that in comparisons of e.p.r.s institutions a concept of e.p.r.s transformation is also needed. In general, clubs are allowed to be under a variety of economic policies and those implemented interfere with relations among clubs. Let us specify an e.p.r.s transformation more precisely.

Definition 4.3 (E.p.r.s policy). *An e.p.r.s policy or e.p.r.s transformation concerns formation of appropriations. If F_{ap_1} and F_{ap_2}, are two appropria-*

tions, $F_{ap_1}, F_{ap_2} : M^{c_l} \to M^{c_k}$, *then a transformation from* F_{ap_1} *to* F_{ap_2} *is an e.p.r.s rule that assigns to each enterprise* H^{c_l} *of the club* M^{c_l} *an e.p.r.s transaction* $\mathcal{P}_{et(H^{c_l})} : F_{ap_1}E^{c_l} \to F_{ap_2}E^{c_l}$ *of the club* M^{c_k} *in such a way that associated with every transaction* $t^{c_l} : H_i^{c_l} \to H_j^{c_l}$ *in* M^{c_l} *there is a commutative diagram*

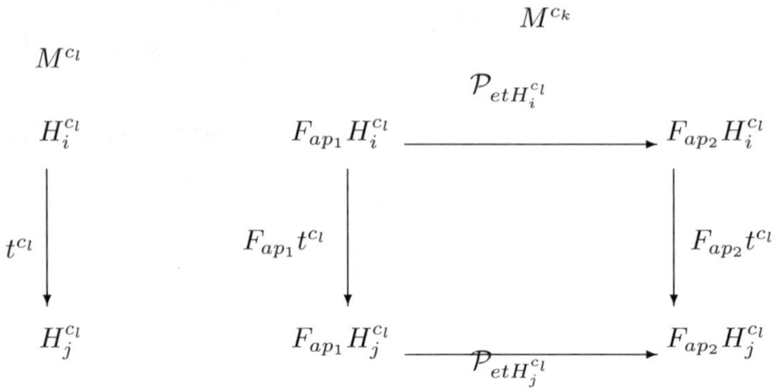

An e.p.r.s transformation that satisfies the above definition is denoted by $\mathcal{P}_{et} : F_{ap_1} \to F_{ap_2}$. In these circumstances, the associated transformations $\mathcal{P}_{etH^{c_l}}$ are often also said to be e.p.r.s natural. As far as comparison of clubs is concerned, notion of e.p.r.s transformation is particularly useful in identifying equivalent clubs from point of view EPRT. Namely, one may say that two clubs are equivalent, i.e., M^{c_k} is equivalent to M^{c_l}, if there exist appropriations $F_{ap_1} : M^{c_l} \to M^{c_k}$ and $F_{ap_2} : M^{c_k} \to M^{c_l}$ such that both way of their composition $F_{ap_1} \circ F_{ap_2}$ and $F_{ap_2} \circ F_{ap_1}$ are equivalent, as e.p.r.s transformations, to the appropriate mapping that preserves e.p.r.s within the each of clubs, $M^{c_k} \to M^{c_k}$ and $M^{c_l} \to M^{c_l}$, respectively. This is a bit weaker than saying that two clubs are isomorphic from point of view of e.p.r.s transactions.

To understand the above definition within the context of concrete economic application let us recall the economic example discussed extensively in the introductory Chapter 1. Here, the idea is to show explicitly how elements of that example correspond to the concepts of a club, appropriation, and transformation formally proposed above.

4.1.2 Simple Examples

Example 4.4. **A&B club and D-com**

Having in mind explanations of Example 1.1 from Chapter 1 one may say that *A&B club*, refers to a collection of enterprises $\mathbf{h}_A \equiv H_A^{A\&B_p}$, $\mathbf{h}_B \equiv H_B^{A\&B_p}$, $\mathbf{h}_{A\&B} \equiv H_{A\&B}^{A\&B_p}$, $\mathbf{h}_k = H_k^{A\&B_p}, k = 1, 2, \ldots, n_{A\&B}$. Denote it by $M^{A\&B_p}$. Recall that $\mathbf{h}_A \equiv H_A^{A\&B_p}$, corresponds to Ann's individual enterprise, i.e. her private endowments of investment capital and human capital, in the particular form of her privately owned computer, software, and other tangible and intangible assets that can be potentially used for computer service, her knowledge and variety of economic relations and transactions that she may carry in the private fashion concerning computer service. Similarly we have for Bob's individual enterprise, $H_B^{A\&B_p}$, while $H_{A\&B}^{A\&B_p}$, is their private partnership enterprise, capturing their private endowments they are ready to include into this enterprise, as their 'parallel' computer, software of more sophisticated programs, and knowledge of those programs and mutual relations of Ann and Bob in their private partnership in this particular enterprise. Other private institutions that may be involved in flows of information concerning computer service, hardware and software are captured under $H_k^{A\&B_p}$. A set of transactions among $H_i^{A\&B_p}, i = A, B, A\&B, 1, 2, \ldots, n_{A\&B}$, denoted by $Trn_{A\&B_p}$ primarily concerns flows of information on computer services as well as other assets among the enterprises of the cub. Then it is obvious that for every pair of enterprises $(H_i^{A\&B_p}, H_j^{A\&B_p})$, $i, j = A, B, A\&B, 1, 2, \ldots, n_{A\&B}$, of A&B private computer club, $M^{A\&B_p}$, there is a set of information flows, as well as transactions of other assets from $H_i^{A\&B_p}$ to $H_j^{A\&B_p}$. Sets of these voluntary transactions are specific to each enterprise. This actually means that $Trn_{A\&B_p}(H_i^{A\&B_p}, H_j^{A\&B_p})$, and $Trn_{A\&B_p}(H_l^{A\&B_p}, H_k^{A\&B_p})$, are disjoint unless Ann and/or Bob are dealing with the same enterprises respectively, i.e. unless $(H_i^{A\&B_p} = H_l^{A\&B_p})$, and $(H_j^{A\&B_p} = H_k^{A\&B_p})$, $i, j, k, l = A, B, A\&B, 1, 2, \ldots, n_{A\&B}$. In that case, sets of information and other asset flows coincide. Now, let us choose three enterprises from A&B private club, $H_i^{A\&B_p}, H_j^{A\&B_p}, H_k^{A\&B_p} \in M^{A\&B_p}$. It is not hard to see that there is an e.p.r.s mapping carrying information and other assets,

$$Trn_{A\&B_p}(H_i^{A\&B_p}, H_j^{A\&B_p}) \times Trn_{A\&B_p}(H_j^{A\&B_p}, H_k^{A\&B_p}) \to \\ Trn_{A\&B_p}(H_j^{A\&B_p}, H_k^{A\&B_p})$$

described by $(t_2^{A\&B_p}, t_1^{A\&B_p}) \mapsto t_1^{A\&B_p} \circ t_2^{A\&B_p}$. Namely, as was already sketched by the Example of Chapter 1 and wildly discussed in sections above, there is an e.p.r.s collection resulting from aggregation procedure concerning information and other assets of enterprises, denoted by $\otimes$. It has the properties that for every enterprise $H_i^{A\&B_p}$ there is an elementary flow of information, one may think of updating hardware and self-learning, for example, $id_{M^{A\&B_p}} \in Trn_{A\&B_p}(H_i^{A\&B_p}, H_i^{A\&B_p})$ which preserves quality argumentation of the ith member of the A&B club over all possible transactions with other members within the club, i.e. those of $Trn_{A\&B_p}(H_i^{A\&B_p}, H_j^{A\&B_p})$, and preserves her/his cost (price) argumentation over all transactions $Trn_{A\&B_p}(H_i^{A\&B_p}, H_j^{A\&B_p})$ with other members within the club. In addition, a rule of aggregation of e.p.r.s is 'associative' in the sense that when the compositions $t_1^{A\&B_p} \otimes (t_2^{A\&B_p} \otimes t_3^{A\&B_p})$ and $(t_1^{A\&B_p} \otimes t_2^{A\&B_p}) \otimes t_3^{A\&B_p}$ are defined, they are equal. Then it is obvious that for this example a composition $\circ$ takes the form of $\otimes$ and satisfies conditions given in definition of a club.

Similar can be shown for capital and human assets concerning Department's computer room and graduate students involved, including Ann and Bob, and computer services that can be obtained 'publicly' within a Campus or from some other nonprivate institutions, $\mathbf{h}_1 \equiv H_{1D}^{D_{pb}}, \mathbf{h}_2 \equiv H_{2D}^{D_{pb}}, \mathbf{h}_{1\&2} \equiv H_{1\&2D}^{D_{pb}}, H_l^{D_{pb}}, l = 1, 2, \ldots, n_D$ as described in detail in Chapter ??. Let us call this club, *D-computer club*, and denote it by $M^{D_{pb}}$.

E.p.r.s relations between these two clubs define economic 'maps' and we have a particular interest in those which respect their e.p.r.s structure. Using our example it can be shown that conditions for a properly determined appropriation are satisfied as defined in 4.2 above. Obviously, an economic flow of information from D-com club, $M^{D_{pb}}$ to A&B private club $M^{A\&B_p}$ exists. We may always think of information (knowledge) that Ann and/or Bob have got through a learning process within the Department and which they have applied in their individual or private partnership computer club. Obviously it is an e.p.r.s functor, called an appropriation, and can be denoted by $\otimes_{ap}$. Namely, there are general rules of behavior in cybrospace, rules concerning Department's authority(s), and graduate students that are agreeable to all and regulate in the form of Department's enterprise transfers of e.p.r.s. In this particular example we are interested in both types of clubs. Thus, in that way to every enterprise $H^{D_{pb}}$ of $M^{D_{pb}}$ an enterprise $\otimes_{ap} H^{D_{pb}} = H^{A\&B_p}$ of $M^{A\&B_p}$ can be assigned, and for every transaction $t^D : H_i^{D_{pb}} \to H_j^{D_p}$ of $M^{D_{pb}}$ an information flow $\otimes_{ap} t^{D_{pb}} : \otimes_{ap} H_i^{D_{pb}} \to \otimes_{ap} H_j^{D_{pb}}$ of A&B private club $M^{A\&B_p}$. That $\otimes_{ap}$ is suitable as an appropriation, can be see from the statement that an appropriation of a concept of preservation of e.p.r.s within Department's assets gives the same concept of preservation of e.p.r.s implemented to the private club. Thus, $\otimes_{ap} id_{H^{D_{pb}}} = id_{\otimes_{ap} H^{D_{pb}}}$. At the same time an aggregation of two transactions $t_1^{D_{pb}} \otimes t_2^{D_{pb}}$ defined in $M^{D_{pb}}$ corresponds to appropriation of aggregates, $\otimes_{ap} t_1^{D_{pb}} \otimes \otimes_{ap} t_2^{D_{pb}} = \otimes_{ap}(t_2^{D_p} \otimes t_1^{D_p})$. Obviously these two clubs can be considered as e.p.r.s isomorphic if there exist mutually inverse appropriations between them. Thus, for our example we may consider two appropriations, i.e. those concerning appropriation of e.p.r.s from A&B private club, $M^{A\&B_p}$, to D-com, $M^{D_{pb}}$, and let us denote this appropriation by A_{stx}; and another appropriation from D-com club, $M^{D_{pb}}$, to A&B private club, and denote it by A_{sap}. An economic intuition of opposed relation of these two appropriations is consistent with the extension of e.p.r.s domain. The following diagram may be useful in understanding relations between these two clubs where $M^{A\&B_p}, M^{D_{pb}}$ denote A&B private, D-com club, respectively, and $t^{A\&B_p}, t^{D_{pb}}$ transactions of information and other assets within private and public club, respectively.

$$\begin{array}{ccc}
M^{A\&B_p} & \overset{\longleftarrow}{\underset{\longrightarrow}{t^p}} & M^{A\&B_p} \\
A_{sap} \Big\uparrow & & \Big\downarrow A_{stx} \\
M^{D_{pb}} & \overset{\longleftarrow}{\underset{\longrightarrow}{t^{pb}}} & M^{D_{pb}}
\end{array}$$

The concept of e.p.r.s transformation or policy may be less obvious in this example. Nevertheless, roughly speaking, we say that it refers to restructuring some of established relations between two clubs. Here we may have in mind relations between two types of appropriations from above, A_{sap}, and A_{stx}. Then an e.p.r.s transformation concerns $A_{sap_1}, A_{sap_2} : M^{D_{pb}} \to M^{A\&B_p}$, in a form of economic mappings, $\mathcal{P}_{sap} : A_{sap_1} \to A_{sap_2}$, or one may write $\mathcal{P}_{sap}(A_{sap_1}, A_{sap_2})$. This means, in fact, an entire collection $\{\mathcal{P}_{sap}(H_i^{D_{pb}}) \mid H_i^{D_{pb}} \in M^{D_{pb}}\}$, where each $\mathcal{P}_{sap}(H_i^{D_{pb}}) : A_{sap_1}(H_i^{D_{pb}}) \to A_{sap_2}(H_i^{D_{pb}})$, is a transaction of club $M^{D_{pb}}$, and such that for any transaction $t^{D_{pb}} \in Trn_{D_{pb}}(H_i^{D_{pb}}, H_j^{D_{pb}})$ we have $\mathcal{P}_{sap}(H_j^{D_{pb}}) \circ A_{sap_1}(t^{D_{pb}}) = A_{sap_2}(t^{D_{pb}}) \circ \mathcal{P}_{sap}(H_i^{D_{pb}})$. Similar is valid for a restructuring of A_{stx}, which is denoted by $\mathcal{P}_{stx}$, so that e.p.r.s natural transformation $\mathcal{P}_{et} = (\mathcal{P}_{stx}, \mathcal{P}_{sap})$ can be associated to above appropriations. Thus, we have the collection of e.p.r.s transformation or an e.p.r.s policy that is coherent or appropriatorial. In that way we have shown that elements of the example studied in Chapter 1 can be expressed in terms of a club.

In general in EPRT one may have a geometric and/or an algebraic picture in mind to get intuition about clubs, at least in the simplest cases. From point of view of geometry the idea is simple as structural relations are somehow ignored and one can think of the elements of a club as 'points' in a set. The morphisms (economic transactions) are arrows or 'paths' connecting the points (agents). Thus, in a simple economic application one may simply think of the agents as members of an economic club. The relations between agents are varieties of economic transactions connecting them which are expressible as set maps. Then a functor (an appropriation) maps the points and paths of one club over to points and paths of the other. We are dealing with economic relations between two clubs, where mapping that links agents and economic transactions within one club are transferred over to agencies and transactions of the other, defining an appropriation relation between those two institutions, denoted by F_{ap}. Sometimes it is convenient to think of an appropriation $F_{ap} : M^{c_l} \to M^{c_k}$ as defining a kind of fibre bundle over the club M^{c_i}, and connection (or gauge economic field) on it. The fibre over each agency, E_i^c in the club M^{c_i}, is $F_{ap}(t_i^c)$ and the analogous flow of economic transaction (parallel transport) along each economic transaction ('path') t^c in club M^c, is given by $F_{ap}(t^c)$. Another fibre bundle is to have fibre $Trn_c(F_{ap}(E_i^c), F_{ap}(E_i^c))$ over each agency, which works better because each fibre is a set. In this case we can speak of 'sections' of this bundle. They are just functions θ which have a value $\theta_{E_i^c} \in Trn_c(F_{ap}(E_i^c), F_{ap}(E_i^c))$ for each agent E_i^c in the club M^c. In this case, the appropriation F_{ap} defines analogous flow of economic transactions (parallel transport) $F_{ap}(t^c) \circ (\ ) \circ F_{ap}(t^c)^{-1}$, along the economic transaction t^c in the club M^c, where it is assumed, for the sake of our simple geometric picture, that appropriation $F_{ap}(t^c)$ is invertible. Then an economic implementable policy $\theta \in Eprsnat(F_{ap}, F_{ap})$ is just a section of this fibre bundle which is flat or covariantly constant under this flow. This is just the content of the coherence conditions, concerning simple economic relations between two agencies from the same club. Namely, one has $\theta_{E_j^c} \circ F_{ap}(t^c) = F_{ap}(t^c) \circ \theta_{E_i^c}$, as simplicity of the example and the geometric approach allows moving $F_{ap}(t^c)^{-1}$ to $F_{ap}(t^c)$ on the other side in order not to assume that it is invertible. The same remarks could be made in general for e.p.r.s policy $\theta \in Eprsnat(F_{ap_1}, F_{ap_2})$ between two appropriations. The fiber over an agent E_i^c is $Trn_c(F_{ap_1}(E_i^c), F_{ap_2}(E_i^c))$ and the analogous flow of transactions is formally given by $F_{ap_1}(t^c) \circ (\ ) \circ F_{ap_2}(t^c)^{-1}$. So we can think of $Eprsnat(F_{ap}, F_{ap})$ as a certain covariantly constant functions on the club M^c with values in club-internal economic transactions. It is obvious that one can 'poitwise multiply' such coherent functions and that an e.p.r.s policy that preserves existing relations between clubs, i.e. the identity e.p.r.s transformation is the identity for this poitwise multiplication. So we have an agreement $Eprsnat(F_{ap}, F_{ap})$, appropriation equivalence, or at least a unital semirule, associated to any such simple economic club. Recall that traditional economic modeling has extensively used tools sketched above, although they may not be expressed over club terms. Namely, the methodology of traditional economics is based on the category of Set of sets that has all of the above features. Agents and simple institutions are modeled as sets, e.g. subsets of some given universal set of economy, economic relations between them are set maps, and shaping that structure through a variety of economic procedures, a lot of economic phenomena can be expressed and analyzed in a consistent way. Another example of the application of the above tools in traditional economic analysis is the simple economy defined by a process of allocation of economic resources and/or economic activity analyses, as it is usually called in economic literature [41]. Here, modeling is within the category of Vec , where the agents are defined over vector spaces, the economic relations are defined as linear maps, and problem of allocations is given as sequences of linear maps that respect some given economic structure. Obviously these can provide a consistent model of economic allocation. As an example of economic club let us discussed some elements of the simple exchange economy, a well know model in any textbook for economists, and here known economic relations are expressed in terms of e.p.r.s club theory.

Example 4.5.
Club of simple exchange-standardized economy

This example views the known traditional description of a simple exchange process from economics, through methodology from above. Namely, elements of a simple enterprise which properties have been extensively discussed in Section 2.2.1, over several definitions, propositions and examples, and if necessary reader may recall them, are combined with the notions of a club, appropriation, and transformation. Thus, in this particular application let A_{sex} be an agreement (unital) on exchange relations between simple agents, where index stands for an abbreviation of 'simple exchange.' The agreement of exchange, A_{sex}, standardizes quality-value relations of any simple good involved in exchange between agents over that agreement. Let us denote by ${}_{sex}M$ the club of this simple exchange standardized economy. Thus, enterprises of this club are simple agents which accept an agreement A_{sex} as an economic principle to be implemented in exchange their endowments (goods). Formally, agents are described by vector space of their endowments on which an agreement A_{sex} is to be implemented. E.p.r.s transactions between agents take form of exchange of simple goods, and are described by linear maps that commute with (intertwine) the argumentation of exchange A_{sex}. In addition, let us recall the well-known assumption of simple exchange process from traditional competitive economics that each agent in valuation of her exchange transaction does not consider her/his effects at the market itself on quality-value of exchange. In this framework the assumption simply means that, any agent in her/his economic reasoning about a gain in exchange of goods, simply throws away the argumentation of A_{sex}. Thus, it is economically plausible to consider this as an example of appropriation that assigns to each standardized form of exchange its underlying economic vector space. It seems natural to call this particular functor, forgetful appropriation, as in the very exchange transactions agents forget impacts of the simple market device on which the very transactions are run (implied by the assumption of 'impartiality of markets' and/or competitiveness). Then the economic policies regarding this form of appropriation in the exchange are in correspondence with the elements of the agreement on the exchange A_{sex} itself.

Proof and comments: To show that the above elements constitute a club of simple exchange enterprises let us check that our axioms of a club are satisfied. In Subsection 2.2.1 it was shown that simple agents constitute an enterprise of a particular simple form, and if necessary reader is advised to recall what are the properties of a simple enterprise. Here, those already obtained results are further analyzed within the particular context of exchange from the example. Namely, assumed simplicity allows to describe each agent by a concrete set with some economic structure. Note that this simple structure implies private property, and in this particular case each agent has complete private claims on at least one good (actually product of pure nature which is considered free or her/his simple economy). Any other e.p.r.s structure would be in contradiction with concept of simplicity. Note, that economic relations of exchange of simple commodities (nondurable onefold goods - apples, eggs, mushrooms for example), are economic maps that respect the structure among simple enterprises. Thus, to complete the proof we have to check do the properties of forgetful appropriation and exchange policies from the example satisfy conditions of a simple p.p.r.s type of club.

The forgetful appropriation has the property that $F_{frg}(V) = V$, where the first V is as an A_{sex}-standardized space of commodities, and the second is just a plain vector space of goods. Similar, we have for exchange transactions, as this appropriation rule of simple 'market' links any agreeable transaction to simple transaction of goods, i.e. $F_{frg}(t^{sex}) = t^{sex}$.

Now let us see statement concerning exchange policy of this simple market or the implementable p.p.r.s policy. So, if $a_{sex} \in A_{sex}$ is an agreement of exchange then one can define $\theta_V(v) = a_{sex} \overset{a}{>} v$, where $\overset{a}{>}$ is the notation of a price (value) argumentation, and v are goods in exchange on which agreement is implemented. Now let see the properties of exchange policy $\theta \in Pprnat(F_{frg}, F_{frg})$, where $Pprs$ is abbreviation for 'pure private rights' which is the assumed e.p.r.s fixed relation in this simple example. The idea is to show that economic coherence of p.p.r.s reasoning of agents, reduces its policy to the definition of exchange of simple goods. Namely, we are dealing with economic maps that commute with the argumentation of $a_{sex} \in A_{sex}$. Conversely, given an economic policy $\theta \in Pprnat(F_{frg}, F_{frg})$, consider $V = A_{sex}$, as the price (value) regular representation of an exchange process by expansion of p.p.r.s of both agents through exchange of goods. Traditionally trained economist may think of expansion of utilities of both agents due to exchange of goods. In addition, we define $a_{sex} = \theta_{A_{sex}}(1_{sex})$, where 1_{sex} is the identity element of exchange which preserves p.p.r relations in exchange or ensures that no agent is worse of by the exchange. We now check that these two conditions are mutually inverse. If we start with an agreement a_{sex} and define θ by the first construction, then the corresponding elements of A_{sex} by the second construction is $\theta_{A_{sex}}(1_{sex}) = a_{sex} \circ 1_{sex} = a_{sex}$, so one can recover particular exchange agreement a_{sex}. In the other direction, if we start with policy θ and define $a_{sex} = \theta_{A_{sex}}(1_{sex})$, then the corresponding policy of exchange by the first construction is $\theta_V(v) = (\theta_V \circ F_{frg}(t_v^{sex}))(1_{sex}) = (F_{frg}(t_v^{sex}) \circ \theta_{A_{sex}})(1_{sex}) = a_{sex} \overset{a}{>} v$, where $t_v^{sex} : A_{sex} \to V$ defined by $t_v^{sex}(a_{sex}) = a_{sex} \overset{a}{>} v$ is an exchange from the price regular representation of v since argumentation, $\overset{a}{>}$ has been implemented. Now we use condition of consistency and that F_{frg} is a forgetful functor. So we can recover θ. Hence $Pprnat(F_{frg}, F_{frg})$ and A_{sex} are in one-to-one correspondence. The agreeable structure mentioned above on $Pprsnat(F_{frg}, F_{frg})$ just corresponds to that of A_{sex} in this particular case, as is clear since $\overset{a}{>}$ is an argumentation of the exchange agreement. Note that this part of the proof also shows that any p.p.r.s policy concerning simple p.p.r.s type of clubs provides back simple p.p.r.s clubs. □

4.1.3 Leading Club

A leading club is defined by the particular structure of its organization. From point of view of economics we may have in mind some monopolistic form, and from formal point of view we are dealing with a structure of monoid or monoidal category. The emphasis of this type of clubs is that they are equipped with some kind of expansion of e.p.r.s, which we denote with $\otimes_{ap}$, and this need not be based on an aggregation.

Definition 4.6 (Leading club). *A leading club, Ld, is defined by* $(M^{ld}, \otimes_{lap}, E^{ld}_{Ld}, P_{leq}, p_{ld}, q_{ld})$ *where:*
(i) M^{ld} *denotes a club with enterprises* E^{ld}_i, $i \in I_{Ld}$; *defined according to Definition 4.1.*
(ii) $\otimes_{lap}$ *is a leading appropriation,* $\otimes_{lap} : M^{ld} \otimes_{ap} M^{ld} \to M^{ld}$, *which is associative under leading e.r.p.s policy,* P_{leq}, *i.e.* $P_{leq} : (\ \otimes_{lap}\ )\otimes_{lap} \to \otimes_{lap}(\ \otimes_{lap}\ )$.
(iii) E^{ld}_{Ld} *is the leadership preserving enterprise or unit leading enterprise of the club.*
(iv) P_{leq} *an equivalence e.p.r.s policy of the leadership in the club, i.e. there are given appropriational isotransactions within the club*

$$P^{lap}_{E^{ld}_i, E^{ld}_j, E^{ld}_k} : (E^{ld}_i \otimes_{lap} E^{ld}_j) \otimes_{lap} E^{ld}_k \cong E^{ld}_i \otimes_{lap} (E^{ld}_j \otimes_{lap} E^{ld}_k),$$
$$\forall E^{ld}_i, E^{ld}_j, E^{ld}_k \in M^{ld},\ i, j, k \in I_{Ld}$$

obeying the following condition, (v) There are leading price (cost) and quality arguments p_{ld}, q_{ld} *respectively, such that leading appropriational isotransactions over price(cost) and quality argumentations,* $p_{E^{ld}_i} : E^{ld}_i \cong E^{ld}_i \otimes_{lap} E^{ld}_{Ld}$ *and* $q_{E^{ld}_i} : E^{ld}_i \cong E^{ld}_{Ld} \otimes_{lap} E^{ld}_i$, *under the leadership of leading enterprise within the club* E^{ld}_{Ld} *satisfy the following triangular condition, (vi) It is also required that a leading enterprise,* E^{ld}_{Ld}, *of the club Ld, has the property to ensure equivalent policies concerning appropriations of e.p.r.s obtained with any enterprise from the club over price and/or quality argumentations* $((\ ) \otimes_{lap} E^{ld}_{Ld}, E^{ld}_{Ld} \otimes_{lap} (\ ))$, *and one that preserves the leading appropriation for the club (* $M^{ld} \to M^{ld}$ *).*

One may note that conditions (v) and (vi) are each others consequence, nevertheless it is convenient to include both as defining properties of a leading club. From the definition and figure 4.1 it can be seen that there are two ways to go from

$$((E^{ld}_i \otimes_{lap} E^{ld}_j) \otimes_{lap} E^{ld}_k) \otimes_{lap} E^{ld}_m$$

to

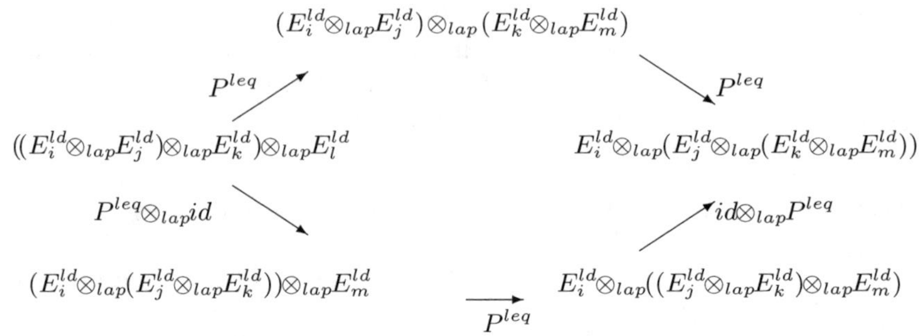

Fig. 4.1. The consistency condition for leading appropriation $\otimes_{lap}$ to ensure associativity.

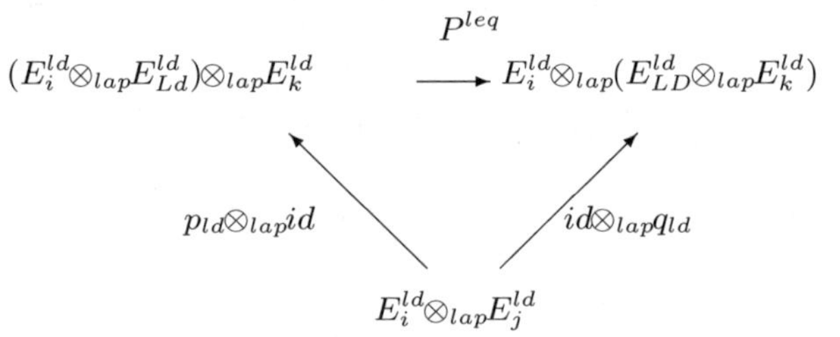

Fig. 4.2. The compatibility condition for the leading enterprise and price and quality arguments.

$$E_i^{ld} \otimes_{lap} (E_j^{ld} \otimes_{lap} (E_k^{ld} \otimes_{lap} E_m^{ld}))$$

by applying leading policy P^{leq} repeatedly. The consistency conditions impose that these two ways of organizing enterprises within the leading club provide the coinciding outcomes. It is worthy to note that, once the condition of consistency is established in the case of all four enterprises, then all other consistency problems of this type within the leading club are automatically resolved. This actually means that we do not have to concentrate too much on which particular procedure in organizing enterprises is used as long as consistency is preserved. There are several ways to organize aggregation of particular enterprises and implementation of policy P^{leq}. They might be perceived on the level of the particular members of the club differently, all lead to coinciding outcome. Formally, one is allowed to omit brackets and write expressions without them.

Now let Ld_1, Ld_2 be two leading clubs. Then one can define an appropriation between them by $F_{ld} : Ld_1 \to Ld_2$, and F_{ld} is a leading appropriation if it respects the leading aggregation, and expansion of e.p.r.s on that basis. Namely, it has the property that the appropriation F^2_{ld} defined by the combination $F^2_{ld}(E^{ld_1}_i, E^{ld_1}_j) = F_{ld}(E^{ld_1}_i) \otimes_{ap} F_{ld}(E^{ld_1}_j)$. Here F_{ld} and the appropriation that combines F_{ld} with the appropriation of the leading club $\otimes_{lap}$ support equivalent e.p.r.s policy. Note that one may think of both F^2_{ld} and $F_{ld} \circ \otimes_{ap}$ as kind of expanded appropriations, as $F^2_{ld}, F_{ld} \circ \otimes_{ap} : Ld_1 \times Ld_2 \to Ld_2$ are equivalent e.p.r.s policies. One may conclude that an e.p.r.s leading appropriation is an appropriation that supports leading e.r.p.s isotransactions $c^{ld}_{E^{ld_1}_i, E^{ld_1}_j} : F_{ld}(E^{ld_1}_i) \otimes_{ap} F_{ld}(E^{ld_1}_j) \cong F_{ld}(E^{ld_1}_i \otimes_{ap} E^{ld_1}_j)$ so that the relevant e.p.r.s policies are respected (implemented). These can be expressed by the Figure 4.3, where to simplify notation we have $F \equiv F_{ld}$, and $\cdot \equiv \otimes_{lap}$, and

$$\begin{array}{ccccc}
(F(E^{ld}_i) \cdot F(E^{ld}_j)) \cdot F(E^{ld}_k) & \xrightarrow{cid} & F(E^{ld}_i \cdot E^{ld}_j) \cdot F(E^{ld}_k) & \xrightarrow{c} & F((E^{ld}_i \cdot E^{ld}_j) \cdot E^{ld}_k) \\
\downarrow P^{leq} & & & & \downarrow F(P^{leq}) \\
F(E^{ld}_i) \cdot (F(E^{ld}_j) \cdot F(E^{ld}_k)) & \xrightarrow{idc} & F(E^{ld}_i) \cdot F(E^{ld}_j \cdot E^{ld}_k) & \xrightarrow{c} & F(E^{ld}_i \cdot (E^{ld}_j \cdot E^{ld}_k))
\end{array}$$

Fig. 4.3. A leading appropriation $F_{ld} \equiv F$ respects the relevant policies P^{leq}.

the conditions for compatibility with the leading enterprise E^{ld}_{Ld} of the club,

$$F_{ld}(E^{ld}_{Ld}) = E^{ld}_{Ld},$$
$$c_{Ld, E^{ld}_i} \circ p_{F_{ld}(E^{ld}_i)} = F(p_{E^{ld}_i}), \qquad c_{E^{ld}_i, Ld} \circ q_{F(E^{ld}_i)} = F_{ld}(q_{E^{ld}_i}).$$

It may be noteworthy that above concept of leading club can be easily linked with the more traditional economic theories and concepts. So for example, traditional general equilibrium economic theory and economic relations among agents are formally based on the category *Set* of sets and this ensures that a leading club can be consistently defined. In this particular case leading appropriation is defined by direct product of sets, i.e. $\otimes_{lap} = \times$, and the leading agents are the singleton sets. It is obvious that in this case concept of an individual agent and pure private economic property rights relations are consistently represented by this club. Similarly, for the simple e.p.r.s institutions, as enterprises on natural recourses as discussed in Chapter 2, the leading club can be defined. The leading appropriation $\otimes_{lap}$ is reduced to simple aggregation $\otimes$. The leading enterprise is then specified by the domain of economic claims **h**. The consistency of these simple institutions is shown and discussed in Chapter 2. Note that formally this simple case is modeled by category of Vec of vector spaces and usual tensor product.

It is worthy to note that in economics there are, of course, plenty of leading groups or groups of economic interests, that are not directly involved with entrepreneurship and entrepreneurial agreements. The best known are economic input-output systems, where some fixed technology defines input-output relations within an economy (among agents, households, industries or whole economies, for example). Formally, it is described by a linear algebra A. Then for any given A, consider the category ${}_A\mathcal{M}_A$ there is an economic arrangement of agents according to each of their economic reasoning shaped by technology A or price and quality standards. Namely, an ${}_A\mathcal{M}_A$, can be considered as a bistandardized economy where economic vector spaces describe standardized price and quality systems of economic activities. Chosen technology, as an agreement A, shapes both sides with price and qualities argumentations. In addition, fixed e.p.r.s relations of chosen technology makes these price and quality argumentations mutually commuting. There is an aggregation procedure $\otimes_A$ over technology A. It has the same properties as aggregation described in Chapter 2 where we were discussing aggregation procedures of agreements on natural resources. Expansions of e.p.r.s of each of the agents is over a field of economic claims on natural resources, but this time quotienting by the relations $v_{Ld_i^p} \overset{a}{<} a \otimes v_{Ld_j^q} = v_{Ld_i^p} \otimes a \overset{a}{>} v_{Ld_j^q}$ for all elements of agreement $a \in A$, where $v_{Ld_i^p}, v_{Ld_j^q}$ denote leading price and quality vector spaces of natural resources on which agents are linked by agreement on technology. One may think of the above equation as 'cleaning conditions' of inputs and outputs of an implemented technology A on the optimal level. Actually, this expresses the price and quality bistandards into an simple leading club from point of view of an ecotechnology. Here I and II welfare theorems are valid, generalizing the category of natural resources in such a way that the role of the domain of e.r.p.s claims is played now by the agreement on technology A. Note that this agreement need not be commutative. The other elements of the leading ecotechnology club, as economic policies, P^{leq} and others, are given by vector spaces ones projected down to $\otimes_A$. There are plenty of other leading clubs.

Example 4.7.

Leading club of simple exchange-standardized economy

Let H be a biagreement or an enterprise and let ${}_HM$ be the club of representations of agreement in Example 4.5. Then a simple aggregation procedure $\otimes$, as defined through standardized notation by $h \overset{a}{>} (v \otimes w) = \sum h_{(1)} \overset{a}{>} v \otimes h_{(2)} \overset{a}{>} w$ from 2.2.1 in Chapter 2 can play here the role of a leading appropriation. Namely, using the coexpansion of e.p.r.s so that defined appropriation is a base for formation of ${}_HM$ into leading club. The leading appropriation is one which treats members of simple exchange standardized club as simple ones and reduce them to concept of natural economic recourses.

Proof: Reader may recall from Chapter 2, that $V \otimes W$ is a representation of simple enterprise H if V and W are. Then the coexpansion of e.p.r.s is used to split an element of enterprise H as requested. Now let us show that other formal defining conditions for a leading club are satisfied:
(i) Check that $\otimes$ is an appropriation. To be an appropriation it must also map an economic transaction of extended club ${}_HM \times {}_HM$, $((\phi, \psi)$ a pair of intertwines, in ${}_HM \times {}_HM$) to an economic transaction, $\phi \otimes \psi$, in ${}_HM$. Here simplicity of the example makes economic transaction $\phi \otimes \psi$ to be defined as the linear map $\phi \otimes \psi$. That such a map is an intertwiner is not difficult to see, and that this is compatible with composition $\circ$ as required.
(ii) Now we are defining the economic policy (isomorphism) Φ to be the same as the usual one at the level of the underlying natural recourses (vector spaces). So $\Phi_{V,W,Z}((v \otimes w) \otimes z) = v \otimes (w \otimes z)$ for all elements v, w, z in their representative spaces. It is an intertwiner or economic transaction since,

$$\begin{aligned} h \overset{a}{>} ((v \otimes w) \otimes z) &= h_{(1)(1)} \overset{a}{>} v \otimes h_{(1)(2)} \overset{a}{>} w \otimes h_{(2)} \overset{a}{>} z \\ &= h_{(1)} \overset{a}{>} v \otimes h_{(2)(1)} \overset{a}{>} w \otimes h_{(2)(2)} \overset{a}{>} z \\ &= h \overset{a}{>} (v \otimes (w \otimes z)) \end{aligned}$$

by coassociativity of Δ. It is clear that Φ is an appropriation isotransaction or economic policy uniformly implemented over all economic resources. The consistency conditions are satisfied as the modeling is based on category of vector spaces Vec.
(iii) The leading agency is the trivial representation $A_{Ld} = \mathbf{h}$ made possible by the coagency in H, $h \overset{a}{>} \lambda = \varepsilon(h)\lambda, \forall h \in H, \lambda \in \mathbf{h}$. It has the desired properties under aggregation $\otimes$ using the axioms of the coagency.
(iv) Price and quantity argumentations are given by $p_{ld} = (\ ) \otimes 1$, and $q_{ld} = 1 \otimes (\ )$, respectively.
(v) Finally, since forgetful appropriation just forgets argumentation of H, while economic policy Φ is the same as for natural resources, it is clear that the particular appropriation which carries forgetful property, ${}_HM \to Vec$, is leading appropriation with $c = id$. □

An economic intuition suggests that e.p.r.s structures imposed on an agreement correspond directly to properties of its club of representations. In the next example it is explicitly shown how this works, to be more formally discussed in next Section 4.2. Also, by a similar calculation, one finds easily that two biagreements have equivalent standardized clubs, in a way compatible with their forgetful appropriations, if and only if the two are related by twisting as in Theorem 3.25 on open enterprises. Similar is valid for open quasibiagreements, as shown by Theorem 3.32 in Chapter 3. Precisely let us consider the following example.

Example 4.8. Let (H, Φ) be an open quasibiagreement or open quasienterprise in the sense discussed in Section 3.4. Then a leading club, ${}_HM$, can be formed with $\otimes$, (as defined above in Example 4.6, recall if necessary), and with opening Φ given by the argumentation of ϕ followed by the usual associativity isotransaction for economic vector spaces so that

$$\Phi_{V,W,Z}((v \otimes w) \otimes z) = \sum \phi^{(1)} \overset{a}{>} v \otimes (\phi^{(2)} \overset{a}{>} w \otimes \phi^{(3)} \overset{a}{>} z).$$

The forgetful appropriation is leading iff enterprise H is twisting-equivalent to an ordinary biagreement or an enterprise, i.e. iff ϕ is a coboundary.

Sketch of proof and comments: The proof is just like one in the preceding example, except that we should carefully deal with the coassociativity as we actually do not have it. So

$$h \overset{a}{>} ((v \otimes w) \otimes z) = (\Delta h) \overset{a}{>} ((v \otimes w) \otimes z) = ((\Delta \otimes id) \circ \Delta h) \overset{a}{>} (v \otimes w \otimes z),$$

where the multiple argumentations are also denoted by $\overset{a}{>}$. Similar for the other round of aggregation of arguments or other bracketing. Then, implementation of opening gives

$$\begin{aligned}
\Phi(h \overset{a}{>} ((v \otimes w) \otimes z)) &= \phi((\Delta \otimes id) \circ \Delta h) \overset{a}{>} (v \otimes w \otimes z) \\
&= ((id \otimes \Delta) \circ \Delta h)\phi \overset{a}{>} (v \otimes w \otimes z) \\
&= h \overset{a}{>} ((v \otimes w) \otimes z) = h \overset{a}{>} \Phi((v \otimes w) \otimes z)
\end{aligned}$$

in view of the axiom (3.14) concerning coexpansion of e.p.r.s of an open quasienterprise. It has been already checked that the 3-cocycle axiom for ϕ precisely corresponds to the consistency condition of a leading club under (iv) in Definition 4.6 for Φ, and that it controls the nonassociativity. Also, the maps Φ are isotransactions because ϕ is invertible. In particular they are of an appropriational type because they are all defined 'uniformly' by the argumentation of an element of $H \otimes H \otimes H$. This is given in the sense that isotransactions commute with any maps that commute with the argumentation of H. Thus, they commute with any economic transactions. Similarly, one has for 2-cocycles. Then appropriational isotransactions can be determined by the argumentation of any invertible element $\chi \in H \otimes H$, in the particular form $c_{V,W}(v \otimes w) = \chi^{(1)} \overset{a}{>} v \otimes \chi^{(2)} \overset{a}{>} w$. Now recall that the requirement that twisting by χ^{-1} in Theorem 3.32 gives an ordinary enterprise is that $\phi((\Delta \otimes id)\chi)\chi_{12} = ((id \otimes \Delta)\chi)\chi_{23}$. One can see that this condition precisely corresponds to the condition that a leading appropriation respects the relevant policies of the club as in Figure 4.3 for the forgetful appropriation to be of leading type. These arguments can be pushed backwards as well. Namely, if the forgetful appropriation is leading with some implementable e.p.r.s policy $\{c_{V,W}\}$, then the latter is necessarily of the form given by the argumentation due to an element of $H \otimes H$ (see discussion on confirmation of openings 3.3.1

in Chapter 2). The condition in Figure 4.3, considered in the price (cost) regular representation and evaluate on $1 \otimes 1 \otimes 1$, tells us that ϕ is a coboundary in the sense of the requirement above. In terms of the non-Abelian coboundary operation this requirement is just $\phi = \partial\chi$ for some $\chi \in H \otimes H$, provided we realize that ∂ is to be computed using the coexpansion of e.p.r.s which provides Δ by the twisting, i.e. using the coexpansion of e.p.r.s modified to $\chi^{-1}(\Delta)\chi$. □

It is intuitively clear that leading clubs can be themselves members of a leading club. To specify precisely the construction of such a general inquisition one may use the notion of the dual leading club Ld^0 of representations of a leading club $(M, \otimes_{lap})$. Formally construction is based on the representation-theoretical self duality principle sketched in *Introduction* at page XVI. It claims that the axioms of a leading club are, in some sense, self-dual, similar as axioms of an enterprise are. In this case, one fixes a leading club Ld over which to organize an economy and in which to build representations. Then one shows that the club, which members are leading clubs equipped with the appropriations to fix leading club Ld, is selfdual in the representation-theoretical sense. Economic transactions in a club of leaders so formed are leading appropriations compatible with the given appropriations to Ld.

Theorem 4.9. *Let $F : Ld_1 \to Ld_2$ be a leading appropriation between two leading clubs. A representation of Ld_1 in Ld_2 is defined to be a pair (V, λ_V), where $V \in \mathcal{V}$ and $\lambda_V \in Eprnat(V \otimes F, F \otimes V)$ is an e.p.r.s equivalence implementable policy, i.e. a collection of appropriational isotransactions $\{\lambda_{V,X} : V \otimes F(X) \to F(X) \otimes V\}$, obeying,*

$$\lambda_{V,1_{ld_1}} = id, \quad \lambda_{V,Y} \circ \lambda_{V,X} = c^{-1}_{V,X} \circ \lambda_{V,X\otimes Y} \circ c_{X,Y}, \qquad \forall X, Y \in Ld_1.$$

The collection of such representations forms a leading club Ld_1°, the dual of leading club Ld_1 over Ld_2. Explicitly, the economic transactions $(V, \lambda_V) \to (W, \lambda_W)$ between representations are transactions $\phi : V \to W$ such that

$$(id \otimes \phi) \circ \lambda_{V,X} = \lambda_{W,X} \circ (\phi \otimes id), \qquad \forall X \in Ld_1.$$

The leading expansion e.p.r.s of representations is

$$(V, \lambda_V) \otimes (W, \lambda_W) = (V \otimes W, \lambda_{V\otimes W}) \quad \lambda_{V\otimes W,Z} = \lambda_{V,Z} \circ \lambda_{W,Z}.$$

The agency object is the trivial representation (ld_1, λ_{ld_1}) where ld_1 is a leading enterprise of the leading club Ld_1 and $\lambda_{ld_1,X} = id$. The forgetful appropriation $Ld_1^\circ \to Ld_2$ is of a leading type.

Sketch of proof and comments: From above it is clear that (V, λ_V) can be considered as some kind of representation of the leading expansion of e.p.r.s in the club Ld_1, and that the economic transactions are like some kind of 'intertwiners'. This then explains the formula for their 'aggregate e.r.p.s expansion' as the 'pontwise' compositions of representations. Once the formulae are accepted and known, it is not hard to check directly that they indeed fulfill the axioms of a leading club. We have a club Ld_1° with the well defined compositions of economic transactions because, if ϕ, ψ are transactions, then so is $\phi \circ \psi$ by passing λ first past ψ and then past ϕ. For the leading structure, it is clear that $\{\lambda_{V\otimes W,X}\}$ are appropriational isotransactions, since each of the factors $\{\lambda_{V,X}\}$, $\{\lambda_{W,X}\}$ are. Let us check the representation condition. Here the upper left cell commutes because this is just statement that λ_W

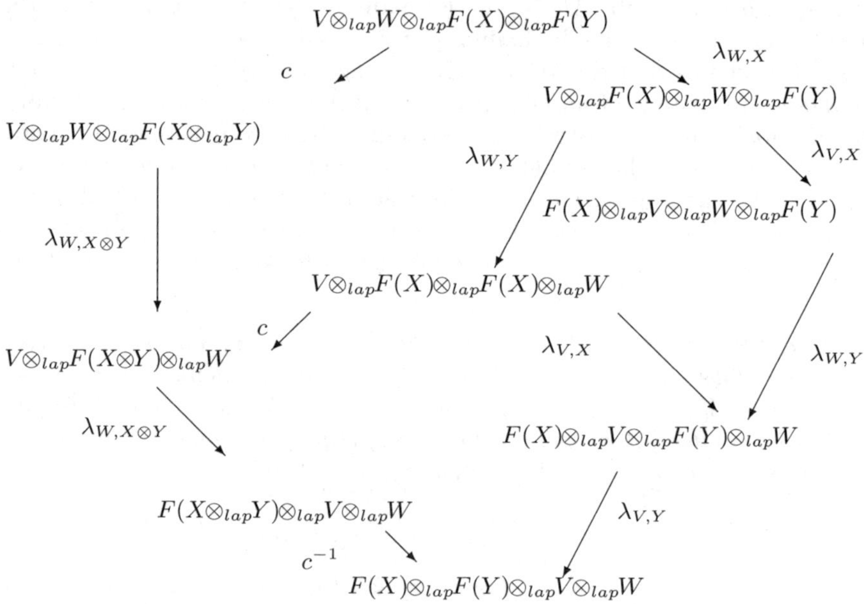

Fig. 4.4. The leading expansion of representations.

is a representation. The isotransactions $c_{X,Y} : F(X) \otimes F(Y) \cong F(X \otimes Y)$ are those that come with the leading appropriation F. We use the existence and coherence of the $\{c_{X,Y}\}$, rather than the condition in Figure 4.3 itself. The lower left cell commutes because this is just the statement that λ_V is a representation. The right hand cell commutes because $\lambda_{W,Y}, \lambda_{V,X}$ act on different members. Hence, the two ways to go around the outside of the diagram coincide. Namely, $\lambda_{V\otimes W}$ is a representation. This defines the leading expansion of e.p.r.s structure for our leading club, Ld_1°. It is associative with the same Φ as that of our underlying club Ld_1. This is an intertwiner of a transaction between the aggregate expansions of any three representations, just from associativity of composition of e.p.r.s natural policies. The leading expansion of transactions between representations is their underlying leading expansion in Ld_2. Finally, it is clear that the appropriation $Ld_1^\circ \to Ld_2$ which forgets λ, i.e. we have $F(V, \lambda_V) = V$, is leading. There are remaining details to be verified in the similar way to get a complete proof. Note that one can also make the same definitions without requiring the appropriation λ_V to be invertible. □

Corollary 4.10. *Every leading club* Ld *has a dual* Ld°, *the dual of* Ld *over itself. Its members are pairs* (V, λ_V), *where* $V \in Ld$ *and* $\lambda_V \in \{\lambda_{V,W} \mid V \otimes W \to W \otimes V\}$, *obeying,*

$$(\phi \otimes id) \circ \lambda_{V,W} = \lambda_{V,Z} \circ (id \otimes \phi), \quad \forall \phi : W \to Z,$$
$$\lambda_{V,ld} = id, \quad \lambda_{V,Z} \circ \lambda_{V,W} = \lambda_{V,W \otimes Z} \quad \forall W, Z \in Ld.$$

Transactions $\phi : (V, \lambda_V) \to (W, \lambda_W)$ *and the leading e.p.r.s expansion of representations are characterized by*

$$(\phi \otimes id) \circ \lambda_{V,Z} = \lambda_{W,Z} \circ (\phi \otimes id), \quad \lambda_{V \otimes W,Z} = \lambda_{V,Z} \circ \lambda_{W,Z}, \quad \forall Z \in Ld.$$

This special case of Theorem 4.15 is also called the center or double of leading club, denoted by $Z(Ld)$ *or* $D(Ld)$.

Proof: A direct proof of the corollary is straightforward. For example, the requirement that the leading e.r.p.s expansion of λ_V and λ_W as a form of aggregation obeys the representation condition is

$$\lambda_{V \otimes W,Z} \circ \lambda_{V \otimes W,U} = \lambda_{V,Z} \circ \lambda_{W,Z} \circ \lambda_{V,U} \circ \lambda_{W,U} =$$
$$\lambda_{V,Z} \circ \lambda_{V,U} \circ \lambda_{W,Z} \circ \lambda_{W,U} = \lambda_{V,Z \otimes U} \circ \lambda_{W,Z \otimes U} = \lambda_{V \otimes W,Z \otimes U},$$

for all $U, Z \in Ld$, as required. Also note that one may just take $Ld_2 = Ld_1 = Ld$ and $F : Ld \to Ld$, as the identity appropriation, i.e. one that preserves the underlying leading structure. We have written the condition for the appropriation explicitly, in this case there is symmetry between the conditions defining λ and the leading club structure. □

It is noteworthy that further generalizations are possible considering $(Ld, \otimes_{Ld})$ as a collection of new e.p.r.s rules, or an enterprise. Then a Pontryagin double-dual theorem can be used, one can construct coadjoint representations, develop e.p.r.s series by applying Fourier theory, ect., at this club level. As has been already mentioned, an appropriation $F : Ld_1 \to Ld_2$ between leading clubs provides a particular economic policy, an $Eprnat(F, F)$ as an agreeable and implementable structure, at least in economic convenient cases. If both clubs are leading and F is a leading appropriation, one also gets a coexpansion of e.r.p.s by policy $Eprnat(F, F)$ by regarding it as something like 'functions' on $(Ld, \otimes_{ld})$. This is studied more completely in next

Section 4.2, where at least in the convenient simple case, with $Ld = Vec$, one obtains an enterprise in this way, such that Ld is essentially its club of e.p.r.s standards. In this case, Ld° is its club of e.p.r.s costandards. A similar phenomenon holds more generally, using the theory of more complex e.p.r.s rules, to be discussed later.

Example 4.11. Let us consider again a leading club of simple exchange - standardized economy. We have H to be a biagreement or enterprise and let $Ld = {}_H M \to Vec$ be its club of standards as in Example 4.7, where the appropriation is the forgetful appropriation. Then Ld°, over a club of natural recourses Vec taken without the invertability condition, is the club ${}^H M$ of costandards.

Proof: Here we work in the familiar club of economies on natural resources and use the same techniques as in Example 4.7. Namely, one can count on nice bijection Lin and $Eprnat$. Precisely, a bijection $Lin(V, H \otimes V) \cong Eprnat(V \otimes F, F \otimes V)$, can be established under which the e.p.r.s implementable policy λ_V corresponds to a map $\beta : V \to H \otimes V$ by $\beta(v) \equiv v^{(\bar{1})} \otimes v^{(\bar{2})} = \lambda_{V,H}(v \otimes 1)$. Here F is the forgetful appropriation and H can be viewed as an H-standardized by the price (cost) regular representation. Thus, λ_V represents $\otimes$ which can be seen over the costandardized property of β, as we have,

$$\begin{aligned}(id \otimes \beta) \circ \beta(v) &= (id \otimes \lambda_{V,H}) \circ (\lambda_{V,H} \otimes id)(v \otimes 1 \otimes 1) \\ &= \lambda_{V,H \otimes H}(v \otimes (1 \otimes 1)) = \lambda_{V,H \otimes H}(v \otimes \Delta(1)) \\ &= (\Delta \otimes id) \circ \lambda_{V,H}(v \otimes 1) = (\Delta \otimes id) \circ \beta(v).\end{aligned}$$

The forth equality is that λ_V is of an appropriation type under the transactions $\Delta : H \to H \otimes H$. Conversely, given a coargumentation $V \to H \otimes V$, it is defined that $\lambda_{V,W}(v \otimes w) = v^{(\bar{1})} \overset{a}{>} w \otimes v^{(\bar{2})}$, and check that it is a policy, ect. Then the transactions in Ld° are the linear maps that intertwine the corresponding coargumentations, and that the expansion of e.p.r.s corresponds to the usual aggregate expansion of costandards. It is noteworthy that the invertability condition on the λ was not considered, and a slightly bigger club was constructed. If one insists on invertability then one has a subclub of ${}^H M$ in which the costandards are invertible in a certain sense. This invertability is automatic if H has a skew mutual understanding map. □

The Example also explains the sense in which the duality of leading clubs generalizes the known duality of enterprises and symmetric e.p.r.s rules. At the same time, one does not have to be limited to the simple case of natural resources, i.e. to condition that $Ld = Vec$. So we have the following Example which statements are left to the reader to prove.

Example 4.12. Consider again a leading club of simple exchange-standardized economy. Let there be given H, a biagreement or enterprise, and let $Ld = {}_H M$. Then Ld° over Ld, in Corollary 4.10, taken without the invertability condition on λ, can be identified with the club of crossed standards and costandards.

Note that the last example uses a convenient way how one might come to the concept of complex institutional doubles from simple ideas of club and its duality. Namely, one takes the dual of an enterprise H, passing from standards to costandards, but at the same time one is doing it in an H-covariant way, which is why the resulting club is the standard of something containing both H^* and H. Moreover, because the construction in the theorem is quite general, we can also apply it to biagreements, open enterprises, and other more complex e.p.r.s institutions. Thus, the e.p.r.s double can be defined, by its club of representations, for these as well. This also shows the power of the methodology of clubs in institutionalization of different forms in EPRT.

Note that we have introduced the term of 'leading expansion' for $\otimes_{ld}$ rather then 'aggregate expansion', because at this level of generality, there need not be any field of e.p.r.s claims of members, $\mathbf{h}$. There need not be any simple extension of e.p.r.s domain (usually expressed by direct sum $\oplus$) either. In our examples connected with the simple enterprises, there is $\mathbf{h}$-linearity and direct sums, and other convenient properties relating to them, such as good behavior for exact sequences under aggregation $\otimes$. Leading clubs with a well-behaved direct sum are symmetric (Abelian).

4.2 Clubs with Transfers

This section provides an introduction for mathematical economists to the theory of enterprises in institutions that is focused on e.p.r.s transfers. The special forms of enterprises induced by a membership to such a club are a kind of generalization of super - enterprises and/or corporations. The idea is to provide basic facts about clubs that allow e.p.r.s transfers, the standards and costandards of enterprises as members of such clubs including the notion of complexity of e.p.r.s transfer rules, braid diagrams to capture these flows, and sketch of technique how to operate with them. From formal point of view we are applying theory of Hopf algebras in braided categories to economic phenomena of interest.

4.2.1 A Few Introductory Notes

One may recall from Chapter 3 that, in spite of its complexity, ordinary open enterprise has a nice property that its e.p.r.s structure can be controlled by a structure of its opening. Obviously, openings are associated to clearing 'market' conditions which solutions are a rich source of e.p.r.s rules. Here the idea is to study some kind of alternative to these e.p.r.s rules, which are to capture nontraditional economic transactions and to develop e.p.r.s transfer rules.

This is also motivated by the ideas coming from theory of super-enterprises or corporations or global corporations. There rather than taking care about complexity of economic rationality of members implying noncommutativity of economic relations between them, one introduces the form of extension of e.p.r.s through aggregation of members' assets (tangible and intangible) in a more complex fashion. The agreements between the partners then remain simple with respect to this new complex form of aggregate extension. Formally, one may think about property of supercommutativity of the collections of e.p.r.s due to this form of aggregation. Then, from this point of view, one can develop super-e.p.r.s rules and/or corporate e.p.r.s rules, provide procedures for constructing super-corporate manifolds as their economic property rights spaces, and super-corporate growth processes. From the point of view of economic theory it is conceptually easier to make an entire shift of a club from economic spaces of natural resources to economic spaces of super-resources. The reader may have in mind a shift from a 'natural' economic rationality of an agent within simple enterprise involving simple economy on natural resources, to an economic rationality supported by an artificial intelligence system of an agent within modern enterprises dealing with information as main economic resources. One can study enterprises in such clubs based on super-e.p.r.s rules. Here the first step in the theoretical development is to generalize such construction to the case of traditional economic aggregate clubs. This ensures an extension of e.p.r.s due to aggregation and supports a collection of isotransactions, generalizing transposition or super-transposition map allowing transfers but retaining its general properties. In this case, it is still valid that transposing of a transposed collection of e.p.r.s provided the collection itself. Simply we have $\Psi^2 = id$ so that these generalized transpositions generate a representation of the simple e.p.r.s rule (symmetric rule). These general properties are needed for most of agreeable constructions of e.p.r.s institutions, for example for enterprises and agreements (programs) to support an economic growth, and these notions can be directly generalized to this 'super' setting. The theory of these clubs under traditional symmetric economic rationality is not fundamentally different from the above mentioned and in previous chapters discussed (super) simple agreements (economies) on natural economic recourses.

More interesting is the further generalization which relaxes the condition on identity mapping and transposition, i.e. that $\Psi^2 = id$, and distinguishes Ψ and Ψ^{-1}. Transpositions are thus more conveniently represented by braid-crossings rather than permutations. They generate an argumentation of the braiding rule concerning e.p.r.s transfers on aggregate extensions of e.p.r.s. Such quasiaggregate or braided-aggregate clubs can be formally introduced into club theory and also arise in the representation theory of e.p.r.s rules. To follow economic flows and study economic agreements and enterprises in such clubs is more complex comparing to the case of clubs with simple and/or open enterprises as members. In this Section it is this theoretical extension of e.p.r.s phenomena that is in focus and the following concrete issues are to be

better understood by introducing e.p.r.s structures that allow transfers:
(*i*) Many economic agreements that are of particular interest in economics, such as the degenerative agreements, domains of e.p.r.s regulation and exchange agreements, for example are not by their intrinsic properties simple e.p.r.s rules but appear to contain elements of complex e.p.r.s transfers. Thus formally we are dealing with braided-matrices $B(R)$ and braided-vectors $V(R')$ associated to R-matrices.
(*ii*) The ordinary club of enterprises in not closed under standardizations in a good sense. So if $H \subset H_1$ is covered by an enterprise projection then $H_1 \cong B \overset{a}{>} H$ where B is an enterprise which includes transfers.
(*iii*) To follow economic flows and to operate with e.p.r.s transfer rules the particular diagrams, so called braid diagrams, are helpful. They also show connections with mathematical knot theory and are a useful technique for reconsideration of some of the properties of ordinary enterprise from the more complex point of view.
(*iv*) In a combination of transfers and restructuring one can obtain useful procedures for studying properties of open enterprises. Namely, by encoding the property of noncocommutativity of these institutions as economic transfers, in a club which allows e.p.r.s transfers, these unfavored properties 'disappear' so that institutions can be considered to be simplifiable from perspective of copartners' rationality implying 'cocommutativity'. Similarly, applying this process on dual open enterprises they can be transformed to institutions which are considered simple from point of view of agents economic rationality implying their commutativity.
(*v*) In particular, properties of some of the e.p.r.s rules that we have already met are more easily understood in terms of the versions that allow transfers.

4.2.2 Definition and General Constructions

This subsection provides the formal definition of the appropriate axioms for transpose mapping, Ψ, and explains a technique of braid diagrams that allows us to easily and intuitively work with transpose mappings and transfers. It is worthy to note that in studying clubs with transfers applying braided structures appears economically natural and comes out of fundamental e.p.r.s structural relations of these settings. Let denote $\otimes^{op}(V,W) = W \otimes V$ and address the economic sense in which $\otimes$ and $\otimes^{op}$ should coincide.

Definition 4.13 (Leading club with transfers). *A leading club with transfers or simply quasiaggregate leading club, is defined by a triple* $(Ld, \otimes, \Psi)$, *where* $(Ld, \otimes)$ *is an ordinary leading club as defined in 4.6 which in addition ensure simplified agents' rationality in the sense that there is an e.p.r.s policy equivalence between the two appropriations* $\otimes$ *and* $\otimes^{op}$, *so that* $\otimes, \otimes^{op} : Ld \times Ld \to Ld$. *Namely, there are given appropriational isotransactions*

$$\Psi_{V,W} : V \otimes W \to W \otimes V, \quad \forall V, W \in Ld,$$

obeying the consistency conditions for a leading club with transfers as follows,

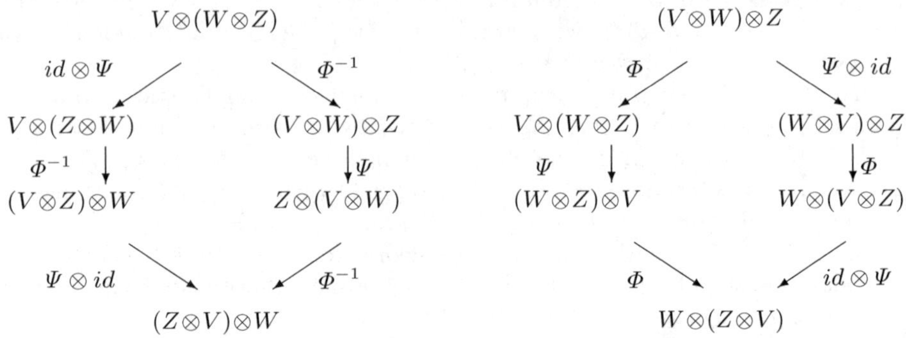

Fig. 4.5. Consistency conditions for leading appropriation in the leading club ($\otimes_{ld} \equiv \otimes$) express compatibility of commutativity and associativity.

Note that to simplify notation, a leading appropriation $\otimes_{ld}$ of an ordinary open enterprise is here denoted simple by $\otimes$, and that above definition just expresses precisely what one might expect for generalized economic transposition maps Ψ as carriers of e.p.r.s transfers.

Generalized transposition map

Generalized transposition maps Ψ from above definition appear to be of crucial importance for understanding e.r.p.s transfers, thus let us discuss some of their properties in more detail. Namely, consistency conditions in Figure 4.5 can be expressed in the following way if one suppress Φ,

$$\Psi_{V \otimes W, Z} = \Psi_{V,Z} \circ \Psi_{W,Z}, \quad \Psi_{V, W \otimes Z} = \Psi_{V,Z} \circ \Psi_{V,W} \tag{4.1}$$

for all enterprises, members of the leading club, $V, W, Z \in Ld$. These conditions express properties of e.p.r.s transfers in the sense that transposing $V \otimes W$ past Z is the same as transposing W past Z and then V past Z. Similar transposing V past $W \otimes Z$ is the same as first transposing V past W and then V past Z. These are economic properties that we might expect of impartial information channels or economic devices for transfer e.p.r.s collections. Here they are formalized by transposition maps. In addition to these proprieties, from the above conditions one can deduce that transposition map Ψ is trivial for the leading member,

$$\Psi_{V,ld} = id_V = \Psi_{ld,V} \tag{4.2}$$

and a host of other e.p.r.s identities that one might expect for some kind of transposition of the elements of a club. One may interpret that any e.p.r.s transfer concerning the leading member and any other member of the leading club with transfers, has actually no impact on the e.p.r.s of the member involved. If $\Psi^2 = id$ then one of the consistency conditions in Figure 4.5 is redundant and a leading club with transfers is actually reduced to an ordinary symmetric leading club which members strictly respect its leading rules.

Note that the appropriational feature of transposition maps means that they are commutative in a certain sense with economic transactions in the club. So, for example, appropriation of Ψ can be expressed by

$$\Psi_{Z,W}(\phi \otimes id) = (id \otimes \phi)\Psi_{V,W} \ \forall \phi \begin{matrix} V \\ \downarrow \\ Z \end{matrix}, \quad \Psi_{V,Z}(id \otimes \phi) = (\phi \otimes id)\Psi_{V,W} \ \forall \phi \begin{matrix} W \\ \downarrow \\ Z \end{matrix}. \quad (4.3)$$

It is noteworthy that conditions (4.1) – (4.3) are automatically satisfied when we are dealing with economic transfers involving natural recourses and simple enterprises. Then transposing concerns ordinary vector spaces or super-vector spaces and Ψ is the twist map or the supertwist respectively, so that

$$\Psi_{V,W}(v \otimes w) = w \otimes v \qquad \Psi_{V,W}(v \otimes w) = (-1)^{|v||w|} w \otimes v, \qquad (4.4)$$

on homogeneous elements of degree $| v |, | w |$, respectively. Here the form Ψ does not depend on the economic spaces V, W and they all connect together as described.

4.2.3 On Tool Kit for Transfers

Symmetric or simple aggregate clubs have properties that are very close to the familiar properties of economic vector spaces. Although these make our modeling easier, they are also less interesting for the same reason. They appear too restrictive to be able to provide more complete understanding of e.p.r.s institutions. Moreover, they sweep under the rug too many interesting issues on flows of e.p.r.s. Presence of e.p.r.s transfers imposes the issues of economic devices for channeling these transfers. An institution that contains e.p.r.s transfers can not be aggregate in the traditional manner. An e.p.r.s transfer, Ψ, as an economic natural transformation between the two appropriations $\otimes_{ap}$ and $\otimes_{ap}^{op}$, cannot assume $\Psi \circ \Psi = id$. But, one is able to distinguish between $\Psi_{V,W}$ and $(\Psi_{W,V})^{-1}$. There are both economic transactions $V \otimes W \to W \otimes V$, so both involve moving V past W to the right, but are distinct. Thus, one may think of Ψ not as transpositions, generating the symmetric e.p.r.s rules for members of a club, but as braids implying quasisymmetry or e.p.r.s transfers.

There is the following convenient notation for working with such transfers. One writes economic transactions pointing generally downwards, and denotes aggregation by horizontal juxtaposition. So instead of a usual arrow for $\Psi, (\Psi)^{-1}$, one uses the following convenient notation to distinguish them.

$$\Psi_{V,W} = \qquad\qquad (\Psi_{V,W})^{-1} =$$

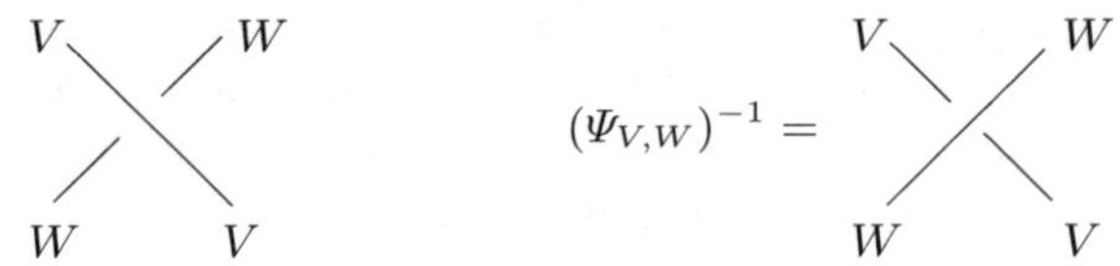

Fig. 4.6. Notation of transfers

Any other economic transaction is denoted by node on a string with the appropriate number of input and output legs. In this notation the consistency conditions in Definition 4.5 and the appropriationality of Ψ are denoted as in Figure 4.7, where the double lines refers to the composite enterprises $V \otimes W$ and $W \otimes Z$ in a convenient extension of the notation. The appropriationality of mapping Ψ is expressed in Figure 4.8, as the assertion that an economic transaction $\phi : V \to Z$ can be pulled through a transfer crossing. Similarly for Ψ^{-1} with inverse transfer crossings.

The coherence conditions for clubs that allow transfers can be expressed very simply in this notation. If two composite economic transactions built from Ψ, Φ correspond to the same transfers, then they coincide as economic transactions. Thus, we have consistency conditions expressed in braiding notation as follows,

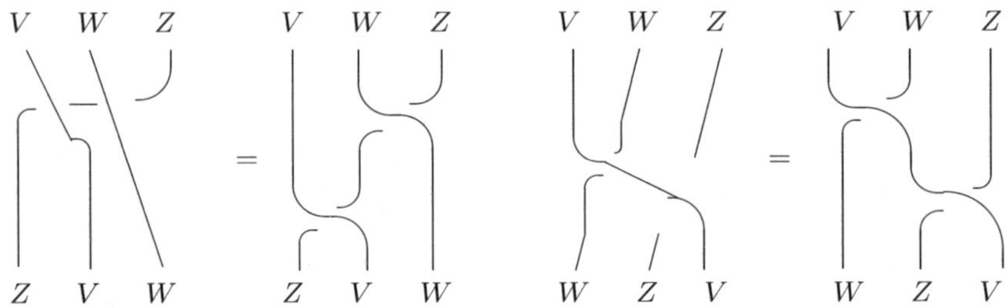

Fig. 4.7. Consistency conditions in the diagrammatic notation

It is not hard to see, for example in Figure 4.9 that two transfers coincide providing the identity,

$$\Psi_{V,W} \circ \Psi_{V,Z} \circ \Psi_{W,Z} = \Psi_{W,Z} \circ \Psi_{V,Z} \circ \Psi_{V,W} \tag{4.5}$$

which holds when the properties of e.p.r.s coherence and appropriational conditions are satisfied, i.e. 'market' clearing conditions are fulfilled. Namely, in Figure 4.8 two transfers coincide because one carried by $\Psi_{V,W}$ on the left can

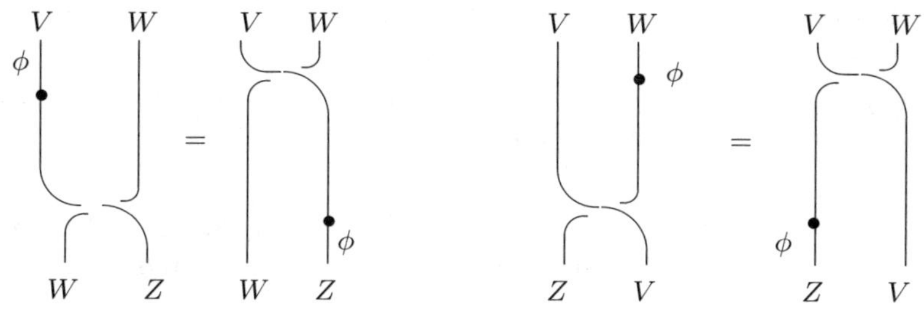

Fig. 4.8. Appropriation in the diagrammatic notation

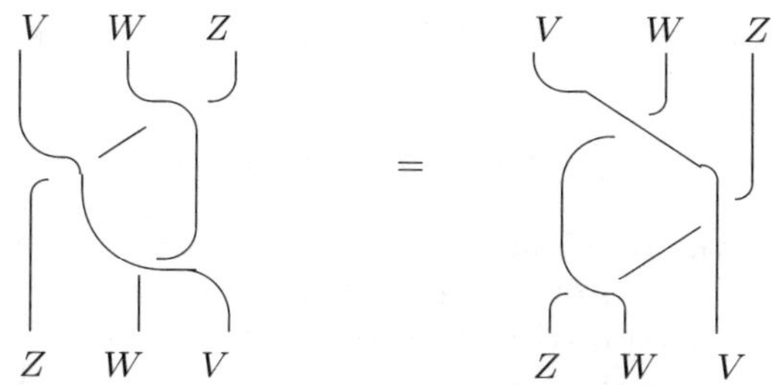

Fig. 4.9. Clearing conditions of transfer relations

be pushed up over a channel of Z member. The general proof in the simple, symmetric case or simple aggregate is based on a presentation of the symmetric rule in terms of transfer Ψ. The proof in the case where transfers are involved is exactly the same with the role of the symmetric rule now played by the transfer rules modeled by the Artin braid group. The transfer rules on a given number of channels (strands) is the rule generated by positive, receiving transfers or over braid crossing and by negative, giving transfers, or under braid crossings of adjacent strands or channels, regarded as mutually inverse, and the clearing conditions in Figure 4.9 for three strands. Note that the coherence theorem can be extended to include branches to ensure that notation is consistent when we include other economic transactions with various numbers of inputs and outputs. In this case we are dealing with symmetric rules, ones that concern a given number of members (enterprises) where the rules are generated by negative and positive transfers of adjacent enterprises, regraded as mutually related. The transfer relations above are given for three enterprises. As mention above, one can introduce rules concerning other economic relations using branches.

4.2.4 Some Basic Properties

The following statement can be undertaken from the properties of λ discussed in Corollary 4.10.

Proposition 4.14. *Let Ld be any leading club. The dual leading club Ld° described in Corollary 4.10 carries transfers in the form $\Psi_{(V,\lambda_V),(W,\lambda_W)} = \lambda_{V,W}$.*

Proof: According the properties of λ discussed in Corollary 4.10 it directly implies that Ψ, as stated, satisfies the conditions of consistency. □

One may recall (if necessary see Chapter 2) that every enterprise carries argumentation on itself by the adjoint argumentation of the agency, denoted by Ad. Any enterprise also carries coargumentations on itself by price regular coargumentation Δ provided by the e.r.p.s coexpansion of the coagancy. In addition it can be shown that they are compatible in the way required for the club of crossed H-standardized club, ${}^H_H M$. The Corollary then describe how transfers are involved,

$$\Psi : H \otimes H \to H \otimes H, \qquad \Psi(h \otimes g) = \sum h_{(1)} g \gamma h_{(2)} \otimes h_{(3)}, \tag{4.6}$$

This necessarily obeys the relations concerning transfers and clearing conditions of openings by transfers from Figure 4.9. This is valid for any enterprise. For example, in the case of simple agreement on growth, given by $H = U(g)$, it also restricts to the subspace $V = \mathbf{h} \oplus g$ as a transfer, where $\mathbf{h}$ is an e.p.r.s field of claims and g a growing factor,

$$\Psi : V \otimes V \to V \otimes V, \quad \Psi(\xi \otimes \nu) = [\xi, \nu] \otimes 1 + \nu \otimes \xi, \quad \forall \xi, \nu \in g, \tag{4.7}$$

and $\Psi(1 \otimes \xi) = \xi \otimes 1$, etc., as usual for the leader of the leading club. Thus, we have a nontrivial transfer or a clearing e.p.r.s operator associated to any nontrivial growth agreement. One also can recall that if H is finite dimensional then a club of crosstandardes ${}^H_H M$ can be identified with the club of representations of the e.p.r.s double. The transfers in this case can also be understood as an example of the following general form.

Theorem 4.15. (Opening and transfer) *If H is an open biagreement or an open enterprise, then the club ${}_H M$ of H-standards is one that allows transfers. Transfers are shaped by the argumentation of opening $\mathcal{R}$ followed by the usual transposition map. Precisely,*

$$\Psi_{V,W}(v \otimes w) = \sum \mathcal{R}^{(2)} \overset{a}{>} w \otimes \mathcal{R}^{(1)} \overset{a}{>} v.$$

Sketch of proof and comments: One has to verify first that Ψ as stated is indeed an e.p.r.s transaction, i.e. that it is an intertwiner for the argumentation of H. We have,

$$\Psi(h \overset{a}{>} (v \otimes w)) = \Psi((\Delta h) \overset{a}{>} (v \otimes w)) = \tau(\mathcal{R}(\Delta h) \overset{a}{>} (v \otimes w))$$
$$= \tau((\Delta^{op} h)\mathcal{R} \overset{a}{>} (v \otimes w)) = h \overset{a}{>} \Psi(v \otimes w),$$

as required. Note that expression $\overset{a}{>}$ was used also to denote the argumentation of $H \otimes H$ on $V \otimes W$. In general, the usual transposition map alone is not an intertwiner. Thus, openness appears as a crucial property and here one need to explore effects of opening first, i.e. $\mathcal{R}$. So, let us verify the consistency conditions given in Figure 4.5.

$$\Psi_{V \otimes W,Z}(v \otimes w \otimes z) = \mathcal{R}^{(2)} \overset{a}{>} z \otimes \mathcal{R}^{(1)} \overset{a}{>} (v \otimes w) =$$
$$\mathcal{R}^{(2)} \overset{a}{>} z \otimes \mathcal{R}^{(1)}{}_{(1)} \overset{a}{>} v \otimes \mathcal{R}^{(1)}{}_{(2)} \overset{a}{>} w = \mathcal{R}^{(2)}\mathcal{R}'^{(2)} \overset{a}{>} z \otimes \mathcal{R}^{(1)} \overset{a}{>} v \otimes \mathcal{R}'^{(1)} \overset{a}{>} w =$$
$$\Psi_{V,Z}(v \otimes \mathcal{R}'^{(2)} \overset{a}{>} z) \otimes \mathcal{R}'^{(1)} \overset{a}{>} w = \Psi_{V,Z} \circ \Psi_{W,Z}(v \otimes w \otimes z),$$

$$\Psi_{V,W \otimes Z}(v \otimes w \otimes z) = \mathcal{R}^{(2)} \overset{a}{>} (w \otimes z)\mathcal{R}^{(1)} \overset{a}{>} v =$$
$$\mathcal{R}^{(2)}{}_{(1)} \overset{a}{>} w \otimes \mathcal{R}^{(2)}{}_{(2)} \overset{a}{>} z \otimes \mathcal{R}^{(1)} \overset{a}{>} v = \mathcal{R}^{(2)} \overset{a}{>} w \otimes \mathcal{R}'^{(2)} \overset{a}{>} z \otimes \mathcal{R}'^{(1)}\mathcal{R}^{(1)} \overset{a}{>} v =$$
$$\mathcal{R}^{(2)} \overset{a}{>} w \otimes \Psi_{V,Z}(\mathcal{R}^{(1)} \overset{a}{>} v \otimes z) = \Psi_{V,Z} \circ \Psi_{V,W}(v \otimes w \otimes z),$$

where $\mathcal{R}'$ denotes a second implementation of opening (second copy of) $\mathcal{R}$. The form of Ψ, as suggested by the theorem, is used and axioms of an opening structure as given in Chapter 3. The axioms (3.1) for an e.p.r.s opening structure provide directly the two consistency conditions above, while the axiom (3.2) provides directly the intertwiner property. The transfers, i.e. the form of Ψ according to the above is shaped by an element of $H \otimes H$ through argumentation. The property of appropriationality for Ψ is thus directly ensured and takes the form of the usual transposition map for simple economic institutions modeled by economic vector spaces. Finely, the assumption that an opening $\mathcal{R}$ is invertible ensures that the transfers Ψ are invertible. □

The importance of this theorem for understanding openings and their role in transfers is that it tells us that the axioms of a nontrivial open biagreement are exactly what one needs to make the leading club of standards to become one that allows transfers. Even more, one can apply the procedure from the above proof in a reverse sense and derive the axioms for an opening $\mathcal{R}$ from transfers. Similar is valid for the case of nontrivial open quasibiagreement. The formula for Ψ is just the same and, for example, one can modify the club of standards in Example 4.8 by introducing transfers through opening if and only if ordinary opening $\mathcal{R}$ obeys axiom (3.2) and (3.1). Namely, a nontrivial opening structure (quasitriangular one) is just what is needed to get the club of standardized enterprises that allows transfers. This will be seen more clearly and formally studied through the reconstruction theorems in Chapter 5. It is noteworthy that a case of a trivial opening, corresponds precisely to the case where Ψ provides a symmetric or simple aggregate club rather then one with transfers. Nevertheless, it is important to have in mind that even elementary discrete enterprises generate large clubs of enterprises with which one might want or have to work in e.p.r.s modeling. This is quite different role of enterprises comparing to their role in carrying an exclusive fixed e.p.r.s law or symmetric rules. The enterprise serves as a kind of e.p.r.s pattern used as a guide that encode the defining features of the club. One may then work with the club without realizing that it is the club of representations of some of e.p.r.s patterns. It seems that many clubs in economics carry such structures and are actually of this form.

Example 4.16. **Simple growth club with transfers** Let $Z'_{/n}$ be the nontrivial open enterprise concerning simple economic growth as was described in Example 3.5, Chapter 3. Then under the leading club Ld_n^Z of representations one my think of simple economic investors. Precisely, the enterprises are simple e.p.r.s institutions, describable by economic vector spaces which are $Z_{/n}$-graded, and the economic transactions are linear maps that preserve the grading. The club is a leading one which allow transfers where the e.p.r.s extension is due to aggregation and is defined by adding the grading standardized by n, and with transfers $\Psi(v \otimes w) = exp\left(\frac{2\pi\imath|v||w|}{n}\right) w \otimes v$ for homogeneous elements of degree $|v|, |w|$. The club is truly with transfers for $n > 2$.

Sketch of proof and comments: Recall that this enterprise is generated by an economic valuation factor g of investors such that $g^n = 1$. Hence its representations decompose as $V = \oplus_{a=0}^{n-1} V_a$, where g is an argumentation by $g \overset{a}{>} v = e^{\frac{2\pi\imath|v||w|}{n}} v$ for all $v \in V_a$. We say that $v \in V_a$ has degree a. This is the grading. The coexpansion is defined by $\Delta g = g \otimes g$, so the decomposition of an aggregate expansion representation is by adding the degrees. To obtain a formula for transfer one uses the formula for opening $\mathcal{R}$ as explained in Example 3.5, put it into Theorem 4.15, which directly provide the expression for transfers above. Thus, one may recall that this enterprise is actually based on the e.p.r.s rules generated by investment returns and risk management already sketched in Chapter 3. Namely, the club generates, as its representations, the club of investors along with its correct transfers structure and transposition Ψ. The term is derived from economics of externalities, where such an exchange laws are in focus. One may think of borrowing-landing relations from financial markets combined with speculative and corruptible transfers in investments agreements. The case when $n = 2$ one is dealing with simple landing-borrowing relations combined with transfers out of traditional monetary market (see [63]). It is exactly the club of $Z_{/2}$-graded or supervector economic spaces and even transactions. Note that this works because $Z'_{/2}$ has nontrivial opening structure or universal monetary market that is expressible over so called universal $\mathcal{R}$-matrix. It carries complex economic relations of agents (lander and borrower) in the club of financial relations. Note that the universal $\mathcal{R}$-matrix or structure of monetary market is given as a formal power series. Hence the transfers Ψ are given by a power series of matrices and can be perfectly convergent when evaluation over complete monetary market (including unobserved monetary speculations). The condition is that one limits himself to a suitable subclubs of representations. This works fine for the standardized growth economy with any fixed appropriation rule ap, $U_{ap}(g)$, if one limit oneself to finite-dimension cases. □

As a more concrete version of above example we may consider the following.

Example 4.17. **Simple growth club with public transfers** Let $Z_{/n,\alpha}$ be the trivial open enterprise concerning simple economic growth with public support as was described in Example 3.16, Chapter 3. The club of representations is given by simple economic public investors with zero-profit standards. Precisely, the enterprises are pairs (V, D_V), where V is a simple financial institution, describable by $Z_{/2}$-graded or supervector economic spaces as above, and the financial transaction $D_V : V \to V$, is an odd economic operator such that it implementation gives $D_V^2 = 0$. Such a club is a leading one which allow transfers, where outcome of an investment is split in the way that private investor is allowed to transfer losses to public assets, and to retain gains in the cases of profitable investment. The club has a leading e.p.r.s expansion $\otimes_{pr}$

$$(V, D_V) \otimes_{pr} (W, D_W) = (V \otimes_{pr} W, D_{V \otimes_{pr} W})$$

and laws of financial transactions over public financial devices

$$D_{V \otimes_{pr} W}(v \otimes_{pr} w) = D_V(v) \otimes_{pr} w + (-1)^{|v|} v \otimes_{pr} D_W(w)$$

and public institutions of 'welfare' transfer,

$$\Psi_{V,W}(v \otimes_{pr} w) = (-1)^{|w||v|} w \otimes_{pr} w + \alpha(-1)^{|w|(1-|v|)} D_W(w) \otimes_{pr} D_V(v),$$

on homogeneous collections of e.p.r.s.

Sketch of proof and comments: Here any representation splits as $V = V_0 \oplus V_1$ according to the eigenvalue of the projection operator $2^{-1}(1+g)$. Thus, D_V is the representation of x into V. It is odd because $gx = -xg$, and it takes an off-diagonal form in the above decomposition. An economic transaction in the club is an even financial operation that intertwines the corresponding financial transactions of public funds. The form of the coexpansion for copartner are $\Delta x = x \otimes_{pr} 1 + g \otimes_{pr} x$, and $\Delta g = g \otimes_{pr} g$, and trivial opening structure imply the given expansion of e.p.r.s due to aggregation and transfers as stated. One may note that enterprises of a similar type for which we would have $D^2 = 1$ rather than $D^2 = 0$ play an important role in complex wealth redistribution under the heading of derivative financial instruments. □

Now, let us return to the general theory and give the dual version for costandards. We know, of course, that it is a routine matter to dualize the theory, i.e., to go from standards to costandards. Here, it is sufficiently important that is worth to give some statements on duality explicitly which checking is left to the reader.

Example 4.18. Let A be a dual nontrivial open biagreement or an enterprise. Show that the transfers in the club M^A of quality A-costandards are

$$\Psi_{V,W}(v \otimes w) = \sum w^{(1_{ap})} \otimes v^{(1_{ap})} \mathcal{R}(v^{(2_{ap})} \otimes w^{(2_{ap})}),$$

where we denote the coargumentation explicitly as in Section 2.2.3, Chapter 2.

4.2.5 Aggregation with Transfers

Let us now discussed an important application of transfers or quasiaggregate clubs which appears to be crucial for solving concrete economic problems. What is needed is an institution to provide an e.p.r.s natural way to define the aggregate expansion of e.p.r.s-rules covariant agreements. Thus we want to define an agreement concerning the expansion of aggregates involving transfers.

Definition 4.19. *Let $\mathcal{C}$ be a leading club. An agreement in $\mathcal{C}$ is an enterprise B of $\mathcal{C}$ which is involved with transaction of expansion of e.p.r.s, $B \otimes B \to B$ and leading transfer agency $1_{lap} \to B$ obeying the usual axioms concerning agreement (associativity and agency axioms as in Chapter 2), but now in the club $\mathcal{C}$.*

From Chapter 2 we may recall that if H is a biagreement or an enterprise then a price H-standard agreement is nothing other than an agreement in the leading club formed by the price or costs standards of that biagreement or enterprise. This leading club is denoted by ${}_H M$, and it contains costs (price) H-standards. The similar is valid for dual point of view, where the dual statement is that if A is a biagreement or an enterprise then a quality A-costandard agreement is nothing other than an agreement in the leading club M^H of quality A-costandards. The later is clear from the aggregate expansion coargumentation (2.2.3). These statements work for any enterprise, as one need only a structure of a leading club to define the notion of an agreement in it. One may recall that within the traditional economic concept the structure of leadership comes in its extreme form of dictatorship. The above statements become particularly useful if H is nontrivial open or if A is dual of nontrivial opening. The reason is the following general construction which involves transfers in a nontrivial way.

Lemma 4.20. *Let B, C be two agreements in a leading club with transfers. Then the e.p.r.s collection $B \otimes C$ also has the structure of an agreement in the club, denoted by $B \otimes_{lapt} C$. The expansion of this agreement is define by composition of transfers and aggregation by the following*

$$m_{B \otimes_{lapt} C} = (m_B \otimes m_C) \circ (id \otimes \Psi_{C,B} \otimes id),$$

while its agency is the aggregate expansion that preserves economic transactions. This agreement can be called an agreement on aggregate expansion with transfers. Moreover, for any three agreements B, C, D in the club, one has $(B \otimes_{lapt} C) \otimes_{lapt} D \cong B \otimes_{lapt} (C \otimes_{lapt} D)$ via the underlying associativity of economic transaction Φ.

Proof: As above, we suppress writing the Φ, p_{lap}, q_{lap} explicitly. It has to be shown that the e.p.r.s expansion defined in the lemma has the property of associativity. Let do this by using the diagrammatic notation already sketched as a convenient tool for working in clubs with transfers. One write the economic transactions concerning expansion, $B \otimes B \to B$ and $C \otimes C \to C$ downwards as: The left hand side of the Figure 4.10 is then the expansion obtained twice

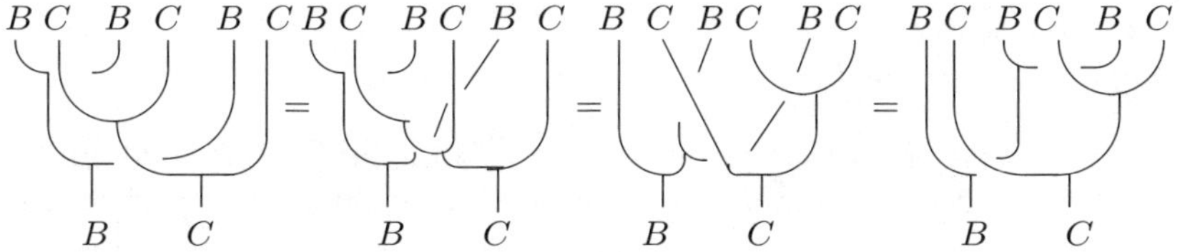

Fig. 4.10. Associativity of the aggregate expansion of two agreements that incorporate transfers.

in price order, and the right hand side is the expansion obtained twice in the quality order. The first equality is obtained by appropriationality under the second of these transactions, using Figure 4.8 to implement it over the quality outcome of B. In the diagram this pushes branches down over the quality outcome of B. Then we use associativity in B and C to reorganize the transactions (branches). Once reorganized transactions are then again object of appropriation under the first of the transactions, implementing the price (cost) argument. In the diagram this pushes the expanding transaction of B up, and under the price outcome of C. The proof that an agency preserves structure is more trivial. Note that the construction itself is associative. It can be seen by writing out the expansions diagrammatically, and using the consistency conditions given by diagrams from Figure 4.7. This imposes the validity of consistency conditions between B, C, D under implementable assumptions that each of agency is e.p.r.s preserving in its economic transactions. □

Corollary 4.21. *Let H be a nontrivial open enterprise and let B, C be cost H-costandards agreements. Then there is an agreement concerning aggregate expansion of H-standards with transfers $B \otimes_{lapt} C$ built on $B \otimes C$ with expansion,*

$$(a \otimes c)(b \otimes d) = \sum a(\mathcal{R}^{(2)} \overset{a}{>} b) \otimes (\mathcal{R}^{(1)} \overset{a}{>} c)d$$

for all $a, b \in B$ and $c, d \in C$, and the argument of aggregate expansion of H.

Hint of proof: The proof follows immediately from the above Lemma and Theorem 4.15. It is also not difficult to verify the statement directly if desired. Here one actually uses axioms of an open enterprise from Chapter 3.

Corollary 4.22. *Let A be a dual nontrivial open enterprise and let B, C be quality H-costandards agreements. Then there is an agreement on aggregate expansion of A-costandards with transfers $B \otimes_{lapt} C$ built on conventional aggregate of B and C, $B \otimes C$ with expansion,*

$$(a \otimes c)(b \otimes d) = \sum ab^{(1^{ap})} \otimes c^{(2^{ap})} d\mathcal{R}(c^{(2^{ap})} \otimes b^{(2^{ap})})$$

for all $a, b \in B$ and $c, d \in C$, and the coargumentation of aggregate expansion given by $\beta_{B\otimes C}(a \otimes c) = \sum a^{(1^{lapt})} \otimes c^{(1^{lapt})} \otimes a^{(2^{lapt})} \otimes c^{(2^{lapt})}$, in terms of the coargumentation on B, C an the expansion of A.

Hint of proof: The proof follows immediately from the Lemma 4.20, and Exercise 4.17. It is also not difficult to verify the statement directly if desired.

Example 4.23. Let B, C be two investment agreements, i.e. $Z_{/n}$-graded agreements for which the expansion map is additive in the degree and the agency has degree 0. There is an agreement on investment aggregate expansion $B \otimes_{lapt} C$ with property,

$$(a \otimes c)(b \otimes d) = e^{\frac{2\pi \imath |c||b|}{n}} ab \otimes cd$$

and an aggregate expansion of agency.

Sketch of proof and comments: The proof is immediate from the transfers in Example 4.16. This also shows how the aggregate expansion with transfers generalizes the notion of $Z_{/2}$-graded or superaggregate expansion of superagreement. More examples of this type are discussed in the next section. The general ideas are the same, one should think of the elements of the agreement as having nontrivial statistics concerning transfers with respect to another independent agreement in the club. At least in the concrete economic setting, where enterprises are simple institutions with simple e.p.r.s gluing structure.

Then they are modeled over vector spaces with conventional additional structure, for example such as discussed in Corollaries 4.21 and 4.22. Thus, it is clear that $B \equiv B \otimes 1$ and $C \equiv 1 \otimes C$ are subagreements, since the transfers are trivial on the unit element. Let write $b \equiv b \otimes 1$ and $c \equiv 1 \otimes c$, then

$$c'b = (1 \otimes c)(b \otimes 1) = \Psi(c \otimes b) = \sum_k (b_k \otimes 1)(1 \otimes c_k)$$
$$= \sum_k b_k c'_k \tag{4.8}$$

if $\Psi(c \otimes b) \equiv \sum_k b_k \otimes c_k$. This means that the two subagreements B, C fail to commute inside the graded aggregate expansion. The statistics of transfers are described by Ψ and can be linear combination rather then simple a phase factor as in this example. □

It may be noteworthy that one may think of $B \otimes_{lapt} C$ as the natural generalization of the trivial aggregate expansion of agreements $(a \otimes b)(c \otimes d) = (ab \otimes cd)$, which one take for granted when working with usual agreement (on simple economic relations). In economic terms, the trivial aggregate expansion of two economic systems corresponds to building joint economic system in which the two subsystems are independent. The superaggregate expansion is implemented in the same way and is the procedure to aggregate expansion of independent private institutions. Then transferred aggregate expansion is a generalization of the notion of combining private institutions. So, more complex economic rationality, needed in this case and implying the property of noncommutativity, is usually thought of as consequence of statistics of transfers rather than an e.p.r.s institutionalization concept or some other origin. This ideas are discussed more precisely over concrete applications in the sequel to this volume.

In addition, it can be seen from Theorem 4.15 that, whenever a nontrivial open enterprise provides an argumentation on an agreement, it induces statistics of transfers. When ordinary e.p.r.s rules cause this, the transfers are trivial so we do not see the phenomenon. In the case when e.p.r.s modifications of ordinary rules are economic arguments they do induce nontrivial statistics of transfers as a corollary of the modification. In this way, two quite different concepts, that of statistics of nontrivial economic transfers and that of covariance under a fixed property law, are unified in the concept of an e.p.r.s rule covariance.

4.3 Duals and E.p.r.s Redistributions

4.3.1 Introduction

Duality is a property of vector spaces and e.p.r.s rule representations, that has been extremely important for modeling and understating economic relations, not just within EPRT but generally in economics. Thus, it seems natural to try to generalize this property to the clubs and other more complex e.p.r.s institutions. Recall, that for simple institutions on natural economic resources, which can be modeled over vector spaces, one has developed concept of duality by well know procedures in forming the dual vector space. It is similar with e.p.r.s rule representations, where one can obtain the dual or conjugate representation using the rule inverse to turn the simple quality argumentation of the e.p.r.s rule on the economic dual vector space back into a simple cost (price) argumentation. Now, the idea is to consider the same construction on the representations of an enterprise. Note that here a mutual understanding map will play an important role in construction theory, as a generalization of an e.p.r.s rule inverse.

It is noteworthy that property of duality and issue of the existence of dual enterprises make economic sense for any club. In the examples that we are discussing it exists in the representations of any enterprise independently of whether or not there is a nontrivial open structure and/or transfers.

There are two approaches to the problem of duality of enterprises in a leading club. The first is to introduce a notion like that of 'linear maps' that describe internal economic transactions between members (enterprises) of a leading club where appropriation of e.p.r.s is according to some accepted $ap(\equiv lap)$ rule. These economic transactions, for any two members (enterprises) V, W of the club, are denoted by $Homt_{ap}(V, W)$. Then, constraining or specializing to $V^* = Homt_{ap}(V, ld \equiv 1_{ap})$, for some fixed ap, should supply a suitable concept for a dual within the considered leading club. In the particular convenient case, one may also get $V^{**} \cong V$. This is how one usually meets the concept of duality, over economic vector spaces, as the vector space of economic linear maps $V \to \mathbf{h}$. Then this property provides the canonical pairing between V^* and V. One should recall that here this V^* is implicitly equipped with an economic evaluation map $ev : V^* \otimes V \to \mathbf{h}$. This approach was used in Chapter 2, which actually defines mentioned canonical pairing. One should have in mind that there is also a coevaluation map, $coev : \mathbf{h} \to V \otimes V^*$, defined as the map whose dualization would be evaluation $V^{**} \otimes V^* \to \mathbf{h}$. For finite dimensional economic vector spaces, there is a symmetry between V^* and V, since in this case one may identify the double dual with the original. Thus, one has explicitly the maps,

$$ev(f \otimes v) = f(v), \quad coev(\lambda) = \lambda \sum_a e_a \otimes f^a, \tag{4.9}$$

for all $v \in V, f \in V^*$ and $\lambda \in \mathbf{h}$, where $\{e_a\}$ is a basis of V and $\{f^a\}$ a dual basis in V^*.

The second and more symmetric approach to the duality problem is to specify $V^*, ev, coev$ abstractly for a leading club and to study how an appropriate formulation of the notion of duality for various types of e.p.r.s institutions can be obtained.

In this section we begin with a formal definition of the appropriate axioms for V^* in a leading club. Then the case of a quasiaggregate leading club is discussed and it is shown how to work with duals in terms of e.p.r.s institutions that allow complex transfer relations over redistribute instruments. Relations of redistributions are modeled using technique of knots and tangle diagrams. The appearance of the redistributing flows of e.p.r.s and redistribution - invariants is fundamental outcome of construction of e.r.p.s institutions that contain variants of e.p.r.s transfers.

4.3.2 Definitions and General Construction

In this subsection we specify $V^*, ev, coev$ abstractly for a leading club and study how an appropriate formulation of notion of duality for various types of e.p.r.s institutions compatible with the leading club can be obtained.

Definition 4.24. (Evaluation, Coevaluation) *Let Ld be a leading club. A member (enterprise) V, of a leading club $V \in Ld$ has a cost (price) dual, or is rigid, if there is an enterprise V^*, $V^* \in Ld$ and economic transactions called evaluation $ev_V : V^* \otimes V \to ld(\equiv 1_{lap})$, and coevaluation $coev_V : ld \to V \otimes V^*$, for fixed leading appropriation, lap, such that*

$$V \stackrel{coev}{\longrightarrow} (V \otimes V^*) \otimes V \stackrel{\Phi}{\to} V \otimes (V^* \otimes V) \stackrel{ev}{\to} V,$$
$$V^* \stackrel{coev}{\longrightarrow} V^* \otimes (V \otimes V^*) \stackrel{\Phi^{-1}}{\longrightarrow} (V^* \otimes V) \otimes V^* \stackrel{ev}{\to} V^* \tag{4.10}$$

compose to id_V and id_{V^*}, respectively. If two enterprises of a leading club V, W have duals and a transaction $\phi : V \to W$ is an economic transaction between them according to e.p.r.s rules of Ld, then

$$\phi^* = (ev_V \otimes id) \circ (id \otimes \phi \otimes id) \circ (id \otimes coev_W) : W^* \to V^* \tag{4.11}$$

is called the dual or adjoint e.p.r.s transaction within the club.

Note that the associativity Φ is omitted in (4.11), and in what follows. It is easy to see that if $(V^*, ev, coev)$ does exist then it is unique up to an isotransaction. Thus, if $(V^{*\prime}, ev', coev')$ is also a dual for V, then one can define an e.p.r.s transaction among duals $\theta : V^{*\prime} \to V^*$, and its inverse by, $\theta = (ev' \otimes id) \circ (id \otimes coev)$, and $\theta^{-1} = (ev \otimes id) \circ (id \otimes coev')$. Relations between two evaluations and coevaluations are then given by

$$ev' = ev \circ (\theta \otimes id), \quad coev' = (id \otimes \theta^{-1}) \circ coev.$$

If every member in the club has a dual, then one may say that leading club Ld is a rigid one.

Let us now explain diagrammatic technique already confirmed as useful and efficient for representations and following e.p.r.s flows within clubs. In notation, the leading (unit) enterprise, ld and transactions Φ are given implicitly, so their symbols are suppressed, and one writes all economic transactions pointing generally downwards. In such notation, the evaluation and coevaluation appear symbolically by $ev = \bigcup$ and $coev = \bigcap$.

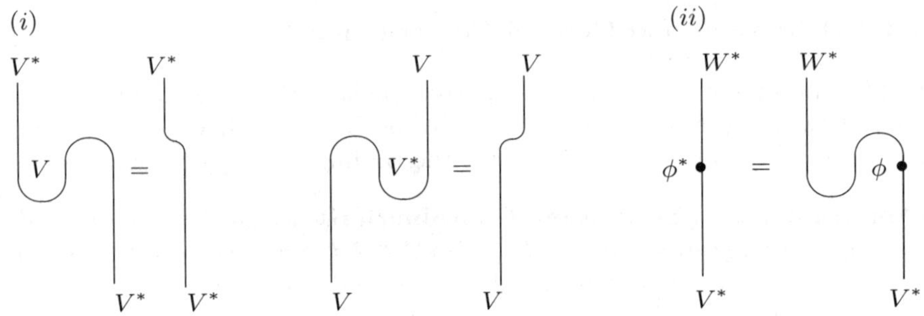

Fig. 4.11. Definitions of: (i) dual enterprise V^*, and (ii) adjoint transaction ϕ^*, in diagrammatic notation.

They are written without marking the node. Then axioms (4.11) in the definition are expressed as the 'bend-straightening axioms' and shown in part (i) of Figure 4.11. The adjoint transaction ϕ^* is shown in part (ii). From traditional concept of economic duality we know that this property also concerns aggregate. Here, Figure 4.12 shows that if two enterprises V, W have duals then their aggregate, where e.p.r.s expansion is given by Ld rule, $\otimes_{lap} = \otimes$, $V \otimes W$, also has dual with

$$(V \otimes W)^* = W^* \otimes V^*, \; ev_{V \otimes W} = ev_W \circ ec_V, \; coev_{V \otimes W} = coev_W \circ coev_V,$$

where unnecessary identity maps, being economic transactions which do not have impacts of e.p.r.s, are suppressed. We take this as the chosen dual of $V \otimes_{ld} W$ in what follows. In a similar way, if V^* has a dual it is natural to choose it so that $ev_{V^*} = (coev_V)^*$ and $coev_{V^*} = (ev_V)^*$. One can also see that if a club Ld is rigid, then $* : Ld \to Ld$ is a contravariant appropriation in the sense discussed in Section 4.1.1.

Let us now address the more interesting e.p.r.s environment where the club is a leading club that allows transfers. Here enterprises within the club, as carriers of variety of e.p.r.s interests, are organized in a transferring manner, so that we are dealing with an aggregated club as described in Section 4.2. Our notation for ev and $coev$ combines with our previous coherence theorem as described above. So one can slide economic transactions between enterprises within the club through transfer crossings, and in the case of ev and $coev$

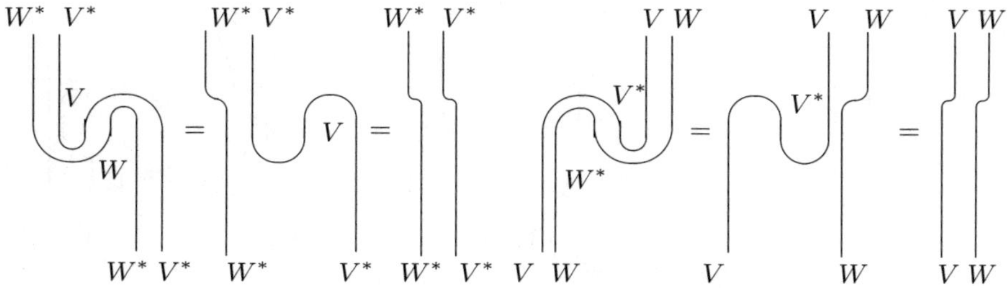

Fig. 4.12. Diagrammatic notation of duality for an aggregate enterprise.

one can straighten the bends of the type shown in the figure. The composite transaction is the same if the diagrammatic picture is the same up to such replacements of transfers.

Proposition 4.25. *In a rigid leading club that allows transfers there are e.p.r.s policies concerning transfers,* $u, v^{-1} \in Eprnat(id, *^2)$ *defined by*

$$\begin{aligned} u_V &= (ev_V \otimes id) \circ (\Psi_{V,V^*} \otimes id) \circ (id \otimes coev_{V^*}), \\ u_V^{-1} &= (id \otimes ev_{V^*}) \circ (\Psi_{V^{**},V} \otimes id) \circ (id \otimes coev_V), \\ v_V &= (ev_V^* \otimes id) \circ (id \otimes \Psi_{V,V^*}) \circ (id \otimes coev_V), \\ v_V^{-1} &= (ev_V \otimes id) \circ (id \otimes \Psi_{V^{**},V}) \circ (coev_{V^*} \otimes id), \end{aligned}$$

for any member V *of the club, and for any aggregate institution within the club,* $V \otimes W$, *among two members, these obey*

$$\begin{aligned} u_{V\otimes W} &= \Psi_{V,W}^{-1} \circ \Psi_{W,V}^{-1} \circ (u_V \otimes u_W), \\ v_{V\otimes W} &= \Psi_{V,W}^{-1} \circ \Psi_{W,V}^{-1} \circ (v_V \otimes v_W), \end{aligned}$$

and, for any economic transaction within the club these policies are such that

$$(\phi^*)^* = u_W \circ \phi \circ u_V^{-1} = v_W^{-1} \circ \phi \circ v_V, \quad \forall \phi : V \to W.$$

These policies are called e.p.r.s equivalence policies as they control e.p.r.s transfers in the way to preserve the leading structure of the club.

Proof: The proof is done diagrammatically in Figures 4.13 and 4.14. It is assumed that both economic spaces V and V^* have duals and we define the economic transactions u_V, v_V in Figure 4.13 part (i), and show their composition in part (ii). They carry appropriational property because any other transaction or node ϕ on the e.p.r.s flow could be pulled through by appropriationality of transfer Ψ and an elementary e.p.r.s rationality of members incorporated into properties of $ev, coev$. So one may think of them

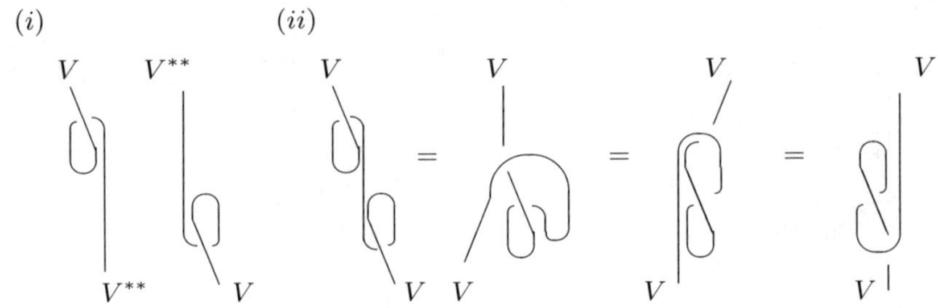

Fig. 4.13. Diagrammatic notation of (i) transactions u and v and (ii) their composition $v \circ u$.

as e.p.r.s policies that transform appropriation rules in the sense explained in Section 4.1. If one club is rigid, then for any member (enterprise) V there is a whole collection of these transactions.

Figure 4.14, under (i) shows that u is indeed invertible, the lower twist on the left being u^{-1}. The proof for v^{-1} is analogous. Part (ii) examines how an equivalency e.p.r.s policy, u, can be implemented on e.p.r.s expansions based on aggregation. Part (iii) computes $u \circ \phi \circ u^{-1}$ and finds ϕ^{**} according to the definition of adjoint economic transactions that corresponds to transfers under opening conditions, (see Figure 4.11(ii)). □

This completes the definition and basic properties of a dual member (enterprise) in a leading club or a leading club that allows transfers. Then having at hand these properties of duals, one can exploit them and identify e.p.r.s institutions within the leading club, by analogy with familiar economic institutions for a simple club (modeled through economic vector spaces). From economic point of view we have particular interest in institutions of e.p.r.s redistribution within the club. Two of these are examples of composite economic transactions of a leading member of the club, i.e. $ld \rightarrow ld$ $(1_{ap} \rightarrow 1_{ap})$, usually captured within concepts of economic redistribution theory. From point of view of EPRT, these economic transactions do not imply expansion of e.p.r.s of the club. Their economic role is to preserve a leading structure of the club. Under their argumentation noting is suppose to happen as far as an e.p.r.s structure is concern, and can be seem to begin in 'nothing' and end in 'nothing'. Formally they look like knots. So, let us here define them more precisely as they are important for understanding role of redistribution within EPRT. Namely, we are dealing with elementary concepts of the e.p.r.s dimension of a member (enterprise) V and the club trace of its endotransaction $\phi : V \rightarrow V$ within a leading club that allows transfers. Precisely we have,

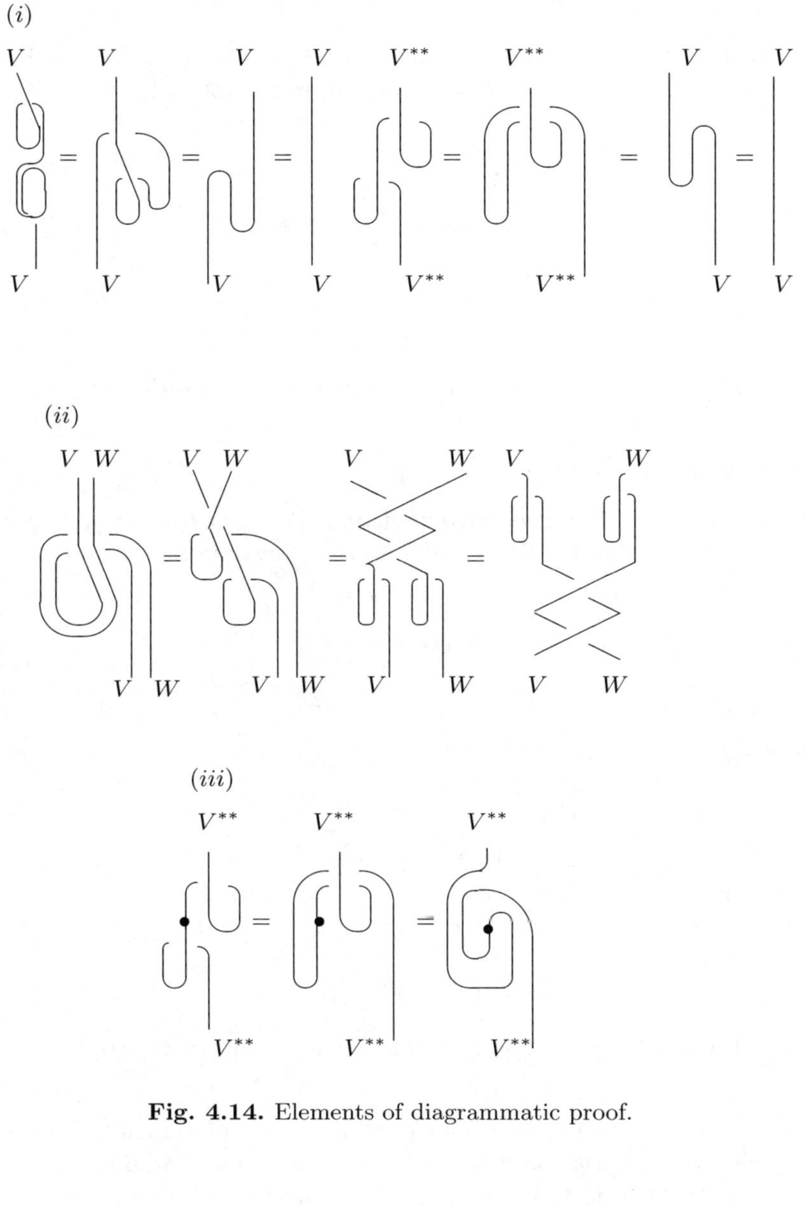

Fig. 4.14. Elements of diagrammatic proof.

Definition 4.26. (E.p.r.s dimension of a member) *The club's e.p.r.s dimension of an enterprise V in a leading club that allows transfers is defined by the following composition of economic transactions,*

$$dim_{ap_{ld}}(V) = ev_V \circ \Psi_{V,V^*} \circ coev_V, \tag{4.12}$$

where ap_{ld} is a fixed appropriation that characterizes the club.

This definition of an e.p.r.s dimension of an enterprise, a member of a leading club, can be expressed by a diagram in the following way,

$dim_{ap}(V) =$

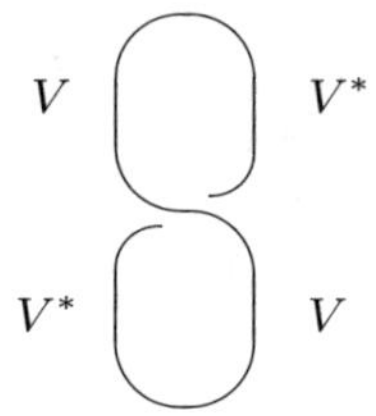

Fig. 4.15. E.p.r.s dimension of enterprise in club with transfers.

Next important instrument is

Definition 4.27. (Trace of transaction) *The club trace of an e.p.r.s endotransaction ϕ of a member V of a leading club with transfers, $\phi : V \to V$, is defined by*

$$Tr_{ap_{ld},V}(\phi) = ev_V \circ \Psi_{V,V^*} \circ (\phi \otimes id)coev_V, \tag{4.13}$$

where ap_{ld} is a fixed appropriation of the club.

In diagrammatic notation we have,

$Tr_{ap}(\phi) =$

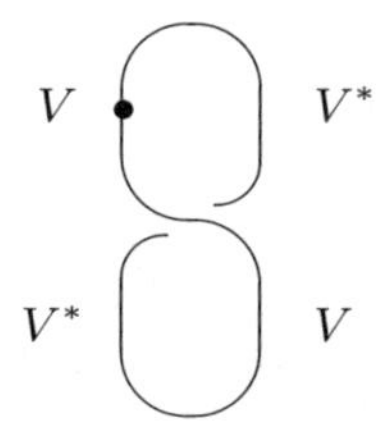

Fig. 4.16. Trace of an endotransaction in a club with transfers.

Note that one can think of the e.p.r.s dimension of a member (enterprise) of the club as the trace of its economic transaction that preserves leading e.p.r.s structure, $dim_{ap_{ld}}(V) = Tr_{ap_{ld},V}(id)$, and that these notions can only make sense in a club with transfers. In addition, in the general case where

$\Psi^2 \neq id$ there is the breakdown of the concept of e.p.r.s expansion within the club, as for dim_{ap}, which explicitly written shows that

$$dim_{ap}(V \otimes W) \neq dim_{ap}(V)dim_{ap}(W),$$

that transcribes diagrammatically as follows,

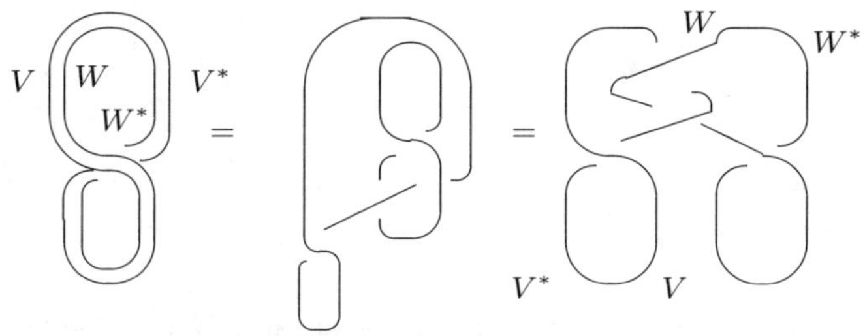

Fig. 4.17. The breakdown of a concept of an e.p.r.s expansion.

A similar problem exists for Tr_{ap}. One does have good behavior with respect to adjoints in the $dim_{ap}(V^*) = (dim_{ap}(V))^*$, as follows easily from definitions. This is as near as one can get in a general club that allows transfers to the usual notations of dimension and trace for simple economic institutions modeled by finite-dimensional vector spaces and linear operators on them. For a more precise further discussion one has to introduce an additional concept of an economic policy that specifies redistribution principle.

Impartial redistribution policy

To be able to get a more precise further insight into e.p.r.s redistribution mappings and their economic effects, concept of an impartial e.p.r.s policy seems useful. It involves *lap*-equivalency policies from Proposition 4.25. One may think of a composition of u and v policies as a provider of a new economic policy $v \circ u$ which properties are suitable by its very construction. Namely, the way its implementation is ensured is grounded on perception that such an e.p.r.s policy is to be seemed the most natural for members of the club from point of view of club's e.p.r.s configuration. Formally, for members V and W one requires that this policy, denoted by ν has a square root $\nu \in Eprnat(id, id)$. It is characterized by,

$$\begin{aligned} \nu_V^2 = v_V \circ u_V, \quad \nu_{V \otimes W} = \Psi_{V,W}^{-1} \circ \Psi_{W,V}^{-1} \circ (\nu_V \otimes \nu_W), \\ \nu_{ld} = id, \quad \nu_{V^*} = (\nu_V)^*. \end{aligned} \tag{4.14}$$

Note that these conditions are not independent. So, for example, one can express the first using the later three. Economic policy ν is called impartial e.p.r.s redistribution policy. Any impartial club is a rigid club that allows transfers and is equipped with such an economic policy. In the case of such a leading club one can restore simple e.p.r.s expansion by using a modified notion of an e.p.r.s dimension, as shown

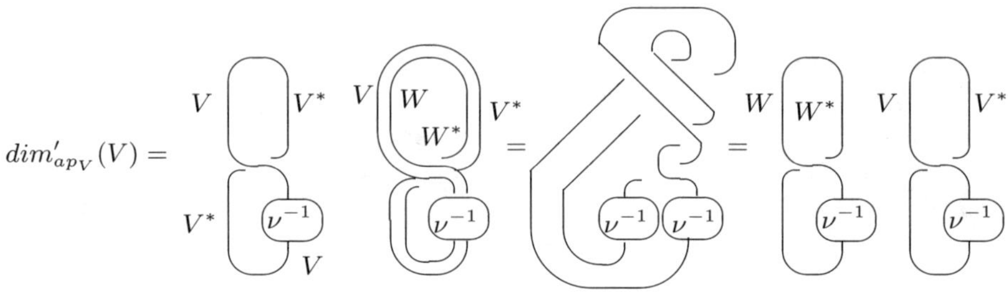

Fig. 4.18. Restoration of simple expansion by an impartial redistribution policy ν.

4.3.3 Redistributing Flows

One should have in mind that any e.p.r.s transaction which, like dim_{ap}, is composed from a transfer, inverse transfer, evaluation and coevaluation maps, i.e. from $\Psi, \Psi^{-1}, ev,$ and $coev,$ and which starts and ends with the leading member, $ld(1_{ap})$, $ld \to ld$ (or in general case $1_{ap} \to 1_{ap}$), is of redistribute type and will likewise look like complex flows of e.p.r.s redistributions. Formally, they can be treated by knot theory. Then the coherence theorem implies that such type of transaction depends only on the redistribution flow of e.p.r.s up to the bend-straightening axioms for duals. This actually means dependence up to the cancellation of transfers with inverse transfers and the transfer relations as before. One may recall from Proposition 4.25 that such economic transactions u, v are generally nontrivial. Thus, the net e.p.r.s transaction, that expresses redistribution flows of e.p.r.s of the leading member, $ld \to ld$ (or in general case $1_{ap} \to 1_{ap}$), is an invariant not exactly of redistributions over all elements, but rather of redistributions up to regular two or more members (enterprises) of the leading club that are considered representative. This implies that the straightening of the twists is excluded. In addition, one may note that not every distinct redistribution can be written down up to regular e.p.r.s representative corresponding to some transactions $ld \to ld$. In other words redistributing invariant is only partially defined.

It may be noteworthy that both problems are resolved in the case of a impartial club. One then obtains a genuine invariant policy, not exactly of redistributions but of framed redistributions.

Now, in an impartial club one has the additional e.p.r.s policy ν, as was shown above, and we can use it to define additional evaluation and coevaluation maps $ev_{ap} : V \otimes V^* \to \mathbf{h}$ and $coev_{ap} : \mathbf{h} \to V^* \otimes V$ by

$$ev_{ap} = ev \circ (id \otimes \nu_V^{-1}) \circ \Psi_{V,V^*}, \quad coev_{ap} = \Psi_{V,V^*} \circ (\nu_V^{-1} \otimes id) coev_V,$$

such that $(V^*, ev_{ap}, coev_{ap})$ is a quality dual for V. This means that it obeys axioms as in Definition 4.24 with the roles of V, V^* interchanged.

Proposition 4.28. *If H is an enterprise, then the club of finite-dimensional price (cost) H-standards is rigid. The price (cost) dual is*

$$(h \overset{a}{>} f)(v) = f((\gamma h) \overset{a}{>} v) \qquad \forall v \in V, f \in V^*,$$

with ev, coev as in (4.9), *for simple economic institutions modeled by economic vector spaces.*

Proof: To prove this proposition we should show that ev, $coev$ are e.p.r.s transactions. Namely, here they take a form of intertwiners for the argumentation of H. Thus,

$$\begin{aligned} h \overset{a}{>} coev &= h \overset{a}{>} (e_a \otimes f^a) = h_{(1)} \overset{a}{>} e_a \otimes h_{(2)} \overset{a}{>} f^a \\ &= h_{(1)} \overset{a}{>} e_a \otimes f^a((\gamma h_{(2)}) \overset{a}{>} (\,)) \\ &= h_{(1)}(\gamma h_{(2)}) \overset{a}{>} (\,) = \varepsilon(h) e_a \otimes f^a \\ &= \varepsilon(h) coev, \end{aligned}$$

where we write $V \otimes V^*$ as a linear map. The reader can explicitly evaluate the terms against an element $v \in V$. For evaluation map we have,

$$\begin{aligned} ev(h \overset{a}{>} (f \otimes v)) &= ev(h_{(1)} \overset{a}{>} f \otimes h_{(2)} \overset{a}{>} v) = (h_{(1)} \overset{a}{>} f)(h_{(2)} \overset{a}{>} v) \\ &= f((\gamma h_{(1)}) h_{(2)} \overset{a}{>} v) = \varepsilon(h) ev(f \otimes v), \end{aligned}$$

as required. In both cases we use exactly the axioms of mutual understanding map γ (from the two sides). We have relations from definition of duality, (4.11) since these hold for the evaluation and coevaluation in the club of finite-dimensional vector spaces. □

One can see that the axioms of a mutual understanding mapping in Chapter 2 are relations that imply $ev, coev$ to intertwine with the argumentation on V^*. The argumentation here is defined by γ, and it specifies the dual or conjugate representation using the dual vector space. To get qualitative duals for some fixed ap_{ld}, $({}^*V, ev_{ap}, coev_{ap})$, one can take similar vector space formulae with ${}^*V$ the predual with basis $\{f^a\}$ and

$$ev_{ap}(v \otimes f) = v(f), \quad coev_{ap} = \sum f^a \otimes e_a, \quad v(h \overset{a}{>} f) = (\gamma^{-1} \overset{a}{>} v)(f),$$

for all $v \in V$, and $f \in {}^*V$, if inverse of mutual understanding map γ^{-1} exists. In fact, one does not need mutual understanding map γ itself, but just that the argumentation denoted γ^{-1} is a skew mutual understanding map in sense of Example 2.10, Chapter 2.

Combining Proposition 4.28 with Theorem 4.15, we see that the finite-dimensional representations of an open enterprise form a rigid leading club with transfers. One also has quality duals (since the mutual understanding map is necessarily invertible in this case), though they will not necessarily be related to the price (cost) duals unless it is the impartial.

Corollary 4.29. *If H is an open enterprise, then the e.p.r.s policies u, v in Proposition 4.28 (concerning the rigid club with transfers of finite-dimensional price (cost) H-standards) are given by the argumentation of u, v in Proposition 3.6 (concerning simple institutions). If H is an impartial enterprise, then the club of standards is also impartial and the e.p.r.s policy ν is given by the argumentation of the element of the simple impartial policy ν in Definition 3.8.*

Proof: Check is based on the definition in Proposition 4.28 and Figure 4.11 (i). Thus,

$$\begin{aligned} u_V(v) &= (ev \otimes id) \circ \Psi(v \otimes f^a) \otimes E_a = (\mathcal{R}^{(2)} \overset{a}{>} f)(\mathcal{R}^{(1)} \overset{a}{>} v) \otimes E_a \\ &= f^a((\gamma \mathcal{R}^{(2)})\mathcal{R}^{(1)} \overset{a}{>} v) \otimes E_a = u \overset{a}{>} v \end{aligned}$$

for all $v \in V$. Here $\{f^a\}$ is a basis of V and $\{E_a\}$ is a dual basis of V^{**}. The result lies in V^{**}. The computation for v is strictly analogous. Hence, if vu determines proper e.p.r.s policy, which is the case when one deals with an impartial club, one can apply such an economic policy and determine its effects by $\nu_V(v) = \nu \overset{a}{>} v$ in the same way. That this policy obeys the condition for $\nu_{V \otimes W}$ follows from the property $\delta\nu$ in Definition 3.8. Implementation then provides the condition for ν_{V^*} which corresponds to $\gamma\nu = \nu$ in view of Proposition 4.28. □

Having above in mind, it appears that every finite dimensional representation of an impartial enterprise gives an invariant of framed redistributions. The trivial representation is domain of e.p.r.s $\mathbf{h}$, so an economic transaction $ld \to ld$ is a map $\mathbf{h} \to \mathbf{h}$. Thus, it can be described by an element of domain of e.p.r.s, $\mathbf{h}$, and it is this element which is invariant. In the case where the enterprise depends on parameters, then so does this invariant. The same remarks concern an open enterprise and suitable redistributions up to regular representative enterprise over all forms.

It is noteworthy that in the above discussion the idea has been that a representation of an e.p.r.s rule leads to a framed-redistribution invariant. However, the concept of club dimension is just to turn reasoning around, and think of each redistribution as a provider of an invariant of representations of the e.p.r.s rule. So, the trivial redistribution provides one of the club's dimensions as explained above, but any other redistribution instrument also determines a generalized dimension. One can think of example of a threfoid dimension of a representation, where we compute the invariant of the threfoid redistribution in representation V. In other words, there is the pairing between e.p.r.s rule representations and redistributions. This pairing can also serve as source for establishing economic relations, on either one or another side, by fixing either the redistribution or the representation.

Let us make a few comments on properties of duals within the general theoretical context in leading clubs. In Section 4.2 it was shown that quasibiagreement also generate leading clubs. Here we have

Proposition 4.30. *Let H be a quasienterprise, then the club of finite-dimensional price (cost) H-standards is rigid with the same argumentation on V^* as in Proposition 4.25 but evaluation and coevaluation are modified so that*

$$ev(f \otimes v) = f(\alpha \overset{a}{>} v), \qquad coev = \sum_a \beta \overset{a}{>} e_a \otimes f^a,$$

where α, β are the elements of extended mutual understanding map in the Definition 3.30 of an open quasienterprise.

Proof: We show that ev, $coev$ are indeed economic transactions, i.e. intertwiners for the argumentation of H. Thus,

$$\begin{aligned} h \overset{a}{>} coev &= h_{(1)}\beta \overset{a}{>} e_a \otimes h_{(2)} \overset{a}{>} f^a = h_{(1)}\beta \overset{a}{>} e_a \otimes f^a((\gamma h_{(2)}) \overset{a}{>} (\,)) \\ &= h_{(1)}\beta\gamma h_{(2)} \overset{a}{>} (\,) = \varepsilon(h)\beta \overset{a}{>} e_a \otimes f^a = \varepsilon(h) coev, \\ ev(h \overset{a}{>} (f \otimes a)) &= ev(h_{(1)} \overset{a}{>} f \otimes h_{(2)} \overset{a}{>} v) = (h_{(1)} \overset{a}{>} f)(\alpha h_{(2)} \overset{a}{>} v) \\ &= f((\gamma h_{(1)})\alpha h_{(2)} \overset{a}{>} v) = \varepsilon(h) ev(f \otimes v), \end{aligned}$$

using the axioms given under (vi) in Definition 3.30. The bend-straightening axioms (4.11) come out as,

$$\begin{aligned} (id \otimes cv) \circ \Phi(\beta \overset{a}{>} e_a \otimes f^a \otimes v) &= \phi^{(1)}\beta \overset{a}{>} e_a \otimes ev(\phi^{(2)} \overset{a}{>} f^a \otimes \phi^{(3)} \overset{a}{>} v) \\ &= \phi^{(1)}\beta \overset{a}{>} e_a(\phi^{(2)} \overset{a}{>} f^a)(\alpha\phi^{(3)} \overset{a}{>} v) = \phi^{(1)}\beta(\gamma\phi^{(2)})\alpha\phi^{(3)} \overset{a}{>} v = v, \end{aligned}$$

$$\begin{aligned} &(ev \otimes id) \circ \Phi^{-1}(f \otimes \beta \overset{a}{>} e_a \otimes f^a) = ev(\phi^{-(1)} \overset{a}{>} \phi^{-(2)}\beta \overset{a}{>} e_a) \otimes \phi^{-(3)} \overset{a}{>} f^a = \\ &(\phi^{-(1)} \overset{a}{>} f)(\alpha\phi^{-(2)}\beta \overset{a}{>} e_a) \otimes \phi^{-(3)} \overset{a}{>} f^a = f((\gamma\phi^{-(1)})\alpha\phi^{-(2)}\beta\gamma\phi^{-(3)} \overset{a}{>} v(\,)) = f, \end{aligned}$$

using the axioms (vi) from Definition 3.30. Thus, these axioms are just what one needs for ev, $coev$, and the argumentation on V^* of this form, to ensure an implementation as claimed. □

Recall that for usual enterprises the freedom in α, β is used to set them to ensure preservation of a chosen e.p.r.s structure. So in the traditional case they are equal to unity. This is not possible when Φ is nontrivial. In dealing with an open quasienterprise we have to consider transfers and hence its e.p.r.s dimension. The same reasoning, as above, provides $dim_{ap}(V) = Tr(u)$, $u = \sum(\gamma\mathcal{R}^{(2)})\alpha\mathcal{R}^{(1)}\beta$, as an argument in the representation V.

Note that the dual constructions to all notions above have the usual meaning. Thus, if A denotes an entrepreneurial agreement, then the club of finite dimensional quality A-costandards is rigid. The dual quality costandard is given by

$$\beta_{V^*}(f) = (f \otimes \gamma) \circ \beta_V, \quad \forall f \in V^*, \tag{4.15}$$

with $ev, coev$ as for simple e.p.r.s institutions modeled by vector spaces. Similar is valid in the dual quasienterprise for suitably modified ev, and $coev$.

One may note that the concept of dimension of an e.p.r.s representation involves an economic transposition or transfer mapping. It is trivial for usual traditional representation of economic rules but it gains an economic importance for better understanding of an e.p.r.s rule and flows. In application of the concept of club dimension, if the representation of the e.p.r.s rule is a canonical one, (which depends only on the e.p.r.s rule structure), then e.p.r.s dimension invariant depends only on the e.p.r.s rule. This is actually the source of the invariants of enterprises. The invariant is the same if two enterprises are isotransactions. Here, the issue seems to be similar as in deciding if two redistribute flows are isotransaction, being a kind of dual problem to that. So for example, the $dim_{ap}(H) = Tr\gamma^2$ is indeed on important invariant of any finite dimensional enterprise.

Another idea for a canonical representation is the price (cost) regular representation. Here, any e.p.r.s rule of H is an argumentation on itself, and is therefore an enterprise in its own club of representations. If H is open, i.e. a strict e.p.r.s rule, then one can define its e.p.r.s order, precisely

Definition 4.31. (Ordering by e.p.r.s) *An e.p.r.s. order of an open enterprise (e.p.r.s rule) is defined by*

$$\mid H \mid = dim_{ap}(H) = Tr(u) \tag{4.16}$$

in the price (cost) regular representation.

Obviously, $\mid \mathbf{h}G \mid = dim(\mathbf{h}G) = \mid G \mid$, the usual order, i.e. the number of elements (members) of a finite rule G. This is behind definition of dimensionally. The usual dimension of the price regular representation exactly counts the number of points in the group, so its club or e.p.r.s dimension generalizes that statement. It may be not so easy to calculate this invariant in practice, but it is certainly an invariant of the enterprise by its club definition.

In the case of *ap*-modification we could consider the e.p.r.s order of the enveloping agreement $U_{ap}(g)$. It is known that, for generic appropriation parameter *ap*, their representations decompose with the same expansions as in the usual case, since these are integers, as we can consider the role of the price regular representation as played by an infinite direct sum of representations with the same expansion as traditional economic circumstances. As particular example, we may consider some V_{price} as a model for $U_{ap}(su_2)$ being self-argumentation. The formal side of the model is the decomposition of the left regular representation of the compact group SU_2. This can be formulated as a decomposition of the e.p.r.s function of an enterprise $*$-agreement $SU_{ap}(2)$, on which $U_{ap}(su_2)$ provides argumentation by the coexpansion. From that point of view V_{price} provides the same answer for the e.p.r.s dimension since it is just the conjugate representation to the price expansion.

Example 4.32. The e.p.r.s order of $U_{ap}(su_2)$, defined by the e.p.r.s dimension of the price regular representation V_{price}, is

$$| U_{ap}(su_2) | \equiv \sum_j dim(V_j) dim_{ap}(V_j)$$

for a formal power series in *ap*. This can be evaluated for real $ap < 1$ where it is finite.

Proof and Comments: The proof is based on definition of the club's e.p.r.s dimension which is extended by linearity to infinite sum. The appropriation *ap* is considered as a formal parameter. However, one has a standard Jacobi theta-function, which converges if one evaluates according an appropriation which is not pure private one. This is an example of regularization of the appropriation. For a suitable range of *ap*, $ap \in (-1, 1)$ members of the club that follows the e.p.r.s rule $U_{ap}(su_2)$ can be obtained. In that way one get an e.p.r.s natural definition of the economic order among members of the club. This order diverges as $ap \to 1$, because, in this limit the usual order of traditional competitive economy is to be obtained, which is infinite. In other words, as appropriation becomes almost pure private the circumstances correspond to traditional competitive case in economics is restored. The particularity here is that, this infinite number of members, trough *ap*-modification, ensure an exclusivity of the appropriation. As known an exclusivity of appropriation is one of the main properties of pure private e.p.r.s structure. □

4.3.4 Generalized Duality

Let us consider an alternative approach to duality that exploits the concept of internal homomorphisms, and get an insight how it is applied in our economic settings. It provides a more general notion of duality than the one discussed above. Namely, duality above was based on the properties of simple economic institutions modeled by finite-dimensional vector spaces, while now the notion of internal homomorphisms is modeled on the properties of the set of linear maps, finite dimensional or not.

In economic applications a homomorphism of interest to us is an economic transaction between two enterprises, $V, W,$ members of a club. It is denoted by $Homt(V,W) : V \to W,$ and has the property that $Homt(v_1, v_2) = Homt(v_1)Homt(v_2)$ for all $v_1, v_2 \in V.$ Note that such type of economic transactions automatically respects the leading structure of the club. The basic idea behind general concept of duality is then to define $Homt_{ap}(V,W)$ for any two enterprises V, W in a leading club with appropriation $ap,$ in such a way that the e.p.r.s collection formed by $Homt_{ap}(V,W)$ is itself an enterprise within the club. In economics this is usually captured under the notion of aggregate operators between economic rule representations. The set of such operators $Homt_{ap}(V,W)$ transforms under the rule argumentation, covariantly in W and contravariantly in $V.$ Here some basic elements of this approach are generalized to the e.p.r.s rule case, using the methods and procedures suitable for understanding economic clubs and other e.p.r.s institutions. As careful reader may note, in conceptualization of $Homt_{ap}$ we explore implementation of the fundamental ideas already discussed in Section 4.1. Recall that in any club $\mathcal{C},$ we have for each enterprise $V \in \mathcal{C},$ a member of the club, a contravariant appropriation mapping $Apr(\,\cdot\,, V) : \mathcal{C} \to Set$ transforming another enterprise of the club, $W \in \mathcal{C},$ over to $Apr(W, V).$ This e.p.r.s transformation also works over economic transactions of the club, as $Apr(\phi, V) = \circ\phi$ for any economic transaction $\phi : W \to Z$ between members (enterprises) W and $Z.$ Precomposition of e.p.r.s with transaction ϕ transforms $Apr(Z, V)$ over to $Apr(W, V),$ as it should be the case for a contravariant appropriation procedure. There is also a similar (covariant) appropriation $Apr(V, \cdot\,) : \mathcal{C} \to Set$ with $Apr(V, \phi) = \phi\circ.$ Now, applying a fundamental fact in category theory in our case of clubs, we know that many contravariant appropriations $\mathcal{C} \to Set$ are equivalent to appropriations of the form $Apr(\ , V)$ for some $V.$ The notion of equivalency in this case means that there are e.p.r.s policies of particular form that are able to equalize outcomes of two forms of appropriations, i.e. $\theta_W : F(W) \cong Apr(W, V),$ where F is a contravariant appropriation. Then one may consider F as representable appropriation and the enterprise V is its representing enterprise. It is determined unequally up to unique isoappropraition $\theta.$

Let us consider a leading club $\mathcal{C}$ as defined in Section 4.1.3. For any two members $V, W \in \mathcal{C},$ we define $Homt_{ap}(V,W)$ as the representing enterprise, when it exists, for the contravariant appropriation $\mathcal{C} \to Set$ that transforms $Z \in \mathcal{C}$ over to $Apr(Z \otimes V, W)$ and an economic transaction ϕ to $\circ(\phi \otimes id).$ Namely, it is defined by the requirement that there are appropriational isotransactions

$$\theta_Z^{V,W} : Apr(Z \otimes V, W) \cong Apr(Z, Homt_{ap}(V,W)) \tag{4.17}$$

for all members of the leading club, $Z \in \mathcal{C}$. This relation actually determines $Homt_{ap}$ and properties of $Homt_{ap}$ which allow us to treat it like the space of linear maps between economic vector spaces.

Proposition 4.33. *Consider a leading club with internal economic transactions as defined by* (4.17). *Then there are following types of e.p.r.s transactions:*
(i) homotransaction,

$$Homt_{ap}(Z \otimes V, W) \cong Homt_{ap}(Z, Homt_{ap}(V, W)) \tag{4.18}$$

(ii) evaluation

$$ev_{V,W} : Homt_{ap}(V, W) \otimes V \to W, \tag{4.19}$$

(iii) composition

$$\circ_{V,W,Z} : Homt_{ap}(V, W) \otimes Homt_{ap}(Z, V) \to Homt_{ap}(Z, W), \tag{4.20}$$

for all enterprises V, W, Z of the club. If leading club allows transfers, as in Section 4.2, then we also have
(iv) direct transfer

$$i_{V,W} : V \to Homt_{ap}(Homt_{ap}(V, W), W) \tag{4.21}$$

(v) aggregative transfer

$$j_{V,W,X,Y} : Homt_{ap}(V, W) \otimes Homt_{ap}(X, Y) \to Homt_{ap}(V \otimes X, W \otimes Y), \tag{4.22}$$

for all enterprises V, W, X, Y.

Proof: Consider a sequence of appropriational isotransactions

$$\begin{aligned} &Apr(U, Homt_{ap}(Z \otimes V, W)) \cong Homt_{ap}(U \otimes (Z \otimes V), W) \\ &\cong Apr((U \otimes Z) \otimes V, W) \cong Apr(U \otimes Z, Homt_{ap}(V, W)) \\ &\cong Apr(U, Homt_{ap}(Z, Homt_{ap}(Z, W))) \end{aligned}$$

for all enterprises. The second isotransaction is defined by precomposition with $\Phi_{U,Z,V}$, while the rest are based on definition of $Homt_{ap}$ and applications of defining relation (4.17). So, we can put $U = Homt_{ap}(Z \otimes V, W)$ and use the identity appropriation, which therefore maps over to an e.p.r.s transaction (4.18) as stated. One takes $U = Homt_{ap}(Z, Homt_{ap}(V, W))$ and the identity appropriation to get the inverse. Also, we can consider in (4.17) the choice $Z = Homt_{ap}(V, W)$ and the identity appropriation on it. This corresponds on the left to a transaction (4.19) as stated. It is analogous to the evaluation of a linear map on the vector space on which it acts. It is important to keep in mind that on this abstract level, the members need not be described by economic spaces and $Homt_{ap}$ need not be appropriation maps. Given such 'evaluation' transactions, we next consider $ev_{V,W} \circ (id \otimes ev_{Z,V})$ as an element of the left hand side of the following

$$\begin{aligned} &Apr(Homt_{ap}(V,W) \otimes Homt_{ap}(Z,V) \otimes Z, W) \\ &\cong Apr(Homt_{ap}(V,W) \otimes Homt_{ap}(Z,V), Homt_{ap}(Z,W)), \end{aligned}$$

and in that way obtain a 'composition map' (4.20) as stated. This is analogous to the composition of operators. One should have in mind that the associativity transaction Φ is suppressed here, but it is implicit in the construction.

Now let us suppose that club we study is not only leading one but that it allows transfers as in Section 4.2. Then $ev_{V,W} \circ \Psi_{V,Homt_{ap}(V,W)}$ is an element of the left hand side of

$$Apr(V \otimes Homt_{ap}(V,W), W) \cong Apr(V, Homt_{ap}(Homt_{ap}(V,W), W))$$

and becomes on the right a transaction (4.21) as stated. Also we have,

$$\begin{aligned} &Apr(Z, Homt_{ap}(V,W) \otimes Homt_{ap}(X,Y)) \cong \\ &\quad Apr(V, Homt_{ap}(X,Y) \otimes Homt_{ap}(V,W)) \\ &\to Apr(Z \otimes V, Homt_{ap}(X,Y) \otimes W) \cong Apr(Z \otimes V, W \otimes Homt_{ap}(X,Y)) \\ &\to Apr(Z \otimes V \otimes X, W \otimes Y) \cong Apr(Z, Homt_{ap}(V \otimes X, W \otimes Y)), \end{aligned}$$

where the first isotransaction is composition with $\Psi_{Homt_{ap}(V,W),Homt_{ap}(X,Y)}$ and the third is composition with $\Psi^{-1}_{W,Homt_{ap}(X,Y)}$. The second and fourth mappings are instances of the general construction

$$Apr(Z, W \otimes Homt_{ap}(X,Y)) \to Apr(Z \otimes X, W \otimes Y), \tag{4.23}$$

which transforms $\phi : Z \to W \otimes Homt_{ap}(X,Y)$ into $(id \otimes ev_{X,Y}) \circ (\phi \otimes id)$. The rest are applications of (4.17), which therefore maps over to a transaction (4.23) as stated. □

Having above in mind we can now connect two concept of duality. Namely, general theory from above is linked with the cost (price) duality and/or rigidity in the sense described previously.

Lemma 4.34. *Let Ld be a leading club and suppose that $V \in Ld$ is rigid in the sense of Definition 4.27. Then for a given leading appropriation lap,*

$$Homt_{lap}(V,W) = W \otimes V^*$$

is an internal homotransaction for any enterprise W in the club. Moreover, in the case of a club that allows transfers, the economic transaction (4.22) becomes an e.p.r.s isotransaction.

Proof: If $\phi : Z \otimes V \to W$, we define $\theta_Z^{V,W}(\phi) = (\phi \otimes id) \circ (id \otimes coev_V) : Z \to W \otimes V^*$. In the other direction, if $\phi : Z \to W \otimes V^*$, we define

$\theta^{-1}(\phi) = (id \otimes ev_V) \circ (\phi \otimes id) : Z \otimes V \to W$. It is easy to see that these constructions are mutually inverse. As usual, there are implicit Φ economic transactions in these formulae. Note also that θ^{-1} is a special case of the more general construction (4.22) already used in the proof of (4.21). If V is rigid, then this map also has an inverse (defined by $coev_V$ in the similar way as θ here). Hence in the case that allows transfers we conclude that (4.21) is also an isotransaction when V is rigid. Actually, in the rigid setting all the transactions (4.17) – (4.21) become quite straightforward using previous shown diagrammatic techniques and this definition for $Homt_{lap}$. □

This lemma explicitly shows that the notion of internal homotransaction includes the notion of duals in the sense described previously. Moreover, it is certainly a more general concept as it allows us to avoid rigidity. Internally homotransaction implies, that one can define $Homt(V, ld_{lap})$ and consider it as some kind of dual of V but without a coevaluation $coev$ and the associated isotransactions in Definition 4.24. In the case that allows transfers we have an economic transaction $V \to Homt(Homt(V, ld_{lap}), ld_{lap})$, as a special case of (4.20), but it need not be an isotransaction as it was in Proposition 4.25. It is isotransaction if and only if V is rigid. One may think of this generalization of duality as a procedure where the properties that are usual for linear maps $V \to W$ are kept, but not those that are special to V being finite dimensional.

Example 4.35. Let H be an enterprise. Then the leading club ${}_HM$ of H-standards has an internal homotransaction as follows

$$Homt(V, W) = Lin(V, W), \quad (h \overset{a}{>} f)(v) = \sum h_{(1)} \overset{a}{>} (f(\gamma h_{(2)} \overset{a}{>} v))$$

for all $h \in H, v \in V,$ and $f \in Homt(V, W)$. The conditions given by (4.17) – (4.19) are valid as the club can be treated as simple e.p.r.s structured and modeled by the appropriate economic vector spaces.

Proof and Comments: One can think of $Homt(V, W)$ as itself an enterprise (member) in ${}_HM$. Namely, we have that an economic activity $\overset{a}{>}$ as it is described in the Example should be considered as an e.p.r.s argumentation. Then to show the statements above one may recall the procedure in proving properties of the e.p.r.s adjoint argumentation in Example 2.30 in Chapter 2. Now one can put

$$(\theta_Z^{V,W}(\phi)(z))(v) = \phi(z \otimes v) \quad \forall \phi : Z \otimes V \to W$$

in the obvious way, and check that it maps any economic transaction $\phi : Z \otimes V \to W$ to an economic transaction $\theta(\phi) : Z \to Homt(V, W)$ as required. Namely,

$$\begin{aligned}(h \overset{a}{>} (\theta(\phi)(z)))(v) &= h_{(1)} \overset{a}{>} (\theta(\phi)(z)(\gamma h_{(2)} \overset{a}{>} v)) \\ &= h_{(1)} \overset{a}{>} (\phi(z \otimes \gamma h_{(2)} \overset{a}{>} v)) \\ &= \phi(h_{(1)} \overset{a}{>} z \otimes h_{(2)}\gamma h_{(3)} \overset{a}{>} v) \\ &= \phi(h \overset{a}{>} z \otimes v) = \theta(\phi)(h \overset{a}{>} z)(v).\end{aligned}$$

Thus one can consider $\theta(\phi)$ as an intertwiner under condition that ϕ is. On the other hand, θ is invertible, and the collection $\{\theta_Z\}$ implies appropriation simply due to the fact that we are dealing with the economic club formed of standardized (simplified) enterprises which economic activities can be modeled by vector spaces. Explicitly, the inverse is

$$(\theta_Z^{V,W})^{-1}(\phi)(z \otimes v) = \phi(z)(v), \quad \forall \phi : Z \to Homt(V, W).$$

One can deduce the required economic transactions (4.17) – (4.19) from Proposition 4.19. The main idea is to exploit the fact that θ and $Homt$ have the same form as for vector spaces, i.e. as for simple enterprises and/or economic institutions. Thus, one may conclude that these maps will also come out in the way as for vector spaces, i.e. in a form of simple institutions. The new point is that they intertwine the argumentation of H. For example, the evaluation and composition operations, $ev, \circ$, respectively, now become

$$ev_{V,W}(f \otimes v) = f(v), \quad \circ_{V,W,Z}(f \otimes g)(z) = f(g(z))$$

for $f \in Homt(V, W)$ and $g \in Homt(Z, V)$ commute with our stated argumentations of H. Note that the ordering in the aggregate procedure is critical here. □

Example above allows one to generalize Proposition 4.28 to include infinite-dimensional standardized institutions. There is also a cost (price) version of internal homotransaction corresponding to a skew mutual understanding map, and generalizing notion of cost (price) duality which are both extremely important for concrete applications in EPRT. The analgue of Corollary 4.29 in the case of nontrivial open enterprise is given by,

Corollary 4.36. *Let H be an open enterprise. Then the economic transactions (4.21) and (4.22) in Proposition 4.28 concerning transfers for internal homotransactions in the club that allows transfers of price (cost) H-standards are modified to*

$$i(v)(f) = \sum \mathcal{R}^{(2)} \overset{a}{>} (f(u\mathcal{R}^{(1)} \overset{a}{>} v)),$$
$$j(f \otimes g)(v \otimes x) = \sum f(\mathcal{R}^{-(1)}\mathcal{R}^{(1)} \overset{a}{>} v) \otimes \mathcal{R}^{-(2)} \overset{a}{>} (g(\mathcal{R}^{(2)} \overset{a}{>} x)),$$

for all $f \in Homt_{ap}(V, W)$, $g \in Homt_{ap}(X, Y)$ and $v \in V$, $x \in X$. Here economic policy u is the canonical element of an enterprise H from Proposition 3.6 in Chapter 3. The second map is an isotransaction in the finite dimensional case.

Sketch of proof: We are using the latter half of the proof of Proposition 4.33 in concrete setting described in the corollary. Also we should recall already shown procedure how an enterprise H imposes argumentation on $f \in Homt_{ap}(V, W)$ from Example 4.35 above. Using this with Theorem 4.15 for the transfers given by $\Psi(v \otimes f)$ to obtain,

$$ev \circ \Phi(v \otimes f) = (\mathcal{R}^{(2)} \overset{a}{>} f)(\mathcal{R}^{(1)} \overset{a}{>} v) = \mathcal{R}^{(2)}_{(1)} \overset{a}{>} (f((\gamma \mathcal{R}^{(2)}_{(2)})\mathcal{R}^{(1)} \overset{a}{>} v))$$

which equals the result stated in using axioms of opening (3.1) from Chapter 3. Now, the procedure, used at the end of the proof of Proposition 4.33 for the sequence of maps, is employed again as follows. One considers an economic transaction $Z \to Homt_{ap}(V, W) \otimes Homt_{ap}(X, Y)$ transforming an element $z \mapsto f \otimes g$, say. The first isotransaction in the sequence provides $z \mapsto \Psi(f \otimes g) = \mathcal{R}^{(2)} \overset{a}{>} g \otimes \mathcal{R}^{(1)} \overset{a}{>} f$. The second isotransaction modifies this by θ as $z \otimes v \mapsto \mathcal{R}^{(2)} \overset{a}{>} g \otimes (\mathcal{R}^{(1)} \overset{a}{>} f)(v)$. The third isotransaction is to introduce transfers Ψ^{-1} to the output of this, so yielding $z \otimes v \mapsto \mathcal{R}^{-(1)} \overset{a}{>} ((\mathcal{R}^{(1)} \overset{a}{>} f)(v)) \otimes \mathcal{R}^{-(2)}\mathcal{R}^{(2)} \overset{a}{>} g$. Next one can view this as $z \otimes v \otimes x \mapsto \mathcal{R}^{-(1)} \overset{a}{>} ((\mathcal{R}^{(1)} \overset{a}{>} f)(v)) \otimes (\mathcal{R}^{-(2)}\mathcal{R}^{(2)} \overset{a}{>} g)(x)$. Finally, one can consider this as $z \mapsto j(f \otimes g)(v \otimes x)$. Computing the argumentation on f, g from Example 4.35 one has

$$\begin{aligned}
j(f \otimes g)(v \otimes x) &= \mathcal{R}^{-(1)} \overset{a}{>} ((\mathcal{R}^{(1)} \overset{a}{>} f)(v)) \otimes (\mathcal{R}^{-(2)}\mathcal{R}^{(2)} \overset{a}{>} g)(x) \\
&= \mathcal{R}^{-(1)}\mathcal{R}^{(1)}_{(1)} \overset{a}{>} (f(\gamma \mathcal{R}^{(1)}_{(2)} \overset{a}{>} v)) \otimes (\mathcal{R}^{-(2)}\mathcal{R}^{(2)} \overset{a}{>} g)(x) \\
&= f(\gamma \mathcal{R}^{(1)} \overset{a}{>} v) \otimes (\mathcal{R}^{(2)} \overset{a}{>} g)(x) \\
&= f(\gamma \mathcal{R}^{(1)} \overset{a}{>} v) \otimes \mathcal{R}^{(2)}_{(1)} \overset{a}{>} (g(\gamma \mathcal{R}^{(2)}_{(2)} \overset{a}{>} x)).
\end{aligned}$$

Here, to get third equality one uses the axiom (3.2) of an nontrivial opening e.p.r.s structure and cancels $\mathcal{R}^{-1}\mathcal{R}$. The result is equal to the expression stated in using these axioms again. One should note that the enterprise Z is irrelevant in this proof since all operations are on a given output $f \otimes g$ of our original map. Alternatively, one can consider that our original map is the identity transaction and that $z = f \otimes g$. We know from Lemma 4.34 that, if V is finite dimensional and hence rigid from Proposition 4.28, then j is an isotransaction. Making a similar computation to the above for this one has the inverse as follows. First, one writes an element of $Homt_{ap}(V \otimes X, W \otimes Y) = Lin(V \otimes X, W \otimes Y)$ as a sum of elements of the form $f \otimes g \in Lin(V, W) \otimes Lin(X, Y)$ in the usual trivial way, as in the club of conventional economic agents modeled over vector spaces. This is where one needs V to be finite dimensional. Then,

$$j^{-1}(f \otimes g)(v)(x) = f(\mathcal{R}^{-(1)}\gamma^2\mathcal{R}^{(1)} \overset{a}{>} v) \otimes \mathcal{R}^{(2)} \overset{a}{>} (g(\mathcal{R}^{-(2)} \overset{a}{>} x)).$$

It is nontrivial to check directly that this is the inverse and that the maps i, j are actually intertwiners for the argumentations of H. Nevertheless, we may consider all of them to be true, having in mind general theory stated above. □

It is noteworthy that the club methods and the possibility of constructions of various types of institutions are quite general and can be implemented also in a quasienterpreneurial setting. In this case one just has to be careful to use the property of the associativity of transfers Φ which were suppressed above. One may take $Homt_{ap}(V,W) = Lin(V,W)$ and the argumentation of H just as in Example 4.35 but now modified to,

$$\theta_Z^{V,W}(\psi)(z)(v) = \sum \psi(\phi^{-1}z \otimes \phi^{-(2)}\beta\gamma\phi^{-(3)}v),$$
$$(\theta_Z^{V,W})^{-1}(\psi)(z \otimes v) = \sum \phi^{(1)}(\psi(z)((\gamma\phi^{(2)})\alpha\phi^{(3)}V)) \tag{4.24}$$

for all $\psi : Z \otimes V \to W$, and $\psi : Z \to Homt_{ap}(V,W)$, respectively. One can check from the axioms of a quasienterprise in Section 3.4 in Chapter 3, that these maps are mutual inverses and are intertwiners. The calculations are a generalization of those in the proof of Example 4.35. The result generalizes Proposition 4.28 to the setting of internal homotransaction. So in the case of quasiopen institutions the resulting relations corresponding to (4.18) – (4.20), and (4.21) and (4.22) are modified by ϕ, in the similar way. They can be computed by tracing through the proof of Proposition 4.25, in just the same way as above.

Note that for internal homotransaction in the club of costandards of an enterprise we have the dual theory as well. Here, $Homt_{ap} = Lin(V,W)$ becomes an enterprise in the club of costandards, which carries coargumentation β defined by

$$\beta(f)(v) = \sum f(v^{(1_{ap})})^{(1_{ap})} \otimes f(v^{(1_{ap})})^{(2_{ap})}\gamma v^{(2_{ap})}, \tag{4.25}$$

for all $f \in Homt_{ap}(V,W), v \in V$, where the coargumentations V, W are denoted in our usual summation notation. The relations (4.18) – (4.20) are as usual for simple e.p.r.s institutions, i.e. vector spaces, while, in the dual opening case, a similar proof to that of Corollary 4.29 gives (4.21) and (4.22) as

$$i(v)(f) = ev \circ \Phi(v \otimes f) =$$
$$f(v^{(1_{ap})})^{(1_{ap})}u(v^{(2_{ap})}_{(1_{ap})})\mathcal{R}(v^{(2_{ap})}_{(1_{ap})} \otimes f(v^{(1_{ap})})^{(2_{ap})}),$$

$$j(f \otimes g)(v \otimes x) =$$
$$\sum f(v^{(1_{ap})}) \otimes g(x^{(1_{ap})})^{(1_{ap})}\mathcal{R}(\gamma v^{(2_{ap})} \otimes g(x^{(1_{ap})})^{(2_{ap})}\gamma x^{(2_{ap})}).$$

Note that to get the case of the dual quasienterprise one has to implement a nontrivial ϕ as well.

The notion of internal homotransaction allows us the variety of applications related to the following elementary lemma.

Lemma 4.37. *In the club of price (cost) standards of an enterprise H, we have $Apr(V,W) = Homt_{ap}(V,W)^H$, the invariant subspace under the argumentation of H. Moreover, $Homt_{ap}(V,V)$ is an H-standard agreement and $Apr(V,V)$ is its fixed point subagreement.*

Proof: For the club ${}_H M$ we have seen that $Apr(V,W)$ consists of those linear maps $V \to W$ that commute with the argumentation of H. If $\phi \in Homt_{ap}(V,W)$ is a fixed point under H, then $h \overset{a}{>} (\phi(v)) = h_{(1)} \overset{a}{>} (\phi((\gamma h_{(2)}) \overset{a}{>} h_{(3)} \overset{a}{>} v)) = (h_{(1)} \overset{a}{>} \phi)(h_{(2)} \overset{a}{>} v) = \varepsilon(h_{(1)})\phi(h_{(2)} \overset{a}{>} v) = \phi(h \overset{a}{>} v)$ so ϕ is an intertwiner. The axioms of an enterprise were used here. Conversely, if ϕ is an intertwiner, then $(h \overset{a}{>} \phi)(v) = h_{(1)} \overset{a}{>} (\phi(\gamma h_{(2)} \overset{a}{>} v)) = h_{(1)}\gamma h_{(2)} \overset{a}{>} (\phi(v)) = \varepsilon(h)\phi(v)$. Namely, ϕ is a fixed point under H. To show the second statement, we use the fact that $Apr(V,V)$ and $Homt_{ap}(V,V)$ are agreements by composition. The latter is covariant under the argumentation of H just because composition $\circ$ is an intertwiner, as has been shown already above. □

For illustration, let V be a given representation of H, and consider maps $V^{\otimes N} \to V^{\otimes N}$ which commute with the argumentation of H. Namely, these maps are self-intertwiners and endotransactions from the aggregate expansion representation. One can identify this as an economic equilibrium in the form of the fixed point subagreement,

$$Apr(V^{\otimes N}, V^{\otimes N}) = Lin_H(V^{\otimes N}, V^{\otimes N}) = Homt_{ap}(V^{\otimes N}, V^{\otimes N})^H.$$

The issues can also be turned around, and we can treat this agreement of endotransaction abstractly by an agreement acting on $V^{\otimes N}$, and that H commutes with it. Namely one has,

$$H \to Lin_{Apr(V^{\otimes N}, V^{\otimes N})}(V^{\otimes N}, V^{\otimes N}).$$

This is a generalization of the phenomena known in the theory of economic behavior as conformed reactions strategies, (formally Schur-Weyl duality). Note that in the enough simple economic environment, when the club of representations is generated by economic vector space V, one can expect to be able to reconstruct an enterprise H entirely. Namely, it can be reconstructed by the set of economic operations that commute with all these endotransaction agreements for all N. This will be discussed more precisely through the general reconstruction theorems in the next Chapter. Let us here recall the known concept of economic growth agreement in an infinite dimensional context. Here one starts with a given equilibrium growth agreement of von Neumann type (formalized by a centralizer of a von Neumann algebra) which becomes an argumentation on a domain of economic claims. Then economic operators (activities) that constitute the double commutant to the agreement

of equilibrium growth, can be identified with the equilibrium agreement itself. Discussion in this Section link up with this growth model on taking a suitably large enough N or suitable limit $N \to \infty$, known within traditional economics as turnpike growth model.
On the other hand, when enterprise H is nontrivialy open one can identify many examples of elements of these agreements of endotransactions which are actually known. So, for example, the economic transactions $\psi_i = id \otimes \cdots \otimes \Psi_{V,V} \otimes \cdots \otimes id$, which transfers V in the ith position of the aggregate with V in the $i+1$ position. Here also, under conditions of convenient economic environments, or well behaved economies, these generate the entire agreement of endotransactions and allows its modeling and computation.

For example, one may recall a model within context of economic growth of a simple economy $U_{ap}(sl_2)$ with two agents. Economic endowments are symmetric and an ownership structure is described by a fixed appropriation parameter ap. Thus, ap denotes appropriation parameter, $ap \in (-1, 1)$, where $ap = -1$ means pure public type of appropriation and $ap = 1$ pure private one. Then $Apr(V^{\otimes N}, V^{\otimes N})$ is the economic agreement generated by first and $N-1$ indeterminates concerning transfers ψ_i that are standardized by the following relations,

$$\psi_i\psi_{i+1}\psi_i = \psi_{i+1}\psi_i\psi_{i+1}, \quad \psi_i\psi_j = \psi_j\psi_i, \quad \forall \mid i-j \mid > 1,$$
$$\psi_i^2 = (ap - ap^{-1})\psi_i + 1.$$

The first two conditions are the assertion that transfer Φ provides an argumentation of the symmetric transfer rule (Artin braid group), as was sketched in Section 4.2, while the additional relation holds when one looks at the representation of market of exchange of two symmetrically powerful type of agents, and its aggregate extension of e.p.r.s power. The same endotransaction agreement is valid for $U_{ap}(sl_n)$ and its fundamental representation of exchange process. This particular agreement over endotransactions is the standard *ap*-hierarchical structured economy with clear ordering, that is usually in mathematical economics described over the special functions. From formal point of view we are dealing with q-Hecke algebra and q-special functions. Note that for the case where one has pure private economic environment in the limit, i.e. when $ap \to 1$, one gets the usual permutation rule. On the other hand, the context of EPRT gives a point of view on such agreements that captures quite generally e.p.r.s environments.

5

Reconstruction Theory

In Chapter 4 the abstract properties of the representations of an entrepreneurial agreement, an enterprise, an open enterprise and an e.p.r.s institution in general, have been formulated and discussed extensively. It is clear now that the representations have an aggregate principle, described by the appropriate expansion of e.p.r.s, duals and in the case of openness transfers. In this Chapter in focus are the converse issues. Namely, the idea is to investigate could a collection of elements of an economic club, which can be strictly identified with simple economic institutions in a certain clear sense, be equivalent to the representations of some enterprise which is to be reconstructed. In addition, within an economic setting where one would allow the identification to be somewhat weaker regarding associatively of aggregate principle, one could hope for reconstruction of a quasienterprise instead. In particular, ones economic principles concerning the procedures of reconstruction are identified, one would like to suggest other weaker concepts of enterprise formation. These can be tailored to have particular properties for their club of representations. In this Chapter, the diagrammatic technique is used, where the elements in our collection need not be identified with the simple economic institutions at all, and where the reconstructed enterprise is an enterprise that allows transfers or is a transferred enterprise. Theorems that concern economic constructions are grouped on those for simple cases, discussed in next Section while more complex cases are studied later on.

5.1 Reconstruction in Simple Institutions

To get economic intuition about the issues first an informal view of the procedures is sketched in Subsection 5.1.1, to be followed by more precise consideration of the procedures for reconstruction an economic institution on collection of simple ones or their clubs.

5.1.1 Basic Forms

The basic idea of an economic reconstruction theorems for simple cases is to build some kind of enterprise of economic functions on collection of enterprises or club of enterprises. So, let us address already known institutions from the point of view of reconstruction.

Club

Let $\mathcal{C}$ be a club, and let $F : \mathcal{C} \rightarrow Vec$ be an appropriation policy to the club of simple enterprises described by vector spaces. In this case, it was already indicated by Example 4.7 in Chapter 4 that there is the procedure to regard $Eprnat(F, F)$ as an 'agreement of flat appropriation sections', or 'an agreement of covariantly constant economic functions' on the club. Thus, $h \in Eprnat(F, F)$ means a family of maps $\{h_X \in Lin(F(X), F(X)) \mid X \in \mathcal{C}\}$ which are carrying appropriation under any economic transaction $\phi : X \rightarrow Y$ within the club or among the members. This is expressed by the condition that $h_Y \circ F(\phi) = F(\phi) \circ h_X$. So, given two such 'economic functions', h and g one can define

$$(hg)_X = h_X \circ g_X. \tag{5.1}$$

The family of economic maps $\{(hg)_X\}$ is also appropriational, since its elements h, g are. Thus, one get an associative agreement. One also have an identity element η, given by $\eta_X = id.$ So obtained agreement is an argument, on each simple economic institution X, in the way that $F(X) \ni v$ by $h \overset{a}{>} v = h_X(v)$.

Leading club

Now let consider the case where $\mathcal{C}$ is a leading club and denote it by Ld, as before. Then one has precisely defined extension of e.p.r.s due to leading aggregation, over the procedure $\otimes_{ld}$, and the fact that $F \equiv F_{ld}$ is leading appropriation. It is leading in the sense that it maps the associatively of aggregate procedure $\times_{ld}$ in $\mathcal{C} \equiv Ld$ over to the usual simple cases of aggregation. Formally it is described by vector space associatively. One may recall the precise definition of a leading appropriation, given in Section 4.1.3. Namely, there were discussed properties of isoappropriations $c_{X,Y} : F(X) \otimes F(Y) \cong F(X \otimes Y)$ obeying the condition in Figure 4.3. (Note that to avoid cumbersome notations, index showing that we are dealing with elements of a leading club, Ld are not written down as there is no danger of confusion). In this case it can be shown that an e.p.r.s policy $Eprnat(F, F)$ implies a coexpansion and coagency,

$$(\Delta h)_{X,Y} = c^{-1}_{X,Y} \circ h_{X \otimes Y} \circ c_{X,Y}, \qquad \varepsilon(h) = h_{1_{ld}}, \tag{5.2}$$

providing an appropriation policy $Eprnat$ into a 'biagreement of covariantly constant functions'. One have a biagreement over a domain of e.p.r.s $\mathbf{h}$ if every economic institution is **h**-linear. Otherwise we have a bileading club, i.e. a leading club with a compatible coleading e.p.r.s structure.

To understand this e.p.r.s coexpansion formula, it has to be a clear what one means by $Eprnat(F,F) \otimes Eprnat(F,F)$. Now, if one is lucky enough so that every economic institution is **h**-linear and the number of enterprises in the leading club, Ld, is finite, one can identify this with $Eprnat(F^2,F^2)$, where $F^2 : \mathcal{C} \times \mathcal{C} \to Vec$ is defined by $F^2(X,Y) = F(X) \otimes F(Y)$. Namely, it consists of 'covariantly constant functions in two variables' on the Ld with values in vector space endotransactions. Similar, for the three or more members of Ld club, when one obtains covariantly constant functions in three or more variables. At this point, let us discuss procedure informally, leaving a more formal approach for next Subsection, as already mentioned.

Namely, from an informal point of view, Δh may be thought of as a function in two variables constructed by the procedure shown. It carries notion of a fixed appropriation or 'covariantly constant' because c, c^{-1} and h, as its constituents, are ensuring a fixed appropriation. The coassociativity of Δ is obtained as

$$\begin{aligned}((\Delta \otimes id) \circ \Delta h)_{X,Y,Z} &= c^{-1}_{X,Y} \circ (\Delta h)_{X \otimes Y,Z} \circ c_{X,Y} \\ &= c^{-1}_{X,Y} \circ c^{-1}_{X \otimes Y,Z} \circ h_{(X \otimes Y) \otimes Z} \circ c_{X \otimes Y,Z} \circ c_{X,Y}, \\ ((id \otimes \Delta) \circ \Delta h)_{X,Y,Z} &= c^{-1}_{Y,Z} \circ (\Delta h)_{X,Y \otimes Z} \circ c_{Y,Z} \\ &= c^{-1}_{Y,Z} \circ c^{-1}_{X,Y \otimes Z} \circ h_{X \otimes (Y \otimes Z)} \circ c_{X,Y \otimes Z} \circ c_{Y,Z}.\end{aligned}$$

Now, $h_{X \otimes (Y \otimes Z)} \circ F(\Phi_{X,Y,Z}) = F(\Phi_{X,Y,Z}) \circ h_{(X \otimes Y) \otimes Z}$ by appropriation notion of h under the economic transaction Φ. Hence, the above expressions are carrying equal appropriate collections of e.p.r.s, from point of view of traditional simple economic functions, or up to the usual vector space associativity. Then a leading appropriation respects the relevant economic transactions, i.e. the conditions in Figure 4.3 holds, and ε is a coagency for Δ and

$$\Delta(hg)_{X,Y} = c^{-1}_{X,Y} \circ h_{X \otimes Y} \circ g_{X \otimes Y} \circ c_{X,Y} = (\Delta h)_{X,Y} \circ (\Delta g)_{X,Y},$$

as required for a biagreement.

Open leading club with transfers

Similarly, if $\mathcal{C}$ allows transfers Ψ as in Chapter 4, Section 4.2, one define an opening $\mathcal{R}$ for a simple institution as a function in two variables by,

$$\mathcal{R}_{X,Y} = \tau^{-1}_{F(X),F(Y)} \circ c^{-1}_{X,Y} \circ F(\Psi_{X,Y}) \circ c_{X,Y}, \tag{5.3}$$

where τ is the usual permutation or transposition map for vector spaces. It is covariantly constant by appropriation notion of c and the image under F of the appropriationality of Ψ. Reader may recall that these definitions were used to check properties of axioms 3.1 for an opening structure:

$$((\Delta \otimes id)\mathcal{R})_{X,Y,Z} =$$
$$c^{-1}_{X,Y} \circ \tau^{-1}_{F(X\otimes Y),F(Z)} \circ c^{-1}_{Z,X\otimes Y} \circ F(\Psi_{X\otimes Y,Z}) \circ c_{X\otimes Y,Z} \circ c_{X,Y},$$

$$(\mathcal{R}_{13}\mathcal{R}_{23})_{X,Y,Z} =$$
$$\tau^{-1}_{F(X),F(Y)} \circ c^{-1}_{Z,X} \circ F(\Psi_{X,Z}) \circ c_{X,Z} \circ \tau^{-1}_{F(Y),F(Z)} \circ c^{-1}_{Z,Y} \circ F(\Psi_{Y,Z}) \circ c_{Y,Z}.$$

These two expressions are equal having in mind that $F \equiv F_{ld}$, i.e. it is leading appropriation and that the equation which is the image under F_{ld} of consistency conditions given in the definition of a leading club with transfers 4.6 in Section 4.2. Similarly, for the other side of the relations. The e.p.r.s content of axiom (3.2) on opening comes out more immediately from the definition of $\mathcal{R}_{X,Y}$ and the appropriation notion of h in the form

$$F(\Psi_{X,Y}) \circ h_{X\otimes Y} = h_{Y\otimes X} \circ F(\Psi_{X,Y}).$$

Rigid club

In the case of a club $\mathcal{C}$ being a rigid club in the sense of Section 4.3 and $F \equiv F_{Ld}$ a leading appropriation, then one has directly

$$\begin{aligned} F(X)^{*\prime} &= F(X^*), \\ ev'_{F(X)} &= F(ev_X) \circ c_{X^*,X}, \\ coev'_{F(X)} &= c^{-1}_{X,X^*} \circ F(coev_X) \end{aligned}$$

and they are a price (cost) dual for $F(X)$. Hence, according to the uniqueness of duals up to e.p.r.s isoappropriations we have induced e.p.r.s isoappropriations,

$$d_X : F(X^*) \to F(X)^*, \qquad d_X = (F(ev_X) \circ c_{X^*,X} \otimes id) \circ (id \circ coev_{F(X)})$$

between this and the usual dual. It is important to note that here, the appropriation F maps to a club of simple institutions. This simple means mapping to Vec. Nevertheless, the same can be implemented although the target may be another leading club. In this setting, we have a mutual understanding map defined by $((\gamma h)_X)^* = d_X \circ h_{X^*} \circ d_X^{-1}$, i.e. more precisely,

$$\begin{aligned} (\gamma h)_X &= (id \otimes ev_{F(X)}) \circ d_X \circ h_{X^*} \circ d_X^{-1} \circ (coev_{F(X)} \otimes id) \\ &= (id \otimes F(ev_X) \circ c_{X^*,X}) \circ h_{X^*} \circ (c^{-1}_{X,X^*} \circ F(coev_X) \otimes id), \end{aligned} \tag{5.4}$$

which appears as a new implementable appropriation policy, i.e. a new element of $Eprnat(F, F)$. The proof that this new appropriation policy obeys the axioms of mutual understanding map is cumbersome. Here, the technique of diagrammatic proof seems to be of great help. Note, that one first computes,

$$((\gamma \otimes id) \circ \Delta h)_{X,Y} =$$
$$(id \otimes F(ev_X) \circ c_{X^*,X}) c^{-1}_{X^*,Y} \circ h_{X^*\otimes Y} \circ c_{X^*,Y} \circ (c^{-1}_{X,X^*} \circ F(coev_X) \otimes id)$$

as an economic map $F(X) \otimes F(Y) \to F(X) \otimes F(Y)$. One then ensures the expansion of e.p.r.s by organizing the elements in the way the outcome of the $F(Y)$ endoappropriation becomes the input of the $F(X)$ part. Then one takes $Y = X$ and obtains a single endoappropriation $F(X) \to F(X)$. Recall that this is the usual composition $End(F(X) \otimes F(X)) = End(F(X)) \otimes End(F(X)) \to End(F(X))$. One then can use appropriational notion of h in the form $F(ev_X) \circ h_{X^* \otimes X} = h_{1_{ld}} \circ F(ev_X)$ to reduce the result to $(m(\gamma \otimes id) \circ \Delta h)_X = h_{1_{ap}} id$ as required. Similarly, for the other half of the mutually understanding axioms, using this time appropriation notion under $coev_X$.

In following Sections we are mostly concerned with above issues, except that they are addressed more formally and in the way that indicates generalizations. One also may recall an idea already exploited in discussion on relevance of the Furier theorem in the application on simple institutions (Chapter 2, Proposition 2.25). Namely, reader may recall the construction of the enterprise $\mathbf{h}(\hat{G})$ of functions on a character rule $\hat{G}$, with the role of the $\hat{G}$ undertake in this case by $\{\mathcal{C}, \otimes\}$. One can think of functions on characters as corresponding to covariantly constant functions defined on the collections of general representations. Thus, one may think of 'function enterprise' $Eprnat(F, F)$ as an e.p.r.s isoappropriation to an enterprise H if $\mathcal{C}$ was given originally as the club of representations of an enterprise H. Also, it is noteworthy that, in concrete applications, one has to be careful in economic interpretation of such an isoappropriation since an original enterprise will typically have it own description. So, for example, a description may be linked with the economic growth by $U_{ap}(sl_2)$, with its usual generators, and one would like to recognize it in terms of elements of the theory.

5.1.2 Reconstruction Theorems

Let us discussed the issues of reconstruction in the simple cases with the more formal treatment. The key idea is already exploited in the previous Section when internal economic transactions where addressed. Namely, appropriations to the simplest economic club are generally representable. Note that the simplest e.p.r.s club is one which trivializes e.p.r.s relations and can be modeled over the category Set. Thus, one could consider a club $\mathcal{C}$ and appropriations, $F, V \otimes F : \mathcal{C} \to Vec$ where $(F \otimes V)(X) = V \otimes F(X)$. In addition, it is assumed that the appropriation that transforms simple e.p.r.s institutions into ones where e.p.r.s are not of an economic concern is representable. Formally, it is assumed that the functor $Vec \to Set$ sending an economic vector space V to $Eprnat(V \otimes F, F)$ is representable. This means that there is some simple economic institution H such that isoappropriations for V can be obtained by

$$\theta_V = Lin(V, H) \cong Eprnat(V \otimes F, F). \tag{5.5}$$

In particular, there is a collection of simple argumentations $\{\alpha_X : H \otimes F \to F(X)\}$ that constitute the implementable economic policies of transformation

$\theta_H(id)$ in $Eprnat(H \otimes F, F)$. Recall that this collection is a collection of linear economic maps $\{\alpha_X : H \otimes F \to F(X)\}$. On the other hand, $\alpha_X \circ (id \otimes \alpha_X) : H \otimes H \otimes F \to F(X)$ is then an e.p.r.s implementation of transformation in $Eprnat(H \otimes H \otimes F, F)$. It can be considered as the map $m : H \otimes H \to H$ under $\theta^{-1}_{H \otimes H}$. Note that this mapping is associative due to associativity of composition of implementable policies of e.p.r.s transformation. In addition, it is managed in such a way that each α appears as an argumentation of enterprise H with this agreeable structure. The agency on domain of e.p.r.s $\mathbf{h} \to H$ corresponds under $\theta_{\mathbf{h}}$ to the e.p.r.s preserving policy (identity in an economically natural transformation) in $Eprnat(F, F)$. This is the formal version of the agreement described by relation (5.1). So, one may consider the club ${}_AM$ of representations of an agreement, A and apply F as the forgetful appropriation. Then one can treat representative enterprise H to be equal to the agreement, i.e. $H = A$, recovering expansion of its e.p.r.s in the proper implementable way. This has been the idea of Example 4.7 in Chapter 4.

One also assumes that the repeated appropriations transforming V to $Eprnat(V \otimes F^n, F^n)$ are similarly representable. One obtains the conditions of representation by service of the expanding the above simple institution so that the appropriations are representable by $H^{\otimes n}$. Here,

$$\theta^n_V : Lin(V, H^{\otimes n}) \cong Eprnat(V \otimes F^n, F^n) \tag{5.6}$$

are given by

$$\theta^n_V(\phi)_{X_1, X_2, \ldots, X_n}(v \otimes v_1 \otimes v_2 \otimes \cdots \otimes v_n) =$$
$$\sum \phi(v)^{(1)} \overset{a}{>} v_1 \otimes \cdots \otimes \phi(v)^{(n)} \overset{a}{>} v_n,$$

where $\phi(v) \in H^{\otimes n}$ is given in an explicit summation notation, $v_i \in F(X_i)$, and $\overset{a}{>}$ denotes the argumentation α. This is automatic if all simple institutions involved are finite dimensional.

Theorem 5.1. (Reconstruction of a biagreement) *Let $\mathcal{C}$ be a leading club, and F a leading appropriation to simple institutions, $F : \mathcal{C} \to Vec$, that obeys representable conditions θ_V and θ^n_V from above. Then H can be organized into a biagreement.*

Proof: The statement in the theorem is an economic interpretation of the reconstruction theorem for vector spaces. Thus, in the proof we should show that applying that theorem the coexpansion of e.p.r.s, Δ, can be defined that, with other given elements, provides biagreemental structure of H. Namely, there is a coexpansion of e.p.r.s, $\Delta : H \to H \otimes H$, defined as the inverse image under θ^2_H of the implementable policy of economic transformation $c^{-1}_{X,Y} \circ \alpha_{X \otimes Y} \circ c_{X,Y}$ that maps $H \otimes F(X) \otimes F(Y) \to F(X) \otimes F(Y)$. We compute the implementable policy of transformation corresponding to both sides by (5.6) of any axiom we want to check. So, we have,

$\theta_H^3((\Delta \otimes id)\circ\Delta)_{X,Y,Z} =$
$((\alpha_X \otimes \alpha_Y) \otimes \alpha_Z)\circ\Delta \otimes id) \otimes \Delta = (c_{X,Y}^{-1}\circ\alpha_{X\otimes Y}\circ c_{X,Y} \otimes \alpha_Z)\circ\Delta =$
$c^{-1}\circ\alpha_{(X\otimes Y)\otimes Z}\circ c^2$

from the definition of coexpansion Δ. On the other side, we have,

$$\theta_H^3((id \otimes \Delta)\circ\Delta)_{X,Y,Z} = c^{-2}\circ\alpha_{X\otimes(Y\otimes Z)}\circ c^2.$$

The implementable policies coincides by leading appropriation F. Also appropriation implied from argumentation of α under transactions $\Phi_{X,Y,Z}$ provides the same procedure as was one in the direct proof for the relation (5.2) above.

Similarly, for the homotransaction property of Δ we have

$$\begin{aligned}\theta_{H\otimes H}^2(\Delta\circ\Delta)_{X,Y} &= c_{X,Y}^{-1}\circ\theta_H(\cdot)_{X\otimes Y}\circ c \\ &= c^{-1}\circ\alpha_{X\otimes Y}\circ c_{X,Y}\circ(id \otimes c^{-1}\circ\alpha_{X\otimes Y}\circ c) \\ &= (\alpha_X \otimes \alpha_Y \otimes \alpha_X \otimes \alpha_Y)\circ(\Delta \otimes \Delta),\end{aligned}$$

where the first equality uses $(\alpha_X \otimes \alpha_Y)\circ\Delta = \theta_H^2(\Delta)_{X,Y} = c^{-1}\circ\alpha_{X\otimes Y}\circ c$ leaving $\theta_H(\cdot)$ evaluated at this stage. Then the obtained definition of coexpansion Δ is used again for the third equality, where the aggregate specifies the position in $H \otimes H \otimes H \otimes H$ what is the main argumentation. The necessary transposition maps τ are suppressed. The result is then linked with $\theta_{H\otimes H}^2((\cdot \otimes \cdot)\circ\Delta_{X\otimes Y})_{X,Y}$. □

The definition of coexpansion Δ in the reconstruction process for biagreement is such that $c_{X,Y} : F(X) \otimes F(Y) \to F(X \otimes Y)$ becomes an isoappropriation of H-standard. Thus, the map $\mathcal{C} \to_H M$ is a leading appropriation and the reconstructed biagreement H is the universal biagreement with this property. So, one may conclude that if there is some other biagreement H' which may be an argument on all the simple institutions $F(X)$ in this way, then there is a unique biagreement on homotransaction $H' \to H$ such that these argumentations are the responses (pull-back) of the argumentations α_X of H. One may think of any collections of argumentations $\{H' \otimes F(X) \to F(X)\}$, as an implementable policy in $Eprnat(H' \otimes F, F)$ and use (5.6) to construct this policy. From point of view of clubs, one may consider H as an universal biagreement with the property that appropriation from the club to the simple institutional forms, $F : \mathcal{C} \to Vec$, factors through ${}_HM$ via the forgetful appropriation.

Proposition 5.2. (Reconstruction of an open biagreement) *For a leading club described in Theorem 5.1 that also allows transfers an open biagreement can be reconstructed.*

Proof: The proof is technically same as in the proof of the preceding theorem. Here, an opening $\mathcal{R} \in H \otimes H$ can be defined as the inverse image under $\theta_{\mathbf{h}}^2$ of the implementable policy of transformation $\mathcal{R}_{X,Y}$ in (5.3). Then using above procedure we have $\theta^3_{\mathbf{h}}((\Delta \otimes id)\mathcal{R})_{X,Y,Z} = c^{-1} \circ \theta^2_{\mathbf{h}}(\mathcal{R})_{X \otimes Y,Z} \circ c$ and

$$\begin{aligned}\theta^3_{\mathbf{h}}(\mathcal{R}_{13}\mathcal{R}_{23})_{X,Y,Z} &= (\alpha_X \otimes \alpha_Z \otimes \alpha_Y \otimes \alpha_Z)(\mathcal{R} \otimes \mathcal{R}) \\ &= \theta^2_{\mathbf{h}}(\mathcal{R})_{X,Z} \circ \theta^2_{\mathbf{h}}(\mathcal{R})_{Y,Z}\end{aligned}$$

from the definitions. There are equal for $\theta^2_{\mathbf{h}}(\mathcal{R})$ as stated, in view of the images under appropriation F of one of the identities for transfers Ψ. Similarly can be shown for other half of the axiom (3.1). For the axiom (3.1) we have

$$\begin{aligned}\theta^2_H(\mathcal{R} \cdot \Delta)_{X,Y} &= (\alpha_X \otimes \alpha_Z \otimes \alpha_Y \otimes \alpha_Z)(\mathcal{R} \otimes \Delta) \\ &= \theta^2_{\mathbf{h}}(\mathcal{R})_{X,Z} \circ c^{-1} \circ \alpha_{X \otimes Y} \circ c.\end{aligned}$$

The calculation for $\theta^2(\Delta^{op}(\ )m\mathcal{R})_{X,Y} = c^{-1} \circ \alpha_{Y \otimes X} \circ c \circ \theta^2(\mathcal{R})_{X,Y}$ is similar. The relation is obtained using the definition of $\theta^2_{\mathbf{h}}(\mathcal{R})$. It is implemented on suitable composition of the appropriation F, and appropriation of transfers Ψ. Note that usual transposition of vector spaces have been suppressed in this proof, and they are given more explicitly in (5.3). □

Proposition 5.3. (Reconstruction of an enterprise) *For a leading club, described in Theorem 5.1, which is also rigid an enterprise can be reconstructed.*

Proof: The proof consists of showing that under the conditions of the proposition a mutual understanding map $\gamma : H \to H$ can be obtained by the implementable policy of e.p.r.s transformation. One may try a map obtained as the inverse image under θ^2_H of the implementable policy of transformation $(id \otimes ev_{F(V)}) \circ d_X \circ \alpha_{X^*} \circ d_X^{-1} \tau^{-1}_{H,F(X)} \circ (coev_{F(X)} \otimes id)$. This determines $\gamma : H \to H$, as $(id \otimes ev_{F(V)}) \circ d_X \circ \alpha_{X^*} \circ d_X^{-1} \tau^{-1}_{H,F(X)} \circ (coev_{F(X)} \otimes id) : H \otimes F(X) \to F(X)$, and ensures H is organized into an enterprise. Details can effectively be shown by the diagram in Figure 5.1. The definition of $\theta_H(m \circ (\gamma \otimes id) \circ \Delta)_X$ is used to lead at anticlockwise path from the institution $H \otimes F(X)$ to institution $F(X)$. The policy $\theta_H(\cdot)$ is recognized and written in the form $\alpha_X \circ (id \otimes \alpha_X)$ in convenient way in the part to the lower left. The part above this commutes one of these argumentations α_X that has been accepted by mutual understanding map γ. The definition of policy of e.p.r.s transformation on mutual understanding map or precisely $\theta_H(\gamma)_X$ specifies the central low square in the diagram. The upper central institution commutes $coev_X$ after implementation of $\alpha_X \circ \Delta$. Note that they are arguments on different economic spaces. The definition of $\theta^2_H(\Delta)_{X^*,X}$ specifies the right hand side on the diagram.

The clockwise path, on the other hand, simplifies procedure further using appropriationality of argumentation α under ev_X in the form $ev_X \circ \alpha_{X^* \otimes X} = \alpha_{Id_{ap}} \circ ev_X$. Then ev_X combines with $coev_X$ to provide argumentation for preservation of leading structure by using one of the rigidity properties of the

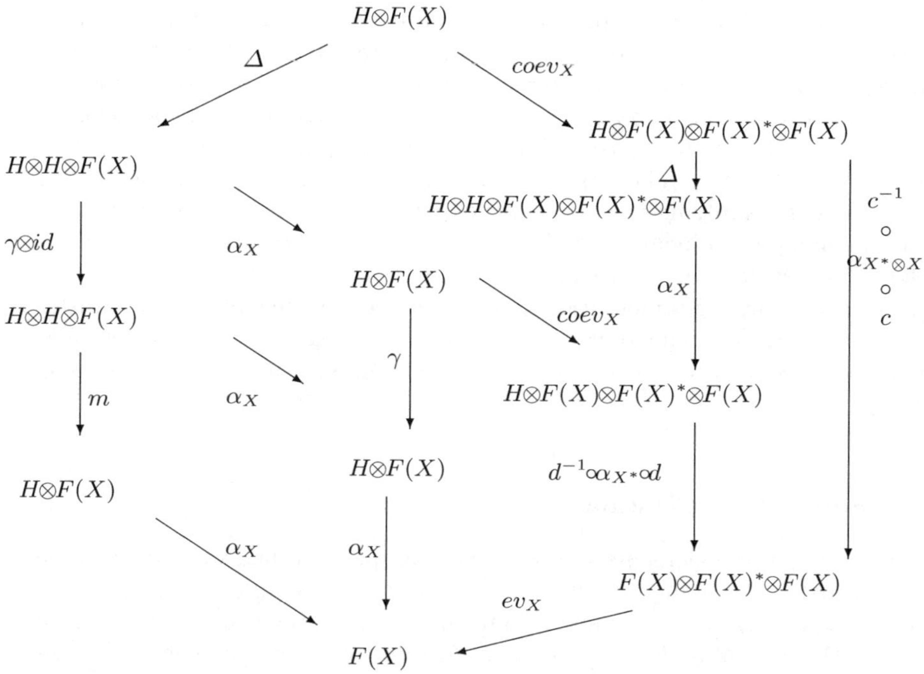

Fig. 5.1. Diagrammatic proof of reconstruction of a mutual understanding map γ.

club give by axioms 4.11 in Definition 4.24. Thus, within a leading club argumentation we have $\alpha_{ld_{ap}} id = \theta_H(\eta \circ \varepsilon)$ as required. The proof for the other axiom of mutual understanding mapping is strictly analogous. □

Example 5.4. Let H be an open biagreement, $\mathcal{C} = {}_H M$ its club of representations, and F a forgetful appropriation as in Example 4.7. Then reconstructed open biagreement corresponds to this open biagreement itself.

Proof: It was shown in Example 4.7 from Chapter 4 that set of implementable policies of e.p.r.s transformation constitutes an enterprise. Namely, $Eprnat(F, F)$ can be identified with $H = Lin(\mathbf{h}, H)$. In the same way, one has now that our representing enterprise in (5.6) can again be taken to be our original H as a simple economic institution. Given an implementable policy of transformation $\theta \in Eprnat(V \otimes F, F)$, one can evaluate it on the leading member or agency, in the price regular representation as before, providing a linear mapping $\theta_H((\ ) \otimes 1) : V \otimes H \to H$. From the other point of view, we treat an economic transaction $\phi : V \to H$ by the implementable policy of transformation θ, so that $\theta(\phi)_X(v) = \phi(v) \overset{a}{>} v$ for all appropriations $v \in F(X)$. Note that, X is an element of the club, i.e. it is given as an

H-standard, and appropriation $F(X)$ is its underling simple institution. In this case two forms of appropriations F and c provide same outcome. Also, an argumentation α_X is equal to the argumentation $\overset{a}{>}$ as expected. Thus, the reconstructed expansion of e.p.r.s correspond to the original one. More directly, this was already shown in Example 4.7. The reconstructed coexpansion of e.p.r.s is such that $(\alpha_X \otimes \alpha_Y)(\Delta h)(v \otimes w) = \alpha_{X \otimes Y} h(v \otimes w) = h \overset{a}{>} (v \otimes w)$, for $v \in X$ and $w \in Y$. The representation of aggregation procedure is defined in Example 4.7 applying the original coexpansion of H, so we see that coexpansions of e.p.r.s coincide. Finally, the reconstructed structure of opening is defined by transfer such that $(\alpha_X \otimes \alpha_Y)(\mathcal{R})(v \otimes w) = \tau^{-1} \circ \Psi_{X,Y}(v \otimes w)$. This coincides with the argumentation of our original opening $\mathcal{R}$ when transfer Ψ is computed from Theorem 4.15. One may note that this exercise compiles elements of reconstruction theory concerning simple institutions addressed so far. □

5.1.3 Some Generalizations

Having some of the elements in the above example modified we can get some of generalized or modified institutions. So, if H is an enterprise and we consider the club of finite dimensional simple institutions, then the reconstruction recovers the mutual understanding map. Also, in above example one may consider nontrivial appropriation $c_{X,Y}$, which through reconstruction provided H_χ, twisted by 2-cocycle of opening $\chi \in H \otimes H$ according to the Theorem 3.25 in Chapter 3, instead of simple H from example above. Nevertheless, twisting is such that χ^{-1} corresponds to the implementable policy of transformation c^{-1} viewed as an element of $Eprnat(F^2, F^2)$ in the trivial way.

One may also consider more general member of the club, for example a quasienterprise. Then one assumes that appropriation F has the property of e.p.r.s expansion in the sense that there are isoappropriations $c_{X,Y} : F(X) \otimes F(Y)$ as before, but without the conditions valid for usual $c_{X,Y}$ as in Figure 4.3. This implies invalidity of the agreement over the economic functions, as implementation of the policy of e.p.r.s transformation can not be ensured any more. Namely, the conjugation by a covariantly constant function of three variables,

$$\phi_{X,Y,Z} = c^{-1}_{Y,Z} \circ c^{-1}_{X,Y \otimes Z} \circ F(\Phi_{X,Y,Z}) \circ c_{X \otimes Y,Z} \circ c_{X,Y}, \tag{5.7}$$

is necessary to recover coassociativity in the weak sense of a quasienterprenerial agreement. From the more formal point of view, this implementable policy of transformation has, as its inverse image under $\theta^3_{\mathbf{h}}$, an element $\phi \in H \otimes H \otimes H$ that can be used to ensure implementation. Namely, this element could have properties of the 3-cocycle condition already discussed in the Chapter 3.

Similarly, in this weak setting combined with the club that allows transfers an open quasibiagreement can be reconstructed. The same formula as above is used for opening $\mathcal{R}_{X,Y}$. The procedure to be implemented is same as for verification of the 3-cocycle condition for ϕ.

Finally, combined with the setting of the rigid club, the extend mutual understanding map (γ, α, β) can be reconstructed, forming a quasienterprise according Chapter 3. Because the appropriation is not leading one, one no longer could obtained $F(X^*)$ as a dual of $F(X)$ as was explained for the leading club above. Nevertheless we may choose invertible implementable policies $\alpha, \beta \in Eprnat(F, F)$ such that

$$\begin{aligned} d_X &\equiv (F(ev_X) \circ c_{X^*,X} \otimes id) \circ \alpha_X^{-1} \circ (id \otimes coev_{F(X)}), \\ d_X^{-1} &\equiv (ev_{F(X)} \otimes id) \circ \beta_X^{-1} \circ (id \otimes c_{X,X^*}^{-1} \circ F(coev_X)) \end{aligned} \tag{5.8}$$

are mutually inverse. For example, one can chose,

$$\begin{aligned} \alpha_X &= id, \\ \beta_X &= (id \otimes F(ev_X)) \circ c_{X^*,X}) \circ (c_{X,X^*}^{-1} \circ F(coev_X) \otimes id), \end{aligned}$$

or β can be made trivial and α typically nontrivial. For an implementable isotransaction U on can define α, β only up to a policy of transformation $\alpha \circ U$ and $\beta = U^{-1} \circ \beta$ that ensure a symmetric relation. Mutual understanding map γ is in the same form as in the first expression in (4.11), and more precisely addressed in Proposition 5.3. In the similar way, as above, it can be shown that that the axioms (3.1) are satisfied. We have extra factors of α, β due to the now definition of the form of appropriation d_X. To verify the axiom (3.2), using the definitions above the expressions that apply extended mutual understanding map (γ, α, β) can be obtained, as $(\sum \phi^{(1)} \beta \otimes \gamma \phi^{(2)} \otimes \alpha \phi^{(3)})_{X,Y,Z}$, ect. from the definitions above and glue the three copies of $End(F(X))$ together when the enterprises, members are treated equal, $Z = Y = X$, but their economic relations are hierarchically organized by convention that output of Z member is the Y input and the Y output into X input. The result can then be obtained easily using the image under appropriation F of the first half of the rigidity axioms 4.11 for the member X. The similar for the second of (3.2) using the second half of (4.11).

5.1.4 Dual Approach

As a lot of other economic phenomena, the issues of reconstructions can be addressed in the dual form. Here, duals are based on costandards, and such an approach can have technical advantages over the above version where standards were in focus. Roughly speaking, the representability assumption for the dual setting states that the appropriation from simple economic institutions to ones that are e.p.r.s free is representable. In this dual version this means that there is some simple economic institution A such that isoappropriations for V can be obtained by

$$\theta_V = Lin(A, V) = Apr(F, F \otimes V) = Trn(F, F \otimes V),$$

where Apr, Trn are collections of appropriations and economic transactions of the club, respectively. These collections transform a simple enterprise V to a free collection of e.p.r.s $Eprnat(F, F \otimes V)$ within this setting, and are representable. One may compare this relation to (5.5) above. In particular, there is a collection $\{\beta_X : F(X) \to F(X) \otimes A\}$ as the implementable economic policies of transformation $\theta_A(id)$. In addition, one defines coexpansion $\Delta \to A \otimes A$ as the inverse image under $\theta_{A\otimes A}$ of the implementable policy of transformation $(\beta_X \circ id) \circ \beta_X : F(X) \to F(X) \otimes A \otimes A$. A coagency can then be specified under the condition that the implementable policy of transformation is persistent. Then an inverse image under $\theta_{\mathbf{h}}$ of this persistent implementable policy of transformation, provides coagency, where $\mathbf{h}$ is the domain of e.p.r.s. In that way A becomes a coagreement which has a coargumentation β on each of the appropriation $F(X)$. One also needs the hierarchical representability where

$$\theta_V^n : Lin(A^{\otimes n}, V) \cong Apr(F^n, F^n \otimes V),$$
$$\theta_V^n(\phi) = \sum v_1^{(1_{ap})} \otimes v_n^{(1_{ap})} \phi(v_1^{(2_{ap})} \otimes v_2^{(2_{ap})} \otimes \cdots \otimes v_n^{(2_{ap})}).$$

It provides conditions to define an expansion of e.p.r.s $m : A \otimes A \to A$, as the inverse image under policy θ_A^2 of appropriation $c_{X,Y} \circ \beta_{X\otimes Y} \circ c_{X\otimes Y}^{-1} : F(X) \otimes F(X) \to F(X) \otimes F(Y) \otimes A$. This gives a biagreement if appropriation F is leading one, and a dual open biagreement if it is merely expansional. In the setting where club is with transfers we have a dual opening structure $\mathcal{R}$ specified as the inverse image under policy $\theta_{\mathbf{h}}^2$ of $\mathcal{R}_{X,Y}$ from (5.3). In addition, if club is rigid one can obtained a mutual understanding map γ as the inverse image under θ_A of

$$(id \otimes ev_{F(X)}) \circ d_X \circ \beta_{X^*} \circ d_X^{-1} \circ (coev_{F(X)} \otimes id). \tag{5.9}$$

To obtain an example of dual reconstruction, one may think of the club that allows transfers over the market clearing conditions $\mathcal{C}(R)$. It is generated by a single R-matrix that expresses market clearing conditions. The result is the dual open biagreement $A(R)$. One can also consider the rigid leading club that allows transfers. Namely, it can be generated in the conventional case of biinvertability that provides a traditional e.p.r.s rule with mutual understanding associated to market clearing conditions R.

5.2 Reconstruction by Transfers

One may recall that the basic idea of economic reconstruction theorems for simple cases, explored above, was to build some kind of enterprise of economic functions on collection of enterprises or club of enterprises, using the simple institutions as building blocks and simple economic relations to glue them together. For complex e.p.r.s relations and institutions it is not always possible to implement this without losing ability to control some of the important e.p.r.s issues. At the same time, one would like to count on the structural support of the leading institutional organizations and their power to preserve an appropriational system. To reach this, one implements a much more crucial generalization of the above reconstruction theorems. So, here the idea is to provide generalized procedures of reconstruction which would be powerful enough to preserve a leading appropriation structure.

Thus, here one operates with an appropriation F, between two clubs $F : \mathcal{C} \to \mathcal{V}$, which, in this generalized case, is such that $\mathcal{V}$ is allowed to be a general leading economic club incorporating transfers. In this setting, the institutions or enterprises that are reconstructed are not going to be simple, usual enterprises, but ones which economic activities are compatible with the club that allows transfers, $\mathcal{V}$. One may note that elements of these institutions may often seem extraordinary, even exotic and unnecessary, but they appear to be needed in many concrete applications for following and control of complex e.p.r.s flows. As in Sections above here discussion is given on abstract level while the concrete forms of economic organizations and institutionalization procedures are discussed in detail in a sequel to present volume.

5.2.1 Forms Incorporating Transfers

One may recall elements of the theory of institutions that allows transfers in the leading clubs given at the end of Section 4.2, Chapter 4 where the discussion was given from point of view of covariant e.p.r.s systems. An enterprise that allows transfers is an institution or member of the club and its expansion and agency characteristics are described by economic transactions including transfers. In addition, by the Lemma 4.20 it was shown that in the case when transfers are allowed, an aggregation procedure of institutions with transfers also carries an agreement on implementable structural policy on e.p.r.s in the generalized leading club that allows transfers. This procedure is considered as an agreement that concerns expansions of e.p.r.s by aggregation that allows transfers. Formally we are dealing with the braided tensor product algebra. The Lemma serves crucially in defining an enterprise that allows transfers or group of rules that allows transfers. Also note that in this Section diagrammatic notation and technic, briefly explained previously, are extensively used as they help us to present statements and proofs quite efficiently. Reader may exercise by turning out all the elementary e.p.r.s theory presented in Chapter 2 in the diagrammatic version. This includes dual enterprises with transfers, standards, costandards, adjoint argumentations, cross expansions of e.p.r.s, and others. For example, one may consider the property of uniqueness of mutual understanding map for simple enterprises, shown precisely in Proposition 2.9, and its diagrammatic version for the case that includes transfers. So, property $\gamma \circ m = m \circ \Psi_{B,B} \circ (\gamma \otimes \gamma)$, is proven by the diagram shown in Figure 5.2. In the graph the loops involving γ are added, knowing that they are trivial from Figure 5.3 below. Transfers are reorganized, and using property

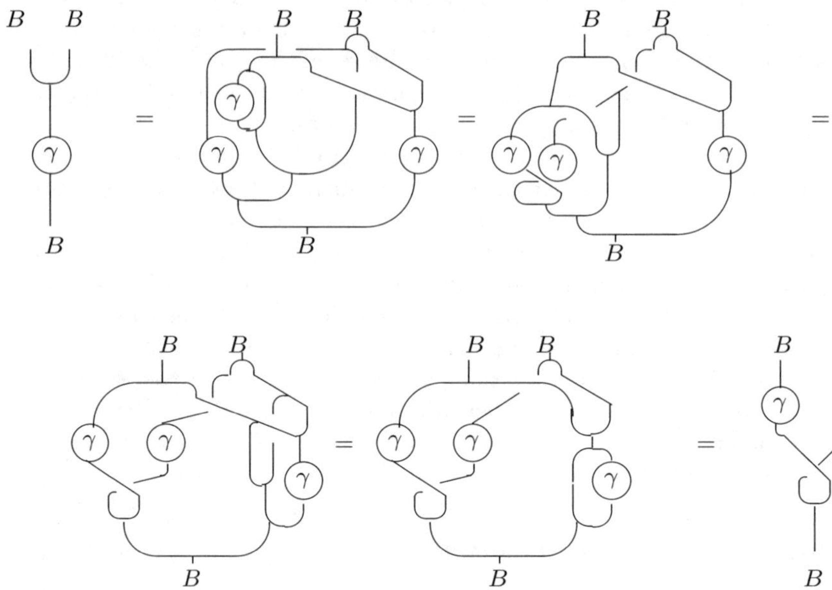

Fig. 5.2. Diagrammatic proof of antihomotransactive property of mutual understanding map γ that includes transfers.

of coexpansion as in Figure 5.3 (a), and then part of (b) again for the final result. To show that antitransaction is also valid for the coagency in this case with transfer, i.e. that $\Delta \circ \gamma = (\gamma \otimes \gamma) \circ \Psi_{B,B} \circ \Delta$, the flows are reversed and the same diagrammatic structure from above can be used.

Definition 5.5. (Biagreement with transfers) *A biagreement in a club that allows transfers or a biagreement with transfers, contains an agreement B, that satisfies conditions of the Definition 4.19 in Section 4.2 and a co-agreement formed of an agreed relation that plays the role of coexpansion $\Delta : B \to B \otimes B$, and another one defining coagency such that $\varepsilon : B \to ld$.*

Definition 5.6. (An enterprise with transfers) *A biagreement from Definition 5.5 is an enterprise in the club with transfers or, loosely speaking, an e.p.r.s rule of transfers, if there is also an economic relation $\gamma : B \to B$ obeying the usual axioms concerning a mutual understanding map but extended to economic transactions in the club that allows transfers.*

These axioms are summarized in Figure 5.3 and 5.4 in diagrammatic notation as was suggested above, and in Section 4.2 and Section 4.3 of Chapter 4. Axioms concerning agency and coagency, η and ε, respectively state that these

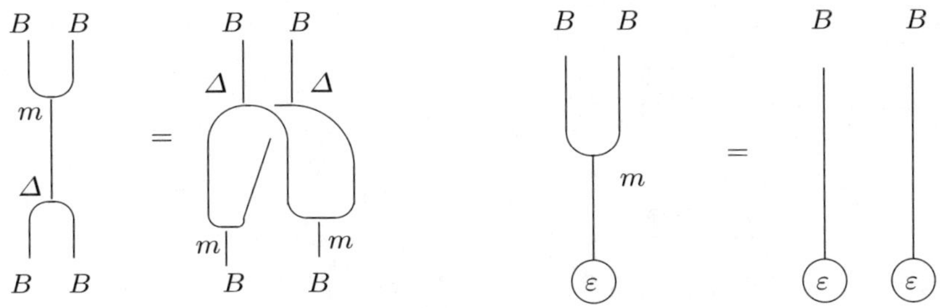

Fig. 5.3. Diagrammatic presentation of axioms of a transfer rule for biagreement showing homotransactive property for a coexpansion.

can involve expansion or coexpansion node without changing the economic transaction. One may note that institutions that allow transfers naturally arise through reconstruction procedures.

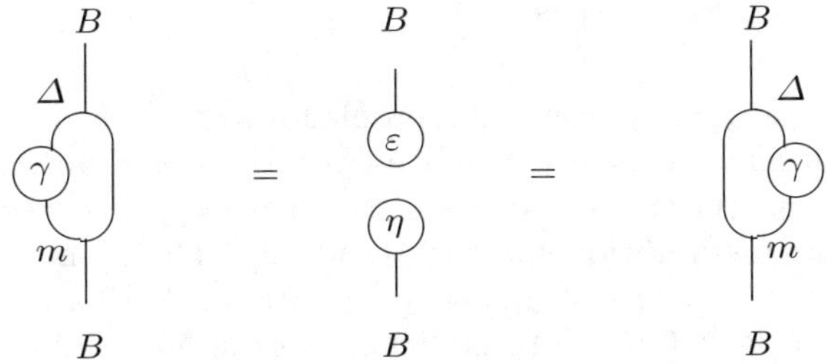

Fig. 5.4. Diagrammatic presentation of axioms of a transfer rule showing properties of a mutual understanding map with transfers.

Definition 5.7. (An open enterprise with transfers) *An enterprise from Definition 5.6 is an open enterprise in the club with transfers if there is also an economic opening $\mathcal{R}$ obeying the usual axiom concerning opening structure but extended to economic transactions in the club that allows transfers.*

5.2.2 Generalized Theorems

The idea is to specify the reconstruction procedures for these settings when economic environment is given by a club that allows transfers $\mathcal{V}$ as the counterpart to the club for the setting of simple institutions denoted by Vec

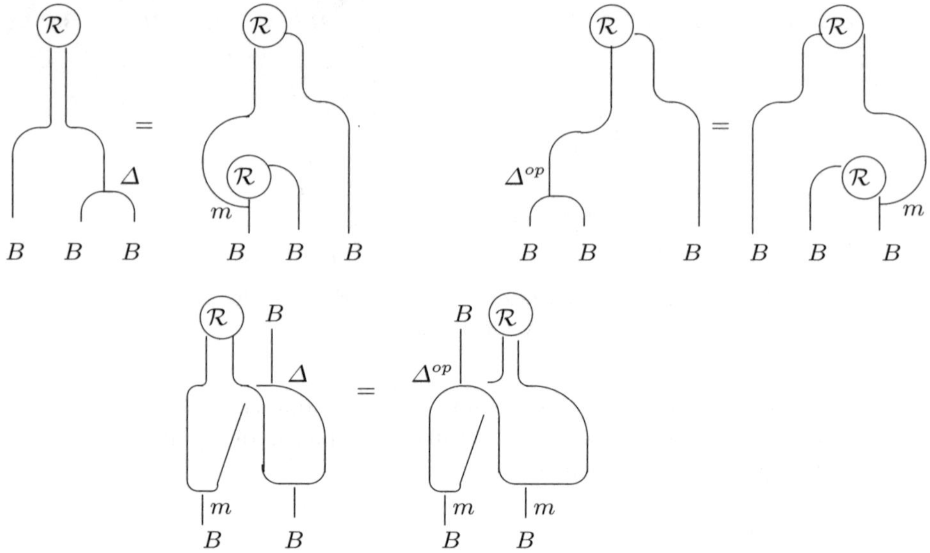

Fig. 5.5. Diagrammatic presentation of axioms of a transfer rule showing opening structure that includes transfers.

and discussed previously. Here, the proofs are the same as in the simple setting, but transfers are involved and we use the diagrammatic notation and technique to incorporate these elements efficiently. The key element is the representability assumption for the standards. Thus, one could consider a club $\mathcal{C}$ that allows transfers and appropriations, $F, V \otimes F : \mathcal{C} \rightarrow \mathcal{V}$ where $(F \otimes V)(X) = V \otimes F(X)$. In addition, it is assumed that there is an enterprise $B \in \mathcal{V}$ such that appropriations $Eprnat(V \otimes F, F) \cong Apr(V, B)$ by appropriational bijections. Then appropriational isoappropriations for V can be obtained by $\theta_V = Lin(V, B) \cong Eprnat(V \otimes F, F)$. In particular, there is a collection of argumentations $\{\alpha_X : B \otimes F \rightarrow F(X), X \in \mathcal{C}\}$ that constitutes the implementable economic policies of transformation and corresponds to the preserving transaction $B \rightarrow B$ within an e.p.r.s institution B, $\theta_B(id)$, in $Eprnat(B \otimes F, F)$. Recall that this collection is given by $\{\alpha_X : B \otimes F \rightarrow F(X), X \in \mathcal{C}\}$. Then using α and the transfers, the induced implementable policies can be obtained as maps

$$\theta_V^n : Apr(V, B^{\otimes n}) \cong Eprnat(V \otimes F^n, F^n) \tag{5.10}$$

and it is assumed that these are also bijections. This is given in Figure 5.6. Under 5.7(*b*) it is shown that expansion $m : B \otimes B \rightarrow B$ is defined in the usual way by the requirement that the economic transactions α_X are arguments. This makes it unique.

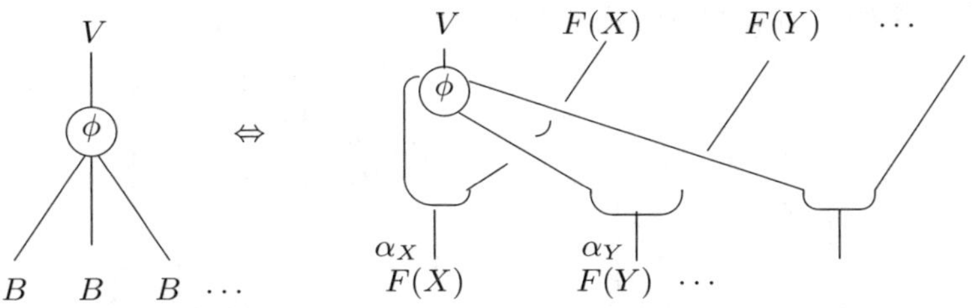

Fig. 5.6. Diagrammatic presentation of reconstruction theorem showing identification of transaction that includes transfers.

Likewise for the leading transaction $ld \to B$, which comes as the inverse image under leading preserving implementation policy of transformation θ_{ld}. The proofs are similar as those before, and do not yet involve the leading structure of the club $\mathcal{C}$ or the transfers in $\mathcal{V}$. One may note that an agreement B that is a member of a club $\mathcal{V}$ can always be obtained applying appropriation $F : \mathcal{C} \to \mathcal{V}$.

Theorem 5.8. (Reconstruction of a biagreement with transfers) *Let $\mathcal{C}$ be a leading club, and F a leading appropriation, $F : \mathcal{C} \to \mathcal{V}$, then B defined as above becomes a member of the club with transfers $\mathcal{V}$, where coexpansion $\Delta : B \to B \otimes B$ is specified by transformation policy θ_V on the composite enterprises, and coagency $\varepsilon : B \to ld$ by an argumentation of the leading member of the club with transfers, $\varepsilon = \alpha_{ld}$.*

Proof: The statement in the theorem is generalization of the reconstruction theorem for simple cases. Here, coexpansion of e.p.r.s, Δ, can be defined which, with other given elements, provides biagreement structure with transfers for B. Namely, there is a coexpansion of e.p.r.s, $\Delta : B \to B \otimes B$, defined as the inverse image under θ_B^2 of an implementable policy of economic transformation built, also as before, from an argumentation on the composite members of the club, $\alpha_{X \otimes Y}$. The policy is formed under the conventions that appropriations $c_{X,Y}, d_X$ are suppressed, being the isoappropriations resulting from the assumption that F is a leading appropriation.

In the diagrammatic presentation of this, given in Figure 5.7(b), the solid node $\alpha_{X \otimes Y}$ is argumentation α on the composite enterprises $X \otimes Y$, which is in this case viewed via appropriation c as a transaction $B \otimes F(X) \otimes F(Y) \to F(X) \otimes F(Y)$. Note that the diagrams refer to transaction within the club that allows transfers $\mathcal{V}$. To prove that Δ is coassociative we also use the diagram. Here, the definition of Δ is used twice, and then again in reverse, using also that F is a leading appropriation and hence compatible with the suppressed associativity in the two clubs. The crucial step is the third equality,

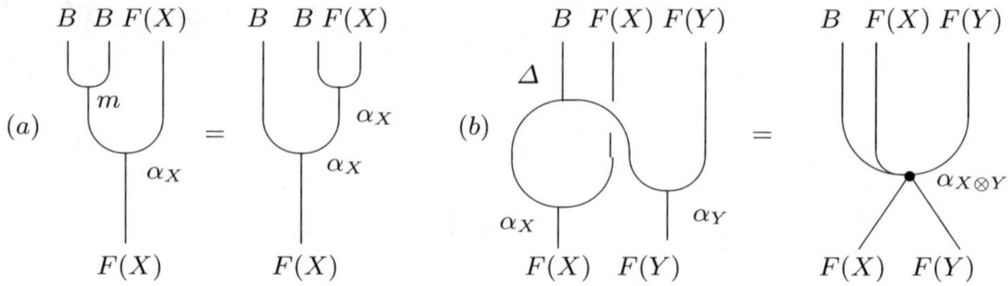

Fig. 5.7. Diagrammatic presentation of reconstruction theorem defining (a) expansion and (b) coexpansion of biagreement with transfers.

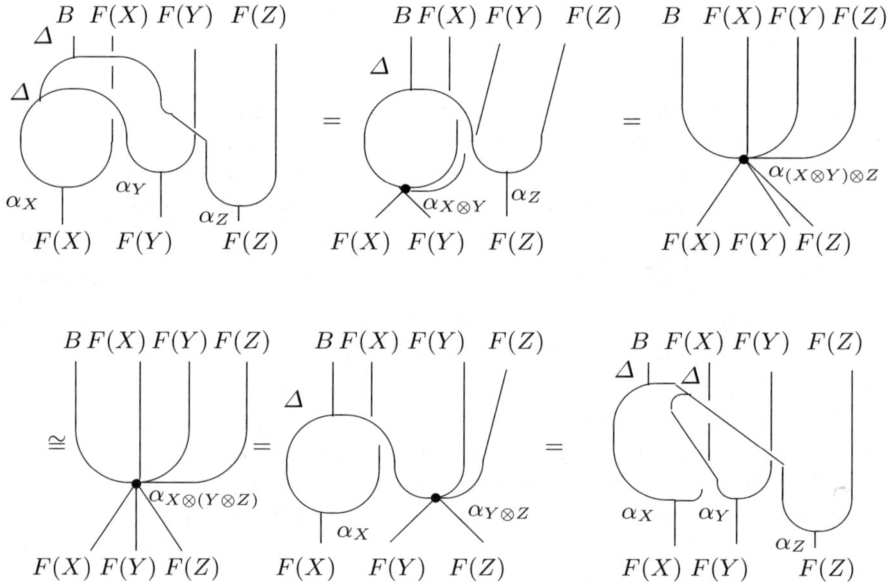

Fig. 5.8. Diagrammatic proof of coassociativity property for the reconstructed coexpansion that includes transfers.

which follows from appropriational character of argumentation α under the associativity transaction $(X \otimes Y) \otimes Z \to X \otimes (Y \otimes Z)$ and from the fact that F is a leading appropriation. In the case where F is not a leading one, but merely expansional appropriation, the coexpansion appears in the form of a quasicoassociative coexpansion. Note that Δ commutes with the expansion, when $B \otimes B$ has the agreed aggregation structure that allows transfers, as in Lemma 4.20. This is actually the proof that Δ is a homoappropriation, given also by the diagram in Figure 5.9, which complites the statement of Theorem 5.8.

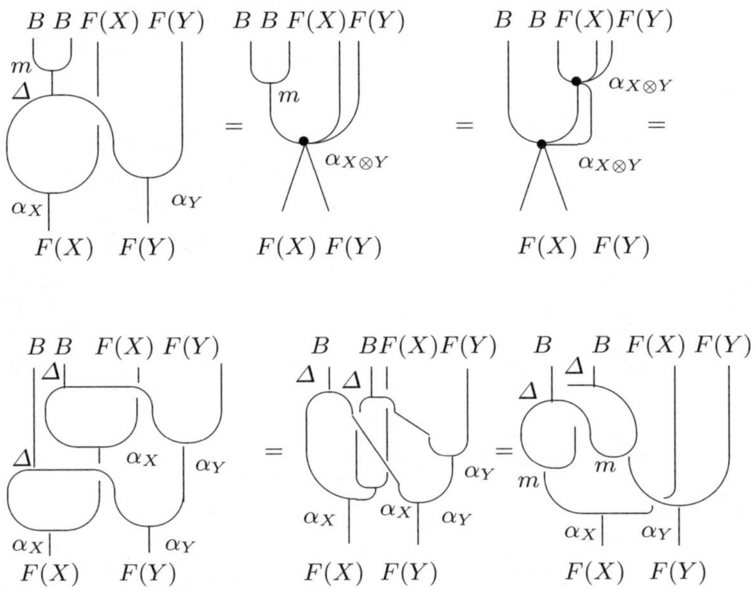

Fig. 5.9. Diagrammatic proof of homoappropriate property for the reconstructed coexpansion in the case that includes transfers.

Proposition 5.9. (Reconstruction of enterprise with transfers) *An enterprise with transfers can be reconstructed for a leading club C that allows transfers, described in Theorem 5.8, that is also rigid.*

Proof: The proof consists of showing that a mutual understanding map $\gamma : B \to B$ can be obtained using a dual argumentation α_{X^*} viewed via appropriation c as transaction $B \otimes F(X) \to F(X)$, implying the required properties of mutual understanding. Thus, map γ defined by Figure 5.10 is

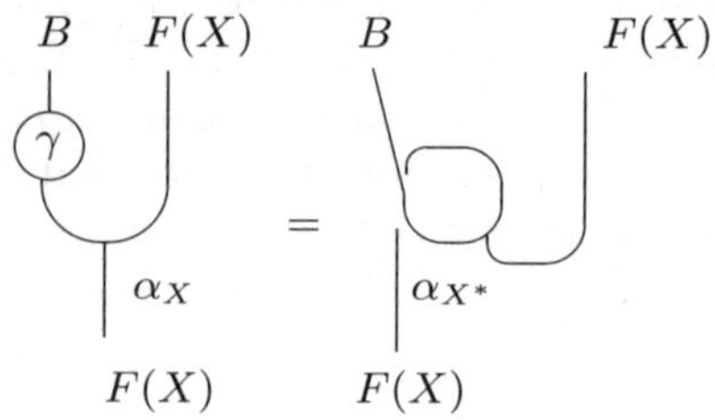

Fig. 5.10. Defining mutual understanding map in the case that includes transfers by reconstruction theorem.

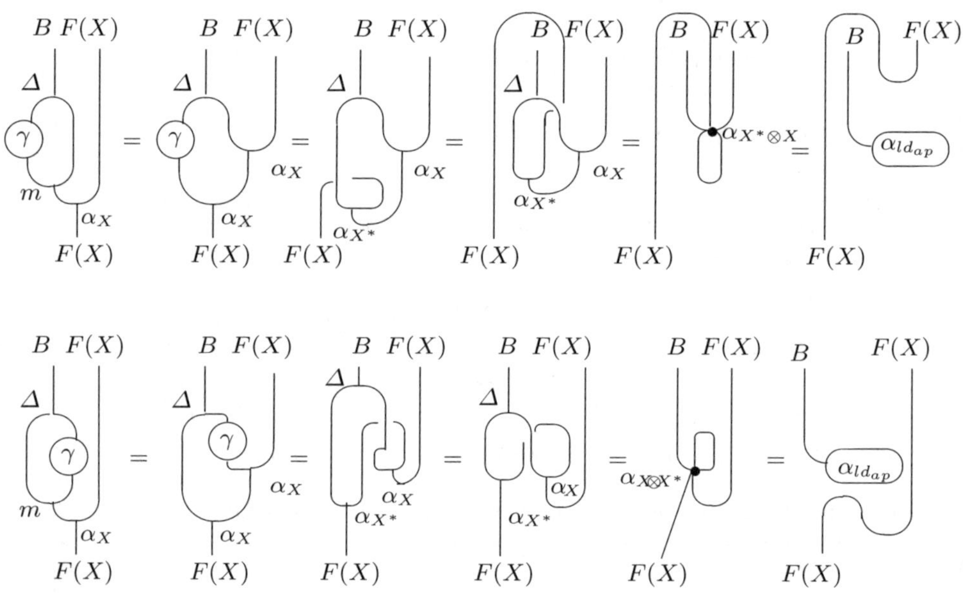

Fig. 5.11. Proof of mutual understanding axioms for reconstructed mutual understanding map in the case that includes transfers.

a mutual understanding map for the coexpansion Δ. This is shown in Figure 5.11. Here the first, second and fourth equalities are definitions of expansion m, mutual understanding map γ and coexpansion Δ. The fifth equality results from appropriationality of argumentation α under the evaluation due to the leading type of the club, i.e. $X^* \otimes X \to ld$. The result is the implementable policy of transformation corresponding to composition of the agency and coagency, i.e. to $\eta \circ \varepsilon$. Similarly for the second line using the appropriation under the coevaluation transaction $ld \to X \otimes X^*$. □

From economics point of view of particular importance is reconstructing procedure that concerns an open structured enterprise with transfers. This case is often a usual consequence of a membership of a club that allows transfers than not. The axioms that are appropriate to these cases have been presented in Figure 5.10 together with the axioms of an enterprise that incorporates transfers. The idea here is that a second coexpansion Δ^{op} and opening $\mathcal{R} : ld \to B \otimes B$, be related to Δ by conjugation. Then this is a slightly more general concept than the one applied for previous cases, as the second coexpansion of e.p.r.s is otherwise not related to Δ. Note that in this case one has an implementable choice of 'opposite coexpansion', as is shown in Figure 5.12 below.

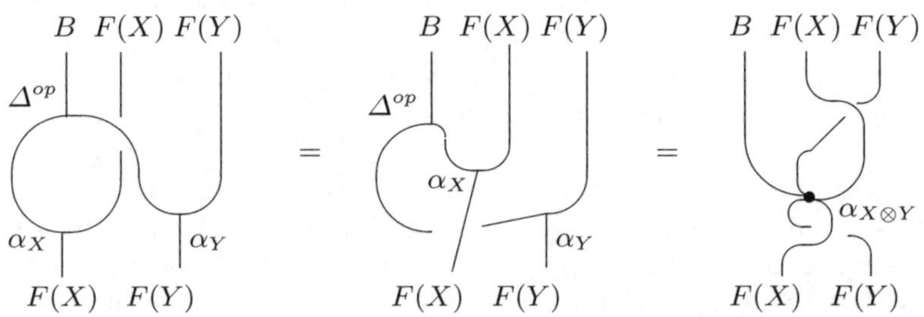

Fig. 5.12. Reconstruction theorem with transfers showing opposite coexpansion.

Here one uses the opposite leading expansion in a club that allows transfers $\mathcal{C}$. Using the analogous procedures to that from Chapter 2 and the procedure in the proof of Theorem 5.8 it can be shown that structure of opposite coexpansion also implies B as a biagreement when club $\mathcal{C}$ is a leading one.

Proposition 5.10. (Reconstruction of an open biagreement) *For a club $\mathcal{C}$ that allows transfers, an opening $\mathcal{R}$ defined in Figure* 5.13 *makes B, with its two coexpansions, into an open biagreement in the club with transfers $\mathcal{V}$.*

Proof: The proof is given in the diagrammatic form. First, let us define an open structure by diagram as given in Figure 5.13. Now in Figure 5.14 the

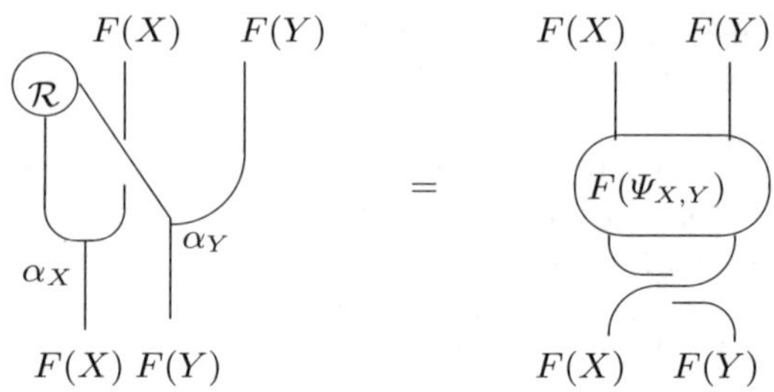

Fig. 5.13. Defining structure of opening by reconstruction theorem with transfers in diagrammatic form.

first axiom on openness is shown, where definitions are evaluated and an appropriation F is used to the hexagon identity in a club $\mathcal{C}$ to get third equality, and then proceed in opposite direction. The proof of the second axiom for the opening $\mathcal{R}$ is shown in Figure 5.15. In the third equality the appropriationality of argumentation α is used, considered from point of view of transfers $\Psi_{X,Y}$. The construction of opening inverse $\mathcal{R}^{-1}$ is based on the implementable policy of transformation inverse to that for opening $\mathcal{R}$. To check that it is inverse in the convolution agreement $ld \rightarrow B \otimes B$ is straightforward using the same techniques. □

Now, results of the reconstruction theory applied to clubs which allows transfers and diagrammatic techniques could be summarized in the following. This theory associates to an appropriation $F : \mathcal{C} \rightarrow \mathcal{V}$ autoappropriate enterprise with transfers. This enterprise appears as canonical argumentation on each of the appropriation $F(X)$ for any X member of the club $\mathcal{C}$. Moreover, the collection of all B-standards that allows transfers is itself a leading club and a standard transfer which makes X become $F(X)$ is a leading appropriation. Thus, one is able to define an enterprise which allows transfers in an abstract manner by $B = Aut(\mathcal{C}, F, \mathcal{V})$. It can be considered as an universal enterprise that allows transfers in $\mathcal{V}$ which has the property.

There are many concrete applications of reconstruction theory that include economic transfers in particular economic circumstances. Here, let us mention two of the best known, i.e. the process of corporatization and investment risk management. Details of these are described in a sequel to the present volume through concrete applications in economics of organizations. At the more abstract level considered here it is of interest to examine the

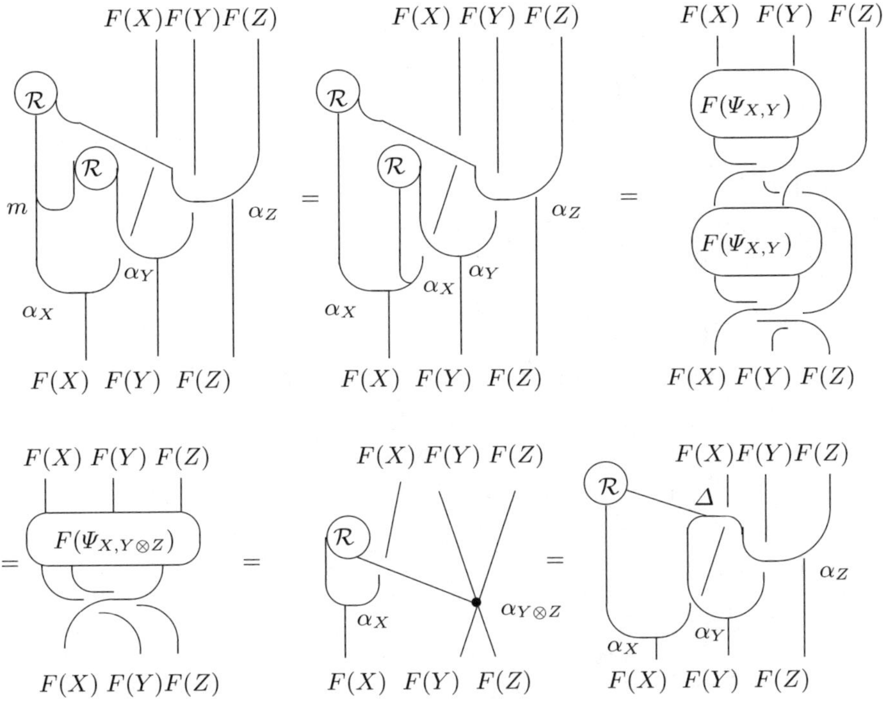

Fig. 5.14. Proof of the opening axioms for the reconstructed opening structure that includes transfers.

simplest case, where appropriation is shaped by intention of preserving existing appropriation structure of institutions within the club or preservation of a club characteristics from e.p.r.s point of view. It appears that every leading club that incorporates transfers, $\mathcal{C}$, has an intrinsic economic rule of transfers, which may be called an autoappropriate rule of transfers $U(\mathcal{C})$. This rule concerns each of the member X of a club $\mathcal{C}$ in an economic canonical manner. In addition, it ensures simplification of e.p.r.s reasoning of copartners. This provides cocommutative relations in the sense that coexpansion and its opposite are equal, $\Delta^{op} = \Delta$, and that opening is defined by the replicative aggregation of agency in the form $\mathcal{R} = \eta \otimes \eta$. As a careful reader may guess these bring us back to the concepts known from traditional economics. Namely, that traditional fixed pure private e.p.r.s rule being axiomatically accepted provide a rather conventional agreement and enveloping structure for a private economy than a more general e.p.r.s rule. More precisely, in this case one needs a suitable completion for the club $\mathcal{V}$, from the point of view of exclusive or

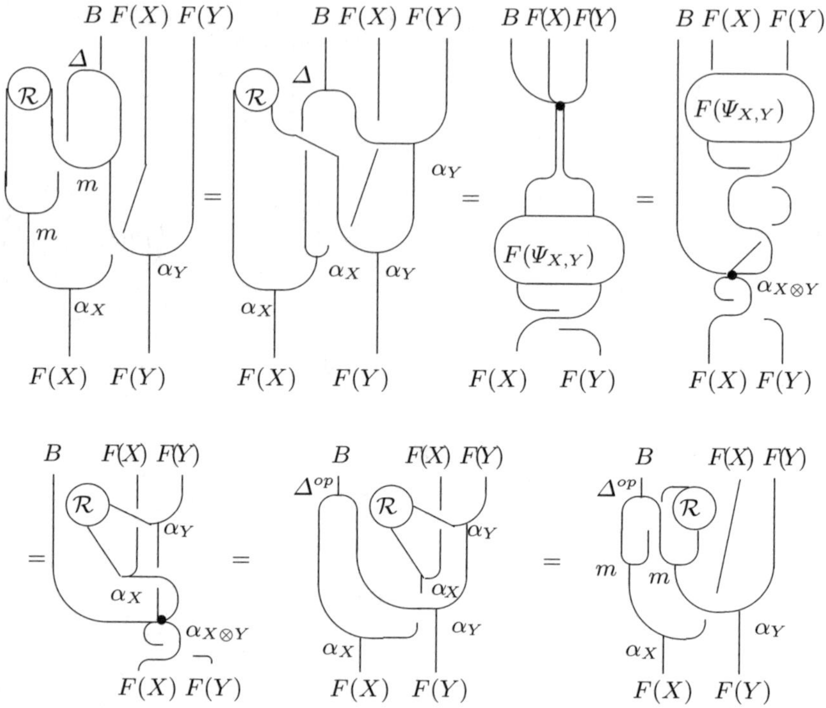

Fig. 5.15. Proof of the opening axioms for the reconstructed opening structure that includes transfers.

dictatorial structure of e.p.r.s, rather than a leading club $\mathcal{C}$ itself, to ensure representative conditions for an implementation of restructuring procedure.

To summarize the above discussions and as an exercise the proof of the following example is left to a reader.

Example 5.11. Every open enterprise H has an analogous e.p.r.s structured institution that allows transfers $H_{apt} = U({}_H\mathcal{M})$. It is given by the same agreement, agency and coagency as the considered open enterprise H, while transfers shape coexpansion by $\Delta_{apt} b = \sum b_{(1)} \gamma \mathcal{R}^{(2)} \otimes \mathcal{R}^{(1)} \overset{a}{>} b_{(2)}$ and a mutual understanding map by $\gamma_{apt} = \sum \mathcal{R}^{(2)} \gamma(\mathcal{R}^{(1)} \overset{a}{>} b)$. The coexpansion Δ_{apt} is perceived as simplified through transfers in the sense that

$$\sum \Psi(b_{(1)} \otimes (\mathcal{R}_{21}\mathcal{R})^{(1)} \overset{a}{>} b_{(2)})(\mathcal{R}_{21}\mathcal{R})^{(2)} = \sum b_{(1)} \otimes b_{(2)},$$

where $(\mathcal{R}_{21}\mathcal{R})^{(2)}$ is a quality expansion of the output of transfers Ψ. Enterprise that allows transfers H_{apt} is a type of rule of enveloping agreement that includes transfers associated to H. It is an element of the club that allows transfers concerning price (cost) H-standards, on the basis of the e.p.r.s adjoint argumentation in Example 2.29, Chapter 2.

5.3 Restructuring

5.3.1 Introduction

This Section discusses an application of recent results in mathematical transmutation theory to modeling of nonstandard transformations in enterprises. The key construction is based on transmutation of once established e.p.r.s relations among partners. Namely, an ordinary enterprise, as described in Section 2.1.2 of Chapter 2, can be turned by this process into one that incorporates a rich complex structure of transfers. Then by considering an agreeable structure of e.p.r.s relations among members in terms of its representations, and targeting these by means of an appropriation policy into some new economic club, an approach is proposed to reconstruct agreeable institution in this new economic club. The idea is that in this way the economic institution or club in which an agreed e.p.r.s structure is economic active and accurate can be changed in a controllable mode.

So for example, referring to the link with traditional economic models, agents may start with the simple type of economies involving natural resources and thus a traditional zero-sum economic game, where their economic rationality could be described with a simple market rationality supported by two fundamental welfare theorems. The collection of economic institutions or club on which agreements, embedding agents' economic rationality, (co)act is in focus. Recall that an obtained aggregate economic institution or economic club is usually an extension of the starting one, and is to some extent a matter of choice of agents. Then, provided we have a concept of representation powerful enough to reconstruct the agreements being represented, economic relations that identify the representations of starting economic club correspond to extended representations, and a new type of agreements can be reconstructed. The point is that these economic relations change the flavor of the economic rationality of members in a fundamental way implying a dynamic extension of the starting economic rationality and a transmutation of agreements between members to a new economic club.

Careful reader may note that Example 5.11 from previous Section has shown, among others, that the theory of open enterprises is contained in the theory of e.p.r.s rules with transfers. The example is also interesting because it shows the concrete and computable point of view in an implementation of EPRT. Namely, it shifts consideration from the problem of institutions and/or members with complicated e.p.r.s structures, in the usual club of simple economic institutions, to the more traditional or symmetric economic structures, but considered from perspective of a club with transfers. Thus, it makes economic sense to call this procedure restructuring, as it is turning one kind of enterprises (members of a club) into another.

In an understanding of restructuring procedures and their applications to EPRT one may also recall issues and procedures in coordination games in economics. Namely, the point is to define the rules of coordinations among agents and using one of these to determine basic economic coordination relations, in which the chosen rule is understood and accepted by agents. Note, that here we may use the open enterprise to determine a club with transfers, and consider it as the collection of the rules of e.p.r.s coordinations among agents. Then it appears accepted and is perceived by partners as simple and most natural for the given economic circumstances.

5.3.2 Restructuring Theorems

The process of e.p.r.s restructuring is quite general, and is one of the main sources of the reconstruction of economic institutions. As mentioned, the idea is that if an institution can be characterized entirely by its club $\mathcal{C}$ of representations, then the appropriation from this club to some other club $\mathcal{V}$ allows reconstruction of the considered institution. Thus, roughly speaking, the main theorem asserts that any enterprise H_2 into which an open enterprise H_1 maps, has induced on it the e.p.r.s structure of an enterprise in the transferred leading club $\mathcal{C}_1$ of H_1-standards. If H_2 is open in the usual sense, then the induced e.p.r.s structure is also open to economic transactions in the club $\mathcal{C}_1$. Throughout this section an open enterprise $(H_1, \mathcal{R}_1)$ is fixed, and the transferred leading club of H_1-standardized enterprises is denoted simply by $\mathcal{C}_1$.

Theorem 5.12. *Let H_2 be a biagreement and f a biagreeable map from an enterprise H_1 to H_2. Then there is a biagreement $B = B(H_1, f, H_2)$ in the club $\mathcal{C}_1$ defined as follows:*
(i) Any simple economic transaction is undertaken from biagreement H_2 so that $B = H_2$ as a linear space.
(ii) The argumentation of B is specified by a membership of the club $\mathcal{C}_1$.
(iii) The structure of agreement (agency and expansion) in B coincide with those of H_2.
(iv) The structure of coagency in B coincide with those of H_2, while the coexpansion of e.p.r.s is modified by opening conditions to Δ_{rs}.

Sketch of Proof: First, we should search for coexpansion based on restructuring, Δ_{rs}, (rs is acronym of restructuring) that would be compatible economic transaction with unchanged expansion of e.p.r.s, m in the club $\mathcal{C}_1$ of H_1-standardized institutions. We may take a modification, so that $\Delta_{rs} = \sum b_{(1)} f(\gamma \mathcal{R}_1^{(2)}) \otimes \mathcal{R}_1^{(1)} \overset{a}{>} b_{(2)}$, in terms of the original coexpansion of e.p.r.s, $\Delta = \sum b_{(1)} \otimes b_{(2)}$ in H_2. Here, the argumentation of the club is undertaken by a member and is given by $\alpha(h \otimes b) = h \overset{a}{>} b \sum f(h_{(1)})bf(\gamma h_{(2)})$, for all $h \in H_1$, and $b \in B$, where the mutual understanding map γ is undertaken from enterprise H_1. As mutual understanding map for enterprise H_1 is given by γ, it can be set $f^{-1} = f \circ \gamma$, and shown that expansion of e.p.r.s due to argumentation of the enterprise H_1 corresponds to influence that this expansion has within the club,

$$\begin{aligned} m(h \overset{a}{>} (b \otimes c)) &= \sum (h_{(1)} \overset{a}{>} b) m(h_{(2)} \overset{a}{>} c) \\ &= \sum f(h_{(1)(1)}) b f^{-1}(h_{(1)(2)}) f(h_{(2)(1)}) c f^{-1}(h_{(2)(2)}) \\ &= h \overset{a}{>} (bmc). \end{aligned}$$

This simply means that argumentation $\overset{a}{>}$ makes biagreement H_2 an H_1-standardized agreement for the ajoint argumentation induced by the agreeable mapping f. For economic transactions that assume an opening arrangement, these have to be considered with particular care and subtlety. So, using defining properties of argumentation and an opening, it can be shown that $h \overset{a}{>} (\Delta_{rs} b) = \Delta_{rs}(h \overset{a}{>} b)$. Agency is supposed to be unchanged, thus it is H_1-standard invariant providing e.p.r.s preserving map as an economic transaction $1_{rs} \to B$, and the unchanged coagency is likewise given by economic transaction $B \to 1_{rs}$. Next, one has to verify that these economic transactions are undertaken according to the rules of a biagreement or an enterprise in the club $\mathcal{C}_1$. More precisely, one shows that Δ_{rs} defines a coagreement on B, where conditions of opening are applied to the transferred e.p.r.s structure on enterprise H_1. Then one shows that Δ_{rs} is an agreeable map to $B \otimes B$. This map incorporates e.p.r.s transfers over the transferred leading expansion of e.p.r.s, $\otimes_{rs}$ as explained in 5.2, so that $\Delta_{rs} = \sum b_{(1_{rs})} \otimes b_{(2_{rs})}$, and one can show that $(\Delta_{rs} b) m (\Delta_{rs} c) = \Delta_{rs}(bmc)$. Then the unchanged coagency is a coagency for Δ_{rs} and the relation $\Delta_{rs}(1) = 1 \otimes 1$ is valid which all together constitute the biagreement concerning e.p.r.s on B. □

Proposition 5.13. (Restructuring enterprise) *Let H_2 be an enterprise and $f : H_1 \to H_2$ as above, then $B = B(H_1, f, H_2)$ constitutes an enterprise in the club $\mathcal{C}_1$. The e.p.r.s structure of this enterprise is given by the structure of biagreement B from Theorem 5.12, and by a mutual understanding map γ_{rs}. It is a modified mutual understanding map of the enterprise H_2 by restructuring and opening. New mutual understanding map γ_{rs} supports restructuring and such an enterprise may be called restructuring enterprise.*

Proof: First, we should check that a modified mutual understanding map, γ_{rs} is an economic transaction in the club $\mathcal{C}_1$ of H_1-standardized institutions. For γ_{rs} we may take $\gamma_{rs} b = \sum f(\mathcal{R}_1^{(2)}) \gamma(\mathcal{R}_1^{(1)} \overset{a}{>} b)$, and it is convenient to express it in the equivalent form, that emphasizes opening conditions,

$$\gamma_{rs} b = f(\sum \mathcal{R}_1^{(2)} \gamma^2(\mathcal{R}_1^{(1)})) f(\gamma \mathcal{R}_1^{(2)})(\gamma b) f(\mathcal{R}_1^{(1)}).$$

Note that here an element $\sum(\gamma\mathcal{R}_1^{(2)})\mathcal{R}_1^{(1)}$ has as its inverse the element $\sum\mathcal{R}_1^{(2)}\gamma^2(\mathcal{R}_1^{(1)})$. Thus an argumentation can be extended to mutual understanding map, γ_{rs} in the sense that relations $h \overset{a}{>} \gamma_{rs}b = \gamma_{rs}(h \overset{a}{>} b)$, and

$$\sum b_{(1_{rs})}\gamma_{rs}b_{(2_{rs})} = \sum b_{(1)}\gamma b_{(2)} = \varepsilon(b)$$
$$= f(\sum\mathcal{R}_1^{(2)}\gamma^2(\mathcal{R}_1^{(1)}))f(\gamma\mathcal{R}_1^{(2)})\varepsilon(b) = \sum(\gamma_{rs}b_{(1_{rs})})b_{(2_{rs})}$$

are satisfied. Here one applies the conditions of opening $\mathcal{R}_1$, as described in [62], to show the validity of the relation that provides the coagency for an enterprise with required properties, implying that B forms a restructuring enterprise. □

It is noteworthy that in considerations of restructuring procedure within the leading transferred club the notion of an opposite coexpansion for an enterprise is of particular importance. The point is that in the circumstances of transfers $\Psi_{H,H}^{-1} \circ \Delta$ does not give an enterprise in leading transferred club $\mathcal{C} =_H \mathcal{L}$, but rather one in the club $\mathcal{C}$ with the inverse transfer. By a similar argument, $\Psi_{H,H} \circ \Delta$ is also not suitable for expressing an opposite coexpansion under the circumstances of nontrivial transfers. Thus, here we have no canonical notion of a simplified economic rationality of copartner(s). So, open enterprises cannot be established in a transferred leading club. One way to overcome this difficulty is to study all possible opposite coexpansions simultaneously. Namely, one may adopt a 'weak' notion of opposite coexpansion in which any second coexpansion at all can be regarded as an opposite one with respect to a class of standards for which it behaves as one would expect for an opposite structure to do.

Definition 5.14. (Weak opposite coexpansion) *Let H be a biagreement in transferred leading club $\mathcal{C}$. We say that $(\Delta^{op}, \mathcal{O})$ is a weak opposite coexpansion for H if $\Delta^{op} : H \to H \otimes H$ is a second coexpansion for H, so that the agreement of H is a biagreement in the club $\mathcal{C}$ in two ways, and $\mathcal{O}$ is a class of H-standards in the club $\mathcal{C}$ such that*

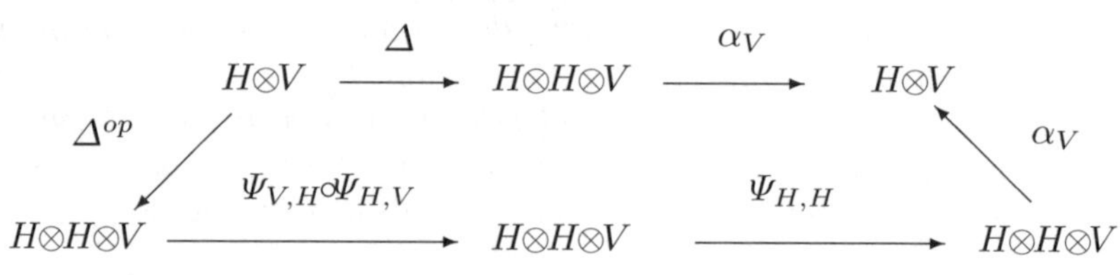

commutes for all (V, α_V) in $\mathcal{O}$.

A price H-standard in $\mathcal{C}$ is of course just a member or enterprise in the club $\mathcal{C}$ and an economic transaction $H \otimes V \to V$, such that $\alpha \circ (id_H \otimes \alpha) = \alpha \circ (m \otimes id_V)$ and $\alpha \circ (\eta \otimes id_V) = id_V$. This notion is studied further in

Section 5.3.3. A transfer rule then appears as an enterprise in the club $\mathcal{C}$ with an opposite coexpansion such that $\Delta^{op} = \Delta$. It is weakly cocommutative with respect to a class of standards $\mathcal{O}$. An economic importance of this weak notion of 'opposite coexpansion' is that it provides new insight into opposite coexpansions and simplified e.p.r.s rationality of copartner on it, providing cocommutativity. This is also useful in the case of ordinary enterprises in the club of simple economic institutions, where transfers are trivial and economies can be expressed over vector spaces. So for example, notion of weak opposite coexpansions make one able to 'measure' level of simplification of e.p.r.s rationality of copartners within an enterprise in the sense that it is present in the greater or lesser degree depending on how large is the class of standards for which it behaves as a cocommutative one. Then one may extend convenient economic properties usually reserved for strictly cocommutative institutions to any enterprise that has argumentation on standards in the class. Thus, it seems rewarding to study the subclub $\mathcal{O}(H, \Delta^{op})$ of all standards obeying the condition in Definition 5.14 of an enterprise H equipped with the second coexpansion Δ^{op} in the club. This is done in Section 5.3.3 where we show that $\mathcal{O}(H, \Delta^{op})$ is closed under the aggregate expansion of H-standards. One should have in mind that in practice it is not easy to describe full class $\mathcal{O}(H, \Delta^{op})$ explicitly. One way out of this problem is not to consider an opposite coexpansion to be fully specified until a subclub $\mathcal{O} \subseteq \mathcal{O}(H, \Delta^{op})$ has been described. In the cases where a construction does not depend on the specific form of $\mathcal{O} \subseteq \mathcal{O}(H, \Delta^{op})$, one may as well take $\mathcal{O} = \mathcal{O}(H, \Delta^{op})$ and proceed with construction.

Proposition 5.15. *Let H_2 be a biagreement, f a biagreeable map from an enterprise H_1 to H_2, and $B = B(H_1, f, H_2)$ a restructuring biagreement in the club $\mathcal{C}_1$ as defined in Theorem 5.12. Then B contains an opposite coexpansion of e.p.r.s of coagency in the club $\mathcal{C}_1$, Δ^{op}_{rs}.*

Sketch of the proof and comments: The procedure to obtain Δ^{op}_{rs} follows the Definition 5.14. It is applied with respect to the subclub of B-standardized agreements (V, α_V) in the club $\mathcal{C}_1$, for which V is a member of the club $\mathcal{C}_1$ being a pullback by argumentation α_V, i.e. $\overset{a}{>}_V$ via $f : H_1 \to H_2$. One may also recall that $B = H_2$ is an agreement by the construction. We may try with the form, $\Delta^{op}_{rs} b - \sum f(\gamma \mathcal{R}_1^{(1)}) b_{(2_{rs})} f(\gamma \mathcal{R}_1^{\prime(2)}) \otimes (\mathcal{R}_1^{\prime(1)} \mathcal{R}_1^{(2)}) \overset{a}{>} b_{(1_{rs})}$, where $\mathcal{R}'_1$ is another outcome (copy) of opening of $\mathcal{R}_1$, and $\Delta_{rs} b = \sum b_{(1_{rs})} \otimes b_{(2_{rs})}$ is the coexpansion of e.p.r.s in B. Now to show its validity, first, it should be checked that the modified coexpansion map, Δ^{op}_{rs}, is an economic intertwiner for the influences of argument α of H_1. This helps us to show that $\Delta^{op}_{rs}(h \overset{a}{>} b) = h \overset{a}{>} (\Delta^{op}_{rs} b)$. Next, one has to verify that this modified coexpansion of e.p.r.s makes B into a biagreement in the club $\mathcal{C}_1$ of H_1-standards. Note, that the procedure is similar to that for Δ_{rs}. Also one has to check if Δ^{op}_{rs} is indeed an opposite coexpansion of e.p.r.s on B according to Definition 5.14 as for the stated subclub of standards in $\mathcal{C}_1$. To ease the notation denote by $\mathcal{M}$

the appropriate aggregate of opening effects, $\mathcal{M} = \sum \mathcal{R}_1^{(2)} \mathcal{R}_1'^{(1)} \otimes \mathcal{R}_1^{(1)} \mathcal{R}_1'^{(2)}$. Then having in mind the transfer relations valid in a club, this condition can be expressed by,

$$\sum \mathcal{R}_1^{(2)} \mathcal{M}^{(1)} \overset{a}{>} b_{(2_{rs})op} \otimes (\mathcal{R}_1^{(1)} \overset{a}{>} b_{(1_{rs}op)}) \overset{a}{>}_\alpha (\mathcal{M}^{(2)} \overset{a}{>} v)$$
$$= \sum b_{(1_{rs})} \otimes b_{(2_{rs})} \overset{a}{>}_\alpha v,$$

for all standards (V, α) and $v \in V$, where $\overset{a}{>}_\alpha$ denotes the argumentation of α. Now, we want this relation to be valid for the subclub of B-standards (V, α) in the club $\mathcal{C}_1$ for which the H_1-standard structure is described over argumentations by $h \overset{a}{>} v = f(h) \overset{a}{>}_{rs} v$. This standard e.p.r.s structure appears to be valid and implementable on all such standards of B in the club $\mathcal{C}_1$ if combination of opening conditions and those that specify opposed e.p.r.s relations satisfy the equation in $B \otimes B$, as follows,

$$\sum \mathcal{R}_1^{(2)} \mathcal{M}^{(1)} \overset{a}{>} b_{(1_{rs})op} \otimes (\mathcal{R}_1^{(1)} \overset{a}{>} b_{(1_{rs}op)}) f(\mathcal{M}^{(2)}) = \sum b_{(1_{rs})} \otimes b_{(2_{rs})},$$

and it can be shown that Δ_{rs}^{op} satisfies such an equality, applying repeatedly the opening conditions $\mathcal{M}$ above. □

Theorem 5.16. *Let H_2, $f : H_1 \to H_2$, B be defined as in Theorem 5.12, and Δ_{rs}^{op} the opposite coexpansion of e.p.r.s as defined in Proposition 5.13. If H_2 is open, then B is also open to economic transactions in the club $\mathcal{C}_1$, with specified structure of the opening, $\mathcal{R}_{rs}$.*

Sketch of the proof and comments: Note that in order for $\mathcal{R}_{rs}$ to be well defined as an opening structure of members in the club $\mathcal{C}_1$, it has to be H_1-invariant. This means that it is an intertwiner $1_{rs} \to B \otimes B$. We may take that the structure of e.p.r.s of this opening is given by $\mathcal{R}_{rs} = \sum f(\mathcal{R}_1^{-(1)}) \mathcal{R}_2^{(1)} f(\gamma \mathcal{R}_1^{(2)}) \otimes \mathcal{R}_1^{(1)} \overset{a}{>} f(\mathcal{R}_1^{-(2)}) \mathcal{R}_2^{(2)}$. To show its validity, one has to calculate impacts of h-argumentation on configuration of the opening structure, $h \overset{a}{>} \mathcal{R}_{rs}$. These can be obtained by the repeated application of conditions of opening given by Definition 3.8 in Chapter 3. In particular, applying the axiom 3.2 on the enterprise H_1 to bring collections of e.p.r.s h together within each aggregate factor. Then eventually, one gets an expression, containing the relations that correspond to the conditions of the opening in the enterprise H_2 and $\mathcal{R}_2 \varepsilon(h)$, that provide the outcome $h \overset{a}{>} \mathcal{R}_{rs} = \varepsilon(h) \mathcal{R}_{rs}$, as desired. Next one verifies that $\mathcal{R}_{rs}$ is an opening structure for B in the club $\mathcal{C}_1$. The procedure is straightforward although cumbersome, and similar to the verifications that were already performed above, where the expressions are written in terms of H_1 and H_2. Note, that since $\mathcal{R}_{rs}$ is H_1-invariant, the argumentation of transfers is trivial. □

Example 5.17. Let H be a biagreement or an enterprise over a field of claims of characteristics not two. If H contains a rule-like element g of order two, then it has the structure of a super-biagreement or super-enterprise, B. If H is open with the opening structure $\mathcal{R}$, then B is super-open. The structure of agreement and coagent of B coincides with that of H. The coexpansion is given by $\Delta_{rs} = \sum b_{(1)} g^{|b_{(2)}|} \otimes b_{(2)}$, coagency by $\varepsilon_{rs} = \varepsilon$, mutual understanding map $\gamma_{rs} b = g^{|b|} \gamma b$, and opening structure $\mathcal{R}_{rs} = \frac{1}{2}(1 \otimes 1 + g \otimes 1 + 1 \otimes g - g \otimes g) \sum \mathcal{R}^{(1)} g^{|\mathcal{R}^{(2)}|} \otimes \mathcal{R}^{(2)}$. Here g carries argumentation on H in the adjoint representation $\overset{a}{>}$ with $g^2 = 1$, hence $p = \frac{1}{2}(1 - g)$ acts as a projection. The above formulae are defined on homogeneous elements of eigenvalue $p \overset{a}{>} b = |b|\, b$. This defines the Z_2-grading of B, and establishes the link with the traditional economic models.

Sketch of the proof: Recall from Chapter 2 the case of a simple enterprise defined by 2-dimensional enterprise generated by 1 and g with the relation $g^2 = 1$, coexpansion $\Delta g = g \otimes g$, coagent $\varepsilon g = 1$ and mutual understanding map $\gamma g = g$. This is just the rule agreement of the finite rule of order two. This becomes a nonstandard closed agreement with trivial opening $\mathcal{R} = 1 \otimes 1 - 2p \otimes p$, $p = \frac{1}{2}(1 - g)$, where p is a projection. Let us denote it by $H_1 = Z_2'$, where the prime is to remind us of the nonstandard structure of closure. Then, the club of super **h**- standards can be determined by ${}_{Z_2'}\mathcal{L}$, where **h** is a domain of e.p.r.s claims with characteristic other then 2. (See Chapter 2 if necessary). One may recall that it is because in an H-standard V the operator $p = \frac{1}{2}(1 - g)$ is the projection so that p as a degree operator, or e.p.r.s gluing operator so that $V = V_0 \oplus V_1$. Economic transactions, that take the form of intertwiners of H, are just superspace economic transactions. The transfers are determined by $\Psi_{V,W}(v \otimes w) = (1 - 2 \mid w \mid\mid v \mid)$ $w \otimes v = (-1)^{|w||v|} w \otimes v$ on homogeneous elements. One may recall that this is just the usual symmetry for super **h**-standards. If V is finite dimensional the V^* is just V^* as an **h**-standard, having in mind that mutual understanding is the e.p.r.s preserving. Now we may take $H_2 = H$ in Theorem 5.16. The existence of an e.p.r.s rule-like element of order two in H implies a map $Z_2' \hookrightarrow H$, and one may apply the construction for $B = B(Z_2', id, H)$ as above. These ensure that the definitions given above are all well formulated and obey the axioms of a super-open super-enterprise. The opposite coexpansion is simply $\Delta_{rs}^{op} = \Psi_{B,B}^{-1} \circ \Delta_{rs}$ where Ψ is the economic super-space law concerning symmetry of isotransactions and in fact, we have $\Psi^2 = id$. In addition, one may consider an example where $H = Z_2'$. The super agreement corresponding to Z_2', is $B(Z_2', id, Z_2') = \mathbf{h} Z_2$. This is the ordinary e.p.r.s rule agreement of Z_2 with trivial opening structure, regarded as a super-enterprise with all elements of degree 0. From Theorem 5.16 the opening structure $\mathcal{R}_{rs}$ on $B(Z_2', id, Z_2')$, is trivial because $f(\mathcal{R}_1^{-1})\mathcal{R}_2 = 1 \otimes 1$. □

One may think of a sub-open enterprise to be used to generate the club with transfers in which the entire open enterprise is then viewed by restructuring. In this process opening structure of the enterprise reduces because the part from the sub-enterprise is divided out. This can be understood that the part corresponding to the sub-enterprise is in some sense simplified.

Corollary 5.18. (Simple restructured enterprise) *Every open enterprise* H *has a transferred rule analogue* $B(H,H)$, *denoted by* H_{rs}. *It is simply transferred in the sense that modified restructuring opening is trivial,* $\mathcal{R}_{rs} = 1 \otimes 1$, *as well as e.p.r.s rationality of copartners on restructuring, implying* $\Delta_{rs}^{op} = \Delta_{rs}$.

Sketch of the proof and comments: Note that the transmutation principle is taken to its logical extreme in this case. Any open enterprise H is viewed in its own club that allows transfers ${}_H\mathcal{C}$, by $H \subset H$. One may think of a process where one uses a metric to determine geodesic coordinations of an economic system. A coordinate system, determined in such a way, implies that the metric looks locally linear. Similarly, for the circumstances that we have interest in, original open enterprise viewed in its own club that accepts and obeys a transfer rule, appears as a transferred institution that can be simplified by e.p.r.s rationality of copartner, and thus can be accepted. We know from Subsection 5.3.2, that if a club is one that allows transfers and F is an aggregate appropriation (in the sense that the transferring is mapped on to the transferring of $\mathcal{V}$) then: (i) $\Delta_{rs}^{op} = \Delta_{rs}$, i.e. $\mathcal{R}_{rs}$ is trivial, and (ii) B is a transfer rule. This transfer rule contains transferred simplified copartner reasoning with respect to the e.p.r.s effects of the appropriation $\mathcal{C} \to_H \mathcal{V}$. Thus, in particular as we have $\Delta_{rs}^{op} = \Delta_{rs}$, opening is trivial and this gives the explicit formula $\sum \Psi(b_{(1)_{rs}^{op}} \otimes (\mathcal{R}_1)_{21}^{(1)} (\mathcal{R}_1)_{12}^{(1)} \overset{a}{>} b_{(2)_{rs}^{op}}) f((\mathcal{R}_1)_{21}^{(2)} (\mathcal{R}_1)_{12}^{(2)}) = \sum b_{(1)_{rs}} \otimes b_{(2)_{rs}}$. The $B(H,H)$ appears as type of transferred rule of enveloping agreement associated with enterprise H. As was already mentioned this completely shifts our consideration from the point of view of an e.p.r.s institution in the usual simple economic club, expressed by vector spaces, to a more traditional perspective but with institutions that allow transfers. Thus, the economic theory of ordinary open enterprises is contained in the economic theory of transferred rules. The transferred enterprise B in Theorem 5.12 above, is equivalent to the original one in that the economic spaces, agreements, and other elements on which H_2 has argumentation also become transmuted to corresponding ones for B. Partly this is obvious since we have that $B = H_2$ as an agreement, so any H_2-standard V of H_2 is also a transferred B-standard. The main point is that V also has argument upon H_1 through the mapping $H_1 \to H_2$. So the argumentation of H_2 is used in two ways. They define the corresponding argumentation of transferred enterprise B and also define the grading of standard V as a member of a transferred club, ${}_{H_1}\mathcal{L}$. This actually extends the process of transmutation to standards.
□

5.3.3 Standards in a Club and Restructuring

The interesting issue is to get some insight into the representations in an arbitrary transferred leading club ${}_H\mathcal{L}$ of an enterprise H that is the member of $\mathcal{C}$. The idea is to apply the results of the transmutations obtained above by biagreement $B = B(H_1, f, H_2)$ and to search for the intrinsic club-theoretical characteristics of an H_2-standard that is invariant under restructuring.

Proposition 5.19. *Let H be a biagreement in the club $\mathcal{C}$, then the club of H-standardized members in $\mathcal{C}$ forms a leading club, denoted by ${}_H\mathcal{L}$. If H is an enterprise and $\mathcal{C}_0$ is a full rigid subclub of $\mathcal{C}$, then the club of H-standards in subclub $\mathcal{C}_0$ is full rigid subclub of the leading club ${}_H\mathcal{L}$.*

Sketch of the proof: One may recall the notion of H-standard in a club $\mathcal{C}$ from Sections 4.1 and 4.2. If (V, α_V) and (W, α_W) are two H-standards in the club $\mathcal{C}$, then their aggregation provides a member of the club, of the form $V \otimes W$, and an argumentation is given by

$$\alpha_{V \otimes W} : H \otimes V \otimes W \overset{\Delta}{\to} H \otimes H \otimes V \otimes W \overset{\Psi_{H,V}}{\to} H \otimes V \otimes H \otimes W \overset{\alpha_V \otimes \alpha_W}{\to} V \otimes W.$$

Having in mind the property (coassociativity) of Δ that is compatible with the expansion of e.p.r.s, and the appropriation due to e.p.r.s transfers Ψ, one can show that the conditions of an H-standard structure in the club $\mathcal{C}$ are satisfied. The property of associativity of agency in the leading club ${}_H\mathcal{L}$ is induced by that of the club $\mathcal{C}$ considered as an intertwiner. In addition, let V be defined as a member of the rigid sub-club of $\mathcal{C}$. Then this means that the dual structure for V has already been specified, and if H is an enterprise, then V^* is also an H-standard in the following sense: It defines a standardized quality-evaluation concept of the following form, $(\alpha_V)^* : V^* \otimes H \overset{\pi_V}{\to} V^* \otimes H \otimes V \otimes V^* \overset{\alpha_V}{\to} V^* \otimes V \otimes V^* \overset{ev_V}{\to} V^*$, and in this case the price-argumentation is necessarily given by $\alpha_{V^*} : H \otimes V^* \overset{\gamma}{\to} H \otimes V^* \overset{\Psi_{H,V^*}}{\to} V^* \otimes H \overset{(\alpha_V)^*}{\to} V^*$ in the club $\mathcal{C}$. Here, properties of the appropriation $\otimes_{rs}$ and coherence of economic transfers were applied. That the transferred leading club ${}_H\mathcal{L}$ is closed under aggregation can be shown using diagrams as follows in Figure 5.16. A qualitative standard, as $(V^*, (\alpha_V)^*)$, above, can be converted by mutual understanding to a price H standard as given by the diagram in Figure 5.17. □

Proposition 5.20. *Let H be a biagreement or an enterprise in the club $\mathcal{C}$, with an arbitrary second coexpansion of e.p.r.s Δ^{op}. Then the club ${}_{Op}\mathcal{C}$ or simply $\mathcal{O}(H, \Delta^{op})$ of standards in the leading club ${}_H\mathcal{L}$, for which Δ^{op} is an opposite coexpansion of e.p.r.s, is a leading subclub of ${}_H\mathcal{L}$. If H is an open enterprise and $\mathcal{O}$ is a leading subclub of ${}_H\mathcal{L}$ with respect to which Δ^{op} of H is an opposite coexpansion of e.p.r.s, $\mathcal{O} = \mathcal{O}(H, \Delta^{op})$, then the club $\mathcal{O}$ is a transferred leading club.*

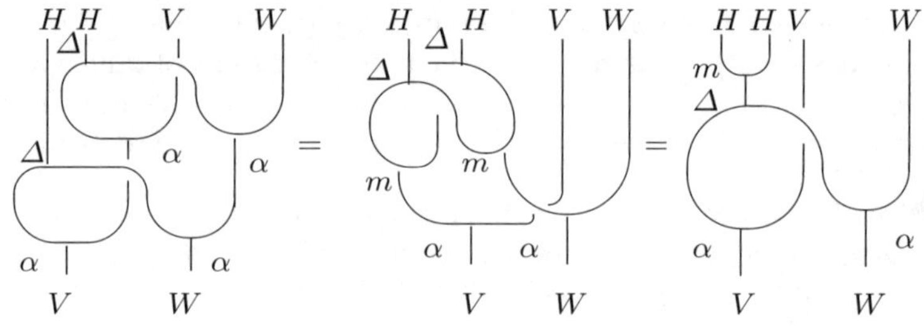

Fig. 5.16. Closeness of H-standard club under appropriation.

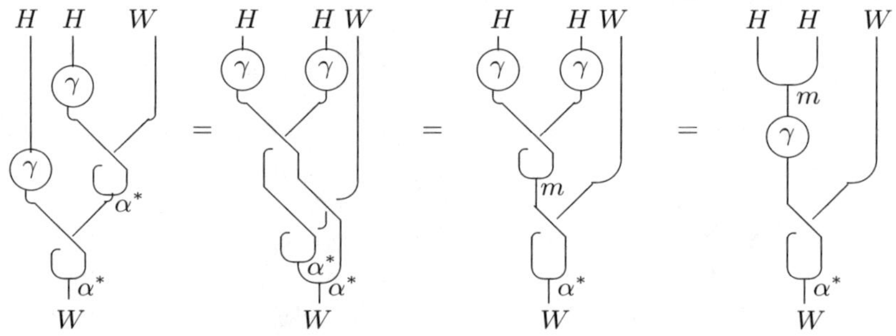

Fig. 5.17. Mutual understanding map, γ, converts a quality standard (W, α^*) into a price standard (H, m) .

Sketch of proof: Note that the institution $\mathcal{O}$ with respect to which an opposite coexpansion of e.p.r.s is defined, can always be taken to be a leading one. An efficient way to show that $\mathcal{O}(H, \Delta^{op})$ is closed under the aggregation, $\otimes_{ap}$, having in mind the Definition 5.14, is by a diagram, see Figure 5.18. Subclub $\mathcal{O}(H, \Delta^{op})$ is closed under aggregation, thus it means that $\mathcal{O}(H, \Delta^{op})$ is leading. In the case of openness of institutions, for any two H-standards in the club $\mathcal{C}$ within the subclub $\mathcal{O}(H, \Delta^{op})$, one can specify an intertwiner for the argumentation $\alpha_{V\otimes W}$,

$$\tilde{\Psi}_{V,W} : V{\otimes}W \overset{\mathcal{R}}{\to} H{\otimes}H{\otimes}V{\otimes}W \overset{\Psi_{H,V}}{\to} H{\otimes}V{\otimes}H{\otimes}W \overset{\alpha_V \otimes \alpha_W}{\to} V{\otimes}W \overset{\Psi_{V,W}}{\to} W{\otimes}V.$$

This defines an e.p.r.s quasisymmetry that can be shown most efficiently using diagrams (left to a reader as an exercise). □

Proposition 5.21. *Let H_1, H_2 be open enterprises, $f : H_1 \to H_2$ an entrepreneurial map between a pair of given enterprises, and $B = B(H_1, f, H_2)$*

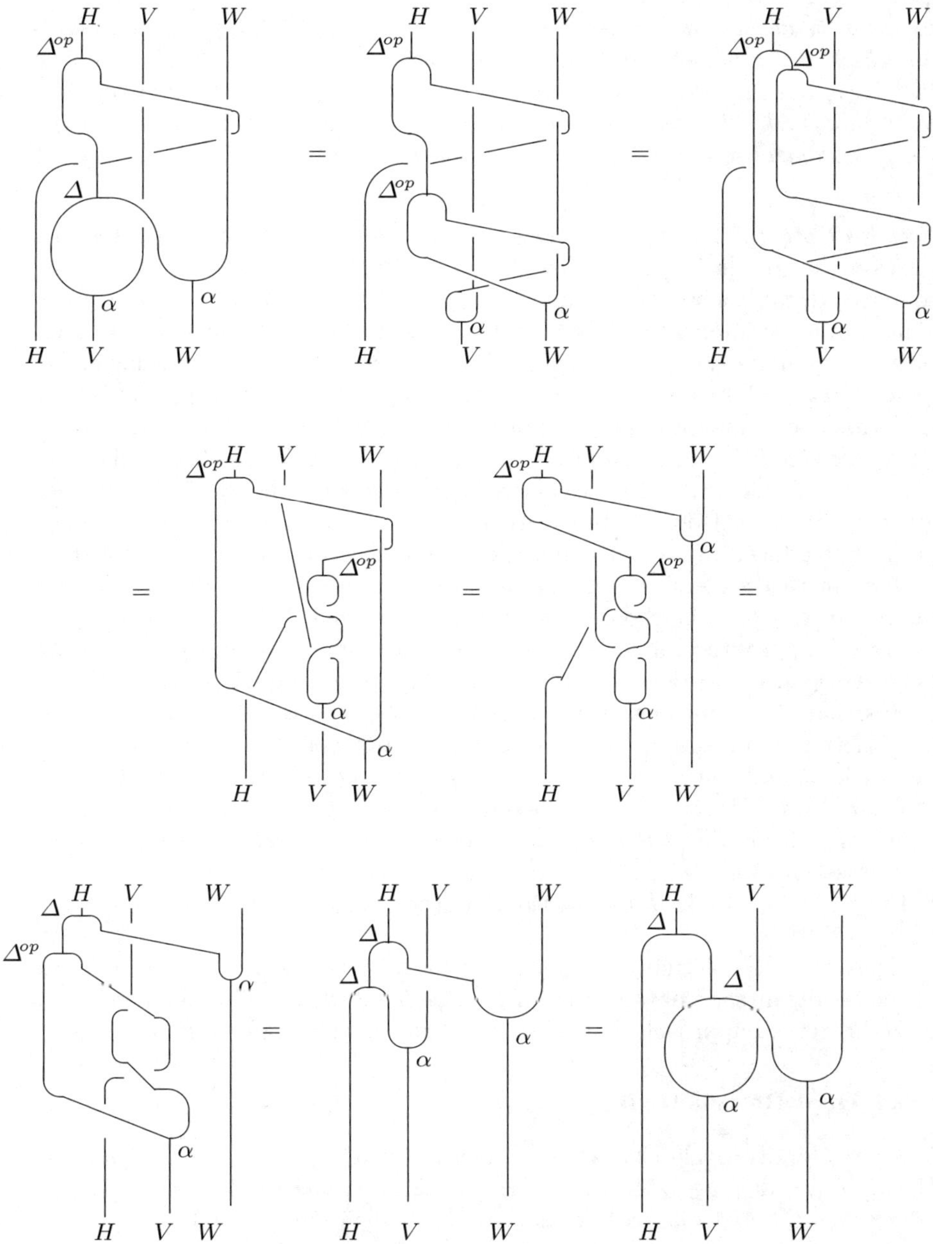

Fig. 5.18. Subclub $\mathcal{O}(H, \Delta^{op})$ is closed under aggregation.

the induced enterprise in the club $\mathcal{C} =_{H_1} \mathcal{L}$ *obtained by restructuring as described in Subsection 5.3.2. Then* ${}_{H_2}\mathcal{L}$ *and* ${}_{B(H_1,f,H_2)}\mathcal{C}$ *are properly defined leading clubs. In addition, there is an appropriation* F_{rs} *that ensures transformation* ${}_{H_2}\mathcal{L} \overset{i}{\hookrightarrow}_{B(H_1,f,H_2)} \mathcal{L}$, *as leading clubs. The outcome of this restructuring appropriation is the transferred leading club,* $\mathcal{O}$ *of* $B(H_1, f, H_2)$*-standards for which the argumentation,* α, *of enterprise* H_1 *is the pullback of that of the enterprise* H_2 *in the sense that* $h \overset{a}{>} v = f(h) \overset{a}{>}_\alpha v$. *Similar is valid for their full rigid subclubs. The composition of restructuring* F_{rs} *and forgetful* F_{frg} *appropriations is the pullback appropriation* $F_{pb} :_{H_2} \mathcal{L} \rightarrow_{H_1} \mathcal{L}$ *induced by* f.

Sketch of proof: The appropriations are all given here by the simple e.p.r.s relations on the underlying simple e.p.r.s institutions as those on natural resources. (Recall their definitions and properties from Chapter 2 if necessary). This simplicity implies the convenient formal structure of linear functors applied on the underlying linear spaces. The structure of the restructuring enterprise $B(H_1, f, H_2)$ is particularly organized so that these appropriations have the properties required in proposition. This may be obtained by application of the generalized Tannaka-Krein type reconstruction theorem. It associates to a monoideal functor $F : \mathcal{C} \rightarrow \mathcal{V}$ between quasitensor categories, a quasitriangular bialgebra or Hopf algebra $Aut(\mathcal{C}, F, \mathcal{V})$ in $\mathcal{V}$, as automorphism braided group, introduced in order to make the reconstruction possible when there is no functor to Vec, e.g. $Aut(\mathcal{C})$. Namely, in the economic application we are interesting in here, the theorem is applied in the case $\mathcal{C} =_{H_2} \mathcal{L}$ and $\mathcal{V} =_{H_1} \mathcal{L}$ where the appropriation is induced by an entrepreneurial map $f : H_1 \rightarrow H_2$ between open enterprises H_1 and H_2. Then in an e.p.r.s interpretation it means that the autotransaction of transferred e.p.r.s rule, $Aut(\mathcal{C}, F, \mathcal{V})$, exists. In the circumstances when we have no appropriation to simple e.p.r.s institutions, and could not specify $Aut(\mathcal{C})$, we may use the identity appropriation, $F = id$, and $\mathcal{V} = \mathcal{C}$ to overcome the difficulties and be able to obtain a club transform. So, $Aut(\mathcal{C}, F, \mathcal{V})$ can be considered itself as a restructuring enterprise and we may write $Aut(\mathcal{C}, F, \mathcal{V}) \cong B(H_1, f, H_2)$. Namely, they are linked by an economic isotransaction, i.e. they are isomorphic. □

Note that this actually offers an alternative proving procedures for some of the results already obtained in Subsection 5.3.2 with an emphasis on e.p.r.s club theoretical approach. For more detail see page 205 and Section 5.3.5.

5.3.4 Dual Restructuring

It is already intuitively clear that the restructuring theory has a dual version. Here, we are dealing with a given A_2 dual open enterprise, A_1 at least a biagreement, and a biagreeable map $p : A_1 \rightarrow A_2$. Thus, we have

Theorem 5.22. (Transferred rule analogous for dual) *Let* A_2 *be a biagreement and* p *a biagreeable map from a biagreement* A_1 *to* A_2. *Then*

there is a biagreement $B = B(A_1, A_2)$ *in the transferred club* $\mathcal{L}^{A_2}$ *defined as follows:*
(i) Any simple economic transaction is undertaken from biagreement A_1 *so that* $B = A_1$ *as a linear space.*
(ii) The structure of coagreement, coagency and agency in B *coincide with those of* A_1, *while the expansion of e.p.r.s,* m_{rs} *is modified.*
(iii) If A_1 *is an enterprise, then* B *has a modified mutual understanding map which is transferred.*

Sketch of Proof: First, we should specify a modified expansion based on restructuring, m_{rs}, and check that this expansion, m_{rs}, and unchanged coexpansion, Δ, of are compatible economic transactions in the club $\mathcal{L}^{A_1}$ of A_1-costandardized institutions. A mutual understanding map, if it exists for enterprise A_1, γ is used to set $p^{-1} = \gamma \circ p$, and show that coexpansion of e.p.r.s due to coargumentation of the enterprise A_1 corresponds to influence that this coexpansion has within the club. This simply means that coargumentation makes biagreement A_2 an A_1-costandardized coagreement for the quality adjoint coargumentation induced by the agreeable mapping p. (See also Example 2.37 and 5.11, and Propositions 5.13 and 5.15.) Agency is supposed to be unchanged, thus it is an A_1-costandard invariant providing e.p.r.s preserving map as an economic transaction $1_{rs} \to B$, and the unchanged coagency is likewise given by economic transaction $B \to 1_{rs}$. Next, one has to verify that these economic transactions are undertaken according to the rules of a biagreement or an enterprise in the club $\mathcal{L}^A$. Namely, we may apply the dual form of Theorem 4.15 to clubs $\mathcal{C}$ and $\mathcal{V}$, both being considered as $\mathcal{L}^A$, and taking appropriation F to be e.p.r.s preserving, i.e. $F = id$. Thus a transferred enterprise B is to be reconstructed in this club. For the reconstruction, the diagrams are again useful. So, from Figures 5.6 - 5.10 with appropriate modification for dual consideration and with careful relabeling, the general formula for m_{rs} in terms of the structure of A_1 can be specified. We may take $m_{rs} = \sum a_{(2)} b_{(2)} \mathcal{R}((\gamma a_{(1)}) a_{(3)} \otimes \gamma b_{(1)})$. Similarly from 5.12 we derive the opposite modified expansion m_{rs}^{op} in terms of m_{rs}. Then expending the inverse of opening, and rearranging the elements by the elementary properties of dual open structures from Chapter 3, one obtains the transferred cocommutativity, when $m_{rs} = m_{rs}^{op}$. Figures 5.12 and 5.13, finally help us to derive the transferred mutual understanding map, γ_{rs} that takes the form $\gamma_{rs} a = \sum \gamma a_{(2)} \mathcal{R}(\gamma^2 a_{(3)} \gamma a_{(1)} \otimes a_{(4)})$, where the mutual understanding map γ is undertaken from A_1. One may note that if $p : A_1 \to A_2$ is a map to a dual open enterprise A_2, then A_1 acquires a new restructuring expansion, mutual understanding and dual opening structure, making it a dual open enterprise $B(A_1, A_2)$ in the transferred club of quantity A_2-costandards. The expression for its restructured expansion and mutual understanding can be obtained as above, where opening $\mathcal{R}$ is modified by $\mathcal{R}_1 \circ (p \otimes p)$. The transferred simplified e.p.r.s rationality of partners now becomes quasisimplified up to the transferred dual quasiopen structure. □

It is noteworthy that the correct club formulation of duality in the transferred setting is necessary to be able to make precise sense of duality concept. Thus, if a transferred enterprise B is rigid as discussed in Section 4.3.3, the B^* is also a transferred enterprise with expansion Δ^*, coexpansion m^*, and mutual understanding map γ^*, where $*$ is the adjoint transaction as in Figure 4.11.

In the case where e.p.r.s intuitions are simple, which members are modeled by vector spaces, it means

$$ev(b \otimes ad) = ev \circ ev(\Delta b \otimes a \otimes d) \quad ev(bc \otimes a) = ev \circ ev(b \otimes c \otimes \Delta a)$$
$$ev(b \otimes \gamma a) = ev(\gamma b \otimes a) \qquad \forall b, c \in B^*,\ a, d \in B.$$

Here evaluation $ev : B^* \otimes B \to 1_{rs}$ first concerns the middle two factors, then the remaining two. It is this dual biagreement and enterprise structure that is denoted by $B^\star$. It is noteworthy that it does not involve any transposition in its definition. Thus, the result obtained does not concern reduction in the untransferred case to usual enterprise duality. Instead it reduces the opposite agreement and opposite coagreement to the usual dual. Precisely,

Proposition 5.23. (Club dual) *Let H be dual to A, then the transferred rules H_{rs} are dual to A_{rs} in the club sense.*

Sketch of proof: One should get $H_{rs} = (A_{rs})^\star = (A_{rs})^{*op/op}$. Here, duality is given by $b \in H_{rs}$ mapping to a linear functional $\langle \gamma b, (\ )\rangle$ on A_{rs}, where γ is the usual mutual understanding map of given enterprise H. First, it can be shown that $\langle \gamma b, am_{rs}d\rangle = \langle(\gamma \otimes \gamma)\Delta_{rs}, d \otimes a\rangle$, for all $a, b \in A_{rs}$ and $b \in H_{rs}$ as required. In addition, we have pairing $\langle \gamma b \otimes \gamma c, \Delta m_{rs} a\rangle = \langle \gamma(cb), a\rangle$, resulting from coincidences between the expansion of H_{rs} and the coexpansion of A_{rs} with the usual expansion and coexpansion. Similar can be obtained for the pairing of the agencies and coagencies. Now one shows that the mapping $\langle \gamma(\ ),\ \rangle$ is an economic transaction in the club of H-standards by $(\langle \gamma(h \overset{a}{>} b),\ \rangle)(a) = (h \overset{a}{>} \langle \gamma b,\ \rangle)(a)$, where the argumentation on $f \in (A_{rs})^\star$ is as discussed in Proposition 4.28. □

In addition, one may recall from discussion on open enterprises, Chapter 3, that the modified opening form, as given by Definition 3.11, $\mathcal{R}_{21}\mathcal{R}$ plays a role of economic homotransaction of the agreements and coagreements that are covariantly linked. Now, this can be understood better as an economic transaction of transferred rules,

$$\mathcal{R}_{21}\mathcal{R} : A_{rs} \to H_{rs}, \qquad \mathcal{R}_{21}\mathcal{R}(a) = (a \otimes id)(\mathcal{R}_{21}\mathcal{R}).$$

In the case when H is factorizable in the strict sense that modified opening is invertible, one gets $H_{rs} \cong A_{rs}$. Namely, the factorisable condition expressed in this way actually implies the associate enveloping agreed transferred rule and activity (function) agreed transferred rule are isotransactive. Namely, they are self-dual from point of view given in Proposition 5.23 above. This is an important application of the concept of transferred rules, which is not at reach within traditional concepts in economic theory.

5.3.5 Generalization of Restructuring

It is already intuitively clear that procedures for following dynamics of e.p.r.s allow generalizations. So for example, it appears that results obtained in formulation of simple e.p.r.s institutions of an elementary club (which members are standardized on simple economic claims, on natural resources for example) can be generalized on e.p.r.s relations, flows and transfers of economic wealth among agents and their institutions using the concept of an open enterprise and considering them as members of a transferred leading club. Similarly, the restructuring theorems discussed in Section 5.3.2 have a straightforward analogue for pairs of open restructuring enterprises $B_1 \to B_2$ in the club $\mathcal{C}$. The outcome of restructuring process is a new restructuring enterprise $B(B_1, B_2)$ in a transferred leading club. The necessary economic relations can be obtained applying the same procedures as in Section 5.3.2 and using the general restructuring theorems.

The following theorem describes how a restructuring enterprise can be specified by a generalized Tannaka-Krein reconstruction procedure applied in these particular economic circumstances. As already mentioned, the idea is that a leading appropriation $F : \mathcal{C}_1 \to \mathcal{C}_2$ between open leading clubs can be associated to an open biagreement or enterprise specified by autotransactive transferred rule $Aut(\mathcal{C}_1, F, \mathcal{C}_2)$ in the institution $\mathcal{C}_2$. To show that such an enterprise exists we need the following.

Definition 5.24. *Let* $F : \mathcal{C}_1 \to \mathcal{C}_2$ *be a leading appropriation between transferred leading clubs* $\mathcal{C}_1$ *and* $\mathcal{C}_2$. *For each member (enterprise)* H_{2i} *in* $\mathcal{C}_2$ *let* ${}_{H_{2i}}F_n : \mathcal{C}_1^n \to \mathcal{C}_2$ *denote the induced appropriations defined by* $(X_1, X_2, \ldots, X_n) \mapsto \mathcal{C}_2 \otimes F(X_1) \otimes F(X_2) \otimes \ldots F(X_n)$. *We say that* $\tilde{F} : \mathcal{C}_1 \mapsto Eprnat({}_{H_{2i}}F, F)$ *is fully representable if:*
(i) $\tilde{F}$ *is representable, i.e. there exists a member* $H \in \mathcal{C}_2$ *and appropriational isotransactions* $\theta_{H_{2i}} : Trn(H_{2i}, H) \cong Eprnat({}_{H_{2i}}F, F)$.
(ii) The maps $\theta^n_{H_{2i}} : Trn(H_{2i}, H^n) \to Eprnat({}_{H_{2i}}F^n, F^n)$ *defined by*

$$\theta^n_{H_{2i}}(k)_{X_1,\ldots,X_n} =$$
$$(\alpha_{X_1}, \ldots, \alpha_{X_n})\Psi^{\mathcal{C}_2}_{H,F(X_1)} \circ \cdots \circ \Psi^{\mathcal{C}_2}_{H,F(X_1)\otimes\cdots\otimes F(X_{n-1})} \circ (k \otimes id^n)$$

are all isotransactions. Here argumentation is given by $\alpha = \theta_H(id_H)$.

The above definition implies that $\tilde{F}$ are also representable by H^n, where associatively isotransactions are suppressed. Note that $\bar{\theta}$ can also be defined in the same way with $(\Psi^{\mathcal{C}}_{Y,X})^{-1}$ in place of $\Psi^{\mathcal{C}}_{X,Y}$. Also, the setting of standards of clubs appears to be suitable for the discussion. So, the following existence theorem can be stated.

Theorem 5.25. *Let $F : \mathcal{C}_1 \to \mathcal{C}_2$ be a leading appropriation between transferred leading clubs. If $\tilde{F}$ is fully representable (at least up to $n = 3$) by a member (an enterprise) H the latter becomes an open biagreement in $\mathcal{C}_2$, such that $H = Aut(\mathcal{C}_1, F, \mathcal{C}_2)$. There is an appropriation $\mathcal{C}_1 \to_H \mathcal{C}_2$ into the club of H-standards in $\mathcal{C}_2$, which composes with the forgetful appropriation to provide F. Moreover, H is universal with this property, i.e. any other such standardized member H' has an e.p.r.s transaction $H' \to H$ or biagreements in $\mathcal{C}_2$. The opposite coexpansion is defined with respect to the image $\mathcal{O}$ of $\mathcal{C}_1 \to_H \mathcal{C}_2$. If $\mathcal{C}_1$ and $\mathcal{C}_2$ are rigid then H is an enterprise.*

Sketch of the proof and comments: The expansion is defined as the transaction $H \otimes H \to H$ corresponding under $\theta_{H \otimes H}$ to the implementable transformation in $Eprnat({}_{H\otimes H}F, F)$ defined on $F(X)$ by $\alpha_X \circ (id \otimes \alpha_X)$. The leading identity $\eta : 1_{ld} \to H$ corresponds to the identity in $Eprnat(F, F)$. The coexpansion is the inverse image under θ^2_H of the element of implementable policy $Eprnat({}_HF^2, F^2)$ defined on $F(X) \otimes F(Y)$ by $c^{-1}_{X,Y} \circ \alpha_{X\otimes Y} c_{X,Y}$. Here $c_{X,Y} : F(X) \otimes F(Y) \cong F(X \otimes Y)$ are the appropriate isotransactions that make F the leading appropriation. We also have $\alpha_1 : H \otimes 1_{ld} \to 1_{ld}$ where $H \otimes 1_{ld}$ is identified with H. Note that above relations and elements of clubs imply from the usual Tannaka-Krein theorems, where $\mathcal{C}_2$ is **h**-standard. Then by extensive use of the transferred relations for $\Psi^{\mathcal{C}_2}$ it can be shown that with θ in the form given above, these theorem can be applied also when the club is transferred leading one. After some tedious computations it can be concluded that the implementable restructuring policies corresponding to the expressions on the left and right in Definition 5.14 holds when $\theta^2(\mathcal{R})$ is determined as $\theta^2(\mathcal{R})_{X,Y} = (\Psi^{\mathcal{C}_2}_{F(X),F(Y)})^{-1} \circ c^{-1}_{Y,X} \circ F(\Psi^{\mathcal{C}_1}_{Y,X}) \circ c_{X,Y}$. Also $\mathcal{R}^{-1}$ determined as the inverse image under θ^2 of $F(\Psi^{\mathcal{C}_1^{-1}}_{X,Y} \circ \Psi^{\mathcal{C}_1}_{F(X),F(Y)})$ is properly defined, which complete the sketch of the proof of the structure of H. The appropriation $\mathcal{C}_1 \to_H \mathcal{C}_2$ is defined by $X \mapsto (F(X), \alpha_X)$. It respects properties of aggregation, transactions and transfers (on the subclub $\mathcal{O}$) in the relevant clubs, and composes with the forgetful appropriation to $\mathcal{C}_2$ to provide F. To show that H is universal with this property, suppose that B is some other biagreement or enterprise in $\mathcal{C}_2$ and an appropriation from $\mathcal{C}_1$ to B-standard in club $\mathcal{C}_2$ is given with these properties. The appropriation associates to each of member X in $\mathcal{C}_1$ a standard that is identified with $F(X)$, and a transaction $\alpha'_X : B \otimes F(X) \to F(X)$. It constitutes an e.p.r.s implementable policy in $\alpha' \in Eprnat({}_HF, F)$. The inverse image of this under θ_B is a transaction $B \to H$ which satisfies conditions of being a biagreement map. $\square$

Proposition 5.26. *Let* $f : H_1 \to H_2$ *be an entrepreneurial map between a pair of open enterprises as in Section 5.3.2. (i) Let* $\mathcal{C}_1$ *and* $\mathcal{C}_2$ *be the transferred leading clubs of* H_1*-standards and* H_2*-standards respectively, and let* F *be pullback appropriation mapping analogous to* f*. Then* $\tilde{F}$ *is fully representable and a restructuring biagreement is specified by* $Aut(\mathcal{C}_1, F, \mathcal{C}_2) \cong B(H_1, f, H_2)$ *as open biagreements in* $\mathcal{C}_2$*. (ii) If enterprises* H_1, H_2 *are finite-dimensional and clubs* $\mathcal{C}_1, \mathcal{C}_2$ *are finite-dimensional standards then* $\mathrm{Aut}(\mathcal{C}_1, F, \mathcal{C}_2) \cong B(H_1, f, H_2)$ *as enterprises in the club* $\mathcal{C}_2$*.*

The validity of this particular application can be shown in a cumbersome and long proof that is omit here.

Now the intention is to sketch how a restructuring theorem of a generalized Tannaka-Krein type works on transferred leading subclubs of B_1-standards and B_2-standards in the club $\mathcal{C}$ for which the respective opposite coexpansions are defined.

Theorem 5.27. *Let* H_1, H_2, H_3 *be three open enterprises, and* f, g *a biagreeable map from an enterprise* H_1 *to enterprise* H_2*, and* H_2 *to* H_3*, respectively. The mapping* g *induces* g_{rs} *as an entrepreneurial restructuring map* $g_{rs} : B(H_1, f, H_2) \to B(H_1, g \circ f, H_3)$*, between a pair of open restructuring enterprises in the club of* H_1*-standards. Then* $B(B(H_1, f, H_2), g_{rs}, B(H_1, g \circ f, H_3)) = B(H_2, g, H_3)$ *is the club of* H_2*-standards.*

Sketch of the proof and comments: Let us fix an open enterprise, H_1, and its transferred leading club of H_1-standards, $\mathcal{C}$. The restructuring procedure discussed in Section 5.3.2 provides an e.p.r.s appropriation to be between the club of pairs (H_2, f) (consisting of an enterprise H_2 and entrepreneurial map $f : H_1 \to H_2$), to the club of such pairs in the club of H_1-standards $\mathcal{C}$. The economic transactions within the first club are entrepreneurial transactions $g : H_2 \to H_2'$ such that $g \circ f = f'$. Here we take $H_2' = H_3$ and g maps to the economic transactions compatible with its appropriation rule rs, denoted by g_{rs}. Then for the simple case discussed here all relevant appropriations are local ones and are implementable in the sense of preserving the e.p.r.s structures. Namely, they are given by identity mappings at the level of linear spaces $g_{rs} = g$ as local restructuring activities that can be described by usual economic transactions within the club. It is then possible to verify the theorem explicitly using the formulae already given in Section 5.3.2. □

The result of Theorem 5.27 suggests that there are aspects of open enterprises that are in some sense invariant or independent of restructuring. Namely, one should not be constrained to e.p.r.s structures in agreements over a fixed domain of claims $\mathbf{h}$, but rather think of transmutation class of agreements. Thus, dynamics of economic flows can be formulated with e.p.r.s structures over other arbitrary e.p.r.s structure in a club, rather than over some fixed one or some fixed institution. In particular, given any agreeable mapping $H_i \to H_j$ one can think of H_j by transmutation as an open enterprise formed over $B(H_i, H_i)$. Here the induced map $B(H_i, H_i) \to B(H_i, H_j)$ can be considered as an agency preserving appropriation procedure ('unit map') in the dynamic economic environment. In this way, any open enterprise H_i can be considered as a 'domain' of e.p.r.s claims over which, allowing for restructuring, agreeable structures can be treated as definable. It is noteworthy that if H_j is merely closed enterprise, i.e. not equipped with the structure of an e.p.r.s opening of market or any other type of opening (new technology, organization and similar), then $B(H_i, f, H_j)$ is also closed type of restructuring enterprise. If H_i is closed enterprise then one cannot reconstruct an enterprise at all. Nevertheless applying the generalized Tannaka-Krein approach, of which particular application is sketched above, one can still regard $H_i \to H_j$ as some form of virtual enterprise and perform an e.p.r.s restructuring.

5.3.6 Examples

In this Section the idea is to address economic restructuring through examples where focus is on procedures that make us able to reduce economic issues about e.p.r.s transfers, inherit to a more complex economic club, to questions about the ordinary enterprise. Only two of those are sketched here, a process of economic restructuring by privatization and a process of economic restructuring by fixed market valuation . More detail and concrete economic analyses of these is given in the sequel of the volume.

One may note that the applications of diagrammatic theory on transferred e.p.r.s rules have been presented only in the simple cases in above Sections. The diagrams will be taken up in combination with more concrete economic applications in a sequel to the present volume. In economic theory and applications it is not unusual to use the diagrams where economic transactions are nodes and a flow chart or wiring diagram or spin network to show the economic flows. Applications on e.p.r.s phenomena discussed above make us, for the first time able to distinguish between economic transfers by under and over crossings in such an economic flow chart. Here, one has to be careful to choose between type of transfers so that constructions provide a consistent e.p.r.s institution without becoming tangled up in an economic unfavorable way. One may note that in the more traditional and convenient economic cases, where we deal with super enterprises or enterprises within symmetric clubs, problem of tanglements does not exist and the generalization from the case of usual enterprises is direct. Naturally, symmetric structures have made the issue of economic transfers either trivial or not actually present, and in that way reduce the economic analysis on ordinary enterprises.

Privatization

Privatization is a particular form of institutionalization, which detail are given in the sequel, as already mentioned. Roughly speaking, the problem of an economic institutionalization is the problem of unifying concepts of an e.p.r.s and an ownership. Once established, proper institutionalization provides a frame of convenient economic analyses analogous to the case of pure strictures, as pure private economies for example. Here we may start with an intuitive understanding of an economic process under the term 'privatization'. The process is to turn a complex structure of e.p.r.s of an enterprise (a member of club that allows transfers), into an ordinary enterprise. The idea is to show how some of transferred enterprises can be privatized back into equivalent ordinary enterprises. It is noteworthy that not all transferred e.p.r.s rules are of the type coming from the restructuring discussed above, so privatization is not simply some reverse process of transmutations applied in economics.

Example 5.28. Let H be a biagreement over domain of claims $\mathbf{h}$ and $\mathcal{C} = {}_H\mathcal{L}$ the transferred leading club of H-standards. Then there is a simple institution, central member of the club, $\mathcal{Z}(\mathcal{C})$, which is both a price H-standard and an invertible price H-costandard. In this form it coincides with the club ${}^H_H\mathcal{L}$ of H-crossed standards as defined and discussed in Sections 2.2.2 and 2.2.3 in Chapter 2. The transfer and its inverse are well defined.

Sketch of the proof and comments: The proof is a direct application of methods described in Section 5.3 so far. A central member of the club, $\mathcal{Z}(\mathcal{C})$, is a simple institution V, which is both a price H-standard and an invertible price H-costandard such that $\sum h_{(1)} v^{(1_{rs})} \otimes h_{(2)} \overset{a}{>} v^{(2_{rs})} = \sum (h_{(1)} \overset{a}{>} v)^{(1_{rs})} h_{(2)} \otimes (h_{(1)} \overset{a}{>} v)^{(2_{rs})}$ for all $h \in H$ and $v \in V$. Then $\mathcal{Z}({}_H\mathcal{L})$ coincides with the club ${}^H_H\mathcal{L}$ of H-crossed standards. The economic transfer is given by $\Psi_{V,W}(v \otimes w) = \sum v^{(1_{rs})} \overset{a}{>} w \otimes v^{(2_{rs})}$. The invertability condition on the costandards ensures that Ψ^{-1} exists, and is automatic if the biagreement H has a skew mutual understanding map. Namely, by Tannaka-Krein reconstruction methods we can reconstruct H as the representing member of a club $\mathcal{C}$ for a certain appropriation. This will give us a bijection of implementable restructuring policies, $Lin(V, H \otimes_{rs} V) \cong Rsnat(V \otimes id, id \otimes V)$ under which λ_V corresponds to a map $V \to H \otimes_{rs} V$. That λ_V represents restructuring aggregation $\otimes_{rs}$ corresponds then to the costandard property of this map. That λ_V is a collection of economic transactions corresponds to the stated compatibility condition between the coargumentation and the argumentation on V as a member of $\mathcal{C}$. This can be seen in detail using the elementary properties of agreements and enterprises already discussed in Chapter 2. So, let H_P denote H as a member of $\mathcal{C}$ under the price argumentation. Given λ_V as reconstruction policy one defines

$$\sum v^{(1_{rs})} \otimes v^{(2_{rs})} = \sum \lambda_{V,H_P}(v \otimes_{rs} 1) \tag{5.11}$$

and check

$$(id \otimes \lambda_{V,H_P})(\lambda_{V,H_P} \otimes id)(v \otimes_{rs} 1 \otimes_{rs} 1) = \lambda_{V,H_P \otimes H_P}(v \otimes_{rs} (1 \otimes_{rs} 1))$$
$$= \lambda_{V,H_P \otimes H_P}(v \otimes \Delta_{rs}(1)) = (\Delta_{rs} \otimes id) \circ \lambda_{V,H_P}(v \otimes_{rs} 1)$$

where the first equality is the implication of λ_V being representation of $\otimes_{rs}$ and the last that λ_V is appropriation under the economic transaction $\Delta_{rs} : H_P \to H_P \otimes_{rs} H_P$. The left hand side is the map $V \to H \otimes_{rs} V$ in (5.11) applied twice so we see that this map is a price coargumentation. In addition,

$$\sum h_{(1)} v^{(1_{rs})} \otimes h_{(1)} \overset{a}{>} v^{(2_{rs})} = h \overset{a}{>} \lambda_{V,H_P}(v \otimes_{rs} 1)$$
$$= \lambda_{V,H_P}(h \overset{a}{>} (v \otimes_{rs} 1)) = \lambda_{V,H_P \otimes H_P}(h_{(1)} \overset{a}{>} v \otimes_{rs} R_{h_{(2)}}(1))$$
$$= \sum(\lambda_{V,H_P}(h_{(1)} \overset{a}{>} v \otimes_{rs} 1))(h_{(2)} \otimes_{rs} (1))$$

where the first equality is based on the definition 5.11 and the argumentation of H on $H_P \otimes V$. The second equality is valid as λ_{V,H_P} is an economic transaction in $\mathcal{C}$. The final equality results from the application of appropriation under the particular economic transaction (regular price formation mechanism for restructuring process) $R_{h_{(2)}} : H_P \to H_P$ given by quality expansion to obtain the right hand side of the compatibility condition. The converse direction of the proof is as follows: Given a coargumentation $V \to H \otimes_{rs} V$ it is not difficult to define $\lambda_{V,W}(v \otimes w) = \sum v^{(1_{rs})} \overset{a}{>} w \otimes v^{(2_{rs})}$. Note that this also directly implies the transferring $\Psi = \lambda$ as stated. Having in mind discussion on a central element and a double dual from Section 4.2.4 in Chapter 4 one may recall that the λ_V were invertible. If this assumption is relaxed then we would get a leading club which is just that of crossed standards as in Sections 2.2.2 and 2.2.3 in Chapter 2. In that case Ψ would not necessarily be invertible and thus transfers would not be completed. The invertibility of λ_V corresponds to price costandards which are invertible in the sense already discussed in Chapter 2. Namely, there exists a linear map $V \to V \otimes_{rs} H$ sending v to $\sum v^{[2]} \otimes_{rs} v^{[1]}$ say, such that

$$\sum v^{[2](1_{rs})} v^{[1]} \otimes v^{[2]} v^{(2_{rs})} = 1 \otimes_{rs} v = \sum v^{(2_{rs})[1]} v^{(1_{rs})} \otimes v^{(2_{rs})[2]}, \quad \forall v \in V. \tag{5.12}$$

Note that if such an inverse exists it is unique and a quality costandard. In addition, it can be shown that the invertible costandards are closed under the aggregations. They correspond to λ_V^{-1} in the similar way as in (5.12) and with $\lambda_{V,W}^{-1}(w \otimes v) = \sum v^{[2]} \otimes_{rs} v^{[1]} \overset{a}{>} w$ for the converse direction. In the case of finite dimensional institutions invertible costandards provide price duals V^* with price coargumentation $\beta_{V^*}(f)(v) = \sum v^{[1]} f(v^{[2]})$. In the case where H is an enterprise with a skew type of mutual understanding, every price costandard is invertible by composing with the skew mutual understanding. Thus in this case invertibility condition appears redundant. It is noteworthy that from the point of view of club theory and discussion in Chapter 4, if $\mathcal{C}$ has quality duals then every $\lambda_{V,W}$ is invertible. The inverse is the quality adjoint of λ_{V,W^*}, or precisely $\lambda_{V,W}^{-1} = (ev_W^{rs} \otimes id) \circ \lambda_{V,W^*} \circ (id \otimes coev_W^{rs})$. In the case when $\mathcal{C} =_H \mathcal{L}$, the finite dimensional price standards have quality duals if the biagreement H has a skew mutual understanding. So in this case the invertibility of λ_V is automatic. This completes computation of a central of transferred leading club, $\mathcal{Z}({}_H\mathcal{L})$, consisting of compatible standard - costandard structures as stated. One may recall that the notion of a crossed standard is an immediate generalization of the notion of a crossed G-standard with $H = \mathbf{h}G$, the e.p.r.s rule agreement of a finite e.p.r.s rule G. In this case the club of crossed G-standards is well known to contain transfers. Moreover, when the members of the club can be identified with underlying simple economic institutions or enterprises on natural recourses modeled over vector spaces, the Tannaka-Krein reconstruction theorem can be used to show that there exists a biagreement $coD(H)$ such that the club with transfers is equivalent to the club of quality $coD(H)$-costandards, $\mathcal{L}^{coD(H)} =^H_H \mathcal{L}$. Here the standards are taken to be finite dimensional as sufficient condition for the Tannaka-Krein reconstruction theorem to apply, and codouble, $coD(H)$, to exist. Note that finite dimesionality is not a necessary condition for existence. In the convenient case the club can be standardized by doubles so that we have also ${}_{D(H)}\mathcal{L}$ for some $D(H)$. This can be understood as an abstract definition of e.p.r.s double, already used in Example 4.17 Chapter 4. In the case where H is an enterprise with the invertible mutual understanding map, one gets that ${}^H_H\mathcal{L}$ is rigid and so $coD(H)$ and $D(H)$ will be enterprises. The club conditions imply that ${}^H_H\mathcal{L}$ is rigid and this duality extends to $\mathcal{Z}(\mathcal{C})$, with the dual of λ_V defined by the price adjoint of $\lambda^{-1}_{V,W}$ as $\lambda_{V^*,W} = (ev_V \otimes id) \circ \lambda^{-1}_{V,W} \circ (id \otimes coev_V)$. This again confirms how very powerful the club methods of restructuring are. □

Lemma 5.29. *Let H be an open biagreement or enterprise, and B a price H-standard with argumentation $\overset{a}{>}$. Then there is a coargumentation β which makes B into a price H-costandard. In addition, this coargumentation is compatible with $\overset{a}{>}$ and invertible.*

Sketch of the proof and comments: Using the axioms of an open biagreement from Chapter 3 it can be shown that a coargumentation given by $\beta(b) = \sum \mathcal{R}^{(2)} \otimes \mathcal{R}^{(1)} \overset{a}{>} b$ is well defined coargumentation. Given in such form, it is compatible in the sense of the Example 5.28 above. In the case when H is only a biagreement we have to check invertibility defined by the relation (5.12) above. The required inverse is provided by inverse of opening in place of opening in the definition of β. This defines an appropriation ${}_H\mathcal{L} \rightarrow^H_H \mathcal{L} = \mathcal{Z}({}_H\mathcal{L})$. Since the appropriation takes economic transactions to economic transactions, or by direct computation, it can be seen that when B is an H-standard (co)agreement then it becomes in this way an H-costandard (co)agreement. □

Theorem 5.30. (Privatization of a transferred enterprise) *Any transferred enterprise B in the transferred leading club ${}_H\mathcal{L}$, (for an open enterprise H), gives an ordinary enterprise $Prv(B)$ by privatization. The argumentation of H on B (as a member of the club) makes a cross expansion and the induced coargumentation β (from Lemma 5.29) makes the cross coexpansion.*

The process $Prv(B) = B {>\!\!\!\triangleleft\kern-.33em\cdot\,} H$ is called privatization of B. The standards of B in the transferred leading club correspond to the ordinary standards of $Prv(B)$.

Sketch of proof: Here the sketch of proof is given from point of view of club restructuring discussed above, although one can also perform a direct proof using properties of an ordinary enterprise as discussed in Chapter 2. So let us consider the leading club of standards of B in the transferred club of H-standards. Members are the simple e.p.r.s institutions on which both H and B perform argumentations. Then using the forgetful appropriation on the level of the club of simple enterprises Vec and reconstructing by Theorem 5.1, one obtains an ordinary enterprise. This is the abstract definition of privatization process such that its representations are the standards of B in the transferred leading club. In the first stage, transferred version of $Prv(B)$ is constructed. Here one can forget only the argumentation of B, giving a forgetful appropriation to the club of H-standards, and apply the transferred reconstruction Theorem 5.8. Since B is economic active in the club of H-standards, it is argumented upon covariantly by H, and hence by H_{rs}. In the other words, B is made to a transferred $B(H,H)$-standard leading agreement. Because it is transferred cocommutative in a sense of restructuring, and one can make a transferred cross product $B {>\!\!\!\triangleleft\kern-.33em\cdot\,} B(H,H) = B {>\!\!\!\triangleleft\kern-.33em\cdot\,} H_{rs}$, by this argumentation. Thus, it contains $B(H,H)$ and it can be shown that this is the transmutation of an ordinary enterprise inclusion, $H \hookrightarrow B {>\!\!\!\triangleleft\kern-.33em\cdot\,} H$, obtaining the required structure of $B {>\!\!\!\triangleleft\kern-.33em\cdot\,} H$ in this way. Thus, $Prv(B) = B {>\!\!\!\triangleleft\kern-.33em\cdot\,} H$ has the structure of a semidirect (co)expansion both as an agreement by $\overset{a}{>}$, and as a coagreement by the coargumentation β from Lemma 5.29. □

Thus, the approach promoted by club theory provides an equivalence between ordinary enterprise $Prv(B)$ and the original B in the sense that its ordinary representations correspond to the transferred representation of B. This is valid as much for super enterprises as for enterprises on other clubs. One may say, that the property known for superstructured simple institutions, that they can be reduced to ordinary ones, can also be recovered in these cases dealing with more complex institutions.

Fixed Market Valuation(FMV)

Connected to the restructuring and privatization is a process of a fixed market valuation. In the economic literature it also comes with notion of projection or more precisely with a notion of an enterprise with projection. Let us consider two ordinary enterprises $H_1, H,$ and let p and i be biagreemental maps $H_1 \underset{i}{\overset{p}{\rightleftarrows}} H,$ with property that composition of these mappings is identical map, so that $p \circ i = id$ forms an enterprise projection. Then there is an agreement and a coagreement B such that, $Prv(B) \cong H_1$ is a simultaneous cross expansion and cross coexpansion which correspond to projections. One may recall that B is actually an enterprise in the transferred club ${}^{H}_{H}\mathcal{L} = {}^{H}_{D(H)}\mathcal{L}$, already addressed by Example 5.28.

Proposition 5.31. (Privatization and FMV) *Let $H_1 \underset{i}{\overset{p}{\rightleftarrows}} H$, be an enterprise FMV and let H have invertible mutual understanding map. Then there is an enterprise B in the transferred leading club which privatization corresponds to H_1.*

Sketch of the proof and comments: Recall that B is the subagreement of H_1 and a member of the transferred leading club ${}^{H}_{H}\mathcal{L}$ by argumentation $\overset{a}{>}$, and coargumentation β. Explicitly, we have

$$B = \{b \in H_1 \mid \sum b_{(1)} \otimes p(b_{(2)}) = b \otimes 1\}, \;\; h \overset{a}{>} b = \sum i(h_{(1)}) b \circ i(h_{(2)}),$$
$$\beta(b) = p(b_{(1)}) \otimes b_{(2)}$$

where $h \in H$. The transferred coexpansion, transferred mutual understanding map and transferring of B are,

$$\Delta_{trr} = \sum b_{(1)} \gamma \circ \gamma p(b_{(2)}) \otimes b_{(3)}, \qquad \gamma_{trr} b = \sum i \circ p(b_{(1)}) \gamma b_{(2)},$$
$$\Psi_{B,B}(b \otimes c) = \sum p(b_{(1)}) \overset{a}{>} c \otimes b_{(2)}.$$

The isotransaction $\Theta : B \rtimes\!\!\!\lhd H \to H_1$ is $\theta(b \otimes h) = bi(h)$, with inverse $\theta^{-1}(a) = \sum a_{(1)} \gamma \circ i \circ p(a_{(2)}) \otimes p(a_{(3)})$ for $a \in H_1$. Now, B as a twisted enterprise can be identified as an enterprise that is a member of a transferred leading club. The set B coincides with the image of the projection $\Pi : H_1 \to H_1$ defined by $\Pi(a) = \sum a_{(1)} \gamma \circ i \circ p(a_{(2)})$. The pushed-out price adjoint coargumentation of H, H_P, on B then reduces to the price coargumentation as stated. The structure of transfer corresponds to the one described in Example 5.28. The axioms of an enterprise as a member of the transferred leading club require that $\Delta_{trr} : B \to B \otimes B$ is an agreed economic transaction with respect to the transferred aggregate agreed structure on $B \otimes B$ Using $\Delta_{trr} = \sum b_{(1)_{trr}} \otimes b_{(2)_{trr}}$, one obtains,

$$\begin{aligned}\Delta_{trr}(bc) &= \sum b_{(1)_{trr}} \Psi(b_{(2)_{trr}} \otimes c_{(1)_{trr}}) c_{(2)_{trr}} \\ &= \sum b_{(1)_{trr}} (b_{(2)_{trr}}{}^{(1_{trr})} \overset{a}{>} c_{(1)_{trr}}) \otimes b_{(2)_{trr}}{}^{(2_{trr})} c_{(2)_{trr}}\end{aligned}$$

which derives the condition of proper defined projections or FMVs. The structure of $B \rtimes\!\!\!\lhd H$ is one that corresponds to the standard price structured cross expansion given by the argumentation and coargumentation as stated. Then by applying θ to these structures and by evaluating them one obtains θ as an enterprise isotransaction. The case when H_1 is only a biagreement implies B being only a biagreement in a transferred club. In this case one can use the convolution inverse $i \circ \gamma$ in the above. Note that the restriction to invertible mutual understanding on H is needed only to ensure that transfer Ψ is invertible as explained in Example 5.28. This is part of interpretation of B as transferred enterprise rather then part of traditional economic concept of FMV. The enterprise projections may have a simple interpretation as examples of trivial or naive e.p.r.s principle bundles, and at the same time as e.p.r.s mechanisms. These put us back to the forms of economic institutions where simple e.p.r.s reasoning of copartners could not be taken as granted. Note also that in the above enterprise H need not be open or dual open. In the case it has the property of openness, the above construction becomes related to the privatization theorem as given above. □

References

1. Abe, E. (1977) *Hopf Algebras*, New York, W. A. Benjamin.
2. Alchian, A. A. (1965) 'Some Economics of Property Rights'. *Il Politico*, 30, 816-29.
3. Aliprantis, C. D. and O. Burkinshaw (2003) *Locally Solid Riesz Spaces with Applications to Economics*, Providence, RI, AMS.
4. Aliprantis, C. D., Turkey R. and N. C. Yannelis (2001) 'A Theory of Value with Non-linear Prices: Equilibrium Analysis Beyond Vector Lattices' *J. Economic Theory* 100, 22-72.
5. Alkan, A., C. D. Aliprantis, and N. C. Yannelis (eds) (1999) *Theory and Applications: Current Trends in Economics*, Berlin, New Your, Springer.
6. Allais, M. (1943) A la Researche d'une Discipline Économique, Paris., Allais, M. and O. Hagen (eds) (1979) *Expected Utility Hypothesis and the Allias Paradox*, Boston, Reidel.
7. Arrow, K. (1964) 'The Role of Securities in the Optimal Allocation of Risk-bearing', *R. Economic Studies*, 31, 91-6.
8. Arrow, K. (1979) 'The Property Rights Doctrine and Demand Revelation under Incomplete Information' in M. Boskin (ed) *Economics and Human Welfare*, New York, Academic Press.
9. Arrow, K. (1995) 'Information, Learning, and Economic Equilibrium' in *Intellectual Property Rights and Global Competition*, (eds) H. Albach and S. Rosenkranz, Sigma, Berlin.
10. Aubin, J. P. (1982) *Mathematical Methods of Game and Economic Theory*, Amsterdam, North-Holland.
11. Aumann, R. J. and S. Hart (eds) (1982, 1994) *Handbook of Game Theory with Economic Applications*, vol.1-2, Amsterdam, Elsecier-North-Holland.
12. Axelrod, R. (1984) *The Evolution of Cooperation*, New York, Basic Books.
13. Bajt, A. (1988) *Forms of Social Partnership*, Zagreb, Globus, (in Slovinian).
14. Barzel, Y. (1989) *Economic Analysis of Property Rights*, Cambridge, Cambridge University Press.
15. Becker, G. S. (1964) *Human Capital: A Theoretical and Empirical Analysis, with Special Reference to Education*, New York, Columbia University Press.
16. Berberian, K. S. (1961) *Introduction to Hilbert Space*, New York, Oxford University Press.

17. Bergen, J. and S. Montgomery (eds) (1994) *Advances in Hopf Algebras*, LNPAM, M. Dekker.
18. Buchanan, J., R. Tallison and G. Tullock (eds) (1980) *Toward a Theory of the Rent-Seeking Society*, College Station, A&M University Press.
19. Chase, S. and M. Sweedler, (1969) *Hopf Algebras and Galois Theory*, LNM, 97, Berlin, Springer-Verlag.
20. Coase, R. (1937) 'The Nature of the Firm', *Economica*, NS, 4, 386-405.
21. Coase, R. (1960) 'The Problem of Social Costs', *J. Law and Economics*, 1, 1-44.
22. Cohn, P. M. (1991) *Algebra*, Vol. 3, Chichester, Johm Wiley & Sons.
23. Connes, A. (1990) *Géométrie Non Commutative*, Paris, InterEditions, see also (1994) *Noncommutative Geometry*, San Diego, Academic Press.
24. Debreu, G. (1959) *Theory of Value: An Axiomatic Analysis of Economic Equilibrium*, New Haven, Yale University Press.
25. Demsetz, P. A. (1967) 'Toward a Theory of Property Rights', *American Economic R.*, 57, 347-59.
26. Demsetz, H. (1988) *Ownership, Control, and the Firm*, Oxford, Basil Blackwell.
27. Dierker, E. (1974) *Topological Methods in Walrasian Economics*, Berlin, Stringer-Verlag.
28. Drinfeld, V. G. (1987) 'Quantum Groups,' in *PICM*, Providence, Rhode Island, AMS, 789-820.
29. Drinfeld, V. G. (1989) 'Quasi-Hopf Algebras' *Algebra i Analiz*, 1 (6), 21-38, (in Russian).
30. Drinfeld, V. G. (1989) 'On Almost-cocommutative Hopf Algebras', *Algebra i Analiz*, 1 (2), 30-46, (in Russian).
31. Eggertsson, T. (1990) *Economic Behavior and Institutions*, Cambridge, Cambridge University Press.
32. Furuboton, E. and S. Pejovich (1974) *The Economics of Property Rights*, Boston, Ballinger.
33. Grossman, S. and O. Hart (1986) 'The Costs and Benefits of Ownership: A Theory of Vertical and Lateral Integration,' *J. Political Economy*, 94, 691-719.
34. Glycopantis, D. and N. C. Yannelis (eds) (2005) *Differential Information Economies*, Berlin, Springer.
35. Harsanyi, J. C. and R. Selten (1988) *A General Theory of Equilibrium Selection in Games*, Cambridge, Mass., MIT Press.
36. Hahn, F. (1989) (ed) *The Economics of Missing Markets, Information and Games*, Oxford, Clarendon Press.
37. Hart, O. and J. Moore (1990) 'Property Right and the Nature of the Firm,' *J. Political Economy*, 98, 1119-58.
38. Hildenbrand, W. (1974) *Core and Equilibria of a Large Economy*, Princeton, Princeton University Press.
39. Kantorovich, L. (1948) 'Functional Analysis and Applied Mathematics,' *Uspehi Math. Nauk*, 3, 89-187, (in Russian).
40. Klein, B. and K. Leffler (1981) 'The Role of the Market Forces in Assuring Contractual Performance,' *J. Political Economy*, 89, 615-41.
41. Koopmans, T. C. (1951) (ed) *Activity Analysis of Production and Allocation*, New York, Wiley.
42. Kreps, D., P. Milgrom, J. Roberts, and R. Wilson (1982) 'Rational Cooperation in the Finitely Repeated Prisoners' Dilemma,' *J. Economic Theory*, 27, 245-52.
43. Lewis, D. K. (1969) *Convention: A Philosophical Study*, Cambridge, Mass., Harvard University Press.

44. Lyubashenko, V. V. (1995) 'Tangles and Hopf algebras in Braided Categories,' *J. Pure and Applied Algebra*, 98, 245-278.
45. MacLane, S. (1974) *Categories for the Working Mathematician*, GTM, Vol. 5, Berlin, Springer-Verlag.
46. Majid, S. (1993) 'Transmutation Theory and Rank for Quantum Braided Groups,' *Math. Proc. Camb. Phil. Soc.*, 113, 45-69.
47. Majid, S. (1995) *Foundations of Quantum Group Theory*, Cambridge, Cambridge University Press.
48. Majumdar, M., T. Mitra and K. Nishimura (2000) *Optimization and Chaos*, Berlin, New York, Springer.
49. Manin, Yu. I. (1988) *Quantum Groups and Noncommutative Geometry*, CRM, University of Montreal.
50. Meade, J. E. (1965) *Efficiency, Equality and the Ownership of Property*, Cambridge, Mass., Harvard University Press.
51. Milnor, J. W. and Moore, J. C., (1969) 'On the Structure of Hopf Algebras,' *Ann. Math.*, 81, 211-264.
52. Modigliani, F. and M. H. Miller (1958) 'The Cost of Capital, Corporation Finance and the Theory of Investment,' *American Economic Review*, 48, 261-297.
53. Montgomery, S. (1993) *Hopf Algebras and Their Actions on Rings*, CBMS, Providence, RI, AMS.
54. Moulin, M. (1988) *Axioms of Cooperative Decision Making*, Cambridge, Cambridge Press.
55. Myerson, R. (1984) *Game Theory: Analysis of Conflict*, Cambridge, Mass., Cambridge University Press.
56. Nash, J. F. (1950) 'Equilibrium Points in N-person Games,' *Proc. NAS USA*, 36,48-49, 1950.
57. Nazaikinskii, V. E., Shatalov V. E. and Sternin B. Yu. (1996) *Methods of Noncommutative Analysis: Theory and Applications*, GSM, 22, Berlin, Walter de Gruyter.
58. Neumann, van J. (1928) 'Zur Theorie der Gesellschaftsspiele' *Mathematische Ann.*, 100, 295-320.
59. Neumann, van J. and O. Morgenstern (1953) *The Theory of Games and Economic Behaviour*, Princeton, Princeton University Press. (1st ed. 1944, 2nd 1950).
60. Pasetta, V. (1978) *Mathematical Aspects of Integration Processes of Enterprises*, Belgrade University.
61. Pasetta, V. (1989) *Methods of Dynamic Economic Analysis*, Belgrade University.
62. Pasetta, V. (1998) 'Modeling Economic Restructuring: An Economic Application of Transmutation,' EPRSA, Working Paper.
63. Pasetta, V. (1999) 'Dynamics in Divide Money Game with Bribing,' *Annals of OR*, 88, 361-377.
64. Pasetta, V. (2004) *Axiomatic Models of Exceptional Economic Agreements*, Preprint EPRSA, Ithaca.
65. Roth, A. E. (1979) *Axiomatic Models of Bargaining*, Berlin, Springer-Verlag.
66. Sato, R. (1999) *Theory of Technical Change and Economic Invariance:* Application of Lie Groups, Edward Elgar, Cheltenham, UK.
67. Schelling, T. C. (1960) *Strategy of Conflict*, Cambridge, Mass., Harvard University.
68. Selten, R. (ed) (1992) *Rational Interaction*, Berlin, Stringer-Verlag.

69. Sen, A. K. (1970) *Collective Choice and Social Welfare*, San Francisco, Holden-Day.
70. Shell, K. (1969) 'Applications of Pontryagin's Maximum Principle to Economics,' in *Mathematical Systems Theory and Economics*, H. W. Kuhn and G. P. Szegö (eds), Vol.1, 241-292, Springer-Verlag, Berlin.
71. Stojanovic, D. (1980) *Models of Economic Growth Matrix*, SA, Belgrade University, (in Serbian).
72. Sweedler, M. E. (1969) *Hopf Algebras*, New York, Benjamin.
73. Thomson, W. and Lensberg T. (1989) *Axiomatic Theory of Bargaining with a Variable Number of Agents*, Cambridge, Cambridge University Press.
74. Takayama, A. (1985) *Mathematical Economics*, 2nd. ed., Cambridge, Cambridge University Press.
75. Ulbrich, K-H. (1990) 'On Hopf Algebras and Rigid Monoidal Categories,' *Israel J. Math*, 72, 252-256.
76. Vind, K. (2003) *Independence, Additivity and Uncertainty*, with contributions by Birgit Grodal, Berlin, New York, Springer.
77. Vobob'ev, N. N. (1984) *Foundations of Game Theory*, Nauka, Moskva, (in Russian).
78. Werin, L. and Wijkander H., (eds), (1992) *Contract Economics.* Cambridge, Blackwell.
79. Williamson, O. E. (1985) *The Economic Institutions of Capitalism: Firm, Markets, Rational Contracting*, New York, Free Press.
80. Yannelis, N. C., C. Herves and E. Marino, 'An Equivalence Theorem for a Differential Information Economy', *J. Mathematical Economics* (forthcoming).

Index

6

Symbol Key

Symbol	*Element*	*Typical EPRT interpretation*	*Typical math interpretation*
$\mathbf{h}$	λ, μ	domain of e.p.r.s claim	ring, field
C	λ, μ	claims	complex numbers
R	λ, μ	claims	real numbers
Z	n, m	claims	integers
N	n, m	claims	natural incl. 0
$Z_{/n}$	n, m	standardized claim on n	modulo n
$Z'_{/n}$	g	debt - e.p.r.s rule	anyon group
$\imath$		virtual claim	$\sqrt{-1}$
V, W	v, w	simple institution	vector space
V^*	ϕ, ψ	simple dual institution	linear dual
e_a, f^a		basic factors	basis, dual basis
Lin		simple e.p.r.s relations	linear maps
End		endotransactions	endomorphisms
$\oplus$		simple e.p.r.s gluing	direct sum
$\oplus_{ap}$		*ap*-modified gluing	
$\otimes$		simple aggregation	tensor
$\otimes_{ap}$		*ap*-mod. aggregation	braided tensor
A_A, A	a, b	agreement	algebra
A_B, A	c, d	coagreement	coalgebra
B		biagreement	bialgebra
H		enterprise	Hopf algebra
H	h, g	e.p.r.s rule	quantum group
G	u, v	economic rule, game	group
M	s, t	market, e.p.r.s device	manifold, set, group
op		opposite expansion	opposite product
$coop$		opposite coexpansion	opposite coproduct

Symbol	*Elem.*	*Typical EPRT interpretation*	*Typical math interpretation*
Δ	$h_{(1)}\otimes h_{(2)}$	coexpansion	coproduct
m		expansion	product
ε		coagent, copartner	counit
η		agent, partner	unit
γ		mutual understanding	
τ		transposition	transposition
$\langle\,,\,\rangle$		valuation	duality pairing
$\mathbf{h}G$		enterp. agreement rule	group Hopf algebra
$\mathbf{h}(G)$		enterp. activity rule	group function algebra
$U(\,)$		enveloping agreement on	enveloping algebra
χ		cocycle	character or cocycle
α	$h \overset{a}{>}$	price argumentation	left action
α	$h \overset{a}{<}$	quality argumentation	right action
β	$\upsilon^{(1_{ap})}\otimes\upsilon^{(2_{ap})}$	coargumentation	coaction
Ad		adjoint (co)argumentation	adjoint (co)action
L		price regular (co)argum.	left reg. (co)action
R		quality regular (co)argum.	right reg. (co)action
L^*		price regular (co)argum. on dual	left reg. (co)action on dual
R^*		quality regular (co)argum. on dual	right (co)action on dual
$\mid\;\mid$		grading	grading
$\int$		e.p.r.s gain	integral functional
$\int\!\!\!\!p$		price gain	integral functional
$\int\!\!\!\!q$		quality gain	integral functional
Λ		gain element	integral element
W		welfare	fundamental operator
$*$			antilinear antiinvolution
$\mathcal{R}$	$\mathcal{R}^{(1)}\otimes\mathcal{R}^{(2)}$	opening structure	quasitriangular structure
u, v		implementable policies	
ν		impartial policy	ribbon element
Ω	x, y	universal set	universal set
Ω	x, y	probability space	probability space
$\langle\;\rangle$		expectation value	expectation value
$\mathcal{C}(\Omega)$	a, b	function on	function on
$L^\infty(\Omega)$	a, b	function on	function on
$C^\infty(M)$	f, g	smooth function on	smooth function
$Vec(M)$	f, g	bundle of claims	vector field
$H^\star, A^\star$		club dual	categorical dual

Symbol	*Elem.*	*Typical EPRT interpretation*	*Typical math interpretation*
$D(H)$		e.p.r.s. double	quantum double
$D(g)$		traditional double	classical double
$\mathcal{H}(,)$		conformal e.p.r.s space	cohomology space
$\sigma(,)$		game partnership	skew-pairing
ap		appropriation parameter	deformation parameter
$\mathcal{C}, \mathcal{V}$	V, W	clubs and members	category and objects
Trn, Mor	ϕ, ψ	set of transactions	set of morphisms
F, G		appropriation	functor
$Eprnat(,)$	θ, λ	implement. approp. policy	natural transformation
$1_{ap}, ld$		leading member	unit object
Ψ		transfer	braided transposition
ev		evaluation	evaluation
$coev$		coevaluation	coevaluation
dim_{ap}		dimension of club	categorical dimension
Tr_{ap}		trace of club	categorical trace
$\mid H \mid$		e.p.r.s order	quantum order or rank
Trn_{ap}		internal transaction	internal hom
B, C	b, c	transfer rule, agreement	braided group or algebra
$B(,)$		reconstruction	transmutation construction
$\succ\!\!\!\alpha\!\!\lhd$		price cross expansion	
$\rhd\!\!\alpha\!\!\!\prec$		quality cross expansion	
$\succ\!\!\!\epsilon\!\!\lhd$		price cross coexpansion	
$\rhd\!\!\epsilon\!\!\!\prec$		quality cross coexpansion	

7

Acronyms

Acronym	*Compound Term*
EPRS	economic property rights space
EPRT	economic property rights theory
e.p.r.s	economic property rights
GET	general equilibrium theory

Printing and Binding: Strauss GmbH, Mörlenbach